Building decent
societies.

Building Decent Societies

The International Labour Organization

The International Labour Organization was founded in 1919 to promote social justice and, thereby, to contribute to universal and lasting peace. Its tripartite structure is unique among agencies affiliated to the United Nations; the ILO's Governing Body includes representatives of government, and of employers' and workers' organizations. These three constituencies are active participants in regional and other meetings sponsored by the ILO, as well as in the International Labour Conference – a world forum which meets annually to discuss social and labour questions.

Over the years the ILO has issued for adoption by member States a widely respected code of international labour Conventions and Recommendations on freedom of association, employment, social policy, conditions of work, social security, industrial relations and labour administration, among others.

The ILO provides expert advice and technical assistance to member States through a network of offices and multidisciplinary teams in over 40 countries. This assistance takes the form of labour rights and industrial relations counselling, employment promotion, training in small business development, project management, advice on social security, workplace safety and working conditions, the compiling and dissemination of labour statistics, and workers' education.

Other recent publications by ILO and Palgrave Macmillan:

INTERNATIONAL AND COMPARATIVE LABOUR LAW (by Arturo Bronstein)

IN DEFENCE OF LABOUR MARKET INSTITUTIONS: CULTIVATING JUSTICE IN THE DEVELOPING WORLD (edited by Janine Berg and David Kucera)

MICROFINANCE AND PUBLIC POLICY: OUTREACH, PERFORMANCE AND EFFICIENCY (edited by Bernd Balkenhol)

GLOBALIZATION, EMPLOYMENT AND INCOME DISTRIBUTION IN DEVELOPING COUNTRIES (edited by Eddy Lee and Marco Vivarelli)

UNDERSTANDING GLOBALIZATION, EMPLOYMENT AND POVERTY REDUCTION (edited by Eddy Lee and Marco Vivarelli)

Building Decent Societies

Rethinking the Role of Social Security in Development

Edited by

Peter Townsend
Professor of International Social Policy, London School of Economics

First published 2009 by
PALGRAVE MACMILLAN

Palgrave Macmillan in the UK is an imprint of Macmillan Publishers Limited, registered in England, company number 785998, of Houndmills, Basingstoke, Hampshire RG21 6XS.

Palgrave Macmillan in the US is a division of St Martin's Press LLC, 175 Fifth Avenue, New York, NY 10010.

Palgrave Macmillan is the global academic imprint of the above companies and has companies and representatives throughout the world.

Palgrave® and Macmillan® are registered trademarks in the United States, the United Kingdom, Europe and other countries

ISBN: 978–0–230–23525–0   hardback
ILO ISBN: 978–92–2–121995–8

This book is printed on paper suitable for recycling and made from fully managed and sustained forest sources. Logging, pulping and manufacturing processes are expected to conform to the environmental regulations of the country of origin.

A catalogue record for this book is available from the British Library.

A catalog record for this book is available from the Library of Congress.

10 9 8 7 6 5 4 3 2 1
18 17 16 15 14 13 12 11 10 09

Printed and bound in Great Britain by
CPI Antony Rowe, Chippenham and Eastbourne

Contents

List of Figures

List of Tables

List of Boxes

Notes on Contributors

Armando Barrientos is Senior Research Fellow at the Brooks World Poverty Institute at the University of Manchester, in the UK, and a Senior Researcher with the Chronic Poverty Research Centre. His research interests focus on the linkages existing between welfare programmes and labour markets in developing countries, and on poverty and vulnerability reduction. His work has been published widely, including articles in *World Development, Applied Economics*, the *Manchester School* and *Geneva Papers on Risk and Insurance*. His most recent book is *Social Protection for the Poor and Poorest: Concepts, Policies and Politics* (Palgrave, 2008, edited with David Hulme).

Christina Behrendt has recently moved from the Social Security Department of the International Labour Office in Geneva to the position of regional Social Security Specialist in the ILO's Regional Office for Arab States in Beirut, Lebanon. Prior to this, she worked as a consultant for the International Social Security Association and others, and as a research fellow and lecturer at the University of Konstanz, Germany, where she also earned her PhD in social policy. She has published on social security in both developed and developing countries, including on minimum social protection benefits, public and private pensions, social assistance, and the effectiveness of social security benefits in alleviating poverty.

Bea Cantillon is Professor and Director of the Herman Deleeck Centre for Social Policy at the Antwerp University in Belgium. She teaches on social policy and welfare democracies. She has published widely on issues relating to poverty, inequality, social and economic policies and indicators. She has acted as a consultant to the Belgian government, the OECD and the European Commission. She is a member of the Royal Academy of Sciences of Belgium and President of the National Office of Family Allowances.

Michael Cichon holds a Master's degree in Pure and Applied Mathematics (Technical University, Aachen, Germany), a Master's degree in Public Administration (Harvard University) and a PhD in Economics (University of Göttingen, Germany). He is a member of the German Actuarial Association (DAV), and joined the ILO in 1986 as senior actuary and health economist. Between 1992 and 1995 he served as social security specialist on the ILO advisory team for Central and Eastern Europe in Budapest. Between 1995 and 2005 he was the Chief of the Financial, Actuarial and Statistical Services Branch of the Social Security Department of the ILO. In May 2005 he was appointed Director of the Social Security Department. He undertook and supervised technical cooperation projects in more than 30 countries, writes on social security policy, financing and governance issues and teaches in the joint ILO/University of Maastricht Master's course on social protection financing.

Chris de Neubourg has studied philosophy, sociology and economics at the Universities of Antwerp and Louvain and holds a PhD in Economics. As Professor of International Comparative Studies at the Maastricht University, he is currently the Academic Director of the Maastricht Graduate School of Governance. As the School specializes in research and training in policy analysis, his research is directed towards social protection and social policy in an international comparative perspective. He has published several books, monographs and articles on labour markets, social protection and migration. Chris de Neubourg has been an adviser and consultant with many governments and international organizations including the ILO, the OECD, the World Bank, United Nations Development Programme (UNDP) and United Nations International Children's Emergency Fund (UNICEF).

John Farrington has worked as a Research Fellow in the Rural Policy and Governance Group at the Overseas Development Institute (ODI) for over 20 years. He has recently worked and published on livelihood diversification in South Asia, the future of aid to Asia, on cash transfers, and on the interface between social protection and the productive sectors, taking agriculture as an example.

Krzysztof Hagemejer is the coordinator for Social Security Policy Development in the Social Security Department of the ILO (since 2005) and actively participates in the ILO fieldwork on extension of social security coverage, particularly in Africa (Mozambique, Tanzania and Zambia). Prior to this, he served as Research and Statistics Coordinator and Deputy Chief of the Social Security Financial, Actuarial and Statistical Services Branch (1998–2005), as social security specialist in the ILO advisory team for Central and Eastern Europe in Budapest, with responsibility for social security projects in the region (1995–1998) and as a policy analyst in the Social Security Department of the ILO in Geneva (1993–1995). Before joining the ILO in 1993, he worked as assistant professor at the Department of Economics of Warsaw University, adviser on social and economic policies to the National Committee of the Independent Trade Union 'Solidarnosc' (1980–1991) and adviser to the Minister of Labour and Social Affairs in Poland (1991–1993). He holds a Master's degree in Econometrics and a PhD in Economics, both from Warsaw University. He writes on various economic issues in social security, particularly on problems related to affordability of basic social protection in developing countries and on social reforms in the transition countries of Central and Eastern Europe, and teaches 'Social Budgeting' at Maastricht University, Netherlands.

Paul Harvey is a Research Fellow with the Humanitarian Policy Group at ODI. His recent work has focused on cash-based responses in emergencies, minimizing corruption risks in relief, the concept of dependency and the role of the state in humanitarian action. Prior to joining ODI he was an aid worker with various non-governmental organizations in a range of humanitarian crises.

Rebecca Holmes is a Research Officer at ODI. She currently works on the effectiveness of social protection policies in poverty reduction and livelihood promotion strategies; synergies between social protection and economic growth; impacts and feasibility of cash transfers; and gender relations and gender dynamics of poverty and vulnerability.

Pongpisut Jongudomsuk is MD, MPH in Public Health, Royal Tropical Institute of Belgium. He served as the director of community hospitals in Thailand for ten years. Then, he was appointed to be the Director of the Bureau of Health Policy and Planning, Ministry of Public Health, and the Director of the Bureau of Policy and Strategy, National Health Security Office. Currently, he is the Director of Health Systems Research Institute (HSRI), Thailand.

Stephen Kidd is the Director of Policy and Communications at HelpAge International and leads HelpAge International's work on social protection, with a particular focus on pensions. Before joining HelpAge International last year, he led the DFID policy team responsible for social protection. Previously, at DFID, he also worked as a Social Development Adviser on DFID's China and Latin America programmes. Stephen Kidd has a PhD in Social Anthropology which he also taught for two years at the University of Edinburgh. He has lived for over ten years in Latin America, working for non-governmental organizations, including Tierraviva in Paraguay, supporting the land rights of indigenous people.

Rüdiger Krech, MPH, Dr PH, is Head of Social Protection Section at GTZ in Germany. He joined GTZ in 2003 and is assigned to numerous national and international task forces on social protection and is a member of the German delegation at the UN Social and Economic Commission. Between 1992 and 2003 he worked at the World Health Organization Regional Office for Europe, where he coordinated the WHO European strategy 'Health for all for the 21st century' and held various senior management positions. Previously, he worked in child psychiatry before he took up a position as a senior lecturer for health in social work at a German college. Dr Krech has a professional background in educational sciences, medicine and public health.

Supon Limwattananon has a BSc (Pharmacy) from Chulalongkorn University, Thailand (1982), an MPH (Primary Health Care Management) from the ASEAN Institute for Health Development (1991), and PhD in Social and Administrative Pharmacy from the University of Minnesota (2000). He served as a pharmacist in a community hospital in north-eastern Thailand for seven years (1982–1989). Currently, he is Assistant Professor and Head of Department of Social and Administrative Pharmacy at Khon Kaen University, Thailand. He received the US Health Care Financing Administration Dissertation Award in 2000. His research interest falls into health economics and econometric modelling, and health equity.

Peter Lindert is Distinguished Professor of Economics at the University of California – Davis and a Research Associate of the National Bureau of Economic Research (NBER). His latest book is *Growing Public: Social Spending and Economic Growth since the Eighteenth Century*.

Francie Lund combines her part-time post in the School of Development Studies at the University of KwaZulu-Natal, Durban, with being Director of the Women in Informal Employment: Globalizing and Organizing (WIEGO) Social Protection Programme. Her South African research and policy work focuses on poorer people's access to social security, and she has recently published a book on the introduction of the child cash transfer, *Changing Social Policy: the Child Support Grant in South Africa*. Her WIEGO activities focus on the extension of social protection to informal workers globally. She publishes widely in academic journals and for popular audiences.

Walaiporn Patcharanarumol has a BSc in Pharmacy from Khon Khaen University, Thailand (1992), an MSc in Health Development from Chulalongkorn University, Thailand (1998), and an MSc in Social Protection Financing from Maastricht University, the Netherlands (2003). She gained work experience in public hospitals of Thailand for several years. Since 2001 she has become a researcher in health care financing at the International Health Policy Programme (IHPP–Thailand). Her interests are in hospital costing, National Health Account (NHA), health insurance, and estimation of health expenditures both in short-term and long-term projection. Currently, she is a PhD candidate in the Health Policy Unit at the London School of Hygiene and Tropical Medicine. Her thesis topic is 'Health Care Financing for the Poor in Lao PDR'.

Phusit Prakongsai has an MD degree from Mahidol University, Thailand (1988), and a Certificate in Preventive Medicine from Thai Medical Council (1993). He has ten years of field experience in public health and health service management at three district hospitals in the rural area of Thailand (1988–1998). He was the principal investigator of several research studies on health policy, health insurance, and health care finance at the International Health

Policy Programme, Thailand (1999–2002). Currently, he is doing a PhD in Public Health and Policy at the London School of Hygiene and Tropical Medicine on 'Equity in Health Care Finance and Benefit Incidence Analysis Before and After Universal Health Care Coverage in Thailand'.

Michael Samson is Research Director of the Economic Policy Research Institute (EPRI, South Africa) and a visiting professor at Williams College (USA). He conducts social protection research, advises government and civil society on social transfer initiatives and teaches in capacity-building programmes with EPRI as well as the Institute for Development Studies (Sussex), Maastricht University and others. Holding a PhD from Stanford University, he is an associate member of the Department of Social Policy (Oxford) and an associate researcher at the Centre for Social Science Research (University of Cape Town). Michael wrote the book *Designing and Implementing Social Transfer Programmes* and other books, journal articles and policy reports on social protection. He currently works on social protection projects in Ghana, Kenya, Mozambique, Pakistan, Papua New Guinea, Rwanda and South Africa, as well as for the OECD/DAC/POVNET and the International Social Security Association.

Wolfgang Scholz is an economist at the Social Security Department of the International Labour Office, Geneva. His academic interests include the interdependencies between demography, economy, labour markets and social protection finance. He is author/co-author of books on social budgeting and social protection finance and of articles on similar or related subjects. In recent years his professional focus has been on the financial evaluation of social protection systems, including health finance, in contexts of technical cooperation projects with ILO member States, among these Aruba, Bulgaria, Germany, Luxembourg, Panama, Thailand and Turkey. He teaches Social Budgeting at the Graduate School of Governance, Maastricht (Netherlands) and offers a course on actuarial practice in international social protection at the Haute École de Commerce, University of Lausanne, Switzerland. From 1989 to 1994 he was appointed professor at the Sozialakademie Dortmund (University of Dortmund), Germany. He holds the position of a ministerial adviser of the German government; since 1994 he has been seconded to the ILO.

Rachel Slater is a Research Fellow in the Rural Poverty and Governance Group at ODI. She works on social protection, food security and rural livelihoods, and has particular experience in sub-Saharan Africa. She currently leads ODI's social protection programme including long-term projects on the linkages between social protection and agricultural growth, and on cash transfers in emergency and development contexts.

Viroj Tangcharoensathien is Director of the International Health Policy Programme, Ministry of Public Health, Thailand, Doctor of Medicine 1980, and served seven years in rural district hospitals before doctoral training in Health Planning and Financing in 1987–1990. He received in 1991 the Woodruff Medal Award for the outstanding PhD thesis of the London School of Hygiene and Tropical Medicine, on 'Community Financing: the Urban Health Card in Chiangmai, Thailand'. Upon return, he focused his work on research into financing health care and health insurance development and reforms and research on equity in health. He initiated and updated the National Health Account and National AIDS Account. He works closely with decision-makers in the Ministry of Public Health and other government levels while maintaining his independence as a policy researcher, and provides consultancies, capacity-building as well as technical support for countries in the region.

Peter Townsend was Professor of International Social Policy, LSE and Emeritus Professor of Social Policy, Bristol University. Over the course of a long career his research interests included international social policy; the sociology of poverty; inequalities in health; and ageing, disability and the family. His most recent publications include *The Right to Social Security and National Development: Lessons from OECD Experience for Low-Income Countries* (ILO, 2007), *Child Poverty in the Developing World* (co-authored with David Gordon and others, Policy Press, 2003) and *World Poverty: New Policies to Defeat an Old Enemy* (co-editor, Policy Press, 2002). He visited China to lecture about Human Rights and Poverty in 2005 and 2006, and also, in these years, debated, and, wrote about, the subject in the Mediterranean region, and in Brasilia. From 2005 until his death in June 2009 he was a consultant to the ILO and the DFID.

Raymond Wagener holds a PhD in Mathematics. He is the head of the Statistics, Actuarial Studies and Social Planning Department of the Luxembourg General Inspection of Social Security (IGSS). As a representative of Luxembourg he is a member of the EU Social Protection Committee. He is a member of the Luxembourg Interministerial Commission for Development Cooperation and of the Board of Lux-Development. At the Maastricht Graduate School of Governance of the University of Maastricht he is a lecturer on health care financing. Between 1992 and 1997 he was the project leader of the bilateral cooperation project for the computerization of the Cape Verde Social Security. He also worked as a consultant for the ILO and the World Bank in various countries in Africa, Asia and Latin America.

Foreword

For a long time, social security was considered a feature of rich societies, which was out of the reach of poorer countries. However, little thought has been given to how social security helped today's rich countries to get to where they are today, and how social security contributed to their economic and social development. Fortunately, the tide is turning. Universal access to social security, which helps to bolster and promote high levels of economic growth and social stability, is increasingly being perceived as one of the contributing factors to economic and social development in today's middle and low-income countries. It forms part of a more balanced concept of economic and social development that has been referred to as 'pro-poor growth' or 'growing with equity'. Closely related to these notions, the ILO has been instrumental in developing the concept of 'Decent Work' in which social protection is one of four pillars – together with rights, productive employment and social dialogue – and it works closely with those other pillars. The Decent Work concept has been inspired by countless discussions with the ILO's constituents – governments, employers and workers – and partners, who have also been instrumental in driving the agenda of Decent Work forward.

The ILO believes that social security is a dynamic concept that needs to be adjusted to the circumstances of the changing global society of the twenty-first century. The basis of how we think about social security has been formed by international conventions and recommendations that are anchored in the broader concept of human rights, and have been accepted by the international community.

The ILO is committed to building a global social floor. We believe that every human being has a right to a minimum of social protection. We cannot accept that 1.4 billion people still live in absolute poverty, and that an even higher proportion of the world's population does not have access to effective social security mechanisms when needed.

Effective social security needs to take into account the transformations that societies go through at different stages of their development. We must make every effort to share valuable information and insights about the best ways to build effective institutions that provide social security according to the highest possible standards. We must share knowledge, ideas and experiences on how to achieve effective social security through knowledge transfer and a sharing of ideas and experiences about the way to do so.

In this light, we hope that this book makes a contribution and will speak to an audience of academics and practitioners alike. The academic world will find a rich body of empirical findings that might be valuable to support ever more sophisticated research on the topic. We hope that practitioners, in particular policy-makers and development practitioners, will be inspired by the original ideas that this book presents, which will – hopefully – eventually lead to better and more effective policy-making, both in the developed and the developing world. We also hope that this book will be relevant for the dialogue and exchange of ideas between the stakeholders in social security in the developed and developing world alike.

The book is idealistic, realistic and pragmatic at the same time. It is idealistic because we are convinced that we can accomplish the objective of strengthening social security and extending coverage. At the same time, the book is realistic because it identifies and assesses the obstacles along the way. Finally, it is pragmatic because it shows how to remove these obstacles.

The book has grown out of a joint initiative by three institutions, the Department for International Development, the Gesellschaft für Technische Zusammenarbeit (GTZ) of Germany, and the International Labour Office (ILO). Together, the three institutions planned and sponsored a research seminar which was held in Geneva on 4–5 September 2006 on the topic of 'Challenging the Development Paradigm: Rethinking the Role of Social Security in State Building'. Addressing the need to extend social security to the excluded majority of the world's population, the objective of this seminar was to discuss possible lessons from OECD experience with social security for economic and social development which would be relevant for development practitioners, donor agencies and developing country governments. The seminar considered whether the experience of poverty reduction in OECD countries provides a challenge to the dominant development paradigm in low-income countries, and discussed the case for putting in place low-cost social security systems within low-income countries based on experiences within OECD and middle-income countries.

We are most grateful to the participants of the seminar and their host institutions for the valuable inputs and inspiring exchanges during the seminar and during the subsequent preparation of the book. We would also like to take the opportunity to thank our partners in this endeavour, DFID and GTZ, for their unrelenting support which went way beyond the mere financial contribution. The book has also benefited from the comments and suggestions of an anonymous peer reviewer, for which we are most grateful.

Like the lively discussions during the seminar, the contributions assembled in this book reflect a broad range of different views and perspectives on the role of social security in development, and it should be stressed that the views expressed by the authors do not necessarily reflect the viewpoints of their home institutions and the organizers of the seminar. Nevertheless, the overall message of the book is clear: growing with equity is possible, and more than that, it is the only way to achieve decent societies.

Assane Diop
Executive Director, Social Protection Sector
International Labour Office

Acknowledgements

This book sets out to provide facts, views and new fragments of thought for the exciting global debate on an emerging new development policy paradigm. Juan Somavia, the Director-General of the ILO, generally summarizes that new paradigm in a single statement: 'countries can grow with equity'. This means that countries can pursue a comprehensive Decent Work agenda including the provision of adequate levels of social security to all their residents, while they are developing economically. No country has to wait till economic growth 'trickles down' to the poor and disenfranchised to lift them out of misery. The authors think that the famous trade-off between equity and efficiency in economic development is a myth. More importantly we think that social security is an economic and social pre-requisite for development.

Particular thanks are due to each of the authors and co-authors of the chapters below, who went to considerable lengths to search evidence, update drafts and meet probing questions from colleagues and myself. I am especially grateful to Michael Cichon and Christina Behrendt of the ILO, and Stephen Kidd of HelpAge (formerly of DFID), for advice, technical and editing support and information in the preparation of the draft of the book and its subsequent revision. They gave the work direction and precision that otherwise it would not have had.

Over many years Tony Atkinson has set an example of the ways to link economics, and for me that has also meant sociology, with international social policy – as can be discerned in many pages of this book. David Gordon of the International Poverty Research Centre in the University of Bristol has led a research team measuring poverty in relation to human rights with a steadiness of vision and technical expertise that few could match. During the early years of the new millennium I have enjoyed sharing in the work of that team – who include Ruth Levitas, Shailen Nandy, Christina Pantazis and Simon Pemberton – and examples of some of the results of the research will be found below.

I wish to thank Conor Gearty and Margot Salomon for their friendship and intoxicatingly original and judicious work on human rights and for allowing me to share that work during the last ten years at LSE.

I have had valuable exchanges with Mark Pearson and Maxime Ladaique, and the advice of Raul Suarez, all of the Organization for Economic Cooperation and Development (OECD). Maxime has steered me through statistical minefields, and was invariably patient and constructive with my inquiries.

I owe much to Sue Brattle for preparatory research into international funding for development on behalf of children – a subject of great prospective importance. I am grateful to Marialaura Ena for her swift research support at the London School of Economics (LSE) in 2006; to Krzysztof Hagemejer for wise advice and hospitality; Gordon Fisher for unrivalled precision about past measures of poverty and developments in social security in the United States; Francesca Bastagli, Sarah Clewes, Nic Stavnes, John Hills, David Piachaud, Hakan Seckinelgin, Tony Hall, John Wilkes, Sarah Roberts, Anne Okello, Helen Gordon and Michael Shiner of LSE for various particular acts of generosity; and to Maria Petmesidou and Christos Papatheodoru for data about the countries of Southern Europe. I believe most if not all of them share a belief in the capacity of social security systems to be the principal weapon in the continuing fight against world poverty.

To Jean, my wife, and to our grandchildren, who sustained me through a difficult patch and who unwittingly contributed to the reflections in this book about the rights and needs of children and not just households, I owe you my love.

Last but not least, let me emphasize that the views expressed here are those of the authors and by no means those of the organizations or institutions they are affiliated with.

Peter Townsend
Bristol, May 2009

Note: An obituary written by Tom Clark, detailing Peter Townsend's outstanding career as an academic and as a tireless campaigner against poverty, in particular child poverty, appeared in *The Guardian* on 9 June 2009 (http://www.guardian.co.uk/society/2009/jun/09/obituary-peter-townsend).

1
Introduction

Peter Townsend

This book addresses the question whether and how social protection systems in general, and social security in particular, should be brought nearer the top of the world's policy agenda. Universal social security systems, which are elaborately established in OECD countries, are not yet actively promoted in low-income countries as a prime means of reducing poverty to contribute to economic and social development. Recognizing that economic and social development are inextricably intertwined across countries, new international strategies are required to establish social security, reduce poverty and productively contribute to economic and social development.

Among the key issues identified for urgent investigation are the historical development of social security in OECD countries and what in particular had brought about the relevant institutions in those countries; the relationship between growth, poverty reduction, state-building and social security in OECD and middle-income countries; whether growth, national wealth and an 'effective state' had been necessary preconditions for, or positive outcomes of, social security; whether there are trade-offs in OECD countries between growth and social security; what wider functions were being served by social security systems in, for example, tackling inequality and exclusion, reducing social conflict, managing demand in the economy, improving the efficiency of labour markets, and protecting workforces; how far, and in what respects, social security in high-income and low-income countries is sustainable and affordable, especially in relation to the impact on job markets; and what lessons might be derived from such cross-national analysis for low-income countries in the context of the challenges they currently face in achieving the Millennium Development Goals, building effective states, and accelerating their own economic and social development.

The ILO has been foremost among international organizations in working up these ideas. The first international labour Convention on social security was adopted at the First Session of the International Labour Conference in 1919. The mandate about social security was incorporated in the ILO Constitution and reaffirmed on 10 May 1944 in the Declaration of Philadelphia.[1]

This statement greatly influenced the international discussions then taking place in preparation of the Universal Declaration of Human Rights, in which the right to social security (Article 25) was incorporated in 1948. The same right was incorporated subsequently into the International Covenant on Economic, Social and Cultural Rights and other human rights instruments.[2] The European Social Charter (Article 12) and the Amsterdam Treaty of 2002 (Articles 136 and 137) went on to reaffirm the right.

Since 1919 the International Labour Conference has adopted 31 Conventions and 23 Recommendations on social security (Kulke and Morales, 2006; see also Humblet and Silva, 2002). Of the eight social security Conventions currently being considered up to date, the flagship Convention is the Social Security (Minimum Standards) Convention, No. 102 (1952), which sets minimum standards for the seven branches of social security: medical care; sickness benefit; unemployment benefit; family benefit; maternity benefit; invalidity benefit; and survivors' benefit. This Convention is also wider in coverage than some earlier conventions that concentrated largely on social insurance. Certain benefits are guaranteed. But signatory states are allowed flexibility in two respects – their minimum obligation is to meet at least three of the nine branches of guaranteed social security benefit and to improve coverage of population progressively rather than comprehensively at once.

The idea has been to progressively realize a comprehensive plan for the social security of entire populations (Kulke and Morales, 2006: 4). A distinction was made between universal schemes of public service, social insurance schemes with earnings-related or flat-rate components, or both, and social assistance schemes. By 2006, 42 countries had ratified Convention No. 102 and have thereby 'incorporated its provisions into their legal systems and, in many cases, their national practice' (Kulke and Morales, 2006: 6). Many developing countries are said to have been inspired by Convention No. 102 'even though nearly all their systems are more modest in scope and, in general, do not yet encompass unemployment and family benefits' (ibid.). Because of the priority given to children in the Millennium Development Goals it is surprising that many of the ILO's member states have not given greater attention to children's allowances within family benefit and to child benefit in particular.

Despite burgeoning international expressions of support in the last half-century for the establishment of institutions conferring the right to social security, huge sections of the world's population continue to be denied this right. For example, as lately as 2006 the Committee on Economic, Social and Cultural Rights (CESCR) stated that it was 'concerned at the extremely poor levels of access to social security ... Over half the world's population lacks access to *any* type of social security protection and only one in five people have adequate social security coverage' (Committee on Economic, Social and Cultural Rights, 2006: 3).

This book is based on a broad understanding of social security which is defined as 'the set of institutions, measures, rights and obligations whose primary goal is to provide – or aim to provide – according to specified rules, income security and medical care to individual members of society' (Cichon and Hagemejer, 2006). Social protection or social security systems[3] incorporate '(1) those cash transfers in a society that seek to provide income security and, by extension, to prevent or alleviate poverty; (2) those measures which guarantee access to medical care, health and social services; and (3) other measures of a similar nature designed to protect the income, health and well-being of workers and their families' (ibid.).

The review is deliberately global in its approach, but limited space made it necessary to single out some aspects of the role of social security in development, and leave other aspects of the subject, which would require more exhaustive research, for future discussion. Among the issues which have been identified as deserving a separate discussion are the relationship between international labour migration and access to social security, the implications of the rapid demographic change in many parts of the developing world for the livelihoods of the population and their access to social security, and the role of cultural factors in extending social security coverage.

The right to social security and national development: drawing together the high- and low-income countries

The book is organized in four parts, the first of which provides a summary account on the right to social security and national development in high- and low-income countries. Peter Townsend in Chapter 2 maps recent public spending on social security systems by the 30 OECD countries, and traces the consequential reduction in poverty. The chapter looks at the varied historical developments in close detail and a typology of welfare states is characterized. The social security systems had been built up in these countries for many decades, and despite recent fluctuations in particular countries, spending as a percentage of GDP had continued to rise during 2000–5, reaching an average percentage of 13 per cent of GDP in 2005, with 20 per cent of GDP committed altogether to public social expenditure. The analysis finds that when applying the conventional European poverty line, average poverty in the 30 countries would have been 45 per cent in 2005 if public social security did not exist, but was in fact 15 per cent.

By striking contrast, the percentage of GDP assigned to public social security in many low-income countries is less than 4, and in India and most of sub-Saharan Africa as little as 1.5 or 1. Without social security there is little chance of 'trickle down' from economic growth, debt relief or overseas aid to seriously reduce poverty. The difference is explained in part by history but also by the disposition globally of economic power today which discourages or disables low-income countries from following the historical path taken by the OECD countries. The lack of social security institutions is difficult to justify in relation to global economic developments and social and economic needs.

The need to bring together the management of social security policies in industrialized and developing countries is demonstrated not only by deepening world poverty but also by the rapid growth in a number of human rights treaties. Mounting acceptance throughout the world of human rights puts pressure on all countries to recast development policies and eliminate poverty. Human rights have come to play a central part in discussions about economic and social development, and the various instruments have been ratified by the great majority of governments in the world. The chapter traces the divergent historical experience in 'developed' and 'developing' countries of putting into practice the fundamental rights to social security, including social insurance, and an 'adequate' standard of living. These rights have not been routinely investigated during a long period of intensifying world concern about the persistence of large-scale extreme poverty.

Thus, they were not regarded as a necessary element of the discussions of structural adjustment policies and then the Social Fund in the 1980s and 1990s, in the fraught regions of sub-Saharan Africa, Latin America, South Asia and Eastern Europe, nor later at the time of the introduction by the UN of the Millennium Development Goals. The international financial agencies focused attention on targeting and short-term means-tested benefits at least expense rather than also, or instead of, minimal living standards for all. This mistake was compounded by an over-generalized, ambiguous and undirected international anti-poverty strategy – concerned in the broadest and most indirect terms with economic growth, overseas aid, debt relief and fairer trade. Whether there was 'trickle down' or even proportionate benefits derived by the poorest sections of population was not investigated and monitored.

In more than three decades economic development policies advocated by the international financial agencies and leading governments have not incorporated sufficient information and direction about the course of corresponding, not to say consequential, social development. Policies designed to establish and invigorate universal public social services and social security payments came to be treated as aberrations of the past rather than as institutions as necessary to the future as to the past. Attempts to restrain and roll back social security were made with too little understanding of the accumulating historical impetus in all OECD countries of its elaborate institutions and multiple functions. This report has sought to review that history.

The strength of a universalistic, human rights, approach to social security, is in turning to future advantage what, after extraordinary struggle, proved to be a highly successful strategy in the past. Working people responded to extreme individual need by combining in collective interest to contribute creatively to economic development and the alleviation of the poverty of others in their midst. Collective protest and action led to the social good – often by the extension of the ideas of representative democracy and citizen participation.

Through social security, coalitions can be built between groups in society of a more varied kind, say, than those representing familiar ethnic or religious divisions. Again, social security systems have created and continue to create cross-cutting and three-generational social identities and have moderated multiple forms of discrimination. Nationalism reinterpreted as universalism reinforces good multi-cultural and multi-generational values that promote stability.

Issues for the global society of the twenty-first century

The following chapters identify issues of concern for the global society of the twenty-first century and highlight the role of social security for economic and social development.

Multiple social and political functions of social security

Chris de Neubourg (Chapter 3) shows that social protection systems have multiple functions which have to be understood. Thus, they have helped to establish democratic statehood in the different countries of Europe. Quoting T. H. Marshall, he points out that political developments have induced the realization of increments of citizenship rights, with civil rights becoming universalized in the eighteenth century, political rights in the nineteenth and social rights in the twentieth century.

Thus in 1878 Bismarck in Germany proposed social policy 'to destroy the growing social democrat movement' by creating a tight bond between the state and the workers. Already the 1870 unification had integrated the mass of workers in the different regions. In 1911 Lloyd George followed the promptings by Churchill as well as Beveridge by introducing the National Insurance Act. And in Sweden between 1889 and 1913 social policy helped to cement the ties between 'the new semi-urban proletariat, the rural poor and the free peasantry as well as the industrialists and older fractions of the ruling class'.

The First World War and its aftermath of economic crises in the late 1920s and early 1930s reinforced the need for unified and systematic social policies. In conditions of social unrest extensive schemes for social protection were accepted to secure social cohesion. And in 1942 the Beveridge report brought institutions and individuals into partnership with the state in 'a common condemnation of the scandal of physical want'. After the Second World War, most of Europe developed systems of 'cradle-to-grave' universal benefits and compulsory contribution-based insurances. The war had left deep divisions and rebuilding the social infrastructure played an important role in that process.

There are two main forms of social transfers: universalist benefits and benefits targeted exclusively to the (very) poor. In contrast to Anglo-Saxon countries and the United States[4] most of continental Europe largely opted for a universalist system complemented with a quantitatively small targeted component. This leads to discussions about who are the 'deserving', and thus eligible, and who are the 'non-deserving' – and thus non-eligible poor. The Danish constitution of 1849 referred to the 'deserving and non-deserving poor' (see Johansen, 1986 for Denmark and Flora and Heidenheimer, 1981 for Britain). This historical example is a strong illustration of the social stigma that was and still is attached to means-tested social benefits. The resulting discrimination and social exclusion is inimical to the ideals of the democratic ordering and does not exactly turn social policy into the completion of the political rights-based movement that installed democracies in Europe.

There is also a pragmatic argument that makes universal benefits attractive from a democratic state formation point of view. The implementation of alternative means-tested transfers requires a robust and fairly sophisticated bureaucratic apparatus that is often not available in countries that build up their social policy capacity. The capacity needed to fully implement the means testing and monitor applicants in order to decide whether or not they are entitled to receive the transfer in the future, is impressive. Data on the means of households – including income from various sources and means stemming from the availability of assets – are difficult to obtain and even more difficult to control. Protocols and procedures are difficult to design and to implement in a fair way across different regions in a country. All this is particularly difficult for weak states with serious limitations in their educated workforce. The adoption of proxy-means-testing methods is sometimes used to simplify the selection of beneficiaries and the transfer allocation decisions. The accuracy of this method is, however, far from encouraging, as illustrated by a recent study in Mongolia on the proxy-means-tested benefits, which concluded that more than one-third of the target group did not receive a benefit (exclusion error) while two-thirds of the non-targeted group received a transfer (inclusion error).

Economic effects of social protection

In Chapter 4 Michael Cichon and Wolfgang Scholz seek to establish the state of the art on what we know – or seem to know – about the economic effects of social protection. The standard economic arguments on the potential interrelationship between social security and economic performance are revisited, wide-ranging statistical evidence is evaluated and finally the authors refute three of the major myths about the relationship between social protection and economic performance, namely: (1) that at each stage of development societies can only afford a certain level of social expenditure (the affordability myth); (2) that economic growth will automatically reduce poverty (the trickle-down myth); and (3) that there is a trade-off between social expenditure and economic efficiency (the trade-off myth).

They point out that there is clear evidence from Europe and OECD countries that social transfers successfully reduce poverty and social insecurity. They go on with statistical analysis of long-term growth rates in the OECD to show that the correlation between growth performance and the share of GDP that is allocated to social expenditure is weak. The scale of social expenditure does not explain a large part of national economic performance and does not seem to have a significant impact on economic growth. National policies and social security system designs can lead to a wide range of different levels of social expenditure at each level of GDP.

Their technical investigation applies to many countries. A regression analysis of social expenditure expressed as a ratio of GDP and the employment-to-population ratios of the age group 15–64 for OECD countries finds virtually no association between the two. The influence of the SER (social expenditure ratio) on employment levels is statistically not very significant.

Although keenly aware of the desirability of further research to explore economic modelling in detail of the relationship between economic growth and increased expenditure on social protection they conclude that three famous myths have been sufficiently discredited:

1. *The poverty alleviating trickle-down effect of economic growth is not reliable.* A high correlation between low poverty levels and high social security expenditure on the macro-level was found. Economic growth does not automatically reduce poverty unless redistributive mechanisms (such as social security systems) are in place. There is thus a good case for social transfers as poverty alleviation mechanisms and hence as a mechanism to foster social development.
2. *The famous trade-off between social expenditure and economic performance does not hold.* High social security expenditure does not automatically suppress employment. Hence high social expenditure and top economic performance can co-exist. Put more specifically, extensive social protection expenditure per capita and high productivity can co-exist. From the point of view of mathematical logic the neo-classical trade-off between equity and efficiency does not hold true.
3. *There is no strict limit for national social expenditure depending on the level of economic development.* In many discussions on levels of social security expenditure in ILO member States non-affordability arguments are fielded, i.e. that certain countries cannot afford more than a certain level of expenditure at a given state of economic performance. Most of such general arguments appear unfounded. The authors find that at any given level of GDP per capita there is a wide range of social expenditure between different countries. While conditions differ from country to country (for example the demographic situation) there is considerable

policy space with respect to the components of national social expenditure (and incidentally public expenditure in general).

Affordability of social security

Is social security affordable in the poorest countries? Krzysztof Hagemejer and Christina Behrendt (Chapter 5) argue a qualified 'yes'. In 2001 the ILO called for an extension of social security. There were precedents upon which low-income countries might build. Some African countries like Namibia and Mauritius had introduced non-contributory pension and disability schemes for all their elderly residents. At an ILO African regional conference in 2007 specific policies to achieve an extension of social security were agreed.

The chapter explores the feasibility of financing different social security packages in seven African and five Asian countries with a mixture of resources from international grants from donor countries. The African countries are Burkina Faso, Cameroon, Ethiopia, Guinea, Kenya, Senegal and Tanzania. The Asian countries are Bangladesh, India, Nepal, Pakistan and Viet Nam. In determining minimum levels of cost the basic social protection package was divided into four elements: (1) universal basic old age and disability pension; (2) basic child benefit – whether universal or limited to orphans; (3) targeted cash transfers for the most vulnerable households; and (4) universal access to health care.

Second, a daily rate of cost per person had to be fixed. The aim was to reduce poverty in the target groups even if the benefit could not eliminate poverty. One alternative for pensions was to set a proportion of the international absolute poverty line of US$1 PPP per day. The other alternative was to apply a fixed percentage of the average income per person, using GDP per person as a proxy for income, since income information for many countries is not available. The standards set were deliberately low. The test of affordability was set by a model of half US$1 PPP per day for all aged 65+. Variants for children included a low universal benefit for children of only 0.35 US$1 PPP per day, for orphans up to 14 years a benefit of 0.15 US$1 PPP per day, and a cash transfer of less than 0.5 US$1 PPP per day aimed only at the poorest 10 per cent of population.

In planning realistic future steps for social protection the coverage and adequacy of existing institutions as well as their costs in each low-income country had to be reliably established. A balance also had to be struck between expansion of existing schemes and what priority had to be given to new and substitute schemes, taking account of what had happened in middle- and high-income countries. Alternative low-cost models deserved serious appraisal. One option was to assume that governments increased social protection, namely on basic social transfers and health care, to one-fifth of their total expenditure (a lower fraction than reached by middle- and high-income countries). By 2010 it could be calculated, for example, that minimum social protection expenditure in low-income countries would cost between 2.4 per cent and 5.8 per cent of GDP.

The authors argue that the question is not whether the low-income countries can afford social security, but whether they can afford not to have social security. They call attention to ample evidence that investment in health care, education and properly designed cash transfers has positive economic and social effects at any stage of development.

They consider the evidence presented shows that low-income countries not only should but could have social security systems. An affordable basic package of health services for everybody and basic cash benefits for the elderly and families with children could be constructed. As countries achieved higher levels of economic development these systems could also grow in scope, levels and quality of benefits and services. Affordability was demonstrable, as the models applied in detail in the chapter showed. This path of development could be achieved by the joint efforts of low-income countries themselves (reallocating existing resources and raising new ones) and of the international donor community (having to refocus grants providing the direct finance of social protection benefits, strengthening administrative and delivery capacity of the relevant institutions nationally and locally, and providing technical advice and support.

Collective as well as individual shocks that have to be prevented by social protection

Michael Samson (Chapter 6) takes a hard look at developments of cash transfers in South Africa, paying particular attention to other developing countries. He insists that to reach the right answers the breadth of the problem of poverty has to be understood first. Distinctively, he argues that social shocks (contrasted with poor continuing conditions) force people into forms of poverty that oblige wider and more effective social protection strategies to be considered.

There are calamities such as wars, civil conflicts, earthquakes and tsunamis that can suddenly impoverish, indeed devastate, entire populations over immense areas. There are smaller-scale shocks, such as job loss, severe illness, disability and death that unexpectedly impoverish single individuals and households without affecting most of the other people in the community. Government schemes, like social insurance, and the extended family, together with the local community, have been the formal and informal coping mechanisms when there is sudden individual impoverishment. But the traditional coping mechanisms of society can be overwhelmed by sudden collective impoverishment.

The two extremes provoke thoughts about the differences between transitory and chronic poverty – but alleviation, and prevention, of transitory and chronic poverty have much in common. The possibility of shocks creates risk – and the poor must acquire coping mechanisms in order to survive.

Without effective social protection, the poorest often develop survival strategies that perpetuate chronic poverty. Poor farmers may adopt safer but lower yielding crop varieties, helping prevent a slide into absolute destitution but also foreclosing promising opportunities to break free from poverty. Imaginative social planning can compensate for individual risk but also pre-empt individual and collective risk from arising in the first place.

Michael Samson takes examples from different countries. Shocks in Ethiopia are central to the life of the poor – and threaten productive assets and create poverty traps. In a recent study nearly every poor household in the sample experienced a severe shock that intensified their poverty. Over a five-year period (1999–2004), 95 per cent of families listed at least one serious shock that led to hardship, including drought (47 per cent), a death in the household (43 per cent) or a serious illness (28 per cent). The poor are more risk averse when they have no insurance or safety net to protect them. It is the same in Tanzania, where unmitigated risk leads to investment behaviour that lowers the expected returns by about 25 per cent, reinforcing poverty traps. In the absence of risk mitigation instruments, the poor invest in assets with safer but lower expected returns. With insurance-like mechanisms, however, the poor take greater risks with much higher expected returns – and can break the poverty trap.

Drought in Kenya affects the spectrum of the poor in multiple ways. The very poorest face starvation – utter destitution. Those who are poor but have some assets often must sell these productive assets in order to survive, and this intensifies their poverty. Those who are less poor nevertheless face economic decline all around them. As a result they face fewer economic opportunities and a greater likelihood of falling into poverty.

Social transfers now present an increasingly attractive option for poor countries to tackle such multiple dimensions of poverty. They lighten long-term conditions of deprivation and soften the blow of sudden crisis. Social transfers also benefit those poor with productive assets – by enabling them to weather shocks without compromising their future livelihoods in order to survive today. Farmers are less likely to sell the livestock on which their future prosperity depends if adequate cash transfers protect their immediate subsistence.

At a macroeconomic level the redistributional impact of social transfers shifts the composition of demand within the economy. South Africa provides one convincing example. Prior to the 1994 democratic elections, racially skewed social transfer programmes failed to adequately reach the poorest, and economic growth languished. The progressive realization of people's rights to social security during the 1990s did not undermine the pro-growth economic agenda. The acceleration of grant spending after 2000 did not deter the broadest economic expansion South Africa had experienced in half a century.

Empirical studies of the impact of social protection measures on labour markets in developing countries find that an increase in real minimum wages is accompanied by a fall in poverty. The improvements in social services are also found to directly improve human well-being – hunger is reduced, health improves, people benefit from education, people feel more secure, they have jobs, there are macroeconomic benefits. Low-income African and Asian countries can minimally protect the poorest at a cost usually less than 3 per cent of current government budgets. Structural empowerment has to be widely applied in labour and other social conditions that are fluid from day to day.

Brazil is an example of a country rapidly expanding a programme (*Bolsa Família*) that provides grants to poor households, particularly for the purpose of improving health and education outcomes. India is implementing a national public works guarantee programme, scaling up a highly successful social transfer model from the state of Maharashtra. Over the past ten years scores of countries have substantially expanded existing social transfer programmes or initiated new interventions or pilots. They continue to get too little international support and recognition of the need for the multiplication of effective schemes.

The transfers can be unconditional, conditional on households actively fulfilling human development responsibilities (education, health, nutrition, etc.) or else conditional on recipients providing labour in compliance with a work requirement. The transfers can be universal or explicitly targeted to the poor and vulnerable – but more successfully to easy-to-define groups in the population – such as children, people with disabilities, bereaved and older people rather than to individuals or households judged poor according to elaborate tests of means.

Many of the poorest countries in the world, however, provide no publicly funded social transfer to the poor. In the absence of public transfers, the poorest households rely on private remittances – cash payments from other (often poor) individuals. While private transfers provide a critical safety net in the absence of government interventions, private remittances are usually inadequate to address the consequences of severe poverty. In many low-income countries, private remittances are financed largely through the toil of the working poor. The regressive nature of this redistributional mechanism limits its ability to address poverty – particularly in those countries where the poor face severe shocks such as HIV/AIDS, war and natural disasters exacerbated by climate change.

Social protection serves as an effective insurance mechanism to protect the poor – enabling them to take on prudent risks that promote their livelihoods. When the poor have access to insurance-like social protection mechanisms, they take greater risks that yield higher returns – and in some cases break out of poverty. South Africa's social grants counter these negative effects by providing households with more resources to finance education. Children in households that receive social grants are more likely to attend school, even when controlling for the effect of income. The positive effects of social security on education are greater for girls than for boys, helping to remedy gender disparities.

Spending in households that receive social grants focuses more on basics like food, fuel, housing and household operations, and less is spent on tobacco and debt. All major social grants – the Older Person's Pension, the Child Support Grant and the Disability Grant – are significantly and positively associated with a greater share of household expenditure on food. This increased spending on food is associated with better nutritional outcomes. Households that receive social grants have lower prevalence rates of hunger for young children as well as older children and adults, even compared to those households with comparable income levels.

The results from the employment equations yield more significant results. For both rural males and females, the effects of the State Old Age Pension and the Disability Grant are statistically significantly positive. Workers in households receiving either a State Old Age Pension or a Disability Grant are significantly more likely to be employed. The child support grant demonstrates a similar effect. Working age adults that were not participating in the labour force – particularly women – in poor households that receive a child support grant are more likely to look for work and more likely to find employment than comparable adults in households that do not receive the child support grant.

For most developing countries, more effective social protection is likely to promote economic growth and development. Social transfers significantly reduce inequality – supporting social stability and fostering investment and economic growth. Well-designed social transfers do not create dependency – they often break dependency traps, particularly by nurturing productive high-return risk-taking. At a macro level they can help restructure the economy to support job creation and economic growth. Social transfers also create fiscal effects that support long-term affordability and economic sustainability.

Priority for children

Children are at greater risk of being in poverty than women and men. The reasons for this, and possible remedies, are discussed by Peter Townsend in Chapter 7. At the turn of the nineteenth century the industrializing powers introduced laws against the employment of children and women in hazardous conditions, and also introduced universal social security schemes and social services to ensure stability during a period of economic upheaval and very rapid population growth. The market adapted its practices to meet these laws. Poverty was greatly reduced. State action and market collaboration more than 100 years ago hold lessons for the treatment of severe problems experienced today by low-income countries.

A special investigation for UNICEF found that 56 per cent of children in developing countries – 1.2 billion – experienced one or more forms of severe deprivation, over half of them (674 million) at least two forms of severe multiple deprivation like total absence of toilet facilities, lack of nearby clean water, malnutrition and extreme overcrowding and poor shelter. Over 10 million children in developing countries die each year, mainly from preventable causes, including malnutrition, pneumonia, diarrhoea, measles and malaria. Scientific research has shown that many of these deaths could be prevented using readily available medical technologies at comparatively little cost and many more by providing resources for shelter, clean water, sanitary facilities, food and fuel. Many children orphaned by HIV/AIDS could be saved from miserable existence and early painful death. The number in sub-Saharan Africa is expected to rise to 16 million, or a quarter of all children, by 2010.

Studies of enforced child deprivation have attracted wide public attention. In a 2007 report the WHO compared children in the poorest 20 per cent of households with the richest 20 per cent and found that 58 per cent of under-fives in the poorest 20 per cent of households in India, compared with 42 per cent in sub-Saharan Africa and 36 per cent in Latin America, are physically stunted for their age, compared with 27 per cent, 23 per cent and 4 per cent, respectively, in the richest 20 per cent of households. Mortality rates of under-fives in the poorest households in these three regions are also disproportionately high – being 14 per cent, 16 per cent and 9 per cent respectively.

The Convention on the Rights of the Child contains elaborate injunctions to protect children from malnutrition, maltreatment, neglect, abuse and exploitation and ensure they are not deprived of access to clean water, sanitary facilities, shelter, health care services, education and information: governments are enjoined to 'recognize the right of every child to a standard of living adequate for the child's physical, mental, spiritual, moral and social development'. The statements, ratified by nearly all of the 191 nation-states in the world, allow single but also multiple measures or indicators of the denial or fulfilment of the specified rights to be devised and tracked.

The poverty of children arises in part from harsh working conditions in which they, and their parents, are placed. Children as young as 7 are reliably reported to be producing paving stones, footballs, clothing and carpets, operating with dangerous pesticides and other chemicals, digging trenches, picking cotton and working in mines – often for ten or more hours a day. The problem is that routine observance of children's needs and rights is neither widely proclaimed nor enforced. Responsibility extends beyond state laws.

Transnational corporations (TNCs) have become a focus of attention. The largest have much greater powers than the governments of low-income countries and their responsibility for harsh conditions that may be created by sub-contractors and subsidiaries is not easy to assess accurately, even for the TNCs themselves. Peter Townsend argues that TNCs and international agencies can work wonders by committing a tiny percentage of their growing resources in particular to social security in the low-income countries, and also by moving towards acceptance of minimum standards of monthly or weekly income on the part of wage-earners and those not in paid employment who are entitled to social security.

For example, transnational employers could add 1 or 2 per cent of wage costs in different countries towards a child benefit to help banish malnutrition, poverty and premature child death, and also encourage more schooling. One practical possibility would be to extend existing employer contributions towards domestic social insurance schemes in the OECD countries to employer operations in the low-income countries. A small Currency Transfer Tax (CTT) (perhaps 0.2 per cent, raising a minimum of US$280 billion) could produce even larger resources. James Tobin had introduced the idea in 1972 and again in the 1990s. Peter Townsend proposes this as the basis for a UN Investment Fund for child benefit to reduce child poverty.

Universal cash benefit schemes for children (together with other schemes discussed in this book for disabled and elderly people) can be introduced in low-income countries by stages. The administrative infrastructures would become one major source of economic and social stability to pit against the unravelling problems of conflict, AIDS and competitive global avarice.

Social protection in Europe and the OECD

The economic growth of OECD countries, especially of the European member countries, has been accompanied over many years by the steady installation of major institutions of social security. The following four chapters scrutinize the history of this process and the effects of social security policies on poverty reduction, economic growth and political stability.

Models of social security in industrialized countries

Systems of relief for the poor have evolved during the last six centuries in Europe. During the rapid industrialization and democratization of the late nineteenth and early twentieth centuries the methods of relief under the poor laws came to be rejected and individual rights to an income in various forms of adversity gradually established. To explore the potentialities of social security for human livelihood and social stability in the twenty-first century the authors of this book became aware of the value to low-income governments and international bodies of tracing recent developments in the OECD countries. Thus, substantial social security spending in Europe, i.e. more than an eighth of GDP, is often consistent with above-average economic growth.

Every OECD country has exceptional features. Nonetheless there is support on grounds of economic and social performance for a classification into three models, represented in Chapter 8 by Norway ('Nordic' or 'Social Democratic'), Germany ('Corporatist') and the United States and the United

Kingdom ('Liberal' or 'Residual'). Poverty and inequality rates are smallest in the countries of the first of these three models and largest in the third. The evidence about economic performance is less conclusive. In all three models comprehensive social insurance and schemes covering everyone in certain population groups (such as the elderly, disabled, children) account for the great majority of expenditure, and means-tested social assistance for the, usually small, minority. Comprehensive social insurance and benefit schemes for entire social groups (children, disabled, elderly) account for two-thirds of the costs of schemes in the OECD to redistribute income to reduce poverty. Measures to increase the living standards of these three groups can be regarded as the 'bedrock' measures in social security systems everywhere. Means-tested social assistance and tax credits account for only one-third of OECD social security costs and have well-testified social and administrative disadvantages.

The contributions of the Council of Europe and the European Union

Raymond Wagener (Chapter 9) explains the history of the Council of Europe and the European Union in developing common values and the European social model. The social dimension of the European Union was first established in 1951 and especially in the agreement reached by the original six 'Corporatist regime' countries signing up to the European Economic Community. The development of social security systems was a basic assumption. The first three of the Articles of the 2005 Treaty establishing a constitution for Europe call, among other things, for the promotion of social justice, the defeat of social exclusion and discrimination and 'the eradication of poverty and the protection of human rights'. He argues that the European Union is at a defining moment: should it develop into 'a social market economy allowing all its citizens to live in dignity and share the prosperity of the Union, or ... into a pure market economy with a residual social policy of poverty reduction?'

Too few initiatives had been taken at European level to develop a real 'European' social model because of the allegiance to the subsidiarity principle which encouraged the view that social protection policies were a matter of national sovereignty. An urgent programme of European investment and subsidy, led perhaps by introducing a 'super-Tobin' type of tax on all electronic transactions for member states, would be one possible remedy. Without a stronger position on social policies at the EU level there is a danger that the development of the 'free market' based on EU legislation will prevail over national social protection laws. The EU has responsibilities regarding social justice within the globalized world. Based on the rich experience of social protection policies within the EU, Europe is well placed to contribute decisively to the development of a global human development model built on solidarity and social justice for all.

Lessons from the European model

Peter Lindert (Chapter 10) finds that, despite pressure from the current orthodoxy of economic opinion to cut public expenditure to make room for economic development, established welfare state spending in Europe is remarkably resilient. He then tries to establish whether the European model of welfare can be exported to developing countries. Comparing first the existing models of welfare in Europe and the developing world he concludes that rich democracies have relatively egalitarian programmes, some of which are universal and some of which are targeted at the poorest income ranks. By contrast, in developing countries relatively regressive, or even elitist, programmes still prevail while notable changes are underway. The author argues that differences in political voice was and is one of the main reasons for the present different forms of welfare in different parts of the world as well as recent changes. The Latin American and the Indian examples prove the point. These are the two major regions of the world where vibrant democracies are changing the weight of the voice of the poor and disenfranchised. The welfare states in these regions are far from qualifying – with respect to their redistributive dimension – as European-style welfare states but as an effect of the greater weight of the voice of the poor efforts are underway to make them more progressive and even explicitly pro-poor – at least in part. In Thailand an explicitly pro-poor health system was explicitly used to harness the votes of the poor. The European model of welfare may never be fully emulated in developing countries, but the fact that it is resilient in Europe and continues to stabilize societies – despite the fashionable short-sighted criticism that is apparent in many countries – is still providing a useful reference for welfare state reformers and protagonists in the developing world. It is too early to say how far welfare reforms in the developing world will go, aiming at greater income security and more equality. However, what we can observe is a positive gradient.

Social security in the European Union

Bea Cantillon (Chapter 11) examines developments within the European Union, and makes use of key indicators of national income, employment and total public social expenditure to explore how they correlate with the scale of poverty in different member countries.

She finds that poverty in Europe is correlated with relatively low GDP, a low rate of employment and a low level of public social expenditure. The relationship between low public social expenditure and poverty in particular is significant. No European country has succeeded in achieving below-average poverty with below-average social spending.

The Nordic countries, where the risks of poverty are lowest, combine a high level of social spending with high GDP as well as high employment rates. Some countries with low employment rates (such as France, Germany and Belgium) succeed in keeping poverty also relatively low, thanks to a high level of social spending. Likewise, some of the poorer countries succeed in attaining below-average poverty thanks to social spending. In other words, low employment rates and low GDP in certain EU member states is compensated for through high social expenditure. However, no country succeeds in compensating a low level of social spending by means either of economic growth or high employment. Rich, high-employment countries where social spending is low end up with rates of poverty that are high. This leads to the conclusion that, if it is possible to attain a low risk of poverty without substantial public spending, it has yet to be demonstrated.

The high economic growth attained in post-war Western Europe has been a necessary condition for achieving social progress. Conversely, rising social expenditures have also contributed to economic growth. The successful combination of economic growth and greater social redistribution in the post-war era was built on social security systems that had gradually evolved since the end of the nineteenth century and this combination was generalized and institutionalized immediately after the 1939–45 war. In Western Europe, economic growth is thus firmly based upon social redistribution and vice versa.

The experience of enlargement seems to suggest that in the new member States low poverty is associated with relatively high social expenditures. It is true that, in most new member States, the same level of spending on social protection (in percentage of GDP) is associated with a poverty risk that is lower than that in the EU-15. However, in those new member States displaying a poverty risk below the EU-25 average, social expenditure levels amount to 20 per cent of GDP or more. This is the case in the Czech Republic, Slovenia and Hungary. Conversely, in all those countries where social expenditures are below average poverty is typically high.

Of course, welfare states differ in more respects than scale of public social expenditures. The importance of the structure and the efficiency of social protection should obviously not be underestimated. In Slovakia, Estonia and Poland poverty is high despite relatively generous expenditure levels. This suggests a rather inefficient social protection system in these countries.

However, in Europe the correlation between the generosity of benefits targeted to the poor and poverty is surprisingly weak. Although in a large majority of EU countries means-tested minimum income provisions have been introduced as general safety nets for the poor, only in five EU countries do these benefits equal the poverty threshold. Most countries with below-average poverty risks provide inadequate benefits (by this standard) while in two out of the five countries with adequate benefits overall poverty is high. This suggests that in most European countries universal social insurance programmes are more important in the fight against poverty than are means-tested social assistance systems of social protection.

There is a great diversity in Europe in terms of both social architecture and poverty outcomes, and this diversity has undoubtedly been further increased with enlargement. The newly acceded member States will most likely develop various new models of welfare democracies. Europe's diversity demonstrates that there are many paths towards attaining a social welfare democracy, depending on the socio-economic, demographic and cultural particularities and social practices that can vary widely from country to country.

Given the very weak economic base in many non-European countries, developing an adequate social protection for all citizens of the world will require a massive input from the affluent welfare states.

Experiences from low-income countries

Social security in developing countries: a brief overview

In Chapter 12 Peter Townsend contrasts the findings from Chapters 2 and 8 about social security systems in the rich countries with the early developments in low-income countries. Thus, contributory social insurance schemes for those of working age who became sick, disabled, unemployed or bereaved, and non-contributory tax-based benefit schemes, especially for children, disabled people and the elderly, were introduced in the leading industrial countries and these schemes had a lasting impact.

Existing social security schemes in developing countries are desperately under-resourced and present a diverse picture. Colonial authorities in most of Asia, Africa and the Caribbean had introduced schemes a century or more ago. They were meagre in coverage and cost and applied mainly to civil servants and employees of large enterprises. Small percentages of population gained access to health care, maternity leave, disability allowances and pensions. In general the poor, and especially rural poor, had no access to cash relief.

In the last decades there has been mounting concern about slow progress. The poorest countries have few means and small support from international organizations to build social security. Some middle-income countries have taken initiatives to introduce, and quickly scale up, cash transfer schemes. Elsewhere, as in India, the percentage of GDP committed to social protection has remained very small in comparison with the industrialized countries. There have been demonstration and pilot projects of the value to populations of particular types of scheme. The ILO reported a modelling exercise in which costs turned out to be 'within reasonable affordable limits' if countries were committed to reducing poverty. But the 'mobilization of international resources will be needed in order to make this an achievable target'.

Low-income countries experience conditions very different from those that applied in the nineteenth and twentieth centuries to industrializing countries that have become highly prosperous. At the end of the nineteenth century countries like Germany, the United Kingdom and the United States were not subject to the domination of much more powerful external governments, agencies and corporations. International taxation and not just national taxation is therefore at issue in reformulating appropriate modern policies.

The chapter suggests that national and international bodies may be obliged in the next few years to choose between two alternative grand strategies in the developing countries: (1) staged progress towards a major public system of social security costing substantially more than 10 per cent of GDP; and (2) conditional public cash transfer schemes targeting the extreme poor and costing less than 3 per cent of GDP.

Initiatives in low-income countries

Armando Barrientos (Chapter 13) reviews the main lessons to be learned from a range of social protection initiatives in low-income countries, including Bangladesh, Bolivia, Ethiopia, India, Nicaragua and Zambia. Many economists assume that establishing social protection is that much harder in low-income countries because of underdevelopment, fragmented political and policy processes, poor revenue raising capacity, and deficiencies in operational capacity. He illuminates the strength of these constraints, and the nature of potential remedies. Low levels of social protection can hinder, for example, the development of employment-based social insurance. He shows, contrary to some pessimists, that in fact there are many policy options available to governments of low-income countries, and the initiatives described have many positive effects in reaching the poor and next-to-poor, but are very small in scale. While fiscal deficits and operational capacity are also restrictive, global partnerships can work effectively to lift these constraints.

Strong partnerships between national governments, international donors, NGOs and researchers can work effectively to lift the financing and capacity constraints as well as the paucity of investment. Donors have a role to play in facilitating the expansion of social protection in these countries by reducing the initial costs associated with setting up appropriate programmes and policies, and national governments need to work on guaranteeing their sustainability by strengthening the domestic mobilization of resources and by strengthening capacity with support from NGOs and researchers. This investment will bring large rewards from the significant contribution social protection can make to social and economic transformation.

Lifting hard-hit populations out of poverty

Rachel Slater, John Farrington, Rebecca Holmes and Paul Harvey (Chapter 14) examine some of the poorest countries – Bangladesh, Ethiopia and Malawi – to explore what combination of policies in rural areas may best promote production as well as social protection to lift hard-hit populations out of poverty. Among both governments and donors they report a widespread view that initiatives to reduce risk and vulnerability are a drain on public funds and limit levels of public investment in the productive sectors – including agriculture. However, they go on to argue from emerging research that there can be positive synergies between social protection and agricultural growth policies whereby social protection interventions reduce the risks faced by poor rural households who are dependent on agriculture.

Ethiopia offers a particularly instructive example. Recognizing the damaging effect that food aid distribution has had on local markets and farmers' incentives to invest in agricultural production, the government has sought to move away from a food-first to a cash-first approach. With support from a wide range of donors, the Ethiopian government developed the Productive Safety Net Programme (PSNP), providing six months of support every year to households in designated food insecure *woreda*s (i.e. districts). Payments are made either as cash or food or a combination of cash and food. About 80 per cent of beneficiary households gain their entitlement by participating in public works, while the remaining 20 per cent, in which no one is of an age or in a condition to be economically active, receive direct support with no work requirement. Introduced in 2005 the programme experienced the familiar problem of being eagerly taken up more by those who were not the poorest or most food insecure. Some of the poorest were excluded in the processes of selection and implementation.

However, the programmes had the positive effect of creating community assets, like soil and water conservation and roads, as well as household agricultural assets, like cattle, sheep and goats. The money also helped families avoid selling animals in emergency situations. Through cash transfers households could choose to add to savings, or meet the costs of medicine, school fees and equipment as well as of food. Payment in food attracted many people only because volatile prices in some areas meant that the regular issue of affixed quantity of grain and vegetable oil was stable in value.

The programmes posed many questions about institutional arrangements and finance, and the difficulties of anticipating some kinds of risk. In general, support was found for recurrent and therefore long-term build-up of social protection spending. The evidence from all three countries 'demonstrates that cash may provide a good alternative to food and inputs transfers. Cash enables greater choice on the part of beneficiaries and can stimulate wider economic growth.'

Social security in developing countries

Francie Lund (Chapter 15) explores the similarities but also the major differences in the extent and nature of poverty in the developing countries and in the anti-poverty strategies being applied or considered drawing on the South African experience. The post-apartheid government of South Africa inherited a substantial system of social assistance, and has built on it since 1994 when the transition to democracy brought to power the African National Congress with its commitment to a non-racial and unified South Africa, and a resolve to share the country's wealth more equitably. However, as with increasing numbers of countries globally, inequality endures. South Africa embodies both the affluence of the north, and the unacceptable scale of poverty in sub-Saharan Africa.

The new government inherited an extensive system of social security but despite the generally conservative macroeconomic policy introduced in 1996, expansion has materialized, and spending on the social pensions and grants has increased sharply. The non-contributory cash transfers, which were racially equalized by 1993, now reach about one-quarter of the population of 44 million. Most of the recent growth in numbers of beneficiaries has been driven by the introduction in 1998 of a new cash benefit for young children.

Visitors to South Africa from neighbouring Southern African Development Community (SADC) countries are surprised by the extent of state welfare provision for children, people with disabilities and elderly people. Visitors from countries with well-established welfare systems are surprised that a country in which there is so much wealth has a welfare system that is so uneven and patchy. The coverage for the unemployed, comprising a quarter of the population, is nearly non-existent.

The author explains each of the grants (the Foster Care and Care Dependency grants as well as the Disability and Child Support grants) and pensions (principally the Old Age Pension) now available. She finds that the grants that are being developed are well targeted racially and also geographically. In the past the grants had not reached the poorest tenth of households according to income – because many were young family households with neither disabled nor elderly people among their members. Many of these households with children can now benefit from entitlement to a small level of Child Support Grant – small relative both to the rate of Old Age Pension and Disability Grant. But in the four years 2003–7 the numbers entitled to the CSG grew threefold to 8 million and this has contributed to a reduction in the population in poverty.

By 2010 it is intended that South Africa will have a new mandatory, contributory earnings-related fund which will be the vehicle for retirement savings, unemployment insurance, and disability and death benefits. It is aimed at those who fall outside the scope of the current unemployment insurance and worker compensation schemes, and who cannot afford to buy private insurance. It is specifically proposed as a bridge between social assistance cash transfers and private provision from the occupational and individual retirement funding industry which is beyond the financial reach of many workers and citizens. This will be a major step towards a more comprehensive scheme – but many will still fall outside it. The author suggests that a voluntary scheme aimed at informal workers, such as that introduced successfully in Costa Rica, would extend the coverage.

In calling attention to the urgency of rapidly improving the social security system the author emphasizes the importance of combining action on cash transfers with action on housing and social services such as health, education and welfare. Since 1994, 2 million low-cost houses have been built but the need for more housing remains urgent, together with the need to improve schools and link progress with minimum nutritional status, and the plan to ensure one free meal a day in primary schools.

Improvements in social security depend on greater awareness of certain really big problems. One problem applies worldwide and not only in South Africa – that the large employers and owners of capital are shedding themselves of their responsibilities for their share of the social wage, largely through patterns of contractualization. Large national and multinational companies 'outsource' more and more components of the production process to labour brokers, who in turn arrange for the piece rate production of, for example, clothing. The producers – the thousands of very poor men and women often working from their own homes – do not know who they are working for. They know only the broker who fetches and delivers their products, which they produce under the guise of being 'self-employed'. Deeper poverty among children, disabled or sick and elderly people, as well as low-wage earners is the consequence.

Another problem that applies especially to South Africa but also to many other countries is the lack as yet of a coherent or comprehensive social assistance policy in the face of the HIV/AIDS epidemic. There is confusion about the conditions under which people with AIDS can get access to the Disability Grant; difficulties in administering the grant; no special measures in place to protect the millions of children affected and infected by HIV/AIDS; insufficient appreciation of the impact of HIV/AIDS on (mostly women's) unpaid care responsibilities; and too little awareness of the 'chains of care' which exist in the southern African situation.

One special problem identified is that no social security system can be properly managed without an underlying system of birth registration and citizen identification. This is the basis of any planning for a good society. One reason for the rapid take-up of the CSG in South Africa was that millions of adults had registered for the first time in order to vote in the 1994 elections, and the CSG provided a similar incentive for the poorest to come forward and register births.

As a lower middle-income country with a unique recent history straddling the colonial and developing world South Africa is recognized to have potentiality for influencing the development policies of low-income countries. It can draw on a wealth of indigenous evidence showing the advantages of specific forms of redistribution of cash to poor people. It has also been lauded as a leader in the field of international human rights, and has been positioning itself as keeper-of-the-peace on the African continent and further afield. Starting within the African continent, and taking into account lessons already learned by countries such as Lesotho, Mozambique and Zambia, which have introduced elements of cash transfer systems, South Africa could become an effective champion – in the ends of both social justice and of economic development – of the extension of cash transfers as one component of social and economic policies.

Lessons from Thailand

Viroj Tangcharoensathien and his colleagues (Chapter 16) find worldwide that there are some 150 million people facing catastrophic health care expenditures, of whom about 100 million have been pushed into poverty by medical bills. For the great majority of these, who are in developing countries, the question of organizing universal health care access is acute.

The authors therefore concentrate attention on universal coverage, pointing out that in May 2005, the World Health Assembly endorsed a resolution urging member States to stride towards this goal and ensure access to health care without the risk of financial catastrophe. The core guiding principles in achieving the goal were enhanced pre-payment, risk pooling, contributions fostered according to ability to pay and use of services according to health needs.

In developed countries universal coverage had taken several decades to achieve. Between the first law on health insurance to the final law implementing such coverage the average was seven decades. The time-scale varied from 127 years for Germany, 118 for Belgium, 84 for Israel, 79 for Austria, 72 for Luxembourg, 36 for Japan, 26 for the Republic of Korea and 20 for Costa Rica.

Policies had been incremental, with major variation in organizational arrangement and source of finance. Two common parallel approaches were payroll taxes for formal sector employees and general tax financed schemes especially for the poor. Coverage for the informal sector was the most difficult challenge. The speed of progress in different countries had depended on level of income, structure of the economy, the distribution of the population, the national ability to administer Social Health Insurance (SHI), and the level of solidarity within a society. While varying in importance these factors represent the lessons that can be applied as policy leverage in developing countries.

By early 2002, Thailand had achieved universal coverage after 27 years since the government's first social protection for the poor (the Low-Income Scheme) in 1975. After introducing the tax-financed medical benefit for low-income households (the bottom layer), successive governments had applied a 'piecemeal' approach – gradually extending insurance coverage to the non-poor (the middle layer) by a subsidized voluntary public insurance scheme (Health Card Scheme) from 1983.

In 1990, a Social Security Act was promulgated for the formal private sector employee (the top layer). They are covered under mandatory tripartite payroll tax financed SHI. This was gradually extended from larger enterprises of more than 20 employees to the smallest firms of more than one employee in 2002. In 2001 30 per cent of the population were left uninsured.

For two decades successive governments invested strongly in public health service infrastructure. Three conclusions can be drawn from the Thai experience. First, there was an explicit pro-poor and pro-rural policy to establish health centres and hospitals in all districts and sub-districts. Coverage of health services to distant locations was extensive. A typical health centre could deal with a local population of 5,000 and a hospital with 50,000. Health centres are staffed by teams of 3–5 nurses and paramedics, while a 30–40 bed hospital is staffed by 3–4 general physicians, 30 nurses and paramedics, 2–3 pharmacists and a dentist. Second, public health prevention, disease control and health promotion programmes at all levels of care, including treatment of TB, HIV/AIDS and other sexually transmitted diseases, were devised and introduced. Given the geographical spread of services, this made better health attainable. Third, the difficulties of extending contributory social health insurance quickly to the 30 per cent uninsured – many of whom were in the informal sector – led to the decision to merge existing schemes for 44 per cent of the population and ensure universal coverage through the adoption of tax financed access to health care with only nominal co-payments.

The lessons drawn from Thailand would be useful for other developing countries now confronted with the construction of equitable health care systems that cover the total population while still wanting to promote the manageable development of health insurance.

Social security: new models for development

Christina Behrendt, Michael Cichon, Krzysztof Hagemejer, Stephen Kidd, Rüdiger Krech and Peter Townsend (Chapter 17) draw together the results of this review of global social security developments. A powerful case exists for rapid expansion of universal social security in low-income countries. At this stage global promotion of a social security floor as one of the core elements of poverty reduction policies, and wider development policies which enable countries to grow with equity, deserves to become the prime strategy of the UN and all international bodies. This is a powerful message that has become particularly relevant to the acknowledged financial and social crisis of 2008–9 and should find its way into the international and national debates on development policy.

Notes

1. This recognized 'the solemn obligation of the International Labour Organization to further among the nations of the world programmes which will achieve ... the extension of social security measures to provide a basic income to all in need of such protection and comprehensive medical care' (Declaration concerning the aims and purposes of the International Labour Organization, Philadelphia, 1944), General Conference of the ILO, 26th Session, 10 May 1944, Section III, para. f. See also Committee on Economic, Social and Cultural Rights, 36th Session 1–19 May 2006,

the Right to Social Security (Article 9), General Comment No. 20, agenda item 5, 16 February 2006 – publication awaited.

2. The right to social security has been recognized in a range of treaties, including the International Convention on the Elimination of All Forms of Racial Discrimination of 1965 (Article 5, e iv), the Convention on the Elimination of All Forms of Discrimination Against Women of 1979 (Articles 11.1 e and 14.2 c) and, as we will discuss in Chapter 10, the Convention on the Rights of the Child of 1989 (Article 26).

3. No effort has been made in this book to harmonize the use of the terms 'social protection' and 'social security'.

4. Means-tested benefits accounted in 2003 for less than 10 per cent in continental European countries against 15 per cent in the United Kingdom, 25 per cent in Ireland and almost 40 per cent in the United States.

Part I
The Right to Social Security and National Development

2
Social Security and Human Rights
Peter Townsend

The introduction and confirmation of successive United Nations Charters and Conventions in the last half-century demonstrates the increasing acceptance of human rights as a basis for recasting development policies. Human rights have come to play a central part in discussions about economic and social development, and have been ratified by the great majority of governments in the world. This chapter traces events of recent decades in relation to the fundamental rights to social security, including social insurance, and an 'adequate' standard of living (Articles 22 and 25 of the Universal Declaration of Human Rights; 9 and 11 of the International Covenant on Economic, Social and Cultural Rights; and 26 and 27 of the Convention on the Rights of the Child). The recent history of the OECD countries is given particular scrutiny.

Human rights to social security and an adequate standard of living have not been widely invoked during a long period of intensifying concern about the persistence of large-scale extreme poverty in the world and the formulation of the Millennium Development Goals. Thus, they were not regarded as a necessary element of the discussions around the structural adjustment policies and then the Social Fund in the 1980s and 1990s, in the fraught regions of sub-Saharan Africa, Latin America, South Asia and Eastern Europe.[1] Attention was focused by the international financial agencies on targeting and short-term means-tested benefits at least expense rather than also, or instead of, minimal living standards for all. This mistake was compounded by an over-generalized, ambiguous and undirected international anti-poverty strategy – concerned in the broadest and most indirect terms with economic growth, overseas aid, debt relief and fairer trade – rather than with institutional systems serving the poor directly. Whether there was 'trickle down' or even proportionate benefits derived by the poorest sections of population was not precisely investigated and monitored.

In their reports of the late 1990s and first decade of the 2000s the international agencies have begun to recognize the strengths of comprehensive or universal public social services and benefits, partly at the instigation of international organizations such as the ILO and UNICEF. Recognition of the strengths of social security for all, including social insurance, may follow. The urgent reformulation of development policies to reduce poverty may then be welcomed – and may bring tangible success.

Attempts to restrain and roll back social security in the last three decades have been made with too little understanding of the accumulating historical impetus in all OECD countries of its elaborate institutions and multiple functions. This chapter, which should be read in conjunction with Chapter 8 in this volume, has sought to review that history because of the critical contemporary need to establish an economic and social as well as political consensus about strategy. It is part of the answer to a wider question, expressed sharply by one writer: 'How did the rich countries *really* become rich?' (Chang, 2003: 2). In looking back at the policies and institutions created and used it may be that egg shells have to be broken in the process.

The task is not just to reintroduce a successful historical model. It is to reshape that model to meet new problems as well as problems that have been familiar for generations. The strength of the universalistic, human rights, approach to social security is in turning to future advantage what, after extraordinary struggle in the past, proved to be highly successful. As we will find, working people responded to extreme individual need by combining in collective interest to contribute creatively to economic development and the alleviation of the poverty of others in their midst. Contributory social insurance and group benefit schemes turned out to be favoured instruments. Collective protest and action led to the social good – often by the extension of the ideas of representative democracy and citizen participation.

Human rights to social security and an adequate standard of living have today put these ideas on the international stage. Properly applied, such universalistic measures can reduce poverty more emphatically and quickly than other – usually more costly and indirect – devices and at the same time improve social relationships. As illustrated by the range of research discussed in later pages, coalitions of interest between fractious ethnic and religious groups can be built up patiently on the basis of universalistic social security systems. Much the same is true of groups identified by generation, gender, age and disability. Self-interest and collective interest can be served simultaneously by such systems. Multiple forms of discrimination and social inequality can be moderated by applying international rights to social security and an adequate standard of living. Nationalism reinterpreted as universalism can also reinforce good multi-cultural and multi-generational values that promote stability.

Therefore the case for rolling back social security is far weaker than believed by many mainstream contemporary economists. The promotion of their case for cuts, particularly in contributory social insurance, has also faltered, because of persisting severe world poverty and growing social inequalities; and disturbing evidence of the inconclusive, at best, and negative, at worst, outcomes of the current international anti-poverty policies. The restoration of the social contract is becoming urgent. That contract must take a new form, but one that invokes the institutions that have served many countries so well in the past. Plans for the future of social security have to be compatible with cost controls and economic efficiency in a multi-national world. The human rights and social identity of social security have to be extended at the same time.

The momentum of international agencies, trans-national corporations and the global market compels modernization and a realistic extension of social security, including social insurance. Movement of labour and population between countries, delegating work from a headquarters country to sub-contracted labour in 50 or 100 countries, brokering new social relations and healing divisions, demands corresponding flexibility in those institutions that embody universal values of non-discriminatory support and security.

The scale of the problem to be addressed

It is now widely accepted that the Millenium Development Goals (MDGs) adopted with world acclaim in 2000 have small likelihood of being fulfilled by the intended year 2015 (see Annex 2.1 to this chapter). At current rates of progress, some of the goals are not going to be met for more than 100, or 150, years (Brown and Wolfensohn, 2004). Table 2.1 provides one, conventional, illustration of trends, drawing on World Bank data. According to these figures there has been progress in reducing poverty, though better proportionately than in reducing absolute population numbers. In the 14 years to 2001 numbers in 'dollar-a-day' poverty declined by less than 100 million. On previously published data from the World Bank absolute numbers,

Table 2.1 Population living below $1.08 per day at 1993 PPP (World Bank)

Region	Percentage of population in households consuming less than the poverty line		Number of poor (in millions)	
	1987	2001	1987	2001
East Asia	26.6	14.9	418	271
Eastern Europe and Central Asia	0.2	3.5	1	16
Latin America and Caribbean	15.3	10.0	64	52
Middle East and North Africa	4.3	2.4	9	7
South Asia	44.9	31.9	474	439
Sub-Saharan Africa	46.6	46.4	217	312
Total	28.3	21.3	1183	1098

Source: For 1987, Townsend and Gordon (2002: 363), drawing on Chen and Ravallion, World Bank Development Research Group (2001: Table 2); and for 2001 Kakwani and Son (2006: Table 2).

excluding China, had increased by more than 100 million between 1987 and 1998 (Townsend and Gordon, 2002: 363). However, World Bank data showing progress are no longer acceptable. There has been swelling criticism of the Bank's measurement of poverty, casting doubt on the estimates reproduced in Table 2.1 (Pogge and Reddy, 2003; Reddy and Pogge, 2001; Townsend and Gordon, 2002; Wade, 2004). And the World Bank's formulation of trends up to 2005 when this book was in the press in 2008 has done little to reduce the force of these criticisms (Chen and Ravallion, 2008; Ravallion, 2008; Reddy, 2008; Reddy and Pogge, 2009; and see also World Bank, 2008a, 2008b).[2]

There are two major scientific issues in reaching a conclusion about trends. One is the technical issue of updating the poverty line from year to year, *and* translating that poverty line into the equivalent purchasing power (or cost of consumable goods and services) in the currency of each particular country. A new research study on the updating of the poverty line has brought a number of the cogent criticisms of the last two decades into sharp focus, arguing that the World Bank's poverty line was lowered from 1993, when the former roughly devised 1985 poverty line of $1.00 per person per day was pitched questionably at only $1.08 per person per day, instead of a more representative and much higher figure, estimated at UNDP's International Poverty Centre to be $1.50 (Kakwani and Son, 2006). For 2001 Table 2.2 shows what a big increase there is in world poverty when $1.50 rather than $1.08 is treated as the correct baseline for 1993 and subsequent years.[3] Absolute poverty in the world becomes 36 per cent and not 21 per cent in 2001 – raising

Table 2.2 Population living below $1.08 per day and $1.50 per day at 1993 PPP in 2001

Regions	Percentage of poor		Number of poor (millions)	
	World Bank ($1.08)	IPC ($1.50)	World Bank ($1.08)	IPC ($1.50)
East Asia	14.9	28.5	271	520
Eastern Europe and Central Asia	3.5	8.6	16	41
Latin America and Caribbean	10.0	15.7	52	82
Middle East and North Africa	2.4	9.0	7	27
South Asia	31.9	56.6	439	779
Sub-Saharan Africa	46.4	61.8	312	417
Total	21.3	36.1	1098	1865

Source: Kakwani and Son (2006: Table 2). They reproduced World Bank estimates based on $1.08 per person per day, compared with their calculated estimates based on a poverty line of $1.50 per person per day, i.e. the median of the poverty lines of 19 low-income countries in Africa and Asia in the 1990s.

the population numbers by 800 million to little short of 2 billion. Those are the most critical figures on which to debate current world development.

The second scientific issue is the practice since 1985 of limiting the measure of a 'poverty line' to material needs and not also to social needs – and adjusting that line in subsequent years not for changing needs but only by applying a cost-of-living index to a historically fixed list of consumables and services. In the 1990s the World Bank stated that two elements – material and social needs – had to be combined in the operational definition and measurement of poverty (see the discussion in Townsend and Gordon, 2002: 358–67). Research to establish social needs was promised but not fulfilled (World Bank, 1990: 26; and see also World Bank, 1993a, 1993b, 1996, 1997, 2000a, 2001). Subsequent measures were based only on fixed basic material needs. No official answer from the World Bank has been given to this criticism in the years 2002–9. If we go back to the World Bank's own carefully chosen definition in 1993, their estimates in subsequent years of world poverty must all have been underestimated. By repricing only the cost of meeting the defined material needs of a base year rather than also calculating the changes in those needs, the trend from year to year in such a scale of poverty must also have been underestimated. Were orthodox measures of household and individual needs to be periodically updated to reflect changes in the customary norms of consumption and the roles and obligations being laid on citizens, workers and members of families, the scale of world poverty would be recognizably much more serious.

Whether allegiance is paid to the orthodox World Bank estimates of the scale of poverty, or to the different, more dismaying, estimates based upon the material and social needs of populations swept along by contemporary market and other powerful social, economic and political forces, the slow progress in reducing the vast extent of poverty, and dealing with the remorseless increase in levels of world inequality, is now generally agreed to be unacceptable. The anti-poverty policies of the 1980s and 1990s were unsuccessful, and in the 2000s continue to be unsuccessful. New national and international anti-poverty policies have to be substituted, or added, as a matter of urgency.

The biggest and most practicable contribution to a solution rests in social security. Social security developments in the context of growing commitments to human rights in the last 50 years deserve examination. Has the process of introduction and consolidation of systems of social security continued, among other effects, to substantially reduce poverty nationally? The public argument for and about social security has existed for many years but has been virtually dormant since 1980. The right to social security was expressly included in formal declarations of human rights by the great majority of countries from 1948 onwards. The right formed part of the Universal Declaration of Human Rights in 1948. It was included in the International Covenant on Economic, Social and Cultural Rights in 1966 and the

Convention on the Rights of the Child in 1989, coming into force respectively in 1976 and 1990. It became the documented spur for early statistical handbooks on development (for example Russett et al., 1964). It has also formed a basis of more enlightened appeals for action to reduce poverty.

Three steps in formulating a new approach might therefore be proposed: (i) to explain how human rights, and especially the right to social security, have been reiterated and expanded in legal and quasi-legal form in the last 50 or 60 years; (ii) to show broadly how social security systems of considerable scope and scale were established by the OECD countries and whether the history and structure of those systems, especially in relation to economic growth, hold any lessons for current development policies; and (iii) to describe in what respects early attempts in the developing countries to institutionalize social security do or do not, and perhaps cannot, resemble the pathways to the reduction of poverty through the establishment of systems of social security taken in the history of the OECD countries.

The fundamental right to social security

International human rights instruments provide a legal framework for strategies to reduce poverty:

> A rights-based approach allows links to be made between otherwise disparate issues and gives legal weight and content to many of the concepts that are traditionally seen and analysed in terms of development, management and welfare. It thus moves away from the instrumentalist and utilitarian language of development economists to that of the entitlements and obligations enshrined within the formal legal system, while retaining the moral authority which other approaches lack. (Chinkin, 2001: 564)

One corollary of this argument about entitlement and obligation is to move away from state-oriented international law to international law concerned equally with the rights of individuals and with 'the responsibility of states and other international actors' (Chinkin, 2001: 564).

Social security systems were established in all OECD countries and the history of the process of establishing human rights has much to offer the framing of current and prospective anti-poverty policies in the developing countries. The rights were expressed first in the Universal Declaration of Human Rights but later repeated, with particular reference to social insurance as part of social security, in later instruments, such as the International Covenant on Economic, Social and Cultural Rights and the Convention on the Rights of the Child (see Table 2.3). In the last two decades public discussion of world poverty has been increasingly related to violations of, and future fulfilment of, human rights (see, for example, Commonwealth Human Rights Initiative

Table 2.3 The rights to social security and an adequate standard of living

Authority	Social security	Adequate living standard
Universal Declaration of Human Rights (1948)	**Article 22** – Everyone, as a member of society, has the right to social security and is entitled to realization, through national effort and international cooperation and in accordance with the organization and resources of each state, of the economic, social and cultural rights indispensable for their dignity and the free development of their personality.	**Article 25(1)** – Everyone has the right to a standard of living adequate for the health and well-being of their family, including food, clothing, housing and medical care and necessary social services, and the right to security in the event of unemployment, sickness, disability, widowhood, old age or other lack of livelihood in circumstances beyond their control.
International Covenant on Economic, Social and Cultural Rights (1966; came into force 1976)	**Article 9** – The States Parties to the present Covenant recognize the right of everyone to social security, **including social insurance**.	**Article 11(1)** – The States Parties to the present Covenant recognize the right of everyone to an adequate standard of living for himself and his family, including adequate food, clothing and housing, and to the continuous improvement of living conditions.
Convention on the Rights of the Child (1989)	**Article 26(I)** – States Parties shall recognize for every child the right to benefit from social security, **including social insurance**, and shall take the necessary measures to achieve the full realization of this right in accordance with their national law.	**Article 27(I)** – States Parties recognize the right of every child to a standard of living adequate for the child's physical, mental, spiritual, moral and social development. **Article 27 (3)** – … and shall in case of need provide material assistance and support programmes, particularly with regard to nutrition, clothing and housing.

(CHRI), 2001; Townsend, 2004b; UN, 1995, 1997; UNDP, 1998a, 1998b, 2000, 2004a; UNICEF, 2004).

The apparent correlation between a lack of progress on the MDGs and levels of spending on social security in the developing countries that have remained very low may not be coincidental. Substantial ongoing social security investments in the OECD countries contrast vividly with slow or non-existent progress in creating social security in poor countries. Eighty per cent of people worldwide still do not have access to adequate social security yet a small percentage of GDP (say 5–10 per cent for each population) would be sufficient in development programmes to provide everyone with a minimum standard of social security. Thus the right to social security was taken for granted in early formulations of development programmes (for example in modernization theories of the 1950s and 1960s).

From the 1980s to the 2000s the objectives of the international financial agencies were to advise cuts in public expenditure and encourage privatization, using low-cost targeted welfare sparingly in substitution of basic social security and services for all. In the middle of the first decade of the millennium there have been, as noted earlier, signs of change. The latest positive sign of a change of mood is the circulation of advanced drafts by the Committee on Economic, Social and Cultural Rights of its proposed General Comment No. 20, *The Right to Social Security (Article 9)*, 16 February 2006. Among the listed obligations of States Parties to fulfil the right to social security are steps to legislate and adopt a social security strategy that include, for example, 'establishing a contribution-based social security system or a legislative framework that will permit the incorporation of the informal sector' (Committee on Economic, Social and Cultural Rights 2006, para. 37). This reinforces the value for development in the low-income countries of the earlier history of the establishment of social security systems in the industrialized countries.

Social insurance as a key component of social security

Long-established public social security systems generally have three components. Although many countries have developed a varied mix of the three, they have to be distinguished routinely to reach scientific conclusions about social functions and outcomes as well as desirability. The three are (i) broadly universal social insurance programmes that collect flat-rate or percentage contributions on income from employment of all insured persons and their employers in a contractual exchange for benefits as of right for those insured and for their dependants (accounting for three-fifths or more of total social security expenditure in the member States of the European Union – see Table 2.4 below); (ii) broadly universal tax-financed benefit schemes, usually flat-rate, for all residents of a particular social category determined by age, disability or other qualifying condition – such as benefits for all children, all disabled people, or all people of a particular age, for example above 70 or 75; and (iii) social assistance schemes only for those qualifying on test of means, that provide minimum benefits or income, and now include tax-credit schemes directed at low-income households.

In general, social security in most if not all OECD countries began as fragmented, grudging means-tested social assistance and evolved, because of discriminatory selection of beneficiaries, meagre level of benefits and poor coverage of those theoretically entitled to assistance, into a predominantly social insurance based system. This provided protection to the unemployed, sick, disabled and elderly, and their dependants, and constituted a springboard back into paid employment. The reason for social insurance overtaking social assistance was mass protest against social assistance, and the fact that the working-class were taking initiatives to fill the holes. There were growing demands for more extended and sufficient coverage of benefits for those experiencing severe adversity beyond their control. For technical reasons (marginal rates of tax, difficulties in defining eligibility operationally, and lack of specific conformity to issues of legal residence and identity) as well as public hostility, social assistance remained in many member countries a relatively small component of 'welfare', smaller indeed than 5 per cent in some countries, such as Germany. From being regarded as the norm for most of the nineteenth century it came to be regarded in many countries in the mid and late twentieth century as a kind of adjustable 'top up' for exceptional need.[4]

Social insurance was a compromise to achieve 'affordability' and 'acceptability' – built on charitable scruple, private insurance precedents, and hard-headed deals between government and employers. Pooling of risk was not just a huge benefit to people in paid work, but also to government and employers in resolving prospective disputes and the costs of settling individual and collective claims and the daunting extent of administering workforces. From the viewpoint of the insured the prospective benefits were better guaranteed, more predictable, and more directly participatory than alternative benefits financed by taxation. Fees and management costs were much lower in public than private insurance.

From the viewpoint of employers the cost of making national insurance contributions towards claims for lay-offs, sickness, disability and injury were eventually accepted as some of the necessary costs of manufacturing and services. The private insurance companies acquiesced because the poor were not a source of profitability. They were not attractive clients because the long history of doorstep industrial assurance showed that profits would be very thin and weekly contributions were always hard to extract. The companies expressed relief when government intervened and worked out an acceptable division of labour. From the viewpoint of government, social insurance was easier and much cheaper to administer than selective social assistance or private insurance, more complaints-proof, and of longer-term economic advantage in using surpluses in good times to ride recession and even depression when times got bad.[5]

The preceding paragraphs distinguish the three key components of social security systems. Two of these – social insurance and tax-financed group benefits – are relevant to guaranteeing defined individual benefit and therefore the fundamental right to social security. However, none of the three can be usefully discussed without also distinguishing the corresponding forms of funding. How the funding of particular schemes is shared between individual, employer and government, and is worked out and agreed nationally is integral to the evaluation of different schemes.

The source and character of the revenue is equal in importance to the design and structure of benefits. The two cannot be disconnected. The revenue from the three types of contributor has varied and continues to vary from time to time and country to country – just as the adequacy of defined benefits continues to be questioned and changed. Effectiveness in achieving social and political aims can also vary – as illustrated in UNICEF research into government measures to reduce 'market' poverty rates (UNICEF, 2006b: 455).[6] Even if social insurance is regarded as a tax, it is a general kind of hypothecated tax that each population is more inclined to accept and support – certainly than general taxation. And it leaves much less to chance in government policy on taxation and the possibilities of manipulation and fraud.

The particular virtues of social insurance in contrast to tax-financed group benefits are that individuals have an incentive to register, that parts of the informal economy are consequently formalized, that individuals acquire more tangible citizenship, that individuals belonging to particular groups and categories of the population come to find that they share similar rights and treatments, and therefore have common interests but also common responsibilities in registering and paying their way, and that the establishment of offices in different locations kick-starts administrative institutions of government and positively contributes to social cohesion.

The problem is that the OECD countries established social security institutions early in industrial history, and developing countries are much worse placed to do the same today. Some are at the bottom of the global heap. But inch by inch some of them can begin to build on the right to social security, 'including social insurance', by introducing laws and expecting international companies to bear a reasonable share of the costs of minimal benefits in adversity (as well as a minimum wage) – ensuring that this applies to sub-contracted labour forces. This would begin to reduce the problems posed by the informal economy – by providing incentives to both employees and employers to abide by the terms of contractual social insurance – and hence extend the range of the formal economy. It would be a mistake to assume that only tax-financed benefits have a part to play in new social security measures in developing countries. International organizations and institutions also have to make a necessary contribution.

In identifying the components of social security in history readers will find that the individual, the employer and the government each made a formal contribution to social insurance. In today's conditions each of these three is differently placed. The individual is increasingly interested in his or her entitlement in another country (professional readjustment, migrant labour, remittances, asylum seeker, refugee, resettlement, transfer of pension, family members in different country locations). The employer is increasingly a trans-national company, with costs and responsibilities extending to many countries, and involving indirect, informal or sub-contracted labour. And the government is increasingly dependent on international laws and agreements, including those affecting national tax revenue, and has an interest in harmonizing taxation in different countries, and affording access to benefits and services cross-nationally and nationally. Later in this chapter the implications for the redesign of social security in both developing and industrialized countries will be assessed. In a global society there may have to be greater standardization of social security and services, as well as a more prominent role in funding and designing national and regional schemes for the most powerful industrialized countries.

The history of systems of social security

How were the human rights to social security and an adequate standard of living in practice introduced in the OECD countries? In fact all member countries put in place the right to social security over many years – going back long before the Second World War. As the reader will see, many of them were successful in achieving long-term sustainable economic growth at the same time as they substantially reduced poverty. Whether as cause or effect of economic growth all countries evolved extensive systems of social security. Table 2.4 summarizes what has been happening in recent years.

First, the table compares total public social expenditure with its largest component, social security, as percentage of GDP, in OECD countries for the year 2001. As can be seen, with the exceptions of Mexico and Korea, between 8 per cent and 19 per cent of GDP was committed in that year to social security cash benefits. Most OECD countries are committing more than 20 per cent of GDP to public services and cash benefits. Crucially, more than half of this is cash benefits. This contrasts dramatically with the meagre levels of GDP committed to both services and benefits in the developing countries.

Second, the table shows no marked fall in expenditure in the last five years. On the contrary, in 2005, 10 of the 17 countries for which expenditure on social security could be tracked up to and including 2005, including the United States, increased expenditure as a percentage of GDP. In five countries such expenditure, expressed as percentage of GDP, was reduced

Table 2.4 Total public social expenditure and total public social security expenditure (included), as percentage of GDP

Country	Total public social expenditure as % GDP (2001)	Total public social security expenditure (cash benefits) as % GDP (2001)	Total public social security expenditure (cash benefits) as % GDP (new OECD series)				
			2001	2002	2003	2004	2005
Sweden	29.8	14.4	17.2	17.3	18.1	17.8	17.4
Denmark	29.2	15.2	16.3	16.4	17.0	16.8	16.2
France	28.5	17.9	17.1	17.3	17.5	17.6	17.9
Germany	27.4	15.6	18.6	19.5	19.8	19.4	19.2
Switzerland	26.4	18.2	11.0	11.4	12.1	..	..
Austria	26.0	18.9	18.6	19.0	19.2	18.8	18.6
Finland	24.8	15.4	15.9	16.3	16.7	16.8	16.4
Belgium	24.7	16.2	15.4	15.8	16.1	16.0	16.0
Italy	24.4	17.1	16.2	16.5	16.8	16.9	17.1
Greece	24.3	16.5	16.9	16.9	17.6	17.1	16.7
Norway	23.9	11.6	13.7	14.8	15.6	14.8	..
Poland	23.0	17.9	17.4	17.6	17.5	16.8	..
UK	21.8	14.2	13.7	13.2	13.3	13.3	13.4
Netherlands	21.4	13.3	11.1	11.2	11.5	11.5	11.1
Portugal	21.1	13.2	12.0	12.6	13.8	14.1	14.9
Luxembourg	20.8	14.5	13.9	14.6	15.0	15.0	14.7
Czech Republic	20.1	12.4	12.7	12.5	12.3	11.9	..
Hungary	20.1	13.0	12.8	13.5	14.0	14.1	14.8
Iceland	19.8	8.4	7.0	8.0	9.4	8.9	9.1
Spain	19.6	12.8	11.7	11.8	11.7	11.7	11.6
New Zealand	18.5	11.6	10.9	10.5	..	..	..
Australia	18.0	9.9	8.5	8.2	8.6	8.4	..
Slovak Republic	17.9	11.9	12.0	11.8	10.9	10.4	..
Canada	17.8	8.0	10.8	10.7	10.5	10.2	..
Japan	16.9	9.1	10.5	11.1	11.2	11.3	..
USA	14.7	7.9	11.4	12.0	12.1	12.0	12.0
Ireland	13.8	7.5	8.3	8.7	9.0	9.0	..
Turkey	13.2	..	..	..	..	..	..
Korea	6.1	2.3	2.0	1.9	2.3	2.5	..
Mexico	5.1	1.3	1.8	1.6	..	..	..
OECD 23	22.0	13.6					
OECD 25	–	–	13.2	13.5	13.8	13.7	(13.6)
OECD 30	20.9	12.6					

Note: See the upper part of the OECD chart reproduced as Figure 2.1.
Source: OECD (2004): Social expenditure database, SOCX via www.oecd.org/els/social/expenditure series 2001, 2nd and 3rd columns, and new National Accounts series, 4th–8th columns – showing total public social expenditure and total public social security/cash expenditure for 2001-5.

Table 2.5 Total public social security expenditure as percentage of GDP in selected high-, middle- and low-spending countries

Countries	Total
High-spending	
France	17.9
Germany	15.6
UK	14.2
Middle	
Australia	9.9
Japan	9.1
Chile	8.2
United States	7.9
Low	
Ghana	2.1
China	1.5
India	1.5
Indonesia	1.1
Mexico	1.1
Kenya	0.3
Zambia	0.3

Source: High- and middle-spending countries – see Table 2.4 above. Low-spending countries – data adapted from ILO (2001a: Statistical Annex). The data for the low-income countries apply to 1996 (1995, China) and exclude health care (then counted in 'social security expenditure').

and in two countries expenditure in the two years remained approximately the same.

Most low-income countries commit less than 5 per cent of GDP in total to public social services and benefits, some of them less than 1 or 2 per cent of GDP. Table 2.5 draws a few examples from high- and middle-spending OECD countries to compare with data for developing countries compiled by the ILO (2001a). The table shows the gap in spending between countries such as France, Germany and the United Kingdom and developing countries like China, Mexico, India, Kenya, Ghana and Indonesia. In high-spending countries total public social security expenditure is between 14 per cent and 18 per cent of annual GDP. In low-spending countries it can be a fraction of 1 per cent to 4 or 5 per cent.

The key role of social security becomes striking when the distribution of income in 'developed' countries before and after taxes and social transfers is considered. Table 2.6 gives a summary of the effects on the extent of poverty – by current definitions of poverty in European (and OECD) member countries.

Table 2.6   Percentage of population no longer in poverty – post-social compared with pre-social transfers, by country and welfare regime (1999)

Welfare regime/country	Percentage of total population no longer in poverty after transfers	Percentage of total population in poverty after transfers	Mean percentage in poverty after transfers (grouped by regime)
Social Democratic/ Nordic			
Denmark	30.3	10.8	11.4
Sweden	35.5	10.2	
Finland	33.1	13.3	
Netherlands	31.2	11.4	
Corporatist			
Austria	35.6	14.2	13.8
Germany	29.6	11.8	
France	32.8	15.9	
Belgium	32.0	13.9	
Luxembourg	31.8	13.3	
Liberal/residual			
United Kingdom	25.0	18.7	18.3
Ireland	23.4	17.9	
South European			
Italy	27.5	18.5	19.6
Spain	28.9	17.3	
Greece	25.5	21.9	
Portugal	25.9	20.6	
EE12	28.6	16.5	
EE15	29.8	15.5	

Source: Derived from Papatheodorou and Petmesidou (2004).

Some OECD countries have reduced domestic poverty more than others but everywhere the combined effects on existing institutions of social security are very substantial. In the table it can be seen that there is strong evidence in support of the division of countries by theorists into different types of welfare state, especially in relation to social security, that were established in the twentieth century (see, for example, Esping-Andersen, 1990).

Table 2.6 illustrates vividly the extent of redistribution through social transfers in OECD countries (total public expenditure, including public social security). A 2006 analysis, using the Luxembourg Income Study's micro-level database, concludes that 'the most extensive overall fiscal redistribution occurs in Belgium, Sweden, the Netherlands and Finland, while households in Switzerland, the United States, Canada and Australia experience the least state redistribution' (Mahler and Jesuit, 2006: 8 and Table 1). Another 2006 report from UNICEF's Innocenti Research Centre shows that child poverty in 17 of the 24 OECD countries for which there is information was rising proportionate to median household income during the 1990s – after government measures to redistribute income (UNICEF, 2006a: 239). The report also shows that if OECD governments did not intervene to effect transfers through social security 'market poverty rates' would be more than 40 per cent (UNICEF, 2006b: 455).

The correlation between high social transfer rates and low poverty rates prompts specific questions about cause and effect. One test is to investigate examples of unusual advances in social spending attributable to new or greatly extended schemes introduced by government. Traditionally these have not been closely tracked and the impact on poverty rates of different elements of multiple policies apportioned. But some exceptions of this kind have been documented. Thus, there was a marked decline in 1968, compared with the immediately preceding years of 1966 and 1967 and with years after 1968, of elderly poor in the United States. The direct cause was a 13 per cent increase in social security (Old Age and Survivors Insurance) effective from February 1968 – which was the only across-the-board social security benefit increase enacted between 1965 and late 1969 (Fisher, 1976: 59). The research covered the period 1959–74 and showed that variations in the level of social security benefit, as well as access to benefit, largely accounted for variations in the proportion of aged persons in poverty. A linear least squares regression was run for 1959 and all years in the period 1966–74.

Support for the key role of social security for the elderly, as well as for other groups, in all OECD countries, is found in a number of the statistical surveys of the Luxembourg Income Study (LIS). Thus 'without social security income, a large proportion of the older population would live in poverty in all developed countries' (Wu, 2005).

Another LIS study found a strong correlation between social expenditures (non-elderly cash and near cash social expenditures) as a percentage of GDP, and relative poverty rates in 16 countries in the 1990s ($r^2 = 0.6183$) (Smeeding et al., 2001; building on earlier LIS studies, for example Smeeding et al., 1990, particularly pp. 72–4). The levels and changes in child poverty in 12 OECD countries since 1900 were traced in another study – uncovering the role of income transfers from the state as cause of reductions in poverty rates (Chen and Corak, 2005). More generally a positive correlation was found between social spending as a percentage of GDP and poverty reduction (Smeeding and Phillips, 2001).

Extensive evidence from the LIS questions conventional economic assumptions about measures to reduce poverty. Noting 'the sizeable increases in market household inequality in most countries' of the OECD during the 1980s and 1990s, one pair of research analysts concluded: 'In contrast to widespread rhetoric about the decline of the welfare state, redistribution increased in most countries during the period, as existing social welfare programmes compensated for the rise in market inequality' (Kenworthy and

Table 2.7 Social security transfers as percentage of GDP

Year	United States	Japan	Germany	France	United Kingdom	Italy	OECD
1960	5.0	3.8	12.0	13.5	6.8	9.8	7.0
1970	7.6	4.6	12.7	14.8	8.8	12.4	8.8
1974	9.5	6.2	14.6	15.5	9.7	13.7	10.5
1990	11.1	7.4	15.2	16.9	11.8	15.5	12.2
2000	...	10.0	18.8	18.0	13.2	16.7	12.6*
2005	12.0	11.3	19.2	17.9	13.4	17.1	13.6*

Source: 1960 – OECD (1992: 67); 1970–2000 – OECD (2001b); and 2004 – OECD (2006a). The data for 2005 are provisional and also drawn from a new OECD series on cash benefits.
Note: *In comparison with earlier decades, the admission of new members has slightly lowered average spending.

Pontusson, 2005). Another pair concluded: 'Our results strongly suggest that more generous entitlements to key social insurance programmes are associated not only with lower *relative* poverty, but also lower *absolute* poverty. This supports the contention that promoting relative economic equality can improve the absolute material well-being of the poor' (Scruggs and Allan, 2005).

Before examining developments in more detail, two of the common features of the various OECD systems must be specified. One is that despite periodic levelling off, and sometimes reduction, of the annual sums included in the national budgets, relative investment by OECD countries in social security has, on average, continued to grow. Table 2.7 illustrates the rising cost of social security in six of the highest-profile countries, some of which have a history of reluctance on the part of government to tax substantially or extend the welfare state. The table shows that between 1960 and 1990 the United States more than doubled its share of national income transferred through social security although the percentage of GDP then levelled off during the next decade. In Germany there was also a levelling off in the 1980s but in the four other countries selected in the table – Japan, France, the United Kingdom and Italy – the GDP percentage continued to grow. The latest figures for 2005 show continued or restored growth in the US, Japan, Germany, Italy and the United Kingdom and a reduced share only in France. Compared with 1990 all these six powerful countries are devoting more national income to social security today.

During the last half-century the percentage of GDP devoted to social security transfers on average by OECD countries has continued to grow, albeit more slowly in the last decade. One problem in generalizing trends is the inclusion of new members, including Mexico that has reduced the average.

Total public social expenditure, which includes social security transfers (see the glossary in Annex 2.2), has followed suit. The steady trend indicates the extension of a network of organizations and administrative schemes approved, legislated and financed through government to underpin different forms of social integration, health and welfare systems, and greater stability in living standards, found to be required in all societies. In this case the OECD reports allow long-standing and more recent groups of member countries to be distinguished. The upward trend has persisted, among the new as well as long-standing member countries.

Despite cutbacks in some countries in periods of economic downturn (for example Japan in the late 1980s and Canada and Sweden in the mid- and late-1990s), there has been evidence of recovery on the part of several countries and continuing, if slower, expansion. But during the 1990s the general OECD picture is one of a levelling off of expenditure rather than reduction, with decreases in some elements of spending in many member countries being counter-balanced by increases in others.

Table 2.8 demonstrates the trend for 1990–2001, and also illustrates exceptions to the trend, including periodic fluctuations, that mark national experience. During the decade as many as 18 OECD countries had increased, and 9 had reduced, the share of GDP committed to social transfers.[7] It can also be seen that during the decade three countries becoming OECD members only recently – Korea, Mexico and Turkey – had sharply increased social transfers relative to GDP.

The accompanying chart from the OECD (Figure 2.1) helps readers to understand better the scale of cash benefits in relation to services, and their major components, but also the meaning of the key terms: total public expenditure/social transfers; social security transfers/social protection and basic social service expenditure (predominantly health services and education).[8] The chart gives the main components of both public and private social expenditure to compare with total public social expenditure in Table 2.4 above.

Current trends are variable. Early in the new millennium public social expenditure in the OECD countries amounted on average to 21 per cent of GDP. In Sweden, Denmark, France and Germany the figure for public social spending is close to 30 per cent. In few countries is the figure less than 18 per cent, although in one country, Korea, it is 6 per cent.

Changes in gross public social expenditures over time are also variable. After having almost doubled in the 20 years to 1980, the expansion of gross public expenditure continued at a reduced rate with the OECD average peaking at 23 per cent in 1993. Since then, the figure has settled back slightly, being 22 per cent for OECD-23 in 2001 or 21 per cent when seven new members are included for the current OECD-30.

Expenditures other than on health account for the slight decline. Within the total spending figure of 22 per cent the three largest categories are pensions (averaging 8 per cent of GDP), health (6 per cent) and income transfers to the working-age population (5 per cent). Public spending on other social services only exceeds 5 per cent of GDP in the Nordic countries, where the public role in providing services to the elderly, the disabled and families

Table 2.8 Total public social expenditure (social transfers) as percentage of GDP 1990–2000 – OECD – ranked by percentage change (+/−)

Country	Social transfers as percentage of GDP 1990	Social transfers as percentage of GDP 2000	Percentage of change
Switzerland	17.9	25.4	7.5
Poland	15.5	21.9	6.6
Portugal	13.9	20.5	6.4
Mexico	3.8	9.9	6.1
Turkey	7.6	13.2	5.6
Japan	11.2	16.1	4.9
Germany	22.8	27.2	4.4
Australia	14.2	18.6	4.4
Czech Republic	17.0	20.3	3.3
Iceland	16.4	19.7	3.3
Greece	20.9	23.6	2.7
Korea	3.1	5.6	2.5
Austria	24.1	26.0	1.9
UK	19.5	21.3	1.8
France	26.6	28.3	1.7
USA	13.4	14.2	0.8
Italy	24.8	25.6	0.8
Spain	19.5	19.9	0.4
Belgium	26.9	26.7	−0.2
Finland	24.8	24.5	−0.3
Denmark	29.3	28.9	−0.4
Canada	18.6	17.3	−1.3
Norway	24.7	23.0	−1.7
Luxembourg	21.9	20.0	−1.7
Sweden	30.8	28.6	−2.2
New Zealand	21.9	19.2	−2.7
Ireland	18.6	13.6	−5.0
Netherlands	27.6	21.8	−5.6
OECD-28	19.1	20.7	1.6

Source: OECD *Social Expenditure Database* for 2004 (SOCX www.oecd.org/els/social/expenditure).

is the most extensive. Public support for families with children averages 2 per cent of GDP and has increased in most countries since 1980. Family support exceeds 3 per cent of GDP in the Nordic countries and Austria, as they have the most comprehensive public system of child allowances, paid leave arrangements and childcare. Moreover, governments also help families through the tax system; examples include the 'quotient familial' in France and 'income splitting' in Germany.

Social insurance spending related to work incapacity (disability, sickness and occupational injury benefits) has declined in as many countries as it has

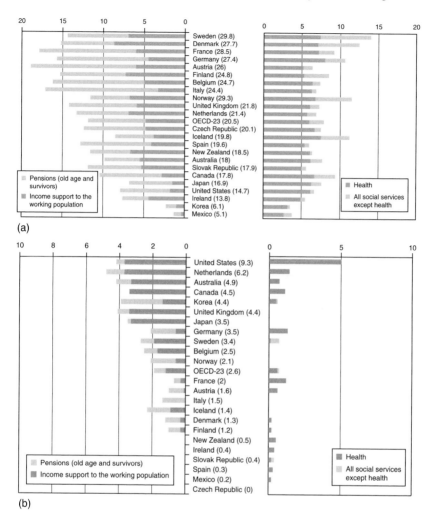

Figure 2.1 Total public and private social expenditure, OECD countries, as percentage of GDP, showing breakdown between cash benefits and services, 2006; (a) Public social expenditure by broad social policy area; (b) Private social expenditure by broad social policy area

Source: Adema and Ladaique (2005).

increased since 1980. Particularly large reductions were found in Belgium, the Netherlands and Portugal (OECD, *Factbook*, 2005).

A feature of social security in nearly all countries is the greater investment in social insurance and non-selective group benefits than in means-tested social assistance. This structural feature suggests that a similar balance will work best for developing countries. Schemes that apply to all members of a

Table 2.9   Trends in the funding of social security (1980–1996)

Funding of social security	1980 (EU-12) (%)	1990 (EU-12) (%)	1996 (EU-15) (%)
All contributions	67.4	65.6	62.9
(employers)	(45.4)	(41.8)	(39.2)
(employees etc.)	(22.0)	(23.8)	(23.7)
General taxes	27.9	27.8	31.9
Other receipts	4.7	6.5	5.2
Total	100	100	100

Source: Ministry of Social Affairs and Health, Finland (1999: 213); Eurostat (1999).

population or group might predominate over schemes dependent on selecting those with the lowest incomes. This bears on the fact that social security, *including social insurance*, is one fundamental right that is included in several of the human rights instruments, to be routinely noted by States Parties. But this could also serve as a structural feature or model for international 'pump-priming' and hold lessons for new or additional forms of international aid to eradicate poverty.

As Table 2.9 shows, around two-thirds of the funding of social security by European member countries is from social insurance contributions and a third from taxes. One noteworthy trend for the member countries during 1980–96 was, as the table also shows, the relative decline in contributions from employers, partly made up by an increase in contributions from employees. Outside the EU contributions to social insurance remain considerable. In the United States, for example, one of the largest member countries of the OECD, employers contribute nearly half the cost.

Economic growth and social security

Do large-scale social transfers handicap economic growth? What came first, growth or social security? National histories of both social security and economic growth, and of their inter-relationships, are of course chequered. Here only a start can be made in identifying cause and effect. However, a sufficient statistical account allows the provisional conclusion to be reached that the institutionalization of social security and economic growth has been mutually interdependent and is a major factor accounting for the relative prosperity and low poverty rates of OECD compared with developing countries.

Among the 'developed' countries high and low levels of economic growth do not correlate uniformly with low and high levels of public expenditure. Countries experiencing relatively high economic growth are not simply those

Table 2.10   Annual economic growth and total public social expenditure as percentage of GDP

Country	Economic growth (annual growth as percentage of GDP)			Public social expenditure as percentage of GDP	
	1991	2001	2005 (projection)	1991	2001
Germany	5.1	1.0	1.4	24.9	27.4
UK	−1.4	2.3	2.6	19.5	21.8
USA	−0.2	0.8	3.3	13.4	14.8
Norway	3.6	2.7	3.2	24.7	23.9
Sweden	−1.1	1.2	3.3	30.7	28.9
Japan	3.4	0.4	2.1	11.2	16.9
Italy	1.4	1.7	1.7	23.3	24.4
OECD total	1.3	1.1	2.9	23.2	22.0

Source: OECD, *Factbook*, 2005.

with relatively low social expenditure. The story is more mixed than sometimes revealed in economic disputes. Table 2.10 starts by illustrating the variability of economic growth in both high- and low-spending countries.

A more acceptable procedure is to examine statistical indicator data over a succession of years. Based on OECD data Table 2.11 shows average growth for the 10 years 1996–2005, compared with average total public expenditure for the first five years (1996–2000) of the decade for relatively high- and low-spending OECD countries. There are clearly exceptions to the correlation presumed to exist by many economists between low spending and high growth. Against the apparently sustained higher growth of some low-spending countries there have been years of little or no growth, for example the United States in 2001–2, Canada in 2001 and New Zealand in 1998. On balance, low-spending OECD countries achieved higher growth in the years just before and just after the turn of the millennium but this does not apply to some earlier periods and is also variable across countries.

Low-spending countries tend to have a more unequal distribution of gross or original incomes, before as well as after social transfers, and higher rates of poverty by EU and OECD standards, as Table 2.11 shows.[9] These are two conclusions, which yield valuable lessons for the necessary social as well as economic basis of future global society. Positive changes in the economy arise as a consequence of invention, initiative and hard work, but also at social expense. The best changes also depend on pre-existing, and deliberately contrived, social strengths. Issues of their national identity and consequential extensive relationships, acknowledgement of their rights to participate in the conventions as well as obey the rules of work and society, matter to people in the satisfaction of their objective needs.

Table 2.11   Annual average economic growth rates and total public social expenditure, as percentage of GDP, compared with inequality and poverty rates

Countries ranked by spending: relatively high and low spenders	Annual average total public expenditure as per cent of GDP, 1996–2000	Annual average real economic growth, 1996–2005	Inequality: richest 10% as a ratio of poorest 10%	Relative poverty: income below 50% of the median %
High				
Sweden	30.5	2.8	6.2	6.5
Denmark	29.7	2.2	8.1	9.2
France	29.0	2.4	9.1	9.9
Germany	27.5	1.3	6.9	8.3
Belgium	27.5	2.2	7.8	8.0
Finland	27.3	3.5	3.8	5.4
Austria	26.1	2.2	7.6	8.0
Low				
UK	21.8	2.8	13.8	12.5
New Zealand	19.9	3.2	12.5	–
Canada	18.0	3.4	10.1	12.8
Australia	17.9	3.8	12.5	14.3
Ireland	15.7	7.5	9.7	12.3
Japan	14.6	1.6	4.5	11.8
US	14.6	3.4	15.9	17.0
All OECD countries	22.5	2.7		

Source: OECD, *Factbook*, 2005; and for cols. 4 and 5, UNDP, *Human Development Report*, 2005, Tables 15 and 4.

The kind of experience people have in general as members of society, and the conditions in which they work and live, cannot be separated from what they are capable of contributing to economic prosperity. The art of state (and multi-state) management lies in constructing growth at minimum social expense and maximum social development.

A generation of research has failed to demonstrate a clear relationship between economic growth and trends in the incomes of poor people. One of the most incisive reports was that of Newman and Thomson (1989) who assembled economic data from a large number of countries and cast doubt on 'trickle down' to such effect that the reverse seemed to be the more correct interpretation (see also Foster and Székely, 2001). World Bank analysts continued to argue for 'trickle-down'. Thus Dollar and Kray purported to show that incomes of the poor rise one-for-one with overall growth, namely that for every 1 per cent increase in GDP the incomes of the poorest 20 per cent also increase by 1 per cent. They concluded that public spending on health and education is of little benefit to the poor (Dollar and Kray, 2000).

However, their findings turned out to be a statistical artefact from a flawed methodology. When applied to random numbers (instead of real data) their method produced the same result (Vandemoortele, 2002: especially 385 and 394–5).

Following study of the concept of 'pro-poor' economic growth and its application to particular countries at UNDP's International Poverty Centre (see for example, Kakwani et al., 2004; Son and Kakwani, 2004; Vandemoortele, 2004), a cross-country analysis of 80 countries was completed. In these countries a total of 237 spells of economic growth were examined. In 106 cases the average real per capita income actually declined. In 131, pro-poor growth, i.e. proportionately more of the average increase in income going to the poorest deciles, could be reliably confirmed for only 55 – or 23 per cent of the total – while less of the average increase in income went to the poorest deciles in the remaining 76 countries (32 per cent of the total). Growth in these countries was 'anti-poor' (Son and Kakwani, 2006).

The influential idea of the last 30 years, therefore, that high investment in public social services and social security deters growth, and that economic growth alone will automatically lead to a reduction in poverty, has not attracted convincing supporting research evidence. There is more support for the alternative idea, that high public social expenditure has positive effects on growth. For example one research team completed an analysis of economic and social data accumulated from panel data over 10 years[10] for the United States, Germany and the Netherlands, representing the neo-liberal, corporatist and social democratic (including Nordic) welfare regimes that came to be separately identified by social scientists in the twentieth century. The welfare regimes of the three countries were compared in terms of their success in promoting efficiency (economic growth and prosperity), reducing poverty, and promoting equality, integration, stability and autonomy. The United States did not turn out to be more efficient than the other two. Overall, the statistical data collected over time suggested that on both economic and social criteria the social democratic regime had advantages over the corporatist, and both had advantages over the neo-liberal welfare regimes.[11] Altogether, there has been a large range of research studies refuting the argument that social security has had a negative impact on economic development (good examples are Atkinson, 1995; Gramlich 1997; Koskela and Viren, 1983; Singh, 1996; and the general review in Hall and Midgeley, 2004: Chapter 8).

Greater distributional equality provides a favourable 'initial condition' for rapid and sustainable growth ... Redistribution of current income and assets, or redistribution of a country's growth increment, is the most effective form of poverty reduction for most countries; and ... mechanisms to achieve the redistributions are feasible for most countries. (Dagdeviren et al., 2001: 23)

The growth and diversification of social protection

Europe is 'the cradle of social protection' (Ministry of Social Affairs and Health, Finland, 1999: 1). Historically the modern welfare state 'took off' in the late nineteenth century, 'between the Italian and the German Unification and the First World War' (Flora, 1986, vol. I: xiii). In the last 100 years systems of social protection have evolved from fragmentary beginnings to systems that are both complex and comprehensive. Although providing modest levels of old age pensions, sickness benefits and invalidity pensions for small minorities in society, conservative and liberal elites as well as more radical social reformers 'in many European countries regarded social insurance programmes as the answer to the "social question" of how to integrate a growing industrial working class into the existing social and political order' (Clasen, 1997: 1).

The speed and scope of urbanization around the end of the nineteenth century led to new as well as larger social problems. Intensified by the new capital-driven economy, hardship arose in the new factory towns as well as the depleted countryside. Protests about conditions easily turned into social conflict. Because the revenues of the state were growing, different social classes were aware of new-found resources and called for state intervention to build the first social welfare institutions. A convincing explanation of the origins of the welfare state in Europe therefore lay in the distinguishing features of the Western European society of that time: fast-developing industrialization and consequently urbanization, and democratization (Flora, 1986, vol. I: xiii). The new European welfare systems shared much in common but also developed differently. First, the evolution of a capitalist market economy in conjunction with a democratic nation-state produced 'a specific type of liberal welfare state'. Second, historical preconditions and the new forms of urban employment allowed strong industrial working classes to emerge to influence how new welfare systems might develop. But, third, there were wide institutional variations that could be exploited differently by individual governments.

It is hard to be exact about the shape and nature of 'the European welfare state'. Many analysts have preferred to argue about sub-categories of the welfare state in order to explain the path taken by one or two particular countries that attracted interest. But there was one widely agreed refrain: 'The modern welfare state started in Europe as an attempt to tackle the problems common to this new social class (the industrial working class): loss of income through accident, sickness, invalidity, unemployment and in old age' (ibid.: xiv–xv). Long-established forms of grudging and punitive social assistance were not the answer. The solution to these problems lay in the institution of social insurance, which was taken up by one country after another. After more than 100 years the social security system as a whole still tends to dominate political discussion about the welfare state. European and American social policy are sometimes differentiated because the United States is said to devote more energy to social citizenship through the development of education than to the expansion of social security (Flora, ibid.) but the scale of United States spending on social security has remained considerable in the last half-century. A review in 1999 concluded that 'by the end of the nineteenth century, governments in the area now covered by the 29 member countries of the OECD typically spent 10 per cent of GDP. One hundred years later, public sector spending in the OECD area averages 47 per cent' (de Kam and Owens, 1999: 176). After 1960 the increase in public outlays 'is mainly explained by higher government spending on public social protection. For 1960–97 social transfers, including subsidies, increased by 11.0 per cent of GDP for the 29 countries to 21.1 per cent of GDP (in a total of 46.6 per cent overall government expenditure' (ibid.: 177). The increase from 1980 to 1995 was 4.7 per cent of GDP.

In 1996 all taxes accounted for 37.7 per cent of GDP,[12] of which 8.8 per cent were employer and employee social security contributions (ibid.: 179). These social security contributions had steadily increased in almost every member country and ranged from 18.1 per cent of GDP in France and 14.5 per cent of GDP in Germany to 1.6 per cent of GDP in Denmark.

After the Second World War social security expenditure grew rapidly and reached 10 per cent of GDP in member countries and in some of them topped 20 per cent. Expenditure was reined back in some member States in the later 1980s, and by others in the 1990s. One intention on the part of government was to save taxation by diverting funds from universal social insurance or tax-financed group schemes to social assistance and means-tested tax credits. The arguable effects have included loss of social cohesion and social reciprocation, and greater instability in living standards and individual life course. However, the average total cost of social security for OECD countries has continued to rise, as percentage of GDP, despite decline for some years before restoration in particular countries, and levelling off or continued growth in others (see Table 2.4 above).

In the mid-twentieth century the member States of Europe came to insure the majority of their populations against the social risks of sickness, disability, old age and unemployment and of welfare deficiencies related to childhood, motherhood, housing and education. They shared a common historical legacy. Expansion of social protection in every member country and a move towards comprehensive coverage did not, however, lead to uniformity.

Despite the common economic and social problems, including poverty, that they faced, member countries continued to develop divergent responses adjusted to their own institutional (socio-political) and structural environments. This seems to have distracted many analysts into making too much of the differences between, or variations among, countries, instead of recognizing that in the scale of resources being used and the protection coverage of entire populations they were following a common path; they were not just trying for domestic reasons to find programmes to deal with small minorities that were exceptional or unique. This will be explained below.

But, more significantly, social insurance contributions rather than taxes came to play the majority role in funding expansion. This was put in place by member countries of the EU. Rarely has this agreement across countries been identified as the key feature of the development of strategies to defeat poverty and simultaneously secure citizens against some of the worst risks to life and livelihood. Table 2.9 above shows that in 1980 social insurance contributions accounted for two-thirds of the financing of social protection. By 1996 there was only a small decline in the role of contributions and they continued to account for 63 per cent of the finance of social protection. Countries that have chosen to give stronger weight in the 1990s and early 2000s to forms of social assistance, including tax credits, have stumbled in their attempts to contain poverty at the same time as maintaining social cohesion and work incentives. Thus comparative analysis of child poverty rates showed that in 16 of 24 OECD countries 'the rate at the end of the 1990s was higher than at the beginning and in only three countries has it declined to a measurable degree' (Corak, 2005). There are major problems in prosperous but increasingly unequal countries of real rates of marginal tax becoming very high when means-tested assistance schemes begin to predominate, of more recognizable wasteful as well as inefficient administration, and of declining public acceptance and support.

It can be also be seen in Table 2.9 above that the (compulsory) contributions made by employers accounted for the larger part of the total contributions made. In only four of the 15 member States in 1996 (Denmark, Ireland, Luxembourg and the UK) were taxes more considerable than contributions (Eurostat, 1999; and Ministry of Social Affairs and Health, Finland, 1999: 213). The predominant trend between 1980 and 1996 was a reduction of employer contributions from 45 per cent of total social protection receipts in 1980 to 39 per cent in 1996. At the same time there was an increase in government taxes and in employees' contributions. One explanation is the growing strength in negotiating conditions of trade on the part of trans-national corporations.

European member States increased, on average, their expenditures on social protection as a whole. Trends are illustrated above in Tables 2.8 and 2.10. As a percentage of the GDP of EU-12 such expenditure grew from just over 24 in 1980 to more than 27 in the early 1990s. In fact, after a sharp rise in the early 1980s the figure levelled out in the remainder of that decade before rising sharply again after 1991 (Eurostat, 1996: 17).

The sensitivity towards social security and social service institutions shown by OECD governments in the final decades of the twentieth century had not been bought lightly. The depression years between the two European wars had taught uncomfortable lessons. In the post-war years the reinvention of government was a 'call to arms in the revolt against bureaucratic malaise' and 'systems of governance can be fundamentally reframed'. Entrepreneurial organizations had to be built round 10 principles, according to one historian, including 'leveraging the market-place, rather than simply creating public programmes' (Gilbert, 1966).

An underlying factor shared in common was the need to develop forms of protection against the risk of loss of income of industrial wage labourers in market economies. When social insurance was introduced in Britain in 1913, for example, unemployment insurance cover was limited to certain industrial sectors, and especially those experiencing trade fluctuations (Gilbert, 1966). Domestic workers, for example, were excluded. In other countries social insurance schemes were established for industrial workers long before schemes for agricultural workers. The histories for example of Hungary, Portugal and Greece confirm the 'path dependency' of this development (Gilbert, 1966).

The purposes and priorities of social insurance have never been comprehensively agreed. The purposes have always been to reduce and prevent poverty through multiple policies; protect living standards; ensure intergenerational and life cycle transfers; promote income equality between different groups; promote social integration; and ensure economic security for entry and re-entry into the labour force.

Conclusion

Throughout history social insurance has been vigorously contested. The institution was established during bitter struggles on behalf of disparate social groups in the principal industrial countries. After attempts to dismiss social insurance on grounds of loss of trade and cuts in profits the institution came to be seen by many elites of different political persuasions as demonstrating how to integrate the growing industrial working class into the existing social and political order – and as an acceptable condition and even incentive for employers. It is a prime example of the far-reaching value and application of the human principle of reciprocity – and its history will be discussed below in Chapter 8.

At first many socialists and trades union activists opposed mandatory social insurance as undermining workers' mutual support schemes and hence workers' solidarity. Some opposed social insurance on the grounds that it gave capitalism a human face. Such opposition eventually bowed to the clear improvement in material living standards brought about by more comprehensive public measures and the fact that social insurance smoothed out shared risks and met the deficits of workers in trades most exposed to injury and sickness, as well as loss of employment. Employees realized they were building up entitlement to a small income if they became sick, disabled or unemployed and when they became old, in return for making regular weekly contributions from their wage in active working life. Members of their families also benefited. Employers realized they could strike acceptable work bargains with their employees because they were also making weekly contributions to a social insurance system for each individual employee, usually of equal scale, to a fund that allowed payments to be made through life to individuals when plunged into, or reaching, conditions of adversity. Elaboration of these schemes of benefit for non-working women and children followed.

The exact form of these schemes continues to be hotly debated. The ambiguities of 'adequate' benefits, like those of the minimum wage, remain, and are subject to acute political exchange and scientific investigation in all countries – as illustrated continuously in research (see, for example, Atkinson, 1991). But data collected from bodies like the OECD, as illustrated in this chapter, routinely demonstrate the resilience in each new generation of the institution.

In the course of more than 100 years social insurance has shown how civil rights can be extended and discrimination between factions reduced. Re-adoption of the system internationally in the twenty-first century – for example by the global corporations and all international agencies – may similarly show how human rights can be extended and racial and religious hostilities lessened.

Annex 2.1

The Millennium Development Goals

1. Eradicate extreme poverty and hunger	Between 1990 and 2015 • Halve the proportion of people whose income is less than US$1 a day • Halve the proportion of people who suffer from hunger
2. Achieve universal primary education	Ensure that by 2015 all children will be able to complete a full course of primary schooling
3. Promote gender equality and empower women	Eliminate gender disparity in all levels of education by 2015
4. Reduce child mortality	Reduce by two-thirds the under-five mortality rate between 1990 and 2015
5. Improve maternal health	Reduce by three-quarters the maternal mortality ratio between 1990 and 2015
6. Combat HIV/ AIDS, malaria and other diseases	By 2015 have halted, and begun to reverse • the spread of HIV/AIDS • the spread of malaria and other major diseases

(Continued)

Continued

7. Ensure environmental sustainability	• Integrate principles of sustainable development into country policies and reverse the loss of environmental resources • Halve the proportion of people without sustainable access to safe drinking water by 2015 • By 2020 have achieved a significant improvement in the lives of at least 100 million slum dwellers
8. Develop a global partnership for development	• Develop the world trading and financial system • Address the special needs of the least developed and landlocked and small island countries • Deal comprehensively with the debt problems of the developing countries

Annex 2.2

Glossary of terms (OECD)

Public social expenditure is the provision by public institutions of benefits to, and financial contributions targeted at, households and individuals in order to provide support during circumstances which adversely affect their welfare, provided that the provision of the benefits and financial contributions constitutes neither a direct payment for a particular good or service nor an individual contract or transfer. Such benefits can be cash transfers, or can be the direct ('in-kind') provision of goods and services. Tax breaks with a social purpose are included. To be considered 'social', benefits have to address one or more social goals. Benefits may be targeted at low-income households, but they may also be for the elderly, disabled, sick, unemployed or young persons. Programmes can be regulated by redistribution of resources across households or by compulsory participation. Social benefits are regarded as public when general government (that is, central, state and local governments, including social security funds) controls relevant financial flows.

Social expenditure consists of public social expenditure (defined above) plus private social expenditure. Thus, social expenditure can be provided by both public and private institutions, but transfers between households are not within the scope of social expenditure. It does not include 'market transactions' – that is, payments in return for the simultaneous provision of services of equivalent value.

Public social security comprises the funds made available at all levels of government by: (1) Social insurance programmes covering the community as a whole or where large sections of the community are imposed and controlled by a government unit. They generally involve compulsory contributions by employees or employers or both, and the terms on which benefits are paid are determined by government. (2) Social assistance programmes generally arise from taxation and cover only those with low incomes. Benefits are transfers made by government units to households and intended to meet the same kinds of needs as social insurance benefits, but are provided outside social insurance schemes and are not conditional on the previous payment of contributions. They are generally conditional on test of means, but sometimes other conditions as well. Tax credits can be included in social assistance, since households with less income than is eligible for tax can have their incomes made up to levels imposed by government through direct benefit payments or the pay received from employers. (3) Social benefits in kind consist of social security including reimbursements) in kind, and social assistance in kind (for example, food, fuel, clothing) excluding transfers of individual non-market goods and services (including gifts).

Social security comprises public social security, as defined above, plus social insurance benefits that are provided by privately funded schemes or by unfunded schemes managed by employers for the benefit of their existing or former employees without involving third parties in the form of insurance enterprises or pension funds.

Social transfers comprise total public and private expenditures as defined above.

Source: Adaptation of OECD *Economic Factbook*, 2005; *An Interpretative Guide to the OECD Social Expenditure Database SOCX*, 2005: 10.

Notes

1. See the extended discussion in Townsend and Gordon (2002: Chapters 1 and 17 but especially Chapters 8 and 9). 'The structural adjustment policies pursued in most developing countries have often contributed to a decline in the small percentage of the working population in the formal sector. The successive waves of structural adjustment programmes have also led to wage cuts in the public and private sectors, thereby eroding the financial base of statutory social insurance schemes. [The programmes have] often resulted in severe cuts in social budgets' (ILO, 2001a: 34).
2. Readers may explore the convolutions of the World Bank in seeking to defend its measurement of poverty and consequential international policies. Exchanges published during 2008–9 represent the lengths to which the bank goes to justify this measurement despite cogent technical and scientific criticisms. The exchanges illustrate growing public acknowledgement of the need for more effective action to defeat poverty and human rights violations. See for example Chen and Ravallion, 2008; Ravallion, 2008; Reddy, 2008; Reddy and Pogge, 2009 forthcoming; and Townsend, 2009.
3. The choice of $1.08 reflected the median of the 10 *lowest* poverty lines among a sample of 33 countries. In 2006, independent examination of the national poverty lines of 19 low-income countries (15 in sub-Saharan Africa and 4 in Asia, including India) constructed in the mid- and late-1990s, produced a different median figure of $1.50 (Kakwani and Son, 2006: 6).
4. By 1960 expert analysts in the United States had come to agree that social assistance must play a 'subordinate role' in relation to social insurance (Hohaus,

1960: 79; more generally Haber and Cohen, 1960; and see examples for different countries of numerous research studies: Braithwaite et al., 2000; Deacon and Bradshaw, 1983; Eardley et al., 1996a, 1996b; Huber, 1996; Oorschot, 2002).

5. This has led to claims about the 'political' misuse of social insurance investment funds, for example, the United Kingdom National Insurance Fund (see Lynes, 2006).

6. For example, Portugal and Finland were found to have roughly the same 'market' child poverty rates but government action brought poverty down to under 3 per cent in Finland while the rate in Portugal 'shows almost no change' (UNICEF, 2006b: 457).

7. All countries experience annual fluctuations in social security and public social expenditure, expressed as percentage of GDP.

8. See glossary in Annex 2.2.

9. The World Bank's latest report confirms the significant difference picked out in the last two columns of Table 2.9, showing corresponding data of the latest gini coefficients for these seven high-spending and seven low-spending countries. Five of the seven low-spending countries have higher coefficients (that is, are more unequal) than any of the high-spending countries (with an average of 0.33 for all seven, compared with 0.27) (see World Bank, 2006: 280–1).

10. Conventional compilations of economic and social statistics have traditionally depended on a succession of cross-sectional snapshots. But there are problems of sample variation and tracing the mechanisms of cause and not just discontinuities in the populations surveyed and analysed. Panel studies have, however, been pioneered and are now coming on stream for a large number of countries. In these studies the same individuals are interviewed time and again, over a protracted period. Experience in early work (for example, Duncan, 1984) showed that 10 years of continuous panel data were required for purposes of drawing conclusive results. The three countries chosen for comparison in the late 1990s were the only ones to have assembled 10 or more years' continuous data (the three organizations being the University of Michigan's Institute for Social Research, from 1968, the Deutsches Institut für Wirtschaftsforschung, Berlin, from 1984, and the Dutch Socio-economic Panel Survey, run by the Centraal Bureau voor de Statistiek, also from 1984 (see Goodin et al., 1999: 2–3 and 9–12).

11. 'It turns out that the social democratic welfare regime is "the best of all possible worlds". [Of the three alternative regimes it] turns out to be the best choice, regardless of what you want it to do. [It] is clearly best on its home ground of minimizing inequality. But it also turns out to be better at reducing poverty than the liberal welfare regime, which targets its welfare policy on that to the exclusion of all else. The social democratic welfare regime is also at least as good in promoting stability (and arguably at least as good at promoting social integration) as is the corporatist welfare regime, which ostensibly attached most importance to those goals. The social democratic welfare regime is also best at promoting autonomy, something valued by all regimes if not necessarily prioritized by any. Thus, no matter which of those goals you set for your welfare regime, the social democratic model is at least as good as (and typically better than) any other for attaining it' (Goodin et al., 1999: 260).

12. In that year social security costs accounted for 25 per cent of all tax revenue, compared with 27 per cent personal income tax, 18 per cent general consumption taxes, 8 per cent corporate income tax, 5 per cent property taxes and 6 per cent other (de Kam and Owens, 1999: 183).

Part II
Issues for the Global Society of the Twenty-first Century

3
Social Protection and Nation-Building: an Essay on Why and How Universalist Social Policy Contributes to Stable Nation-States

Chris de Neubourg

Unmistakably, the growth of social protection systems and the development of nation-states in the advanced capitalist world are closely associated. This chapter argues that universalist elements of social protection systems contribute to state- and nation-building and therefore are potentially strong building blocks for stable political and economic systems in less advanced economies. I will explore:

1. how exactly the development of social protection systems and the building of nations were associated in some European countries;
2. what political theory and political economy teach us about the link;
3. how universal social benefits contribute to stable non-violent nation-building; and
4. how far universal family benefits can lessen poverty and inequality and play their part in relatively extensive but simple social protection systems.

At least two recent examples of modern successful state transformation come to mind when considering how social protection systems may help or are even essential in anchoring new developments in (re)building nations: Germany after its reunification and South Africa after the end of the apartheid regime. In the German case the structured social-democratic welfare state of West Germany was copied in the new 'Bundesländer'. In South Africa, addressing the overt and stunning high level of poverty among the discriminated coloured population was given high priority in an attempt to prevent massive social unrest during the first decade of democracy. In both cases, a fundamental question arises. Would the countries as nation-states have survived if this route had not been chosen and would the political and human rights, and the social rights, of the 'new' citizens have been guaranteed – at some level at least – as a political programme and intention?

European experiences

The history of the European welfare states has to be written in separate periods. The basis for the modern welfare states was formed in the period between the German and Italian unifications and the First World War. The inter-war period and the Second World War consolidated the needs for more assertive government social policy and have put social policy in the context of broader macroeconomic political realities. The full development of a diversified (Western) European welfare state was seen in the period after the Second World War. The Eastern and Central European countries entering the EU a decade after the fall of the Berlin Wall were and are writing their own history when joining the club of modern welfare states established in capitalist countries. In all cases and periods the link between the development of systematic social policy within social protection systems and the strengthening of the nation-state can be illustrated by pointing to specific developments in some countries.

The instrumentality of social policy in the struggle to maintain political stability amidst rapidly transforming economies and new socialist and social democrat movements, is most obviously illustrated by the early nineteenth-century advocates of social welfare state constructions in Germany and Britain. While in 1878 Bismarck in Germany proposed social policy 'to destroy the growing social democrat movement' by creating a tight bond between the state and the workers (Alber, 1986: 5), Otto Hinze had no problem in admitting in 1915 that this objective had not been reached but that social protection policy 'enables the government to take a strong and decisive position vis-à-vis the lower classes and their demands' (Flora and Heidenheimer, 1981: 270). The social policy of the Prussian state had already been extended to all the regions of the unified German nation in 1870 as an element of pragmatic unification for the large mass of workers. In the United Kingdom, Winston Churchill recognized in 1911 that there was a need for what he called an 'averaging machinery' 'bringing the magic of averages to the aid of millions' and introduced together with Lloyd George the National Insurance Act (advised by William Beveridge). Equally, before the First World War the Swedish social policy developments are described by Olson (1986: 4) to rest on a firm national feeling between 1889 and 1913 for 'the profound ties between the new semi-urban proletariat, the rural poor and the free peasantry as well as the industrialists and older fractions of the ruling class'.

Keeping nations together by encompassing all residents under some form of social system (even in the absence of a full implementation of all political rights), seemed to be the major concern of policy-makers when establishing the skeletons of social protection systems in the pre-First World War period. The First World War and its aftermath of economic crises in the late 1920s and early 1930s, reinforced the need for unified and systematic social policies. Even in Italy, where until 1900 social policy had relied on the exclusive monopoly of the Catholic Church, the need for a state social policy became 'the topic of the day' in order to address the social unrest. It found its consolidation in the foundation of the corporatist state in 1927 wherein social policy acquired high political status being regarded as 'a privileged tool for the creation and maintenance of social consensus' (Ferrera, 1986: 389). The idea of a consensual social cohesion mobilizing altruistic motivation and stimulating new kinds of social behaviour was also at the very heart of the further development of the British welfare state (Parry, 1986). Combined with macroeconomic analyses, it turned both Beveridge and Keynes into 'reluctant collectivists' (George and Wilding, 1976). The Beveridge report (1942) and the policies advocated by it, aimed at promoting solidarity by 'bringing institutions and individuals into partnership with the state in a common condemnation of the scandal of physical want' (p. 2). The Weimar republic in interwar Germany introduced a series of social reforms to calm the public unrest (Alber, 1986) and Denmark introduced in 1933 a large-scale reform in its social policy in order to cover a larger part of the population by giving the large majority in the country access to social rights. Before that date, Danish social policy had been resting on the philosophy of the poor laws introduced already in 1824 and modified by the constitution of 1849, excluding beneficiaries from – rather than including them in – political and social life (Johansen, 1986).

The welfare state was developed fully in most (Western) European countries after the Second World War. While the countries under the influence of the Soviet Union embarked on their own specific social model, social policy in the north-western part of Europe gradually developed into a system covering cradle-to-grave risks in a combination of universal benefits and compulsory contribution-based insurances. Especially in the 1950s and early 1960s, the establishment of these fully developed welfare states rested on the sense of national solidarity created by the war and extended by the will to rebuild Europe afterwards. In Italy and Germany the war had left deep divisions. National solidarity had to be re-established in the ruins of the fascists and the national socialist states. Rebuilding the social infrastructure played an important role in that process (Ferrera, 1986). In most countries of North-West Europe,[1] political development had induced the realization of increments of citizenship rights, with civil rights becoming universalized in the eighteenth century, political rights in the nineteenth and social rights in the twentieth century (see also T. H. Marshall in his seminal lecture on 'Citizenship and Social Class', 1950).

After the Second World War, the countries east of Germany followed their own path. In the Soviet Republics social protection was linked to employment providing workers with basic social protection from health services to yearly holidays through their employers (job security guaranteed the access to these services over the lifetime of the workers), supplemented by a complicated system of categorical benefits and privileges favouring special groups and institutionalizing care for all those not well connected to employment such as the handicapped, elderly and orphans.[2] The legacy of the 'state socialist welfare traditions' left a remarkable imprint on the social systems in most Soviet Republics after the break up of the USSR in 1991. Most countries, some more than others, still struggle with persistent elements from the old system. The most hard to change features seem to be the institutionalized care for special groups and the endless list of privileges and special benefits such as in-kind benefits for public transport, electricity and housing for specific groups. On the other hand, some elements of the system were changed in scope and coverage while the basic social legitimating forces are still active. Few countries got rid of universal child benefits or fully abolished state pensions. It should be understood that despite the important changes in the economic systems, the needs and demands of the population for forms of social protection were and are very active and still refer to the experiences and the aspirations under the former regime.

The shaping of the political preferences of the population was subject to contradictory forces. On the one hand, a lot of people were relieved to have abandoned the old state-socialist system. On the other hand, the uncertainties of the new systems were considerable and many voters still felt that the state should take responsibility for many of their needs. This wish was and still is not always easy to reconcile with the self-help mentality that the capitalist system seems to promote. Few countries had stable governments for protracted periods: with the exception of Estonia, all countries showed a picture of changing coalitions after elections and often experienced changing policy modes and moods even within relatively short periods. Promises were broken and half-baked reforms stopped or even reversed after a change of government. As a result, social protection policy is still not unified and revised in a comprehensive way in most countries, showing the political hesitations and illustrating the uncertainties of the new systems further. It is, however, clear in almost all countries that the majority of the populations in these countries still regard the state as the important actor in organizing solidarity across groups, cohorts and classes (de Neubourg, 2006).

Reviewing the sketchy history of social protection systems in Europe, it can be concluded that the development of these systems 'followed the footsteps of the nation state' (Flora, 1986: xii). The history is too diverse to allow the conclusion that the installation and enlargement of social protection systems has been used as an important element in the building of nations. Political rulers explicitly expressed intentions to counteract critical forces by 'buying off' the sympathy of the masses and thus providing basic social protection or by providing privileges to certain groups. They also expressed a sense of responsibility towards large groups of workers in particular, but few, if any, had a blue-print or a master plan to use social protection policy to build up or strengthen the nation-state. To fully understand the role that social protection policy played in anchoring the nation-states, we need theoretical considerations from both political science theory and political economy.

Theoretical considerations

Following the tradition of Durkheim, Weber, Marx and de Tocqueville, Stein Rokkan (1973, 1974, as quoted in Flora 1981: 397–436), Peter Flora (1986) and Jens Alber (1986) developed a theory of what they called 'an analytical framework of modernization'. An essential element of this analytical framework is the reconciliation of capitalism and democracy. They argue that in democratic states, capitalism cannot survive without translation of intended political equality into the realm of the economy; social protection systems serve as the 'mediator' between political equalization and economic inequality. As such, social policy is a firm reaction to the problems of the industrial working class. Even without a full Marxist interpretation, it is not difficult to see how social protection helped in appeasing the conflict between the rhetoric of the 'republic' wherein political 'égalité' was and still is the cornerstone and the harsh economic inequalities and the misery of the masses of workers in the nineteenth-century capitalist industrial economies. Rokkan (1973, 1974, as quoted in Flora 1981) interpreted the development of the welfare state in Europe as 'the completion of the nation state'. He distinguishes four stages in the history of European democracies: state formation, nation-building, participation and redistribution. The nation-state cannot become a democracy if it is not completed by political participation of all the citizens. Redistribution, realized in social protection systems, becomes then the finishing element that anchors the democracies into stable systems where the participation of all the citizens does not lead to overthrowing the capitalist mode of production in order to overcome the apparent contradiction between political equality and large economic inequality.

Despite its simple elegance, the theory does not allow us to understand how social protection systems could be an element contributing to the stability of democratic political constructions in nation-states in the twenty-first century. The service-dominated modern Western economies and the apparent lack of large masses of industrial workers in low- and middle-income economies seem to deprive the theory of its essential conditions. The essential element of the theory is, however, not the co-existence of a large industrial class of workers and political democracy, but the recognition of an underlying mechanism that is necessary for both political equality and economic egalitarianism: solidarity. It is the 'fraternité' in the rhetoric of the French Revolution.

Starting from the third idea in the French revolutionary slogan – 'liberté', generally translated in terms of individual freedom – the existence of nation-states is a puzzle as long as there is no *communality* (as reflected in the ideas of solidarity or reciprocity) in the preferences for public goods of individuals within these nation-states and as long as there are no *economies of scale* – assuming that it is relatively less costly to provide public goods for several or many persons than for a single person. It has to be assumed that the stability of nation-states depends on the existence of economies of scale in the provision of public goods and depends too on at least a minimum level of solidarity, shared beliefs, values and preferences on the part of its citizens.[3] In the absence of economies of scale and/or a minimum homogeneity in preferences (as reflections of beliefs and values), nations would disintegrate.[4] The question to be addressed is therefore how economies of scale and a sufficient homogeneity of preferences are to be translated into solidarity – so that there can be a stable basis for social protection systems to be installed, developed and maintained. (This implies that a minimum solidarity is a condition for installing social protection systems without excluding the possibility that the systems themselves enhance solidarity further.)

The political economy of transfers among regions with differing distributions of income within an economic system is analysed in an important paper by Bolton and Roland (1997). They argue that the major effects that are at work leading to equilibrium or disequilibrium are the political effect (measured by comparing the difference in the desired fiscal policy between the median voter in region A and the median voter in region B), the tax base effect (measured by comparing the contributions of regions being richer/poorer than the unified country) and the economies of scale effect.

Assuming a skewed income distribution to the left with fewer richer people than poorer people (as is the case in all countries) and a democratic state wherein civil rights are guaranteed to all citizens, richer people are regionally not separable from poorer people because the former need the latter in the economic process.[5] Solidarity within regions depends on the willingness of richer people to pay relatively more for public goods than poorer people within the same region/nation or the willingness to redistribute income via taxes or, in other words, the willingness to transfer income from the rich to the poor. This willingness, or preference, depends on perceived economies of scale and the existence of externalities. The economies of scale argument is evident but the externalities argument requires further analysis.

Externalities of poverty come in various forms, roughly to be divided into negative externalities of (relative) poverty and positive externalities of less inequality. Negative externalities refer to increased risks of 'disutility' related to the existence of poor parts of the society. This is, for example, the case when poverty leads to risk of increased ill-health among poorer people but also leads to risk of increased ill-health among richer people. De Swaan (1988), for example, argues that the rich in the Dutch cities of the seventeenth century were prepared to pay for the sewage systems in order to reduce the risks of deadly diseases. Negative externalities are also important when richer people experience disutility from the fact that they are surrounded by too many poor people when that leads to higher criminality. Again, disutility for the rich may arise from the very fact that the daily experience of being confronted with poor people is regarded in contradiction with their preferences related to economic equality or to acceptability of poverty.[6]

Positive externalities of less inequality may arise if richer people profit from a less poor and better educated workforce because the returns on investment are bigger; or, in other words, when expenditures on social protection are seen as productive investment (as elaborated in de Neubourg and Castonguay, 2006).

Finally in the political economy of income distribution we have to consider a negative externality related to the median voter argument. Assuming two groups in a full democracy – a small rich group and a large poorer group which are regionally inseparable – it can be argued that the preferences for the provision of public goods and the related taxes of the poorer group will differ from the preferences of the rich group more if the income distance between the two groups is larger. This provides the small rich group an incentive to close the income gap between the rich and the poor. In other words the rich group may rationally choose to redistribute income even if none of the externalities discussed above is deemed important to the rich.

Universal or means-tested targeted transfers

Solid democratic state formation and social protection are intertwined. But which forms of social protection are more supportive than others for democratic state formation?

There are two main forms of social transfers: universalist[7] benefits and benefits targeted exclusively to the (very) poor.[8] It is remarkable that continental Europe, in contrast to Anglo-Saxon countries and the United States,[9] has largely opted for a firm universalist system complemented with an important but quantitatively small targeted component (de Neubourg et al., 2007). Political theory and political economy provide arguments for this choice. Social transfers may be seen as social rights – complementing civil and political rights are easier to defend if all citizens are provided with these rights. Although discrimination on the basis of needs – usually by means- or income-testing – is strictly speaking not incompatible with the idea of social rights, it is more difficult to implement because social consensus on the actual definition of 'deserving and non-deserving poor' is implied. That is to say, there is supposed to be consensus on how income thresholds are set and measured. This leads to discussions about who are the 'deserving,' and thus eligible, and who are the 'non-deserving', and thus non-eligible poor. These discussions are difficult and lead to social exclusion rather than to social inclusion as is illustrated by the nineteenth-century experiences of Britain and Denmark, two early innovators in social policy. The 'poor law'-based benefits of the nineteenth century in both countries, being income-tested, had serious implications for the political and civil rights of the beneficiaries.

They lost their political rights – for example the right to vote – as long as they received the benefits. In Denmark, they even lost particular civil rights. Beneficiaries had no right to marry without prior consent of the local poor relief commission that provided the benefit. In Britain this political discrimination evaporated in the nineteenth century, but in Denmark the restrictions on the political rights and civil rights for poor law benefit recipients survived even the 1933 large-scale reform of the social policy system. The Danish constitution of 1849 referred to the 'deserving and non-deserving poor' (see Johansen, 1986 for Denmark and Flora and Heidenheimer, 1981 for Britain). This historical example is a strong illustration of the social stigma that was and still is attached to means-tested social benefits. The resulting discrimination and social exclusion are inimical to the ideals of democratic ordering and do not exactly turn social policy into the 'completion of the political rights-based movement' that installed democracies in Europe.

There is also a pragmatic argument that makes universal benefits attractive from a democratic state formation point of view. The implementation of alternative means-tested transfers requires a robust and fairly sophisticated bureaucratic apparatus that is often not available in countries that build up their social policy capacity. The capacity needed to fully implement the means-testing and monitor applicants in order to decide whether or not they are entitled to receive the transfer in the future, is very large. This is especially problematic when the state is young and has to build up legitimacy or when countries are subject to government corruption. Under means-tested transfers, officials or civil servants will have to decide whether or not each applicant is eligible, how the information on the household's means is collected and assessed, for how long the transfer is allocated and when a new cycle of assessment and allocation should be started. Data on the means of households – including income from various sources and means stemming from the availability of assets – are difficult to obtain and even more difficult to control. Protocols and procedures are difficult to design and to implement in a fair way across different regions in a country. All this is particularly difficult for weak states with serious limitations in their educated workforce.[10] The adoption of proxy means-testing methods is sometimes used to simplify the selection of beneficiaries and the transfer allocation decisions. The accuracy of this method is, however, far from encouraging, as illustrated by a recent study in Mongolia on proxy means-tested benefits, which concluded that more than one-third of the target group did not receive a benefit (exclusion error) while two-thirds of the non-targeted group received a transfer (inclusion error) (Hodges et al., 2007).

There is of course an alternative to direct cash transfers, namely social insurance.[11] The administrative and economic management capacity to run sustainable social insurance schemes is, however, also demanding though of a different nature. It may be easier than means-tested benefits regarding the allocation and disbursement decisions, but it is complicated in design particularly in setting contribution levels, accounting rules, discount rates, entitlement rules and benefit levels. Long-term financial sustainability is not easy to assess, let alone guarantee.

The technical difficulties related to implementing means-tested transfer schemes, compared with social insurance schemes, also make them more sensitive to corruption. More decisions have to be made by individual officers and therefore corruption can enter the process more easily. Elsewhere, I have argued extensively that the simpler the scheme, the less corruption will be the result (de Neubourg, 2002); complexity of legislation and levels of corruption are positively related (see also Rose-Ackerman, 1999). This is an important argument in favour of *universal* assistance schemes: weak states in low- and middle-income countries can avoid increasing corruption by installing simpler social protection legislation.

All in all, universal benefits, while requiring also some administrative capacity, are by far the easiest to design, to implement and to monitor.

Political economy considerations reinforce this argument in three ways. First, the distinction between deserving and non-deserving poor means that the population is no longer divided into a small rich group and a large poorer group, but into three groups: a small group of rich, a small group of very poor (deserving poor) and a large group of not-so-poor persons. The median voter argument becomes more complicated, but redistribution of income from the rich towards the very poor only leaves the larger group in the population outside the system. This increases the risk for the rich that the median voter preferences of the large not-so-poor third group are not sympathetic to the rich group's needs and preferences. A social system based on transfers to the very poor only may not result in the desired political stability – at least not in a full democracy.

Secondly, the negative externalities that lead to the installation of a basic social protection system are most probably not counteracted adequately by focusing efforts on the poorest people only. Negative externalities for the rich still exist because they are also related to the consequences of the behaviour of the not-so-poor group. In other words, the rich are no longer adequately protected because the not-so-poor group have fewer prospects from the system than the very poor.

The third way by which the reliance on targeted transfers for the very poor only may be defective in political economy terms, is to refer to economies of scale. Much of the economies of scale argument is linked to the basic idea of risk pooling. Tax-based universalist transfers maximize the tax base in the sense that it is easily defensible to let a large part of the society contribute to the financial coverage of a series of benefits that are accessible for all persons in the economy. Technically it is difficult to cover the transfers to the poor of taxes or contributions from the poor only – known as the 'adverse selection' argument. Politically it is difficult to convince the rich and the middle- and lower-income class – the not-so-poor – to (continue to) contribute to the financing of transfers from which they themselves are excluded by design. This is a traditional argument suggesting that 'benefits for the poor are poor benefits'. It refers to the political resistance of the not-so-poor to social protection systems from which they are excluded as potential beneficiaries. It also increases the danger of social stigma attached to social benefits and of benefits leading to social exclusion rather than social inclusion as in the nineteenth-century British and Danish cases (see above). In a democratic society, social protection systems based solely (or mainly) on targeted benefits for the poor are only sustainable in the long term if they are based on non-economic pressures such as feelings of solidarity and charity requiring a large degree of 'fraternité' among the rich and the middle- and next-to-poor income classes.

I have argued so far that there are sound theoretical reasons to believe that social protection in general can seriously contribute to the creation of stable democratic nations and that this is illustrated in the historical processes of most high-income countries. I have also argued that universal benefits are attractive in terms of administrative capacities, and that political economy arguments reinforce this statement. But can universal benefit really contribute to less poverty and less inequality in a realistic way? It remains to be seen whether universal benefits prove to be affordable, adequate and relevant. These are empirical questions.

Universal benefits are affordable, adequate and relevant

In the following empirical discussion regarding the affordability, adequacy and relevance of universal benefits, the analysis is limited to universal or 'categorical' benefits, namely child or family benefits. The reason for this is that data sources that allow benefits and their effects internationally to be explored only contain information on the type of benefit and not its universality or otherwise. Except for child or family benefits, other benefits tend to be either a mixture of universal non-contributory and contributory benefits – such as pensions and social insurance benefits – or are means-tested targeted benefits – such as social assistance, housing and other benefits.

One of the main arguments against the application of universal benefits is their fiscal *affordability*; it is argued that most countries lack the fiscal space to implement relevant universal benefits. This applies especially to child benefits in low- and middle-income countries because of the combination of the limited tax base and the high fertility rates, and to universal social pensions in high-income countries because of the combination of a limited labour force – and therefore tax base – and high life expectancy. Other chapters in this book demonstrate that this is not necessarily true for low- and middle-income countries: it is argued that for most countries the lack of fiscal space is limited in time and that most countries would be able to finance universal benefits after a limited number of years. Evidently, a lot depends on the level of the benefits set; poorer countries can start by installing relatively modest benefit levels and increase them when economic prosperity allows them to do so. Whether means-tested targeted benefits are better affordable than universal benefits is an empirical issue. The total yearly costs of a benefit system roughly depend on the sum of the disbursed benefits plus the administration costs. The administration costs of universal benefits are lower than the administration costs for means-tested targeted benefits. The level of the administration costs is higher in countries with less capacity to implement the targeted system, since especially in the first years of the implementation, large investments are needed to build up the capacity of the administration to implement the means-testing and the associated benefit disbursement. On the other hand, the sum of the disbursed universal benefits will probably be higher than the sum of benefits for means-tested targeted benefits (depending on the level of the individual benefits in both cases). In wider cost-benefit analysis it has frequently been shown that a large proportion of persons theoretically eligible for a means-tested benefit do not in fact receive it; and many who do receive it, as I have pointed out earlier in this chapter, are theoretically ineligible. As a consequence, it is difficult to state a priori that universal benefits are less affordable than means-targeted social benefits.

For high-income European countries, the total costs of the universal family benefits are limited, as illustrated in Figure 3.1.[12] Even for continental European countries with generous child benefits, the total spending does

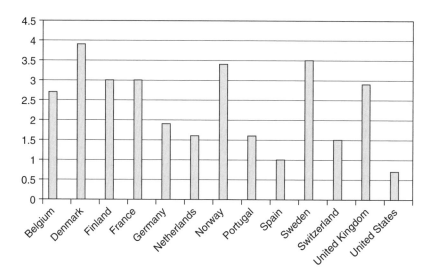

Figure 3.1 Expenditure on family benefits as a percentage of GDP, selected OECD countries, 2004
Source: OECD Social Expenditure Database Edition 2008.

not exceed 4 per cent of GDP. In none of these countries is the existence of universal child (or family) benefits under political pressure, suggesting that, at least in public opinion, universal child benefits are fiscally affordable.

Whether universal benefits (in this case child or family benefits) are *adequate* has to be judged by the relative poverty reduction effect of the benefits and by the expenditure on the benefits according to income deciles. Because of their universal character, child benefits in most European countries can be expected to show a considerable amount of leakage – in benefits paid out to higher incomes – and their effect on poverty reduction is expected to be low. However, the contrary is true, as is illustrated in Table 3.1 and Figure 3.2. Table 3.1 estimates the change in the poverty rate that can be attributed to various categories of benefits, using a relative poverty line, that is, the European Laeken poverty line of 60 per cent of median income, and an absolute poverty line, that is, using the Orshansky poverty line adopted in the United States, for a number of EU countries. From the table it can be seen that a large poverty reduction results from pensions expenditure – for all social and mandatory pensions. Family benefits, however, reduce poverty considerably in all countries with universal benefits (the Benelux countries, the Scandinavian countries, Austria, France, Germany and the United Kingdom). It is remarkable that the impact is much bigger than the impact of means-tested social assistance and 'other benefits' in these countries.[13] This highlights an interesting phenomenon: in advanced European countries means-tested social assistance is designed and used as a social policy instrument of last resort. This implies that both poverty and inequality are reduced by other types of benefits (universal categorical or group benefits and social insurances) lifting the majority of low-income households out of poverty before targeted benefits apply. The relatively small remaining group of households is then addressed by ambitious but quantitatively modest means-tested social assistance schemes (as extensively discussed in de Neubourg et al., 2007).

Figure 3.2 illustrates the disbursement of family benefits by income decile as a percentage of the total family benefits. It can be seen that for most countries the benefit incidence is highest for the deciles 2 to 4 and declining consistently with higher deciles, indicating that family benefits are relatively well targeted towards the lower income families despite their universal nature in these countries. The fact that the lowest decile seems not to profit from the universal family benefits in all countries but Belgium, the Netherlands and the United Kingdom is due to the fact that many (childless) elderly persons belong to the lowest income decile. That is not true for the three quoted countries because they have universal pension benefits: old age pensions in the Netherlands (AOW), guaranteed minimum incomes in Belgium and the basic flat-rate state pension in the United Kingdom.

Universal child (family) benefits not only contribute considerably to the reduction of poverty and inequality, they are also *relevant* in terms of their

Table 3.1 Poverty reduction impact of benefit categories in 2000 using two alternative poverty lines (benchmark: final income)

	Laeken poverty line – 60% median income					Orshansky 'absolute' poverty line (net household income)				
	Pensions	Family benefits	Sickness/disability/ unemployment	Social assistance	Other	Pensions	Family benefits	Sickness/disability/ unemployment	Social assistance	Other
Belgium	-15.6	-4.7	-4.9	-0.1	-0.5	-16.9	-2.8	-4.8	-0.2	-0.3
Denmark	-11.5	-2.2	-5.1	-0.3	-2.9	-14.2	-0.7	-4.3	-0.1	-2.1
Germany	-18.2	-4.9	-4.1	-0.5	-0.5	-18.0	-3.4	-3.1	-0.6	-0.4
Greece	-16.7	-0.8	-1.4	0.0	-0.1	-15.2	-0.4	-1.2	0.0	-0.1
Spain	-12.7	-0.4	-4.0	0.0	-0.2	-12.3	-0.4	-3.6	0.0	-0.2
France	-16.9	-3.6	-3.8	-0.2	-2.4	-17.5	-3.7	-3.0	-0.2	-2.4
Ireland	-6.1	-2.8	-5.4	-0.2	-0.8	-7.0	-3.3	-4.1	-0.4	-0.8
Italy	-19.4	-0.5	-2.0	0.0	-0.1	-18.5	-0.4	-1.9	0.0	-0.1
Luxembourg	-16.6	-6.0	-4.1	-0.3	0.0	-14.3	-2.3	-2.2	-1.3	0.0
Netherlands	-14.7	-3.4	-4.3	-1.4	-0.7	-14.2	-2.4	-3.8	-1.8	-0.4
Austria	-15.6	-6.7	-2.9	0.0	-0.5	-15.2	-3.7	-2.2	0.0	-0.2
Portugal	-11.1	-0.9	-2.5	-0.3	-0.2	-9.8	-1.6	-3.4	-0.5	-0.1
Finland	-12.4	-5.6	-11.3	-0.5	-2.8	-12.3	-2.6	-6.4	-0.4	-1.4
United Kingdom	-14.0	-4.3	-3.9	-0.5	-3.8	-14.1	-3.9	-3.2		-3.9

Source: Authors' calculations: for technical details on the databases and basic poverty estimates as provided in Notten and de Neubourg, 2007; tax credits are not counted as benefits in the data; a breakdown by type of benefit is not possible for the USA due to the lack of data on separate benefit categories that fit the EU definitions.

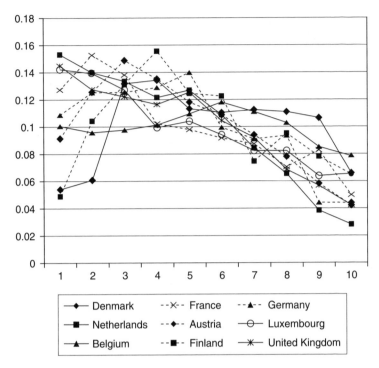

Figure 3.2 Family benefits per decile as a percentage of total family benefits, 2000
Source: Authors' calculations; see also Table 3.1; for technical details see Notten and de Neubourg, 2007.

share in total household income in Europe. This is illustrated in Figure 3.3. The average annual income share of family benefits is considerable for all deciles (between roughly 15 and 30 per cent for the lowest decile and between 2 and 5 per cent for the highest decile, with values in between for the others). Child and family benefits are especially important for the lower poorer deciles – making up a large portion of their annual income.

Concluding remarks

European history in established welfare states teaches us that few countries introduced and elaborated social protection systems with the simultaneous intention of building a stable nation. However, the protection of the weak and the poor contributed undeniably to the inclusion of large masses of industrial workers into capitalist economies and in that way anchored democratic political institutions into a world that showed large economic inequalities. Political theory explains how social policy

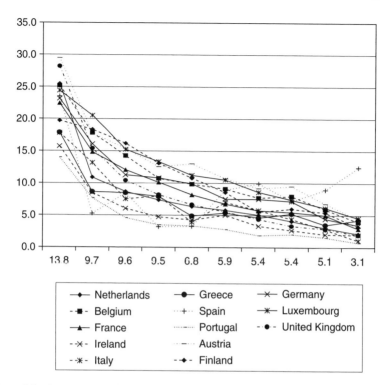

Figure 3.3   Average annual income share of family benefits per decile per household (for all children younger than 25 living in the household), 2000
Source: Authors' calculations; see also Table 3.1; for technical details see Notten and de Neubourg, 2007.

complements political participation in order to 'marry' political equalization to the economic inequality induced by markets. Political economy theory adds several arguments to explain how social protection contributes to stable democracies: communalities in preferences and economies of scale are major elements that bind nations together in the fight against externalities. Social protection tends to soften harsh inequalities.

When we ask what kind of social protection elements contribute most to the stability of nations, we conclude that in the European case universalist benefits fit the theoretical arguments best. Universalist benefits contribute to stable nations convincingly mainly because the alternative of means-tested or conditional provisions require a distinction between deserving and non-deserving poor and therefore divide rather than unite. Moreover, the not-so-poor middle- and low-income classes are excluded from welfare provisions for which they nevertheless have to contribute the most.

Finally, means-testing, and monitoring conditionality, require capacities to design, to implement and to monitor that young democracies seldom possess. The likelihood is therefore that the implementation of a means-tested social protection scheme contributes to corruption and bad governance more than does the implementation of simpler universal benefits. The question remains whether universalist benefits are affordable, adequate and relevant. In the European case we have seen in this chapter that while universal child benefits require only a small percentage of GDP, they reduce poverty and inequality considerably and they form a substantial part of the income for low-income households. Whether this also holds for low- and middle-income countries is analysed in other contributions in this book. It is, however, plausible that the theoretical arguments are not different in these economies and that there are therefore solid arguments to plead for basic universal benefits as an effective and efficient way to contribute to the stability of fragile and troubled nations.

Notes

1. The Mediterranean countries are late developers in this respect with Spain and Portugal characterized by long-lasting dictatorships after the Second World War.
2. This very sketchy description does not suggest either that the entire population was well or even adequately covered by the social system or that there were no inequalities within the systems.
3. We disregard for simplicity's sake the fact that of course the historical formation of states is path-dependent on pre-state coalitions, geographical locations, power distributions in pre-revolutionary elites, simple historical 'accidents', colonialism in the poor countries and the like. Moreover, communality in preferences does not fall from the sky: it is socially constructed.
4. The process of secession and the resulting 'equilibrium' in the size of nations is analysed in the interesting book by Alesina and Spoloare (2003) and the papers on which it is based.
5. Note that the latter is possible under non-democratic states wherein poorer people are granted less or no civil rights than richer people; this is the case, for example, under apartheid or a closed caste system.
6. It is clear that nations may differ in their taste for economic equality. The preferences as revealed by the voting behaviour of the median voter in (Western) Europe are clearly less 'tolerant' towards inequality and poverty than the preferences of the median voter in the United States.
7. I use the concept 'universalist' rather than 'universal' since most of these benefits are not universal in the strict sense of the word. The target groups, however, are usually large demographic groups such as children or elderly; the benefit is called universalist if neither an income- or means-test is attached to the eligibility nor the disbursement of the benefit is made conditional on the behaviour of the recipients.
8. Benefits and social provisions can of course be distinguished in many more ways: according to the way they are financed (taxes versus contributions), administered (as individual accounts or as insurances; as defined benefits or defined

contributions), implemented (in kind or in cash) or organized (private or public). All these distinctions are interesting but less relevant in this context.

9. Means-tested benefits accounted in 2003 for less than 10 per cent in continental European countries against 15 per cent in the United Kingdom, 25 per cent in Ireland and almost 40 per cent in the United States (de Neubourg et al., 2007).

10. In practice direct means-tested income transfers have often to be supplemented by other direct assistance programmes (e.g. budget management assistance, labour exchange, public works, family counselling) in order to avoid recipients becoming benefit-dependent. This increases the capacity requirement for the administration further.

11. In this text social insurances are seen as contributory benefits limiting the benefit entitlements to those who have contributed. The link between contributions and benefit entitlements may be strong or weak but with social insurance we assume here that non-contributors are excluded from the benefit. It should be noted that some benefit categories in some countries require contributions rather than taxes while providing benefit entitlements beyond the group of contributors; in the latter case we do not regard these social protection schemes as social insurances.

12. The costs for the equally universal social pensions in some countries cannot be estimated on the basis of the same comparable sources because the data do not distinguish between universal social pensions and mandatory insurance-based pensions.

13. The calculations provided in Table 3.1 are based on poverty estimates for European countries and the United States using household survey data and adopting both the official US Orshansky method and the semi-official EU Laeken method for all the countries. The estimates require extensive data manipulation: the technical details can be found in Notten and de Neubourg, 2007. The sub-division of benefits into five categories is done by Eurostat and requires decisions on where exactly benefits belong.

4
Social Security, Social Impact and Economic Performance: a Farewell to Three Famous Myths[1]

Michael Cichon and Wolfgang Scholz

Introduction: social protection and its primary objective

Social protection systems consist of the set of (a) all public transfers in a society that seeks to provide income security and prevent and alleviate poverty; (b) all measures that guarantee public access to health and social services; (c) all measures that protect workers' income, health and well-being. Social protection thus seeks to free people from social insecurity and consequential existential fear and is thus inevitably an income redistributive system. If designed, managed and administered well, social protection systems generally achieve that objective.

Social security is a human right (Article 22 of the Universal Declaration of Human Rights) and its roll-out to as many people as possible is a part of the ILO's mandate.[2] The need to extend social security was last confirmed by the International Labour Conference in 2001.

National social security systems – worldwide – achieve demonstrable success in reducing poverty. What remains to be explored is whether these results are obtained through incurring high opportunity cost in terms of reduced economic growth which would inevitably be associated with long-term welfare losses of a society – provided the benefits of growth are equitably distributed. This chapter tries to establish the state of the art on what we know – or seem to know – about the economic effects of social protection.

The chapter first revisits the standard economic arguments on the potential inter-relationship between social security and economic performance, then evaluates some of the statistical evidence and finally applies some simple logic to refute three of the major myths with regard to the relationship between social protection and economic performance. These are:

1. at each stage of development societies can only afford a certain level of social expenditure (the affordability myth);
2. economic growth will automatically reduce poverty (the trickle-down myth);

3. there is a trade-off between social expenditure and economic efficiency (the trade-off myth).

Social security and its social outcomes

There is clear evidence from Europe and OECD countries that social transfers successfully reduce poverty and social insecurity (Cichon et al., 2004). Figure 4.1 shows the net estimated effect of public transfers and taxes on poverty rates (as measured by the poverty head count index, which is perhaps the clearest indicator of income inequality) in OECD countries, i.e. in countries with a fairly extensive social transfer system and well-developed tax systems. The effects are nothing less than dramatic. The reduction of the pre-tax and transfer poverty rates ranges from a minimum of about 10 percentage points, estimated in the United States, to a high of around 30 percentage points, found for Sweden.

Figure 4.1 describes the effects of high spending social protection countries vs. low spending countries on national poverty lines. Higher than average social spending is demonstrably correlated with reductions in national poverty headcount levels.

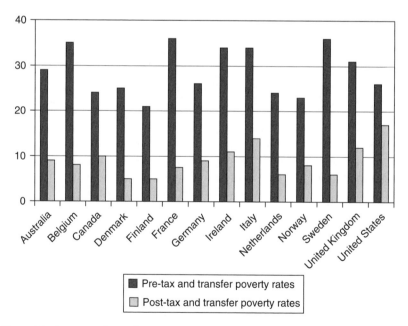

Figure 4.1   Pre-tax and transfer vs. post-tax and transfer poverty rates in selected OECD countries, mid-1990s (total populations)
Source: OECD (2000).

It is not possible to draw clear-cut conclusions in relation to developing countries, since overall volumes of social transfers are comparatively small. However, some basic social protection transfers, such as basic non-contributory pension schemes have proven to be powerful in the fight against poverty. A variety of countries have introduced universal pension schemes in recent years, and while they have mostly provided benefits at modest levels, their effects by way of poverty-reducing effects for whole families have been very positive. Benefits are provided overtly for the old and disabled, but in practice benefits provided for individuals – whose status in their families is often significantly enhanced through their receipt of a cash income – effectively support whole families. Redistribution of cash income within the household means that more families than hitherto are able to finance school fees, medicines, etc. (HelpAge International, 2004). Strong evidence of positive experience comes from countries as diverse as Brazil, Mauritius, Namibia, Nepal and South Africa. The ILO's International Financial and Actuarial Service has calculated that the provision of such a basic package of social transfers in most countries would cost between 1 and 2 per cent of GDP, which would equate roughly to between 5 and 10 per cent of national budgets. Implementing such a package in many countries could represent a rapid first step in a broader attack on the kind of deep-rooted and chronic poverty often found in 'pockets' within countries.

Social transfers also have a marked impact on income equality, which can be interpreted as an indicator of social coherence. Evidence from the Luxembourg Income Study (Ruiz-Huerta et al., 1999) of the mid-1990s (thus before the recent wave of reforms) shows that the combined tax and transfer systems in OECD countries reduce income inequality by between 40 per cent and 50 per cent in countries including Belgium, France, Germany and Sweden, and by between 20 per cent and 30 per cent in countries such as Australia, Canada, the United Kingdom and the United States. Prominent observers of the emerging inequality in Europe and the OECD countries since the mid-1990s, including Smeeding (2002) and Atkinson (2002), attribute increasing inequality within societies, as measured by increasing Gini coefficients, to changes in governments' tax and transfer policies. Atkinson (2002: 24–5) concludes that, when analysing the impact of globalization and public policy on changing income equality, 'we must not lose sight of the role of policy. Changes in tax and social transfer policy have played a major role in increasing inequality in a number of countries. To a considerable extent the development of inequality in disposable incomes – what matters to our citizens – lies in our own hands.'

The key question that remains to be answered in the context of this chapter is whether these positive effects may actually lead to too high opportunity cost in terms of economic performance. In other words, should a country not invest more in pro-growth policies since that would reduce poverty to a larger extent in the long run than social transfers would? The latter is the famous

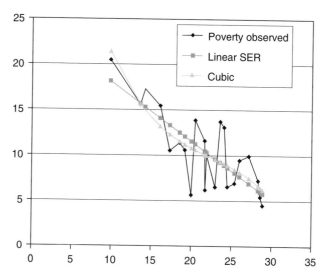

Figure 4.2 Inter-relation between poverty rates and total public social expenditure ratios in 22 selected OECD countries, 2000

Notes: Independent: SER; Dependent Mth Rsq d.f. F Sigf b0 b1 b2 b3; POVERTY LIN .607 20 30.91 .000 24.3699 −.6497; POVERTY CUB .652 18 11.22 .000 56.0540 −5.4098 .2235 −.0033.

'trickle-down' or 'the tide will raise all boats' effect. There is an intellectually difficult problem here. Even if economic growth were to reduce poverty in the long run, how do we 'discount' that reduction of poverty to compare it to the immediate effects that social transfers apparently have on poverty today? That is obviously a difficult question to answer. But we may get around it, by looking at some statistical evidence.

Figure 4.2 shows the relationship between national poverty rates in 22 OECD countries and the national social expenditure ratio (SER) (i.e. total public social expenditure over GDP). Figure 4.3 correlates national per capita GDP levels in purchasing power parities and the same poverty rates. Poverty rates are here defined in line with OECD statistics as 50 per cent of the median national incomes. All data used come from OECD statistical databases. The figures also relay the key statistical results of the regression. Two different types of regressions are tested to broaden the validity of the exercise, i.e. curvilinear regressions using linear and cubic[3] functions.

Poverty drops clearly in association with increasing social expenditure and increasing GDP levels. And so it should. However, interestingly, in the R square, the measure of association between GDP per capita and poverty lines is only in the order of 0.35 in the best case and thus 53 per cent lower than in the 'best' regression line between poverty rates and social expenditure ratios. Both exercises show high statistical significance levels. This means

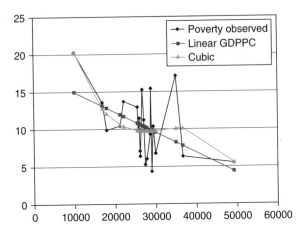

Figure 4.3 Inter-relation between per capita GDP and poverty rates in 22 selected OECD countries, 2000

Notes: Independent: GDPPC; Dependent Mth Rsq d.f. F Sigf b0 b1 b2 b3; POVERTY LIN .228 20 5.92 .024 17.4041 −.0003; POVERTY CUB .354 18 3.28 .045 41.0843 −.0031 1.0E−07 −1.E-12.

that poverty reduction is much more associated with national social expenditure ratios than with levels of GDP. Without entering into the causality debate, one can conclude that increasing GDP levels can and do in many cases reduce poverty. That effect, however, is not certain. It is much more probable that increasing levels of social expenditure will reduce poverty. So the apparent choice between transfer-based poverty reduction and growth-based poverty reduction may be a false alternative. Without redistributive mechanisms such as social security transfers, economic growth may not affect poverty noticeably. Since it takes decades to build functioning social transfer systems, waiting for their introduction until high levels of GDP have arrived is not a realistic option. 'Trickle-down' effects do not occur automatically and depend on whether or not social protection systems are in place.

Figure 4.4 combines the above exercises in one single figure. It shows the relationship between poverty rates, social spending and levels of GDP for a data set that also includes non-OECD countries. It shows that at each level of GDP per capita in purchasing power parities countries with higher than average social security spending have lower poverty rates than countries with lower than average social security spending. Interestingly, the distance between the two lines remains almost constant for major ranges of GDP per capita. If the 'trickle-down' hypothesis were true, the distance between the curves should narrow towards the higher ranges of GDP per capita and the low spenders should improve their relative poverty performance. This does not seem to be the case. More detailed studies are necessary to explore the effect in detail, but what we can say now is that the acceleration of

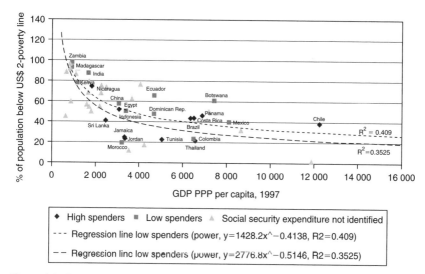

Figure 4.4 Percentage of population below US$2 – poverty line versus GDP PPP per capita (1997); countries grouped according to high and low spending on social security (exponential regression); transition countries excluded

poverty reduction with increasing GDP per capita in the low spending country group compared with the high spending groups does not seem to take place. Another question mark behind the trickle-down effect ...

The graph also shows that at each level of per capita GDP countries have a choice as to how extensively they want to combat poverty through redistributive transfers or not. Countries seem to be able to afford a wide range of different levels of social spending at the same level of GDP per capita – a theme to which we will revert in later sections.

Thus, social transfers are associated with reductions of poverty, much more directly as high levels of GDP. This leaves us with one critical question: Could it be that social expenditure at certain stages of development compresses economic growth so much that the 'loose' anti-poverty effect of a potentially higher GDP would be bigger than the one that can be achieved by social expenditure at the existing level of GDP? In other words, could Sweden, for example, without its extensive welfare state have achieved such a high level of GDP that the resulting level of poverty at that high level would be lower than the level that it achieves today? Or again, in other words, what would be the counterfactual anti-poverty effect of non-welfare states compared with welfare states? The answer – if it exists – can only come from an assessment of the effect of social expenditure on economic growth. Before we try to analyse the evidence we have to recapitulate an inconclusive theoretical academic debate.

The academic debate about social protection as an input to economic growth

National social protection systems and their perceived effects on economic performance have been subject to intense policy debates in many countries during the last decades. On the one hand, experts[4] (notably those working in the international financial institutions (IFIs)) claim that social systems redistributing up to 30 per cent of countries' GDPs – and, thus, since considered too high[5] – are no longer affordable. Social protection expenditure is seen as an impediment to growth creating negative short- and long-term growth effects.

But do social protection systems have detrimental economic effects? What is the position of those arguing they do have such effects? Proponents usually base their reasoning on standard growth theory. Their advantage in reasoning is that they dispense a 'canonical', mathematically formulated set of models, whose results overwhelmingly point in the same direction.[6]

The following are argued to be detrimental:

(a) Financing transfers exclusively through taxing labour can have negative labour market effects if wage structures are rigid.
(b) Financing or subsidizing social protection benefits out of general revenues can contribute to the deterioration of the government budget deficit, increase domestic interest rates and hence reduce private investment and growth. Such financing of transfers might also cause opportunity cost in terms of reduced public investments.
(c) Wrong incentives set by income protection mechanisms in the presence of, for example, unemployment and early retirement schemes, can trigger withdrawals of potentially productive employment from the labour force.
(d) Some national social protection systems cause administrative costs that produce fiscal waste and hence high economic opportunity cost as required contributions/taxes could, alternatively, be used for financing production.

On the other hand, social protection systems are claimed to have positive economic effects:

(a) Social security systems create the social peace that is a necessary condition for the long-term viability of all investments.
(b) Reliable access to social transfers reduces existential angst through providing at least a minimum level of income security, reduces the need to resort to illegal earnings in income, reduces the potential for social discrimination and friction by empowering citizens and hence creates social peace, which is a prerequisite for long-term profitable investments.

(c) Reliable access to unemployment and other social transfer benefits facilitates the adjustment of labour forces to structural changes of economies.

(d) Substantial expenditure on health care, safety and health, and prevention and alleviation of HIV/AIDS can increase labour productivity.

(e) Income smoothing through social transfer stabilizes consumption and hence avoids abrupt contraction of domestic demand in times of recession.

(f) National pension savings have or can become a major source of domestic finance for investments and thus may play an important role in the developing or restructuring of economies.

(g) Social transfers allow unemployed, sick and disabled workers some resources to improve skills through training, bridge transitions to alternative jobs more suited to their experience and qualifications, and explore possibilities to work in more productive and better paid or more secure jobs.

(h) Social protection and the financing of social services through social protection itself generate a substantial proportion of total employment in modern service-based economies.

(i) Social transfer systems can help to redistribute some of the proceeds of economic growth (inter alia, created through globalization) to the most vulnerable persons in societies and can, thus, help to create a broader acceptance of globalization.

(j) Collective social security systems that protect people against partial or total loss of income would have a moderating effect on labour costs as people would not have to build up huge personal contingency reserves financed from wages and other incomes.

It should be added that countries where diversion is low but focus on production is strong, i.e. the large European welfare states, have (meanwhile) made their social protection systems operate at enormously low administration costs, which are usually much lower than in many private insurance schemes and hence are more efficient than those in delivering social security.

The pros and cons of the impact of social protection on economic growth seem to be fairly balanced. However, in political and economic discussions it is those claiming that well-functioning social protection systems are an indispensable prerequisite for growth in open market economies, who are, paradoxically, in the weakest analytical position.[7] This is because social protection is disregarded in the construction and operation of economic models as an input factor to economic growth – social protection plays close to no role in the academic syllabus in economics of universities around the world. This is a sorry fact about the present 'state of the art' in growth economics. Those who argue that the level and quality of social protection might significantly contribute to explaining differences in long-term growth rates – and, thus, of countries' income levels – have, thus far, not undertaken efforts to formalize their argument and consequentially face difficulties competing successfully with ubiquitous standard explanations. Here, we are forced to look at scarce evidence to approach an answer.

Empirical evidence

Historical evidence

Since about the middle of the 1970s, i.e. after the first oil price crisis, countries with well-established social protection systems entered a period of *welfare state containment*. Major welfare states like Austria, France, Germany, the Netherlands and others broadly kept their social expenditure shares in GDP at the levels reached in the mid-1970s. After the fall of the Iron Curtain, these ratios transitorily peaked at high levels in those countries economically most affected by the resulting changes in multilateral trade relations and/or by other factors (for example in Germany by the unification). Subsequently all countries returned to their 'normal' levels (Figure 4.5). In fact, all containment measures reflect the *new paradigm of economic policy*, which

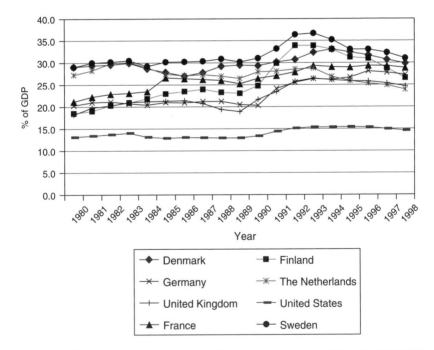

Figure 4.5 Development of social expenditure as a percentage of GDP, selected OECD countries
Source: ILO (2004).

has increasingly dominated political and socio-economic discussions and analyses for the last 20 to 25 years, and which claims that low European growth rates are mainly a result of too high and wrongly designed (badly structured) social protection provisions. If that were true, one would expect continuing reductions of the social expenditure ratios now and in future. In any case, such moves would have to be implemented against counteracting social needs, like increased unemployment, increasing health care costs, changing family structures or increasing old-age dependency rates, which all increase societal insecurity in the industrialized countries. Thus far, what can be observed is that social expenditure in the OECD (measured in percentage of GDP) has stabilized at long-term levels, which equally applies to lower and to higher growth countries.

Contrary to mainstream expectations, this policy has not led to higher economic growth (Figure 4.6). Firstly, it has to be observed that economic growth rates have come down to moderate levels since the mid-1970s. Since then growth rates have hovered around a quite stable 2 per cent trend. While ranking of countries' growth performance changes over time, Figure 4.5 clearly indicates that the industrialized countries – economically – are highly interdependent in their development. The further, slight, decline of rates since the early 1990s must, most obviously, be due to other effects than social spending, which has been contained since the mid-1970s.

In comparing the dominating shapes of Figures 4.7 and 4.8, one can already conclude that there is little correlation between economic growth rates and the share in GDP of social protection spending. Obviously,

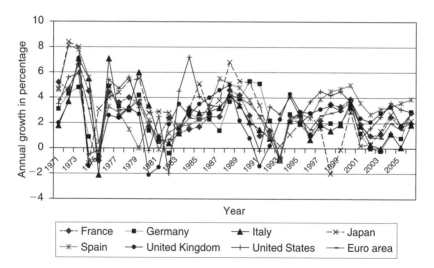

Figure 4.6 Growth rates of GDP in major industrialized countries/regions
Source: Ministry of Health and Social Security, Berlin; EUROSTAT, Luxembourg.

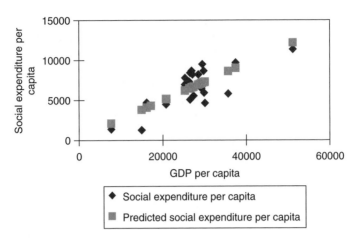

Figure 4.7   Correlation between GDP and public social expenditure per capita in PPP, OECD, 2001

governments of major countries over the past 30 years have continuously taken measures to maintain relative social protection spending at country-specific *constant* levels,[8] while, over the same time, GDP growth rates have been declining trend-wise (Figure 4.6). Whether GDP growth rates will rise to higher average levels is an open question. However, it seems obvious that this is not likely to be triggered through a stabilization of social spending.

The statistical relationship between economic performance and social spending

Figure 4.7 plots the relationship between the GDP per capita and public social expenditure per capita in purchasing power parities in 25 major OECD countries. At first sight there is a positive relationship between these two variables and the R square indicating the fit of the regression curve is sufficiently high (0.62) for relatively crude analysis.

However, the variables GDP per capita and social expenditure per capita have too many common determinants to provide a meaningful correlation. Social expenditure consists to a large extent of the cost of services and income replacing cash transfers. The absolute levels of both variables in the individual countries have direct links to per capita incomes and hence GDP per capita. To be more meaningful, the relationship between GDP and a variable that describes not only the absolute level of social expenditure but also incorporates aspects of discretionary national decision-making should be analysed. The variable used here is the social expenditure ratio SER (i.e. social expenditure expressed as a percentage of GDP).

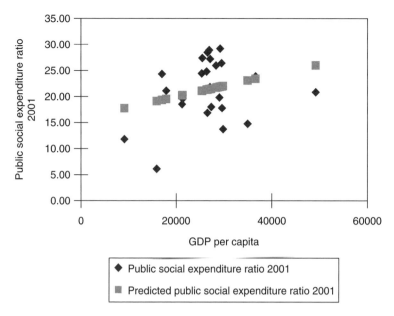

Figure 4.8 Correlation between GDP per capita and (PPP) public social expenditure as a share of GDP (public social expenditure ratio)

The statistical analysis of long-term growth rates in the OECD shows that the correlation between growth performance and the share of GDP that is allocated to social expenditure is weak. Figure 4.8 correlates GDP per capita in purchasing power parities and the social expenditure ratio in 22 major OECD countries in 2001. The R square is extremely small.

Figure 4.9 maps the average growth rates in the same countries between 1980 and 2001 with the average shares of social expenditure of GDP during the same period. While the regression shows a slightly negative slope, the R square is also very low (i.e. 0.09). Limiting the period to the decade 1991 to 2001 only marginally changes the picture.

The figures confirm the earlier observation that there is virtually no direct relationship between the per capita GDP or the rate of growth and the level of the social expenditure ratio. Sweden and the United Kingdom, for example, have a similar level of GDP per capita but a more than 7 percentage points difference in the social expenditure ratio. In both countries, social expenditure is largely of a public nature. Thus, the difference between the composition of total social expenditure between public and private expenditure does not affect the comparability.

Similarly, Ireland and Luxembourg, for example, have similar long-term growth rates, while the average social expenditure ratio in Ireland is 4 percentage points lower than in Luxembourg. Italy, on the other hand, has a

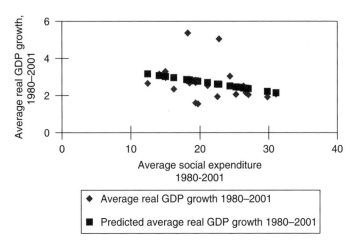

Figure 4.9   Average social expenditure vs. long-term economic growth

similar long-term social expenditure ratio to Luxembourg but its long-term growth rate is only 40 per cent of that of Luxembourg. The GDP growth performance is similar to that of Norway while it has only 40 per cent of the social expenditure ratio.

The above observations lead to one conclusion. Aggregate social expenditure figures do not explain a large part of national economic performance and do not seem to have a significant impact on economic growth. National policies and social security system designs can lead to a wide range of different levels of social expenditure at each level of GDP.

One might argue that levels of GDP per capita are determined by a variety of other factors that are clearly not predominantly influenced by the average level of the social expenditure ratio, such as the demographic structure, consequential national levels of demographic dependency between active members and inactive members of a society, the nature of the national physical and human 'capital stock', and the average number of hours worked per worker.

Social security provisions on the other hand might directly influence the level of employment by providing incentives or disincentives for labour market participation. When correlating social expenditure ratios and employment levels, we face a chicken and egg problem. On the one hand, high levels of unemployment lead to high transfer expenditure, while on the other hand, the availability of transfers may lead to high withdrawal rates. However, a regression analysis of the SERs and the employment-to-population ratios of the 15–64 age group for OECD countries shows virtually no association between the two and the influence of the SER on employment levels is statistically not very significant.[9]

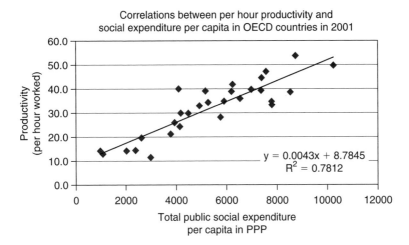

Figure 4.10   Social expenditure and hourly productivity, OECD countries, 2001
Source: ILO calculations, based on OECD/SOCEX database.

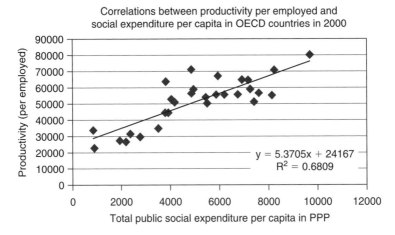

Figure 4.11   Social expenditure and productivity per worker, OECD countries, 2000
Source: ILO calculations, based on OECD/SOCEX database.

In order to exclude all these – partially contradictory – effects we have analysed the effects of social expenditure on hourly productivity. This analysis shows that in the OECD region there is a strong positive correlation between social expenditure (per capita of the population) and labour productivity (GDP per hour worked) (Figures 4.10 and 4.11). The correlation between 'simple' per capita (per worker) productivity and social expenditure (per capita of the population) is still positive but less tight.

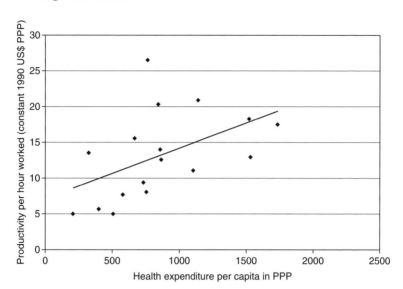

Figure 4.12 Health expenditure per capita and hourly productivity, non-OECD countries, 2005
Source: ILO and WHO.

The above relationship also seems to hold true for non-OECD countries. Reliable data are hard to assemble, so we limit ourselves to analysing the relationship between health expenditure per capita and hourly and per worker productivity (Figures 4.12 and 4.13). Health expenditure as part of overall social expenditure can be seen to have a direct impact on maintaining the productivity of workers.

Interpreting statistics

The above observations can be subject to different (and to some extent contradictory) interpretations:

(a) The standard interpretation is, of course, that social spending can be increased with labour productivity. Only productive economies, it is argued, can devote significant amounts to social protection. The lower the labour productivity, the less can be spent, accordingly.

(b) The second interpretation is that social protection (spending) has direct and indirect positive effects on labour productivity. There can be very little argument contesting that access to health care and occupational health and safety services have positive, productivity-enhancing impacts on health. Sickness, disability and old age benefits allow exhausted and less productive workers to 'escape' from the labour market. Unemployment benefits facilitate the restructuring of labour markets and hence help to ensure that workers are employed in the most productive jobs

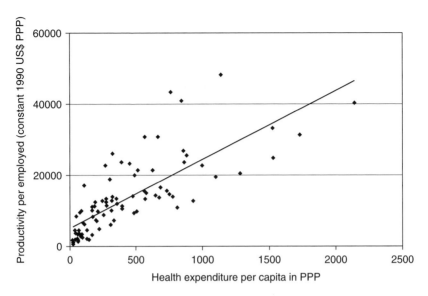

Figure 4.13 Health expenditure per capita and productivity per worker, non-OECD countries, 2005
Source: ILO and WHO.

possible. Positive productivity effects of social security would emerge from the relative financial security and social stability that the system creates.

Even if observers do not feel able to decide on one of the options, one important fact should not be overlooked, when interpreting the above results: there is nothing in the empirical findings on the correlation between productivity and social expenditure suggesting that high spending on social protection is automatically associated with low productivity. On the contrary, there seems to be strong empirical evidence indicating that high productivity (only) materializes if accompanied by high social spending.

If one juxtaposes that finding with the very low level of correlation between employment levels and the social expenditure ratio, the conclusion has to be that some social security systems might discourage labour force participation. This is not a general rule as the cases of Sweden, Norway and Switzerland show: in those countries relatively high levels of social expenditure coincide with high levels of employment. Apparently, the institutional arrangements that govern the transfers can create positive micro-economic incentives as well as disincentives and inefficiencies. Social expenditure thus may facilitate high levels of GDP through the productivity conduit but it may not lead to a full exploitation of countries' production potential if badly designed. However, likewise, there is thus no reason to believe that relatively high levels of social expenditure automatically lead to a compression of potential levels of GDP.

In a recent textbook a group of ILO experts conclude that 'it is probably fair to conclude that economic theory and evidence alone do not give us a clear-cut answer as to what the net effect of the different kinds of welfare states on economic performance and hence the welfare of the population is ... However, what we have learned confirms previous findings that social protection measures can indeed achieve positive social outcomes and do not strangle economic development. That is encouraging' (Cichon et al., 2004: 150).

Conclusion: three famous myths lose credibility

Let us face the facts. What we would like to see is, of course, a solid proof of positive causality between a decent level of social expenditure and economic growth. Our regression analyses – like all regression analyses – fail to provide that proof. That is regrettable, but social policy-makers can probably live without that mathematical proof. In the course of this chapter we think we have sufficiently discredited three famous myths.

(1) **The poverty alleviating trickle-down effect of economic growth is not reliable**
    We can show high levels of correlation between low poverty levels and high social security expenditure on the macro-level. We can also show by micro-analytical instruments how the direct redistributive mechanism can work to reduce poverty. We also showed that economic growth does not automatically reduce poverty unless redistributive mechanisms (such as social security systems) are in place. There is thus a good case for social transfers as poverty alleviation mechanisms and hence as a mechanism to foster social development. The only argument that could discredit the (early) introduction of social transfers is that they would cripple economic growth to such an extent that the resulting loss in welfare would actually lead to higher long-term levels of poverty.

(2) **The famous trade-off between social expenditure and economic performance does not hold**
    What we know is that extensive social protection expenditure per capita and high productivity can co-exist; we know that high social security does not automatically suppress employment and hence we know that high social expenditure and top economic performance can also co-exist. Hence – strictly speaking from the point of view of mathematical logic – the opposite neo-classical trade-off between equity and efficiency does not hold true.

(3) **There is no strict limit for national social expenditure depending on the level of economic development**
    In many discussions on levels of social security expenditure in ILO member States non-affordability arguments are fielded, i.e. that certain

countries cannot afford more than a certain level of expenditure in a given state of economic performance. Most of such general arguments appear unfounded. We have observed at various stages of the above analysis that at any given level of GDP per capita there is a wide range of social expenditure between different countries. The latter implies that conditions differ from country to country (for example the demographic situation) but also that there is considerable policy space with respect to the components of national social expenditure (and incidentally public expenditure in general).

Where does it leave us?

There is certainly a need for more detailed research to remove statistical inconclusiveness and provide a proof of causality. There may also be – or almost certainly is – a saturation point for social expenditure beyond which it becomes economically and socially counter-productive. We do not know where that point is. It will depend on specific national circumstances and the specific design of the transfer systems and the affiliated incentives. But this point is far away for most countries, notably in the developing world. At the moment, countries like Denmark and Sweden with an SER of almost 30 per cent do not show any sign of having passed that saturation point. Others at lower levels may have. So, for the majority of the countries in the world, reaching the saturation point is not a real risk.

When governments, social partners and civic society are shaping policies for low- and middle-income countries, as well as most high-income countries, it should suffice to know that social security systems:

- reduce poverty and inequality;
- are compatible with high economic growth,

provided they are designed correctly and do not lead to waste and perverse objectives. When making national social security systems an explicit feature in national developments policies, the critical question should not be whether this is the right thing to do, but how to do things right.

Notes

1. This chapter draws extensively on the paper 'Social Protection as a Productive Factor' that the Social Security Department presented to the ILO's Governing Body in November 2005.
2. See Declaration of Philadelphia – Article III (f), including clauses (d) and (f), leads to a broad definition of social protection.
3. This regression technique uses a cubic polynomial as a regression function.
4. See, *inter alia*, IMF (2003: Chapter IV).
5. Although it is not always clear when social expenditure is considered 'too high'.

6. The *anti-social protection position* is equally covered by the mainstream proponents of 'neo-historic' economic growth theory. However, they do not (yet) present a similar set of mathematically formulated and generally accepted growth models, which would help to support their reasoning.
7. See, *inter alia*, ILO (2001b: 11–12).
8. There are, of course, exceptions to this observation. Greece, for example, extended its social spending substantially over a period of about 20 years while Ireland significantly reduced its spending share in GDP over the recent past.
9. The results of the regression analysis are as follows:
Independent: SER 2001

Dependent	Mth	Rsq	d.f.	F	Sigf	b0	b1	B2	b3
ER2001	LIN	.043	27	1.20	.283	65.6742	.2637		
ER2001	INV	.055	27	1.57	.221	74.7492	−66.531		
ER2001	CUB	.082	25	.74	.538	39.1246	5.3588	−.2878	.0050

5
Can Low-Income Countries Afford Social Security?

Christina Behrendt and Krzysztof Hagemejer

Proposals to accelerate the establishment of social protection systems in low-income countries have gathered strength in the early years of the twenty-first century. These proposals are being subjected to searching questions. One major question concerns 'affordability' – with which this chapter seeks to deal.

Social security has recurrently been perceived as a luxury that only rich countries can afford. This view has recently been challenged from different angles. From an economic perspective, it is increasingly recognized that pro-growth and pro-poor policies are inseparable and mutually reinforcing also in developing countries (for example, ILO 2006a; OECD 2006b). The lack of social protection mechanisms in many developing countries exacerbates the vulnerability of the population against economic shocks and the vicissitudes of the life course, such as sickness, old age, disability or maternity. If no protection mechanisms exist, these contingencies create poverty traps from which poor households are unlikely to escape quickly. Lack of basic income security prevents men and women from engaging in productive economic activity (always associated with risk) and forces them to focus just on survival. The alleged trade-off between social protection and productivity or growth is not supported by systematic empirical evidence. Today's developed countries have pursued their economic growth in parallel with the expansion of social security. Social security has helped to bolster and sustain economic and social change, and has had enormous positive effects on poverty reduction and living standards as well as on the quality of human capital and social cohesion. Rapidly growing countries, such as the Democratic Republic of Korea in the aftermath of the Asian crisis and more recently China, have acknowledged that sustainable growth and economic development require a solid underpinning by social protection and have taken bold measures to improve social security (Kwon, 2004; Lin and Kangas, 2006; Shin, 2000). There is more and more evidence coming from emerging social protection schemes in low-income countries on the positive economic impacts of social protection measures on the level of economic activity and on productivity.

In addition, rights-based approaches have drawn attention to the human right to social security as affirmed in the Universal Declaration of Human Rights[1] as well as in other international instruments.[2] While these rights-based approaches are increasingly relevant in the international discourse (Townsend, 2007), much more effort needs to be devoted to the implementation of those international standards at the national level (Kulke and López Morales, 2007).

The governments of a number of low-income countries have in fact themselves taken initiatives to call for greater commitments to social security. At a conference in March 2006 hosted by the African Union and the Government of Zambia, high-level representatives of 13 African nations called for a greater role for social protection in national poverty reduction strategies.[3] Delegates also called for costed national social security action plans. In a similar vein, the report of the Commission for Africa in 2005 recommended social protection strategies for vulnerable groups of the population, namely orphans and vulnerable children and their families and communities (Commission for Africa, 2005). The recent White Paper of the Department for International Development of the United Kingdom recognizes that social protection mechanisms have positive effects on health and education outcomes as well as on local economies in poor countries (DFID, 2006). At the 89th Session of the International Labour Conference in 2001, government, worker and employer representatives reaffirmed the ILO's commitment to social security and called for a renewed campaign for the extension of social security coverage to all women and men (ILO, 2001b).[4] At the 2007 ILO African Regional Conference in Addis Ababa, participating countries agreed that 'all African countries (will) adopt coherent national social security strategies, including for the introduction or extension of a basic social security package that includes essential health care, maternity protection, child support for school-age children, disability protection and a minimum pension' (ILO, 2007a: point 17, p. 9).

The question of affordability has to be considered in the context of the fiscal and broader economic environment at the national level (Cichon et al., 2004). In addition, it is important to consider national institutional capacities and governance aspects. However, one has to consider also the international context: with respect to the need to ensure that global competition does not drive countries and their populations below agreed minimum labour and social standards, and to obtain international support in financing provision of minimum basic social protection in low-income countries during the transitional period until these countries have the necessary domestic fiscal capacity to do so themselves.

This chapter summarizes the results of recent ILO research studies into the affordability of social security in low-income countries and puts them into a broader context. It is structured into four parts. First, we present estimates of the cost of the elements of a basic social protection package for twelve low-income countries in Africa and Asia from two recent ILO costing studies, and of the basic social protection package as a whole. Second, we discuss the feasibility of financing such a package – under different options – from a mixture of domestic resources and resources provided through international grants from donor countries. Third, we present results from a recent micro-simulation study which show the potential of cash transfers for the reduction of poverty. Fourth, the concluding section puts the affordability question differently: can low-income countries afford *not* to provide social security to their populations?

Evidence from first costing studies

The ILO has undertaken two costing studies in Africa and Asia that provide a first estimation of the costs of a basic social protection package in low-income countries now and over the coming decades. Twelve countries have been covered by this costing model so far:

- seven counties in Africa: Burkina Faso, Cameroon, Ethiopia, Guinea, Kenya, Senegal and Tanzania (Pal et al., 2005); and
- five countries in Asia: Bangladesh, India, Nepal, Pakistan and Viet Nam (Mizunoya et al., 2006).

In the following, the rationale and results of the ILO's cost estimations are summarized for the following elements of a basic social protection package separately in different variants:

1. universal basic old age and disability pension;
2. basic child benefit, either universal or limited to orphans only;
3. targeted cash transfer for the most vulnerable households;
4. universal access to essential health care.

We will then turn to the cost projections for a selected basic social protection package and the possible financing of such a package. A full description of the methodological background and the underlying demographic and socio-economic assumptions can be found in the original studies (Pal et al., 2005; Mizunoya et al., 2006).

Basic old age and disability pensions

Due to their lower earning capacities, older persons are among the most vulnerable groups of the population in low-income countries. Only a small proportion of older people have access to old age pensions from social insurance schemes. For example, in Burkina Faso, 1.6 per cent of the population over the age of 65 receives an old age pension, and less than 2.8 per cent of today's economically active population of working age is affiliated to an old age pension scheme.[5] The large majority of older persons have to rely on traditional support capacities of families and communities which are being overwhelmed by the impact of HIV/AIDS, migration as well as pervasive chronic poverty and destitution.

A number of middle- and low-income countries have introduced non-contributory old age pensions for their elderly population. Countries with social pension schemes include Brazil, Botswana, India, Mauritius, Lesotho, Namibia, Nepal and South Africa. Some of the schemes cover only targeted groups of the population; others, for example Mauritius or Namibia, have developed schemes widely applied to all elderly residents in their populations. Evidence from those countries shows that such social pensions have a remarkable impact on the living standards of elderly persons and their families, particularly on children (cf. Barrientos 2008b; Barrientos and Lloyd-Sherlock, 2002; Charlton and McKinnon, 2001; Save the Children UK et al., 2005). This experience also shows that social pensions are feasible and accessible for low-income countries.

Variant I: benefit level defined in absolute terms

The ILO model includes two variants of universal basic pensions. In both cases selected amounts are very small, aiming at reduction of poverty in the target groups. In the first variant, the amount of benefit is set as a proportion of the international absolute poverty line of one US$ PPP per day. It was assumed that simulated universal old age and disability pension will amount to half of that poverty line, that is to US$0.50 PPP per day (and thus about US$15 PPP monthly or US$180 PPP annually) and would be paid to all men and women aged 65 or older; and to persons of working age with serious disabilities (the eligibility ratio was assumed to be 1 per cent of the working-age population, which reflects a very conservative estimate of the rate of disability). It was also assumed that the benefit value would be indexed to inflation only over the projection period.

Such non-contributory benefits for older persons already exist in Nepal (Rajan, 2003) and India (HelpAge India, 2003; Rajan, 2001), yet they cover only a small proportion of the elderly population. The simulated projected universal old age and disability pension would capture a much larger proportion of the older population than the existing programmes in these countries.

Based on these assumptions, the annual costs of providing a universal basic old age and disability pension is estimated at between 0.3 and 1.0 per cent of yearly GDP in the countries considered (see Figure 5.1). Projected costs for 2010 remain well below 0.5 per cent of GDP in seven of the twelve countries,

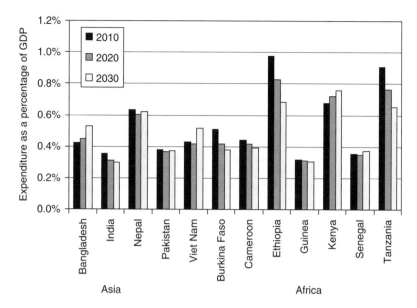

Figure 5.1 Costs for basic universal old age and disability pensions as a percentage of GDP, Variant I

Source: Based on Mizunoya et al., 2006; Pal et al., 2005. These figures include assumed administration costs of 15 per cent of benefit expenditure.

while Burkina Faso, Ethiopia, Kenya, Nepal and Tanzania find themselves between 0.5 and 1.0 per cent of GDP.

Variant II: benefit level defined in respect to GDP per capita

In a second variant, the level of benefits was not linked to absolute international poverty threshold as in the first variant but set as a fixed proportion of the average income level in the country, using GDP per capita as a proxy for average income. Thus, the benefit is assumed to be 30 per cent of GDP per capita.[6] All other parameters were kept the same as in the first variant. Based on these assumptions, the estimated annual costs for a universal old age and disability pension is more homogeneous across countries and becomes between 0.7 and 1.2 per cent of GDP in 2010 (see Figure 5.2).

Basic child benefits

Old age and disability pensions can certainly have a major impact on the livelihoods of households with an elderly person, but more widely spread benefits would be needed to have a substantial impact on the reduction of poverty for the entire population. Benefits for families with children can

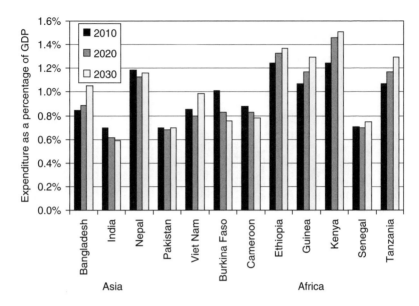

Figure 5.2   Costs for basic universal old age and disability pensions as a percentage of GDP, Variant II

Source: Based on Mizunoya et al., 2006; Pal et al., 2005. These figures include assumed administration costs of 15 per cent of benefit expenditure.

have such an impact, as shown by some cash child benefit programmes in a development context (Save the Children UK et al., 2005). Most of these programmes are found in Latin America and have been set up as conditional cash transfers (see, for example, de la Brière and Rawlings, 2006; Rawlings, 2005). Many of these programmes have had a marked impact on poverty reduction as well as on school attendance. Although evidence on their effects on the reduction of the worst forms of child labour is not conclusive, evaluations suggest a positive effect in some countries, particularly when cash benefits are combined with after-school activities (Tabatabai, 2006).

However, there are some concerns about the transferability of conditional cash transfer programmes into countries with an insufficient infrastructure in the education and health sector (Kakwani et al., 2005). Therefore, the first variant of a child benefit modelled here is a universal benefit paid to all children up to the age of 14. The level of such benefit is assumed very modestly to be equal to half of the universal pension amount; that is US$0.25 PPP per day (Figure 5.3).

Variant I: universal child benefit

The projected costs for a basic universal child benefit vary greatly between countries, yet there is a common trend towards lower costs in the longer

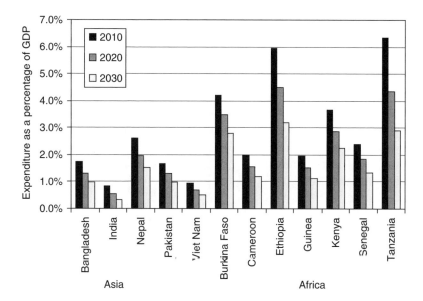

Figure 5.3 Costs for basic universal child benefit as a percentage of GDP, Variant I
Source: Based on Mizunoya et al., 2006; Pal et al., 2005. These figures include assumed administration costs of 15 per cent of benefit expenditure.

run. For the year 2010, the cost estimations remain below 2 per cent of GDP in Bangladesh, Cameroon, Guinea, India, Pakistan and Viet Nam. Burkina Faso, Nepal, Kenya and Senegal find themselves between 2 and just over 4 per cent of GDP while Ethiopia and Tanzania stand out with some 6 per cent of GDP.

Variant II: orphan benefit

The second variant of child benefit represents an even more modest approach to child protection. Benefits are assumed to be targeted to orphaned children only up to the age of 14. It is assumed that the level of this orphan benefit is linked to average incomes in the country and set at a level of 15 per cent of GDP per capita. The number of orphans was based on estimates provided by UNAIDS et al. (2004).

A child benefit for orphans aged 0–14 is estimated to come at between 0.3 and 1.1 per cent of GDP (see Figure 5.4). The lower estimated costs for Asia partly reflect the fact that the African countries considered tend to have a higher proportion of orphans than Asian countries, and that the proportion of orphaned children in the population is higher in the African than in the Asian countries.

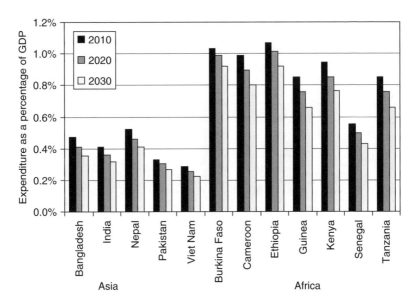

Figure 5.4   Costs for basic universal child benefit as a percentage of GDP, Variant II –
orphans

Source: Based on Mizunoya et al., 2006; Pal et al., 2005. These figures include assumed
administration costs of 15 per cent of benefit expentiture.

Targeted cash transfer

The model calculations also considered a targeted cash transfer similar to one
being provided by a GTZ-sponsored pilot scheme in the district of Kalomo
in Zambia (see Schubert, 2004, 2005).[7] This programme provides very small[8]
cash benefits of about US$14 (PPP) per month and per household (that is
slightly less than half a dollar per household per day and thus much less
per person – or per child in the household) directed only at the 10 per cent
of households in the covered area identified through the targeting procedure as the most destitute.[9] The majority of beneficiary households are older
women caring for children. Eligible households are identified through a
community-based targeting mechanism that focuses on those who are unable
to support themselves due to the lack of an able-bodied person in the household. Because of this relatively complicated administrative procedure that
has to be completed to identify the right households, the administrative
costs assumed for this costing model are higher than for universal benefits,
that is, 33 per cent of benefit expenditure.[10]

The cost projections show that such a targeted cash transfer covering
10 per cent of households in the Zambian scheme would cost annually less
than 0.3 per cent of GDP by 2010 in nine of the twelve countries considered.

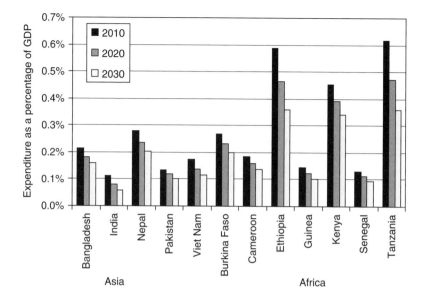

Figure 5.5 Costs for a targeted cash transfer for poorest 10 per cent of households as a percentage of GDP
Source: Based on Mizunoya et al., 2006; Pal et al., 2005. These figures include assumed administration costs of 33 per cent of benefit expenditure.

Only in Ethiopia, Kenya and Tanzania would the estimated cost be higher and reach between 0.4 and 0.6 per cent of GDP. As Figure 5.5 shows, all these costs are very small indeed.

Compared with the universal benefits considered above, this type of benefit comes at a relatively lower cost (although with much higher proportion of total expenditure spent on administration and not on transfers to households), yet poverty reduction is also very much smaller (Gassmann and Behrendt, 2006). There will always be concerns about how effective targeting mechanisms of this kind can be and how efficient they are in reducing poverty at least cost. The targeted cash transfer will not be further followed in this chapter.

Essential health care

A basic social protection package would not be complete without universal access to essential health care. It is well known that ill health is a major poverty risk and that high health expenditure can be financially catastrophic for individuals and their families and drive them into severe poverty from which many cannot recover for years. This is of acute relevance in countries with a high prevalence of HIV/AIDS, but it should not be forgotten that the effects of less prominent diseases, such as malaria, are much more dramatic on morbidity and mortality in many countries.

Providing access to health care, including equitable health insurance mechanisms, is therefore an important contribution to eradicating poverty and vulnerability (ILO, 2007b; Lamiraud et al., 2005; Scheil-Adlung et al., 2006). Such mechanisms address poverty and vulnerability on several levels: by facilitating access to medical care they improve health and restore earning capacities more quickly, and thus ensure that health problems of a family member do not entail unbearable costs for the family as a whole. In addition, impacts on school attendance, employment and human capital can be expected, which will contribute to sustainable economic growth and social development.

The cost projections used in this chapter reflect the calculations of the Commission on Macroeconomics and Health (2001), which are based on an estimate of the per capita costs of scaling up selected priority health interventions in low-income countries to reach universal coverage for the population in need. Largely focusing on communicable diseases, childhood and maternity-related interventions, this cost estimate is based on a detailed costing of the additional expenditure required for extending coverage to 49 priority interventions.[11]

The costing model incorporates essential health expenditure per capita, assumed to be US$34 per year on average in low-income countries by 2007, and US$38 in 2015, as estimated by the Commission on Macroeconomics and Health.[12] After 2015, the costs are indexed in line with inflation.

Current health spending in many low-income countries remains well below this level – in some cases more than ten times below. For example, per capita government expenditure on health in 1999 was US$3.4 in Cameroon and US$1.3 in Ethiopia in 1999 (Pal et al., 2005: 12–13).

Extending access to health care to larger parts of the population is more than just a cost issue. One of the major difficulties in many countries is that not enough qualified medical staff are available to provide the necessary health care services.

Based on the assumptions of the Commission on Macroeconomics and Health, the costs of a minimum package of essential health care would initially require between 4.0 and 14.0 per cent of GDP in all countries but Ethiopia (see Figure 5.6). In the latter, more than 30 per cent of GDP would have to be allocated to health care. These exceptionally high costs in the case of Ethiopia are largely due to the relationship between the modelled health expenditure and currently very low levels of GDP per capita. Taking into account current levels of health expenditure and low coverage of populations, enormous financial efforts would have to be made in the short term to introduce even a minimal medical intervention package and this would be difficult to accommodate within domestically available fiscal space. The gap would have to be filled by international transfers.

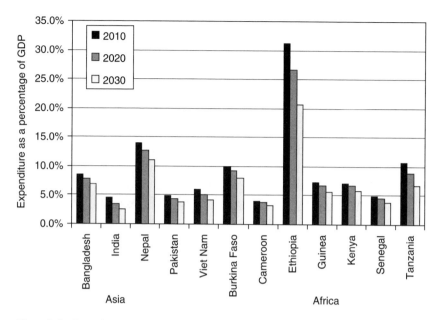

Figure 5.6   Costs for essential health care as a percentage of GDP
Source: Based on Commission on Macroeconomics and Health, 2001; Mizunoya et al., 2006; Pal et al., 2005.

A basic social protection package

Taken together, universal cash benefits and access to health care would provide a basic social protection package that would meet the most basic needs
of the population. While the previous calculations have reflected different
options, now we shall concentrate on just one basic social protection package.
This will include the following elements:

- a basic universal old age and disability pension;
- a universal child benefit for all children up to the age of 14; and
- access to essential health care interventions as selected by the Commission
  on Macroeconomics and Health.

This basic social protection package corresponds to the model calculations
(Mizunoya et al., 2006; Pal et al., 2005),[13] with cash benefit amounts linked
to the World Bank US$1 PPP per day international absolute poverty line (tak-
ing US$0.50 per day per person for pensions and US$0.25 per day for child
benefits).

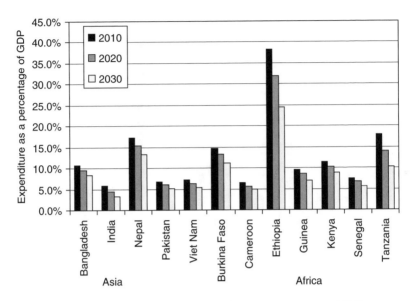

Figure 5.7   Costs for basic social protection package as a percentage of GDP
Source: Based on Mizunoya et al., 2006; Pal et al., 2005.

The cost of essential health care constitutes the largest cost component in the total package (see Figure 5.7). Especially in the case of Ethiopia, which stands out with by far the highest costs for basic social protection, health care is the main cost driver according to the underlying assumptions. Among the other countries, the initial annual costs of a basic social protection package is projected to be in the range of 6.4 to 11.4 per cent of GDP by 2010 in eight of the twelve countries considered, namely Bangladesh, Cameroon, Guinea, India, Kenya, Pakistan, Senegal and Viet Nam. Three countries – Burkina Faso, Nepal and Tanzania – are in a band between 14.7 and 17.3 per cent of GDP. It should also be noted that, according to the underlying assumptions, the cost of a basic social protection package is projected to decrease in all countries by 2030.

The projections show that fully introducing even a basic social protection package requires a level of resources that is much higher than current spending in the majority of low-income countries (that rarely spend more than 3 per cent of GDP on health care and rarely more than 1 per cent of GDP on non-health social security measures). Therefore, a considerable joint domestic and international effort is needed to invest in basic social protection to bring about significant social development and a sharp reduction of poverty. Possible sources of financing of such an effort are discussed in the next section.

Possible sources of financing

The costing simulations entail two contrasting alternative options. The first assumes that governments would not increase the *proportion* of resources allocated to social protection, keeping unchanged the level of spending on social protection in 2003. Available resources are assumed to increase only proportionally, in line with increases in government revenues resulting from economic growth and widening of the tax base. The second option assumes that the governments of the countries in question *will* substantially increase the proportion of available resources allocated to basic social protection to reach one-fifth of their total expenditure (which would still be well below prevailing proportions of public budget spent on social protection in many middle- and high-income countries (usually between one-third and one-half of government expenditure).

Our results are presented for each of these two alternative spending options, as applied in the model calculations developed by Pal et al. (2005) and Mizunoya et al. (2006). In order to ensure comparability of results between the African and Asian countries, the results for the African countries were recalculated to include only health and other social protection expenditure, excluding education expenditure. Therefore, the results presented here are different from the ones presented in Pal et al. (2005).

Option 1: constant share of public expenditure devoted to basic social protection

Under the first spending policy option, it is assumed that governments would not increase the relative size of their allocations to basic social protection. They would keep the current share of total government expenditure unchanged. The estimated current shares are rather low but differ substantially among countries: for example, 0.8 per cent in Pakistan and 8.4 per cent in Tanzania.

Under such spending policy, governments would be able to finance from available domestic resources the modelled basic social protection package only up to the following amounts (expressed as percentages of GDP: see Figure 5.8). Due to their low current expenditure levels, Pakistan and Viet Nam would spend only up to 0.2 per cent of GDP on basic social protection in 2010, slightly rising over time. Countries like Cameroon, Guinea and Senegal could reach spending levels around 0.5 per cent of GDP. A third cluster of countries is found with spending levels around 1 per cent of GDP: Bangladesh, India and Nepal, joined by Burkina Faso, Ethiopia and Kenya at 1.0–1.5 per cent of GDP. Tanzania stands out with spending levels of more than 2.0 per cent of GDP, which reflects high current expenditure levels on basic social protection. The outcome would be as varied and as unrelated

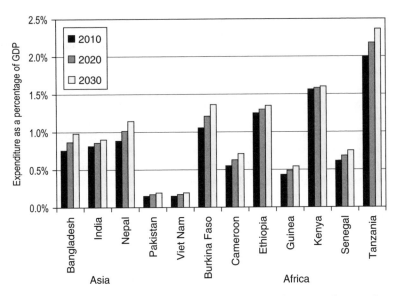

Figure 5.8 Projected domestically financed expenditure on basic social protection as a percentage of GDP (spending option 1: 2003 spending level held constant over time)

Source: Based on Mizunoya et al., 2006; Pal et al., 2005. The figures for Africa were recalculated to make the data comparable to the ones from Asia.

to national needs and international standards as government expenditure is today.

However, the total cost of the basic social protection package that we have constructed (Figure 5.7) is much higher than the estimates of future resources that are likely to be available – shown by projecting current levels of spending in line with economic growth (Figure 5.8). Therefore, if countries are not in a position to break out of the low levels of social protection expenditure within their available domestic resources, they will need to draw heavily on external sources of funding to implement basic social protection.

Figure 5.9 shows what share of government expenditure is covered by the basic social protection package under the above spending policy assumptions. While countries like Pakistan, Viet Nam, Ethiopia and Guinea initially cover less than 5 per cent of the total estimated costs, countries such as India, Kenya and Tanzania could shoulder more than a tenth of the estimated costs in 2010, quickly increasing to roughly one-fifth in Kenya and Tanzania, and to considerably more than a quarter in India by 2030. In all countries, the capacity to increase the share of domestic financing increases over time, but remains insufficient to cover the basic social protection package modelled above.

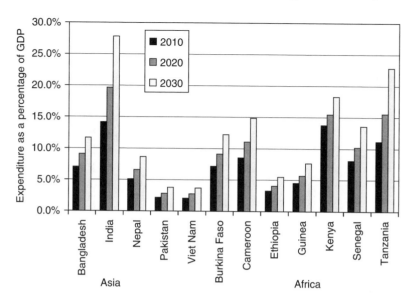

Figure 5.9 Share of total cost of basic social protection package to be covered by domestic resources (spending option 1: 2003 spending level held constant over time)
Source: Based on Mizunoya et al., 2006; Pal et al., 2005. The figures for Africa were recalculated to make the data comparable to the ones from Asia.

Option 2: spending levels increased to one-fifth of government expenditure

Under the second spending policy option, it is assumed that governments increase disproportionately their allocations to social protection (namely health care and basic social cash transfers) to one-fifth of their total budget.

When this alternative model is applied, domestically financed expenditure on basic social protection reaches levels of between 2.4 and 5.8 per cent of GDP in 2010 (see Figure 5.10). The lowest level is projected for Bangladesh, due to the relatively small volume of the government budget; yet the domestic financed social protection spending would rise from 2.4 to 3.1 per cent of GDP between 2010 and 2030. In Burkina Faso, Cameroon, Nepal, Pakistan and Viet Nam, the governments would be able to allocate from 3.4 to 3.9 per cent of their GDP to basic social protection in 2010, increasing these figures from 4.3 to 5.0 per cent of GDP by 2030. In Guinea, Senegal and Tanzania, governments could allocate 4.6 to 4.8 per cent in 2010, with spending levels projected to reach 5.6 to 5.8 per cent of GDP by 2030. The governments of Ethiopia and Kenya could invest 5.5 and 5.8 per cent respectively of GDP into basic social protection in 2010, increasing to 5.9 and 6.0 per cent of GDP by 2030. Starting from a similar level, India is the

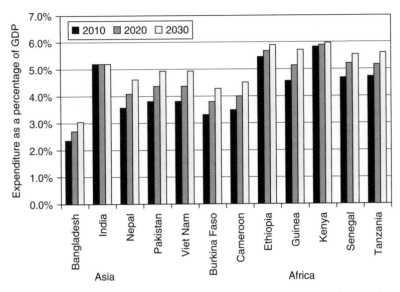

Figure 5.10 Projected domestically financed expenditure on basic social protection as a percentage of GDP (spending option 2: spending on basic social protection reaching 20 per cent of government expenditure)
Source: Based on Mizunoya et al., 2006; Pal et al., 2005. The figures for Africa were recalculated to make the data comparable to the ones from Asia.

only country in which the relative level of domestic financing is assumed to decrease over time under those assumptions from 5.3 per cent in 2010 to 3.2 per cent of GDP in 2030. India's exceptional results are related to the fact that the cost of the basic social protection package remains below the limit of 20 per cent of total government spending starting from 2013.

Figure 5.11 shows that if India increased the share of social protection spending in its total budget, by 2010 it would be able to finance over 90 per cent of the universal basic social protection package domestically and 100 per cent later on. For other countries, even after such reallocation of domestic resources, there would still be a need to fill the substantial financing gap by international transfers. Countries like Bangladesh, Burkina Faso, Ethiopia and Nepal could cover less than 30 per cent of the total financing needs by 2010. While their capacity to finance a basic social protection package is expected to increase over the following two decades, the share of domestic funding remains below 40 per cent of the total needed, which implies that substantial external support would be necessary for some time. Tanzania starts off from a similar situation but is expected to increase its ability to finance basic social transfers domestically more rapidly: to more than 50 per cent by 2030.

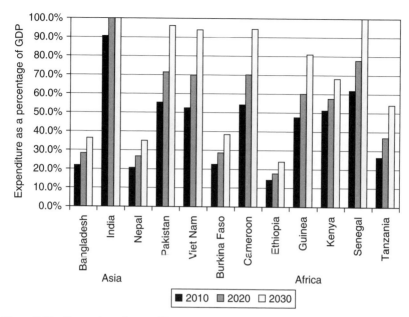

Figure 5.11 Share of total cost of basic social protection package that can be covered by domestic resources (spending option 2: spending on basic social protection to reach 20 per cent of government expenditure)

Source: Based on Mizunoya et al., 2006; Pal et al., 2005. The figures for Africa were recalculated to make the data comparable to the ones from Asia.

For a second cluster of countries, including Cameroon, Guinea, Kenya, Pakistan, Senegal and Viet Nam, the projections sketch a more optimistic picture. These countries would be in a position to cover 48–62 per cent of the total costs of the package by 2010 (i.e. if they were to devote one-fifth of domestic resources to basic social protection). By 2030, 68 per cent (Kenya) and 100 per cent (Senegal) of basic social protection would be covered.

The international context of the social protection models

The above projections were developed under rather rigorous assumptions with respect to the fiscal policies of the countries in question. First, they were all assumed to depend only on revenue raised domestically (thus phasing out current external grants). Therefore the scale of external finance required towards the basic social protection package is net of the projected deduction of such external flows. The idea is to redirect as well as increase current external support, to focus it on providing the very basic social protection package. This is intended to concentrate national attention upon anti-poverty priorities.

Second, all the countries were assumed to cap their overall public expenditure at a level no higher than 30 per cent of GDP. Such an assumption was made to show what is possible within the framework of a relatively 'small state' (as measured by the size of public finances). As countries develop and widen their tax base they may wish to go beyond 'small state' and rather follow relative levels of government revenues and expenditure prevailing in the OECD countries. For the time being, pressures of 'tax competition' developing as part of the spontaneous globalization processes may prevent them from doing so. This, however, may change if global governance of the globalization processes is strengthened and agreement on a global social floor (which would include a guarantee of universal access to basic social protection) is reached.

Impact on poverty reduction

In reducing unacceptable rates of poverty, are there other studies that help to show what is the minimum affordable cost of a social protection package? Complementing the projections illustrated in this chapter, a recent ILO study has simulated the effects of some elements of a basic social protection package on poverty reduction through micro-simulations in the cases of Senegal and Tanzania (Gassmann and Behrendt, 2006). Considered were a universal old age and disability pension and benefits for children of school age only (7–14 years) as opposed to all children or orphans as in the costing model illustrated above. Benefit levels were defined relative to *national* poverty lines, that is, 70 per cent of the food poverty line for old age and disability pensions, and 35 per cent for child benefits. It was estimated that this combination of benefits would require 3.3 per cent of GDP in Senegal and 3.2 per cent of GDP in Tanzania (Gassmann and Behrendt, 2006: 20).

These micro-simulations have shown that the combination of a universal old age and disability pension and child benefits for children of school age (7–14 years) would directly reduce extreme poverty by some 40 per cent in Senegal and Tanzania. In the case of Senegal, such a benefit package is estimated to reduce the proportion of the population living below the food poverty line from 19.7 to 11.5 per cent. In the case of Tanzania, food poverty rates are estimated to be reduced from 22.2 to 13.6 per cent of the population (see Figure 5.12). The poverty gap is estimated to be trimmed down by 58 per cent in the case of Senegal and by 67 per cent in Tanzania (see Figure 5.13).

These estimated effects on the poverty rate and the poverty gap only consider first-order effects, yet it can be expected that the availability of small but regular incomes would also have considerable second-order effects due to better nutrition and hygiene as well as access to social services such as health care and education. In addition, evaluations of existing cash

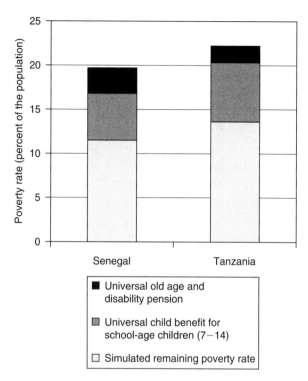

Figure 5.12 Simulated direct effect of social cash transfers on the poverty headcount in Senegal and Tanzania
Source: Based on Gassmann and Behrendt, 2006. Disability pensions could not be included in the case of Tanzania.

transfer programmes show that local economies might also benefit from those transfers, particularly in rural areas.

Conclusion: can low-income countries afford not to have social security?

The models we have chosen to illustrate the possible development of social protection schemes in developing countries sketch a minimum level of protection. We have deliberately taken a modest standard of provision partly to illustrate what is the smallest system that can and must be introduced in the near future to begin to meet the dire needs that exist, but also to illustrate the fact that with economic development such a system is affordable. Social security is not a social cost, but an affordable investment in the prevention of poverty and vulnerability, the quality of work and life, social cohesion and peace, nation-building and global security. In other words,

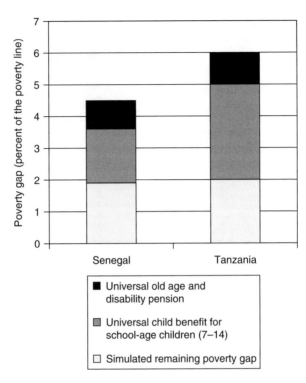

Figure 5.13 Simulated direct effect of social cash transfers on the poverty gap in Senegal and Tanzania
Source: Based on Gassmann and Behrendt, 2006. Disability pensions could not be included in the case of Tanzania.

social security is an investment in people and states. Therefore, the main question is not whether low-income countries can afford social security, but whether they can afford *not* to have social security. There is ample evidence that the investment in health care, education and properly designed cash transfers have positive economic and social effects in countries at any stage of development. Without social security one can hardly imagine countries having sustainable social and economic development and their populations getting out of poverty traps. Various cash transfer mechanisms, as well as mechanisms to ensure access to health care and education, are among the most important means to ensure effective social protection for all.

There is a range of policy instruments to meet these needs and priorities of vulnerable groups which have been tested in middle- and low-income countries, and which have shown positive results. In addition to the available real-life examples, simulations show that such instruments have a substantial effect on reducing poverty and vulnerability.

Experience with various non-contributory cash transfers in a number of developing countries shows that such policy instruments are not only desirable, effective and affordable, but also administratively feasible. Countries have chosen different strategies to administer and deliver such transfers. While some countries have opted for universal benefits to specific categories of the population, others have put in place elaborate mechanisms of administrative or community-based targeting. Both approaches have their specific advantages and disadvantages (Coady et al., 2004). Universal benefits to specific categories of the population tend to be relatively easy and inexpensive to administer, they provide stronger rights and entitlements to the population and are less prone to stigmatization of beneficiaries. In addition, clearer rules, higher transparency and rights of appeal provide a safeguard against nepotism and corruption. Targeted benefits often attract higher political attention because of their focus on the poorest and stronger community involvement, but they rely on more complex and less transparent administrative procedures, tend to convey weaker rights to potential beneficiaries and often face difficulties in actually reaching the very poorest.[14] In any case, this requires a review of institutional capacities at the national, regional and local level, particularly with a view to delivering benefits in rural areas.

Providing a basic level of protection to vulnerable groups of the population must be the cornerstone of national policies. In addition, other instruments, such as social insurance, are needed to complement this basic level of protection. Even if a basic social protection package cannot be implemented at once, a sequential approach can generate immediate benefits in terms of poverty reduction, pro-poor growth and social development. A national forward-looking social protection strategy can help to sequence the implementation of various social programmes and policy instruments and ensure that these are integrated in broader development frameworks.

The evidence presented shows that low-income countries not only should but also can have social security systems, by providing a basic package of health services to everybody and basic cash benefits to the elderly and families with children. As these countries achieve higher levels of economic development, their social security systems can also advance in parallel, extending the scope, level and quality of benefits and services provided. A basic social protection package is demonstrably affordable, as the models discussed in this chapter show. But this is on the condition that the package is implemented through the joint efforts of the low-income countries themselves (reallocating existing resources and raising new resources) and of the international donor community – which would have to refocus international grants on the supplementary direct financing of social protection benefits, on strengthening the administrative and delivery capacity of national social protection institutions in low-income countries and on providing the necessary technical advice and other support. All these steps have begun to be taken in a number of low-income countries in Africa and elsewhere (recent developments in countries like Tanzania, Zambia, Mozambique or Nepal are just a few examples) and there are signs that the process will accelerate in the near future.

Notes

1. Article 22 of the Universal Declaration of Human Rights states that 'Everyone, as a member of society, has the right to social security and is entitled to realization, through national effort and international co-operation and in accordance with the organization and resources of each State, of the economic, social and cultural rights indispensable for his dignity and the free development of his personality.' Article 25 reads '(1) Everyone has the right to a standard of living adequate for the health and well-being of himself and of his family, including food, clothing, housing and medical care and necessary social services, and the right to security in the event of unemployment, sickness, disability, widowhood, old age or other lack of livelihood in circumstances beyond his control. (2) Motherhood and childhood are entitled to special care and assistance. All children, whether born in or out of wedlock, shall enjoy the same social protection.'
2. Such as the International Covenant on Economic, Social and Cultural Rights, the Convention on the Rights of the Child, and the recently adopted Convention on the Rights of Persons with Disabilities.
3. See Government of Zambia et al., 2006.
4. The ILO's mandate in the field of social security is firmly grounded in its constitution of 1919 and in the Declaration of Philadelphia of 1944.
5. Preliminary results from ILO Social Security Inquiry; data refer to 2004.
6. Linking benefit to average income levels makes them substantially higher in relatively richer countries. For example, while in Tanzania benefit set as 30 per cent of GDP per capita was only slightly higher – in local currency units – than benefit equivalent to US$0.5 PPP, in Senegal benefit anchored with average income level was twice as high as benefit linked to the international poverty line. ILO Conventions setting minimum standards for social security cash benefits (like Convention No. 102 (1952) or Convention No. 128 (1967)) specify minimum benefits always relative to country-specific income benchmarks (i.e. 40 or 45 per cent of individual earnings for earnings-related benefits or 40 or 45 per cent of earnings of a typical unqualified manual worker for flat rate benefits) and never in absolute terms.
7. The Zambian cash transfer scheme in 2007 already covered selected areas in five different districts of Zambia and it is envisaged to be gradually upscaled to cover the whole country by 2012.
8. The amount of benefit in Kalomo is supposed just to ensure that covered households can afford two very basic meals per day (the monthly benefit is equivalent to the cost of a bag of maize). Eligible beneficiaries have no other source of income and many of them were begging to get food before the programme started.
9. Despite very modest benefit levels (the monthly benefit is equivalent to the cost of a bag of maize), the first evaluations of the pilot project are rather encouraging. Not only have living standards of recipients considerably improved, but households have also started to save and invest part of the money (Zambia Ministry of Community Development and Social Services and German Technical Cooperation, 2006).
10. The first evaluation of the Kalomo pilot project shows lower levels of administrative expenditure, that is 23 per cent of benefit expenditure (that is 19 per cent of

total expenditure) if government official salaries are included (Zambia Ministry of Community Development and Social Services and German Technical Cooperation, 2006: 32; own calculations). As the scaling up of such a programme to a national level might bring about higher administration cost, our cost projections are based on a higher proportion of administration cost.

11. Kumaranayake et al., 2001. Selected interventions were identified as key in addressing the major health conditions among the poor and cover the following categories: tuberculosis treatment, malaria prevention and treatment, HIV/AIDS prevention, care and treatment, treatment of childhood diseases (like acute respiratory infections, diarrhoea, causes of fever, malnutrition, anaemia), immunization against childhood diseases (vaccinations: BCG, OPV, DPT, measles, hepatitis B, HiB) and maternity-related interventions (including antenatal care, treatment of complications during pregnancy, skilled birth attendance, emergency obstetric care, postpartum care, including family planning).

12. Commission on Macroeconomics and Health, 2001: 55, 165–7. Amounts are expressed in 2002 US$. The respective estimate for least developed countries is US$34 for 2007 and US$41 for 2015. For low- and middle-income countries, the estimate is US$36 and US$40 respectively. The authors note that 'at purchasing power parities ... the minimum cost of the essential package would probably be above $80 per person per year' (ibid., footnote 79, p. 120).

13. The model calculations for African countries (Pal et al., 2005) included also basic education which is not reflected here.

14. This can be due to creaming effects which reflect the fact that the very poorest face various difficulties in accessing such benefits because of a lack of education, knowledge and information, physical distances and transport costs etc., and that not-so-poor groups may have better chances to access benefits than the very poorest.

6
The Impact of Social Transfers on Growth, Development, Poverty and Inequality in Developing Countries

Michael Samson

Effective social transfers reduce poverty and inequality, and these social effects generate important growth and development impacts in many developing countries. This chapter outlines a theoretical framework through which social transfers generate these effects, and discusses experiences in developing countries with a focus on the impact of South Africa's social grants.

Social transfers aim to reduce poverty, which itself is not a uniform or static condition. Poverty is complex and multi-dimensional. Over a billion people in the world have no access to safe drinking water – resulting in an estimated 5,000 children less than five years of age dying each day from diarrhoea. Climate change exacerbates this problem by further eroding the availability of water in some of the poorest parts of the world (DFID, 2006: 82). Hundreds of millions of poor people will never escape poverty, but rather pass the scourge to their children through numerous transmission mechanisms: exploitatively low wages, lack of educational qualifications, and bad forms of housing in poor localities without access to sanitary facilities and drinking water. These are the 'chronically poor', as distinguished from the 'transitory poor', who encounter shocks that push them into a state of deprivation from which they may eventually escape – though some events, such as major injury or loss of a living wage because of age, can bring poverty for the rest of one's life (CPRC, 2005).

The shocks (as distinct from poor continuing conditions) that force people into poverty take a number of different forms. Some of these calamities – such as wars, civil conflicts, earthquakes and tsunamis – can suddenly devastate entire populations within often expansive areas. Termed 'covariate' shocks, these disasters pose special problems because they can severely undermine the traditional coping mechanisms societies develop and affect large segments of population. Other forms of shocks – such as job loss, severe illness, disability and death – unexpectedly impoverish single individuals and households, without affecting most of the others in the community. Termed

122

'idiosyncratic' shocks, these tragedies are more easily mitigated by various informal and formal mechanisms of social insurance. The distinction between chronic and transitory poverty is far from absolute. Shocks – such as military conflict affecting civilians – can disrupt the provision of nutrition, education and health care that children need in order to avoid a lifetime of chronic poverty (Orero et al., 2006). In addition, it is not just the direct impact of the shocks that undermine the well-being of the poor and vulnerable. The possibility of shocks creates risk – and the poor must acquire coping mechanisms in order to survive. Without effective social protection, the poorest often develop survival strategies that perpetuate chronic poverty. Poor farmers may adopt safer but lower yielding crop varieties, helping prevent a slide into absolute destitution but also foreclosing promising opportunities to break free from poverty (Orero et al., 2006).

Social transfers present an increasingly attractive option for poor countries to tackle these multiple dimensions of poverty (Orero et al., 2006). They lighten long-term conditions of deprivation and soften the blow of sudden crisis. Cash transfers to the most destitute protect their consumption, helping to provide for nutrition, health care and access to education. This support can prevent some of the worst consequences of poverty – the transmission of lifelong poverty to children. Social transfers also benefit those poor with productive assets – by enabling them to weather shocks without compromising their future livelihoods in order to survive today. Farmers are less likely to sell the livestock on which their future prosperity depends if adequate cash transfers protect their immediate subsistence.

The International Labour Office demonstrates that social transfer programmes in low-income African and Asian countries can protect the poorest at a cost that could be around 3 to 4 per cent of GDP (Mizunoya et al., 2006; Pal et al., 2005). The cost of providing the poorest in sub-Saharan Africa with modest cash transfers is a small fraction of the additional US$25 billion of aid that the G8 agreed at Gleneagles to provide to Africa (DFID, 2006: 84). Governments often provide more than just the most basic package because they find themselves obliged to deal with the poor and not only the extreme poor. Structural empowerment has to be widely applied in labour and other social conditions that are fluid from day to day. South Africa spends more than 3 per cent of national income on social grants. Lesotho recently decided to increase the value of the social pension by 33 per cent – significantly higher than the inflation rate.

Policy-makers are increasingly recognizing the importance of social transfers (including social pensions, grants for children and families, public works schemes and other programmes) in achieving the Millennium Development Goals. In South Africa, the Minister for Social Development Zola Skweyiya has championed a tripling of spending on social grants over the past seven years, with most of the new benefits intended for poor children. Leaders in neighbouring Lesotho implemented a new social pension in 2004.

Brazil is rapidly expanding the *Bolsa Familia* programme that provides grants to poor households, particularly for the purpose of improving health and education outcomes. India is implementing a national public works guarantee programme, scaling up a highly successful social transfer model from the state of Maharashtra. Over the past ten years scores of countries have substantially expanded existing social transfer programmes or initiated new interventions or pilots.

Social transfers not only tackle income poverty, they also provide effective support for broader developmental objectives. Households in developing countries spend social transfer income primarily on food, improving nutritional outcomes. In many countries, social grants are distributed largely to women, promoting empowerment and more balanced gender relations. Better household living standards facilitate education and improve health outcomes – particularly for women and children. Social transfers also provide a role in the protection strategy for those afflicted by HIV/AIDS, malaria and other debilitating diseases. Long a vital tool for industrialized countries, social transfers are increasingly recognized as an essential policy element for low- and middle-income nations.

In addition to their vital social contribution, social transfers can support critical economic objectives. Many of the world's fastest growing economies over the past several decades have built social protection into their policies at early stages because of its potential to increase productivity and contribute to stabilizing domestic demand. The failure to provide appropriate social protection limits prospects for growth and development at the very foundation of society because household poverty undermines children's nutrition and educational attainment, limiting their future prospects (Asian Development Bank, 2003: 50). Poverty traps individuals and households – even entire countries – stifling human dignity and eroding potential. Poverty reproduces itself generation after generation, challenging policy-makers to take imaginative and bold steps to transform their nations. Social transfers are increasingly acknowledged as an effective tool to reduce this inter-generational poverty.

This chapter defines social transfers as regular non-contributory payments of money provided by government or non-governmental organizations to individuals or households, with the objective of decreasing chronic or shock-induced poverty, addressing social risk and reducing economic vulnerability.[1] The transfers can be unconditional, conditional on households actively fulfilling human development responsibilities (education, health, nutrition, etc.) or else conditional on recipients providing labour in compliance with a work requirement. The transfers can be universal or explicitly targeted to the poor and vulnerable – but more successfully to easy-to-define groups in the population – such as children, people with disabilities, bereaved and older people rather than individuals or households judged poor according to elaborate tests of means.

Social transfers constitute a critical element of social protection strategies in industrialized countries. Chapter 1 of this book documents how OECD countries invest at a far greater rate in social protection than do poor countries – and consequently reduce poverty substantially. The experience of OECD countries provides no evidence that social protection spending inhibits economic growth, and countries that spend substantially on social security often experience above-average rates of economic growth. Chapter 3 provides an analysis of these relationships, suggesting that the weight of evidence indicates a positive relationship between social protection investment and economic growth and development.

Many of the poorest countries in the world, however, provide no publicly funded social transfer to the poor. In the absence of public transfers, the poorest households rely on private remittances – cash payments from other (often poor) individuals. While private transfers provide a critical safety net in the absence of government interventions, private remittances are usually inadequate to address the consequences of severe poverty. In many low-income countries, private remittances are financed largely through the toil of the working poor. The regressive nature of this redistributional mechanism limits its ability to address poverty – particularly in those countries where the poor face severe shocks such as HIV/AIDS, economic crisis, war and natural disasters exacerbated by climate change.

This chapter first discusses the linkages among poverty, inequality, social protection and growth and identifies theoretical relationships. It then discusses the range of evidence for many developing countries – particularly in Africa. The next section focuses on labour market evidence in South Africa, and the final section draws linkages between growth and fiscal affordability.

The theoretical context

While the ongoing debate concerning the relationship between inequality and growth has failed to yield a resolution, few dispute that severe inequality undermines growth prospects. In the context of this discussion, 'economic growth' refers not only to its technical definition – in terms of real increases in national output – but also to the positive developmental outcomes frequently associated with higher incomes. The technical measurement of economic growth reflects the percentage change in real gross domestic product, but the broader appraisal requires a multi-dimensional assessment of health, education, environmental, equity and other outcomes. High inequality certainly reduces the impact of growth on poverty reduction. In a globalized world, growth increasingly depends on high quality human capital – inequality skews the distribution of education and other forms of human capital, and reflects a situation in which the poor cannot participate fully in the economy. And inequality erodes social stability – deterring investment and undermining growth prospects.

Social transfers directly tackle inequality and poverty – they transfer resources from the upper income to the lowest income households in a relatively efficient manner. Part of that transfer is horizontal rather than vertical – from wage-earning households with no dependent children or dependent adults to those with one or more dependants, or from households currently prosperous to those currently poor, with the promise to the prosperous that when or if they experience future shocks they too can count on similar compensating benefits.

In many ways social transfers promote economic growth. They provide households with resources to invest – in nutrition, education, health and other forms of human capital. They also provide security that underwrites the higher risk of more productive ventures. Social transfers also provide immediate liquidity that some recipients employ to finance immediate investments.

Yet some economists continue to posit a conventional view that there is a negative trade-off between social protection and growth. The wealthiest countries in the world – as a group – have the most comprehensive systems of social protection. Social security is an essential basic service in all successful states that have experienced long-term sustainable growth rates alongside successful poverty reduction. This empirical regularity contradicts the notion of a negative trade-off, although some economists continue to speculate about its existence.

The likelihood of a negative trade-off diminishes for the poorest and least protected countries. The lower the level of social protection, the more likely will additional investments in social security promote economic growth. South Africa provides one convincing example. Prior to the 1994 democratic elections, racially skewed social transfer programmes failed to adequately reach the poorest, and economic growth languished. The progressive realization of people's rights to social security during the 1990s did not undermine the pro-growth economic agenda. Grant spending accelerated rapidly after 2000, and this tripling of spending on social protection did not deter the broadest economic expansion South Africa had experienced in half a century. While other economic policy factors have contributed to South Africa's recent positive growth performance, this experience demonstrates the compatibility if not mutual synergy of economic growth and broad-based investment in social protection.

Understanding the relationship between social protection and growth requires a comprehension of the multiple dimensions of poverty. Income and asset poverty undermines human capabilities and traps people in geographic locations deprived of developmental opportunities. The poor often lack the organizational power to make their voices heard, and institutions may fail to serve the poorest.

For example, empirical studies of the impact of social protection measures on labour markets in developing countries find that 'an increase in real

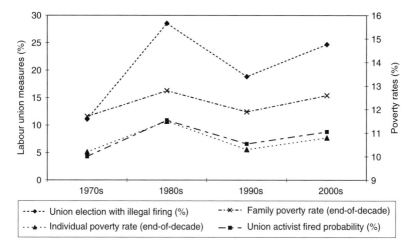

Figure 6.1 Organizational power and poverty in the United States, 1974–2005
Source: US Census Bureau (poverty rates); Schmitt and Zipperer, 2007 (union measures).

minimum wages is accompanied by a fall in poverty'.[2] In many countries, however, the working poor lack the organizational capacity to effectively achieve pro-poor institutional change. Even in rich countries, organizational poverty can be associated with income poverty. For example, in the USA from 1974 to 2005, increases in the illegal firings of pro-union workers have been associated with worsening poverty. From the 1970s to the 1980s, the rate of illegal firings of union workers rose – as did poverty rates. From the 1980s to the 1990s illegal firings fell – and so did the poverty rate. Both of these trends have reversed during the current decade, with worsening poverty accompanying an increase in the rate of illegal firings. The trends are illustrated in Figure 6.1.[3] Clearly, many factors besides labour union power affect poverty, but these trends are consistent with the hypothesis that the weakening of labour unions through illegal firings is one of the contributing factors that increase poverty.

Political factors may be associated with the weakening of the organizational capacity of the poor and pro-poor institutions (Figure 6.2). Over the same time period, a union activist faced a 20 per cent chance of an illegal firing during Republican presidential administrations, and only a 12 per cent probability in years that a Democrat was president. Likewise, 25 per cent of union elections suffered illegal pro-union worker firings during Republican presidential administrations, yet only 16 per cent of the elections were marred in this way during a Democratic president's tenure.[4] (Over this time period poverty rates rose in 60 per cent of the years that a Republican was president, yet in only 27 per cent of the years that a Democrat held this

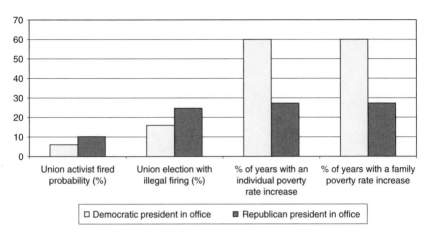

Figure 6.2   Political parties and poverty in the United States, 1974–2005
Source: US Census Bureau (poverty data); Schmitt and Zipperer, 2007 (labour union measures).

office.[5]) The discussion of these correlations is not meant to imply that the presidents themselves are responsible for these effects – but the presidential party in office can serve as a proxy for a range of political forces that affect the pro-poor direction of public institutions. This is consistent with the broader argument that 'the relative strength of different political tendencies with different power bases in society fundamentally shaped the character of welfare states in advanced industrial economies', and that 'different political preferences were translated into different policies when these parties held political power' (Huber and Stephens, 2001: 312).

Each dimension of poverty can reinforce the other dimensions – and addressing one dimension can potentially influence the others. Social transfers directly tackle income poverty – but the interlinkages lead to broader impacts in terms of health, education, security, empowerment and other broadly developmental objectives.

Mapping the dimensions of poverty describes the empirical basis for this theoretical framework. A Poverty Map for one of South Africa's poorest provinces shows the concentration of households living on less than two dollars per day. The map shows that poverty is geographically concentrated in rural areas deprived of infrastructure, particularly in those regions removed from major roads. A map of unemployment shows the same patterns of concentration. The patterns of poverty coincide with the patterns of unemployment – documenting the inter-relationships between these two conditions. In South Africa, poverty and unemployment go hand in hand, highlighting the concern between social protection and labour markets. The dimensions of poverty extend much further. For South Africa maps of

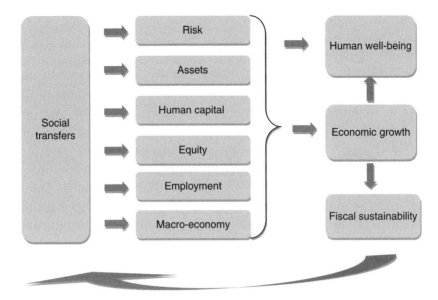

Figure 6.3 Channels through which social transfers affect economic growth

hundreds of social indicators – such as reliance on paraffin as opposed to electricity for lighting, with the numerous resulting poisonings and burns – provide a clearer picture of how poverty affects people. School attendance rates, health indicators, access to safe water, telephones – all of the indicators paint the same pattern across the province and the nation.

Social protection tackles income poverty – and through several intricate linkages, it affects the other dimensions of poverty and inequality. Many of these interactions bolster economic growth. Figure 6.3 illustrates the main channels through which social transfers affect growth – through improved risk management, productive asset protection, human capital development in terms of nutrition, health, education, improved equity from offsetting discrimination, employment and various macroeconomic effects.[6]

Social transfers can serve as an effective instrument for managing social risk. Themba, a mother of three children living in Nyanga, an impoverished township on the outskirts of Cape Town, describes her predicament: 'If I have ten rand, then I can feed my children tonight. I can't take the chance to spend it on a taxi to go look for work. If I don't find a job, we'll go hungry again' (Samson, 2005). The reality of this risk contributes to trapping Themba in poverty. Social transfers can protect the poor against the worst consequences of risky investments, providing protection and thereby encouraging behaviour that can help free poor people from poverty.

Social transfers can also protect the productive assets the poor depend upon for their livelihood. In the face of severe economic shocks, poor people must often sell their assets in order to survive. This makes it more difficult for the poor to lift themselves out of poverty once the shock subsides, and also undermines economic activity in poor communities. By sustaining the vital consumption of the poor, social transfers better enable poor households to maintain their productive assets.

In particular, social transfers protect children's accumulation of human capital. By providing resources at a critical point in a child's development, social transfers protect nutrition and improve long-term educational outcomes.

Many of these effects produce stronger outcomes for girls compared to boys. As a result, social transfers also support greater social equity in terms of redressing gender inequality. Similarly, many of the labour market outcomes are more pronounced for women compared to men. This gender impact is largely a result of an emerging 'good practice' in the design of social transfer programmes – the benefits are increasingly paid to women rather than the formal 'head of household'.

Increasingly evidence is emerging to document the positive impact of social transfers on employment. The section below on labour market outcomes discusses recent evidence for South Africa. Less formal evidence suggests positive employment effects resulting from social pensions in Namibia, as discussed below.

At a macroeconomic level the redistributional impact of social transfers shifts the composition of demand within the economy. Depending on the structure of the economy, these effects may stimulate employment and economic growth. The macroeconomics section below describes these potential effects in the case of South Africa.

The improvements in social services directly improve human well-being – hunger is reduced, health improves, people benefit from education, people feel more secure, they have jobs and there are macroeconomic benefits.

These factors also promote economic growth, and there is a multiplier effect contributing to improving people's well-being from that economic growth. The economic growth also expands the tax base, and supports fiscal sustainability. This can further support the expansion of social transfers, and trigger a virtuous circle. Each of these effects is discussed in greater detail – with documented supporting evidence – in the sections below.

Social protection, livelihoods and employment: a review of some evidence

Social protection provides an opportunity for policy-makers to positively support livelihoods and employment. Experience in Africa and the rest of the world documents the developmental impact of social security.

Shocks in Ethiopia are central to the life of the poor – and threaten productive assets and create poverty traps. In a recent study nearly every poor household in the sample experienced a severe shock that intensified their poverty.[7] Over a five-year period (1999–2004), 95 per cent of families listed at least one serious shock that led to hardship, including drought (47 per cent), a death in the household (43 per cent) or a serious illness (28 per cent). The poor are more risk averse when they have no insurance or safety net to protect them.

Studies in Ethiopia and Zimbabwe demonstrate that droughts and other severe shocks lead to impoverishment at least in part by undermining health. Anthropometric measures reflect the poor's inability to insure against the worst forms of risk, and demonstrate how household dynamics can shift the burden onto women and young children. Young pre-school children tend to be more adversely affected than older pre-school children, and adult women bear a greater burden on average than do adult men. The long-term impacts of the shocks undermine physical stature as well as educational outcomes, creating negative consequences potentially for generations (Dercon and Hoddinott, 2003).

A case study of how communities responded to the disastrous 1999 floods that devastated central Viet Nam illustrates how shocks cause impoverishment, and how social responses can mitigate the impact. The sudden deluge of 2.3 metres of rain over a period of four days caused rivers to flood their banks and destroy lives and property, leaving no opportunity for evacuation to higher land. Yet weaker storms in previous decades had caused more prolonged hunger and impoverishment. For those whom local governments and organizations provided food and necessities in 1999, the shock was less persistent. Affected communities have higher living standards today than prior to the floods, and improvements in social security are reducing the risk of future disasters (Beckman, 2006).

For those societies without adequate social protection, it is not just the shock that is the problem – the poor respond to this unmitigated risk by making decisions that are safer but yield lower returns. They choose crops that are more likely to succeed even if the expected returns are lower than with higher yielding but riskier varieties. They cannot afford to take on that risk. Shocks cause poverty directly through the negative consequences of the disaster. The absence of adequate risk management mechanisms, however, can intensify poverty even before the actual shock occurs. The poor cannot build assets as rapidly if they must engage in relatively low-return activities in response to unmitigated risk.

A similar effect is observed in Tanzania and India (Dercon, 2006), where unmitigated risk leads to investment behaviour that lowers the expected returns by about 25 per cent, reinforcing poverty traps. In the absence of risk mitigation instruments, the poor invest in assets with safer but lower expected returns. With insurance-like mechanisms, however, the poor take greater risks with much higher expected returns – and can break the poverty trap.

One reason the productive impact of risk mitigation is so great is that the adverse consequences of unmitigated risk are so severe – and so persistent. Zimbabwe provides further evidence, where shocks exert negative impacts for decades. One study quantifies a 40 per cent reduction in the capital stock of the poor due to unmitigated risk. Drought and war in Zimbabwe exert a significant negative impact on children sixteen years later – leading to a 7 per cent loss of lifetime earnings. Ethiopia and Kenya demonstrate similar long-term impacts (Dercon, 2006; see also Alderman et al., 2003; Dercon 2005; Dercon et al., 2005).

Drought in Kenya affects the spectrum of the poor in multiple ways. The very poorest face starvation – utter destitution. Those who are poor but have some assets often must sell these productive assets in order to survive, and this intensifies their poverty. Those who are less poor nevertheless face economic decline all around them. As a result they face fewer economic opportunities and a greater likelihood of falling into poverty.

Social protection serves as an effective insurance mechanism to protect the poor, enabling them to take on prudent risks that promote their livelihoods. When the poor have access to insurance-like social protection mechanisms, they take greater risks that yield higher returns – and in some cases break out of poverty. Social transfers support livelihoods across the whole spectrum of poverty, by protecting the consumption of the most destitute, preserving the assets of the poor (which otherwise would be sold for survival) and broadly increasing economic activity.

Many African countries – particularly in Southern Africa – demonstrate experience consistent with a positive pro-poor growth impact of social transfers. In 1950 Mauritius introduced what became a non-contributory universal pension, which today costs approximately 2 per cent of national income. The social pension represents a social contract that has laid a foundation for stability, growth and development. Today, Mauritius has the lowest poverty rate and highest per capita income of any SADC country (Kaniki and Samson, 2007). Similarly, in Botswana the social pension implemented in 1996 has significantly reduced inequality in one of Africa's (and the world's) most unequal countries. Costing less than half a per cent of national income, the pension has provided one of the country's main instruments for sharing growth, supporting the social stability required for ongoing investment.

In Zambia's social cash transfer programme – initiated a few years ago and targeting the poorest households in the pilot districts – many participants immediately invest a significant proportion of the cash transfers. This multiplies the value of the transfer to the recipients while providing employment for others in the community and boosting economic growth. Similar investment effects are observed in South Africa, Brazil and Mexico. Households face serious credit constraints, yet seek to invest when provided the opportunity. Social transfers provide enough insurance protecting against the downside of risk – the guaranteed income provides assurance that they can invest without facing the most dire consequences if the investment fails to pay off. In DFID's pilot in Kenya, for example, one woman used her transfer to buy inputs to make soap, which she sold over the course of the month, multiplying the value of the cash payment.

The world's newest universal social pension – implemented in Lesotho in 2004 – promotes human capital accumulation, particularly for orphans and vulnerable children. While formal evaluations are still in progress, preliminary evidence suggests it plays an important role supporting older people taking care of grandchildren whose parents have died from AIDS. Social transfers in Namibia support labour market participation and local economic activity. Close to universal take-up of the social pension provides a broad impact. Social transfers often provide enough support to households so that woman can migrate to look for work. In particular, access to social pensions is associated with out-migration from rural areas, suggesting that young adults migrate to cities to look for jobs (Adamchak, 1995, cited in Barrientos and Lloyd-Sherlock, 2002). Cycles of economic activity coincide with the cash injected into the local economy on pension day.

Non-contributory pension programmes in Latin American countries generate similar development effects. Extreme poverty is 16 per cent lower in households with pension income than in those without pension income in Argentina (Bertranou and Grushka, 2002). Headcount poverty among households with pensioners is significantly lower than those without in Brazil. There is also a strong association between the presence of female pensioners and school enrolment of girls aged between 12 and 14 (De Carvalho Filho 2000, cited in Barrientos and Lloyd-Sherlock, 2002).

South Africa contributes a substantial body of evidence. The grants are among the most generous in the developing world, and take-up rates are relatively high by international standards. The extensive and high quality data that is available has supported studies by researchers around the world. The studies document the strong growth and development impact in terms of human capital, employment and the macroeconomic effects. Duflo (2000) finds that the household with an eligible woman for Older Person's Pension increases the weight-for-height of girls significantly, while there was no effect on boys and in the household with an eligible man. Other studies in South Africa show that poverty and its associated consequences erode the opportunities for children and youth to attend school, fomenting a vicious cycle of destitution by undermining the household's capacity to accumulate the human capital necessary to break the poverty trap. Many poor children cannot attend school due to the costs associated with education, including the necessity to work to supplement family income. In addition, communities that are resource-constrained provide lower quality educational services, which negatively affect enrolment rates.

South Africa's social grants counter these negative effects by providing households with more resources to finance education. Children in households that receive social grants are more likely to attend school, even when controlling for the effect of income. The positive effects of social security on education are greater for girls than for boys, helping to remedy gender disparities. Both the Older Person's Pension and the Child Support Grant are statistically significantly associated with improvements in school attendance, and the magnitudes of these impacts are substantial. To the extent that social grants promote school attendance, they contribute to a virtuous cycle with long-term dynamic benefits that are not easily measured by statistical analysis.

Spending in households that receive social grants focuses more on basics like food, fuel, housing and household operations, and less is spent on tobacco and debt. All major social grants – the Older Person's Pension, the Child Support Grant and the Disability Grant – are significantly and positively associated with a greater share of household expenditure on food. This increased spending on food is associated with better nutritional outcomes. Households that receive social grants have lower prevalence rates of hunger for young children as well as older children and adults, even compared to those households with comparable income levels.

Social transfers and the labour market impact in South Africa

Conventional economic theory suggests that social grants may undermine labour force participation by reducing the real cost of not working.[8] Models developed for industrialized countries and applied broadly to South African data sometimes corroborate this hypothesis. However, when models are developed that reflect the labour market behaviour of South Africans who receive social grants, the results contradict this hypothesis.[9] The response of very low-income South Africans to an increase in their income is significantly different from the response of South Africans with incomes closer to the national average.

The evaluation of the labour market impact requires the employment of an economic framework that interacts job search by workers (labour supply) with their ability to find a job, which depends on the willingness of firms to hire them (labour demand). A study by EPRI in 2004 (Samson et al.) found that workers in households receiving both pensions and child support grants looked for work significantly more extensively and intensively, and found employment more successfully. Disaggregated analysis into urban and rural areas and by gender documented that these effects are particularly strong for rural women.

In the absence of social protection, poverty demands a private safety net – primarily financed from the meagre resources of the working poor. This amounts to a very regressive tax that erodes worker productivity and stifles demand for labour. Social transfers constitute poverty tax relief and can stimulate job creation.

EPRI's 2004 study takes as a starting point the non-parametric result that, from September 2000 to February 2001, labour force participation rates rose in households receiving social transfers – yet fell in those that did not. The study also observed that unemployment rates fell over the same time period in households receiving social transfers – yet rose in those that did not. This suggests that South Africa's social grants are associated with improved labour market activity.

For the country as a whole, labour market participation rose by 0.6 per cent from September 2000 to February 2001. However, for those households that did not receive social grants, labour force participation fell by 1.1 per cent. Labour force participation rates in households receiving social grants rose by 3.3 per cent – countering the negative effects in non-grant households and accounting for the national increase. More rigorous evidence stems from statistical models built on the survey data that control systematically for differences among households. As discussed below, these econometric results corroborate that social grants are positively and significantly associated with improvements in labour force participation. There is no evidence that social grants foster dependency.

This greater participation was rewarded with greater success in finding employment – suggesting that social transfers are consistent with increased labour demand. While unemployment rates rose in households not receiving social grants, they fell in households that received the grants. Workers in households not receiving grants experienced an increase in unemployment rates from September 2000 to February 2001, while unemployment rates in households receiving grants fell.

For the country as a whole, the unemployment rate rose by 0.6 per cent from September 2000 to February 2001. For those households that did not receive social grants, the unemployment rate rose by 1.5 per cent. However, the unemployment rate in households receiving social grants fell by 1.3 per cent – dampening the negative effects in non-grant households and reducing the national increase in unemployment. The same effect is observed when one analyses the expanded definition of the unemployment rate that does not exclude discouraged workers.

These differences are small but statistically significant. However, the time-span is short due to the limitations of the Labour Force Survey panel. Persuasive non-parametric evidence would require a longitudinal data set over a longer time period, particularly given the importance of focusing policies on long-term rather than short-term impacts.

Again, the statistical models discussed below that control systematically for differences among households provide more rigorous results of what this table implies – that social grants are significantly associated with reductions in the unemployment rate. Again, there is no evidence that social grants foster dependency. This result is consistent with the hypothesis that social transfers help to overcome poverty's impact taxing the working poor.

In order to test the robustness of this non-parametric result, the study analysed Statistics South Africa data from the September 2000, 2001, and 2002 Labour Force Surveys and the 2000 Income and Expenditure Survey, which support the use of both cross-section and panel models. The cross-section models followed the standard approach of setting up a sequential model of individuals in the labour market, with selection into participation, and then into employment. Because household formation is endogenous to labour force status and wages earned (individuals with low or no wages are less likely to set up independent households), the effect of household-level characteristics (such as social grant receipt) on these variables cannot be most efficiently assessed with a cross-section model. Pensions, in this case, might be associated with unemployment or lower wages not because pensions have a negative effect on wages, but because individuals who have low or no wages are more likely to move to a household that receives pensions. The panel model can control to some extent for this effect, by examining households who receive social grants at a given point in time, and then modelling the evolution of labour market outcomes in those households, compared to households that are not receiving social grants.

An important explanatory variable – the household's overall income – is endogenous to labour force participation decisions. Using a household's reported income to explain labour force decisions may produce biased results, as these labour force decisions may also explain household income; household income and labour force decisions may be simultaneously determined. However, the concept of a household's 'earning power' may be viewed as largely insulated from labour force participation decisions and may be used to explain these decisions. Because a household's earning power is not directly observable, however, it is necessary to predict it employing other observable characteristics, including demographic and educational characteristics.[10] The full details of this estimation and its application to these models are available in Samson et al. (2004).[11]

This methodology includes a sample selection correction procedure in order to more accurately assess a particular variable's effects on the given stage of participation or employment. Because the stages are sequential, if no sample selection correction were used, the estimated coefficient on a variable for a given stage might be contaminated by its effects on all previous stages. For a hypothetical example, consider wealth: extremely high levels of wealth may reduce an individual's probability of participation in the labour market while increasing the probability of getting a job if he or she sought one. Without the sample selection correction procedure, one could (hypothetically) estimate wealth having a negative effect on employment solely because of its negative effect on participation. The household cross-sectional model follows in part the methodology of Klasen and Woolard (2005), predicting the share of adults in a household who report to be in the broad labour force, the share of those in the broad labour force who are also in the narrow labour force, and the share of those in the narrow labour force who are employed.[12]

The technical details of the individual labour force participation and employment regressions are reported in Samson et al. (2004). In general, because of sample selection problems and data issues, many of the coefficients on the social grant variables are not statistically significant. Following the example of Bhorat et al. (1999), the econometric analysis estimates separate regressions for males and females, broken down into rural and urban sub-samples. Most notably, with respect to labour force participation rates, the effects of the State Old Age Pension and the Disability Grant are statistically significantly positive for rural females. However, for rural males and urban males and females, all the social grants have effects that are not statistically different from zero.

The results from the employment equations yield more significant results. For both rural males and females, the effects of the State Old Age Pension and the Disability Grant are statistically significantly positive. Workers in households receiving either a State Old Age Pension or a Disability Grant are significantly more likely to be employed. The results identified by the cross-sectional analysis are subject to a sample selection problem referred to as 'unobserved heterogeneity'. While the cross-sectional analysis provides some weak evidence that social grants have positive effects on both labour market participation and employment, the results are not unambiguous. Stronger evidence can be provided through the analysis of panel data, which can more effectively control for the problem of unobserved heterogeneity.

The panel model uses Labour Force Survey data to analyse the effects of social grants on labour force participation, employment and productivity (reflected by wages).[13] The first set of panel data estimates addressed the question of narrow labour force participation, using the official Statistics South Africa definition that excludes discouraged workers. The second set of panel data estimates addressed the question of broad labour force participation, using the expanded Statistics South Africa definition that includes these workers. Both sets of models incorporate explanatory variables for both the State Old Age Pension (SOAP) and the Disability Grant (DG). The Child Support Grant (CSG) did not enter significantly into any of the participation regressions, perhaps due to the relatively small size of the grant during the sample period, and its low take-up rate in September 2001. In addition, to control for the impact of demographic characteristics, age- and gender-related variables were included, including the number of age-eligible pensioners (both those receiving and not receiving the SOAP). In addition, changes in household composition were incorporated into the model through variables reflecting the change in the number of children, the change in the number of women and the change in household size overall.[14] The full details of the econometric results are presented in Samson et al. (2004).

Regardless of estimation technique[15] or model specification, the two key effects tested are corroborated by all the participation models: both receipt of the State Old Age Pension and receipt of the Disability Grant have a significant positive impact on both narrow and broad labour force participation. The results are not significantly different across the various specifications of the models. Other explanatory variables have reasonable effects consistent with economic theory. Estimated exogenous income has a negative impact on both narrow and broad labour force participation – workers in households with sufficiently high incomes tend to withdraw from the labour force. Eligibility for the State Old Age Pension (in the absence of actual receipt of the grant) has a negative effect on household labour force participation. This effect, however, is only statistically significant when controlling for the gender composition of the household. Age composition of the household is consistently statistically significant. The rural/urban distinction is statistically significant only with the two-stage model that corrects for the simultaneity bias. Likewise, the geographical variables are more significant in these corrected models.

The third set of estimates addressed the question of employment using the official definition of the labour force, and the results of models that evaluate the impact of the Child Support Grant are fully documented in Samson et al. (2004). The model incorporates explanatory variables for the three major social grants – the State Old Age Pension (SOAP), the Child Support Grant (CSG) and the Disability Grant (DG). As with the labour force participation models, provincial binary (dummy) variables and a variable to capture the rural effect were also included.

Again, regardless of estimation technique or model specification, the two key effects tested by this model are corroborated by all four regressions: receipt of both the State Old Age Pension and the Disability Grant have a significant positive impact on measured household employment rates. Estimated exogenous income has a negative impact on employment rates – workers in households with sufficiently high non-labour incomes are less likely to be employed. However, as with narrow labour force participation, eligibility for the State Old Age Pension (in the absence of actual receipt of the grant) has a negative effect on employment, but this effect is not statistically significant for any of these models. The provincial variables are statistically significant for the two-stage least squares models, reflecting significant labour market differences across provinces.

More recent data confirms the result that working age adults in poor households that receive a social pension are more likely to look for work and more likely to find employment than comparable adults in households that do not receive the social pension. Matching the September 2004 Labour Force Survey to the March 2005 survey and correcting for mismatched individuals provides a dynamic picture of how labour force participation changes for households receiving and not receiving the social pension.[16]

Table 6.1 Impact of the social pension on labour force participation in households, 2005

Corrected data	Household receives social pension in 2004 (%)	Household does not receive social pension in 2004 (%)	Improvement associated with social pension (%)
Probability that a poor working age adult will:			
Find employment in 2005	9	7	2
Be actively looking for work in 2005	15	13	2
Not participate in the labour force in 2005	76	80	4

Note: Sample includes working age adults (older than 16) in households in the lowest income quintile with older people but with no working individuals in September 2004.
Source: Statistics South Africa Labour Force Surveys and EPRI calculations.

Table 6.1 compares the change in labour market participation for out-of-the-labour-force working age adults (those older than 16 years) in households with no employed individuals in September 2004 but including at least one older person (defined in terms of age eligibility for South Africa's older person's pension). The first row of data shows the proportion of these adults who were employed in March 2005, broken down by status in terms of household receipt of the social pension. The second row shows the proportion of adults who were actively looking for work but not employed. (None of the adults in this sample were employed in September 2004 or looking for work.) The third row shows the proportion of adults with an unchanged status – those who were not participating in the labour force (out-of-the-labour-force).[17]

This methodology follows a standard approach employed to identify the probability that an individual will 'transition' from one labour market state to another – for example, to make the transition from unemployment to employment, or from non-participation in the labour market to active participation.[18] The 'probabilities' refer to the proportion of individuals in each category during September 2000 that made the transition to each respective category in February 2001.[19] For example, of those out-of-the-labour force adults in households receiving a social pension in September 2004, 9 per cent had found employment by March 2005. This 9 per cent figure is interpreted as the simple probability that an out-of-the-labour-force adult in September 2004 living in a household that receives a social pension would find a job and be employed in March 2005. The other entries in the table can be similarly interpreted. For example, of those out-of-the-labour force adults in households that did not receive a social pension in

Table 6.2   Impact of the child support grant on labour force participation

Corrected data	Household receives child support grant	Household does not receive child support grant	Improvement associated with child support grant
Probability that a poor working age adult will:			
Find employment in 2005	15	13	2
Be actively looking for work in 2005	20	17	3
Not participate in the labour force in 2005	65	70	5

Note: Sample includes working age adults (older than 16) in households in the lowest income quintile but with no working individuals in September 2004.
Source: Statistics South Africa Labour Force Surveys and EPRI calculations.

September 2004, only 7 per cent had found employment by March 2005. This 7 per cent probability is lower than that associated with a similar individual in a household receiving a social pension. In this sense, the probability that an out-of-the-labour-force adult finds employment over the time period is greater if the person lives in a household receiving a social pension. Likewise, the probability of beginning to actively look for work is greater if the person lives in a household receiving a social pension.

In households that received the social pension, 9 per cent of adults were employed in March 2005 and another 15 per cent were actively looking for work. In households that did not receive the pension, only 7 per cent were employed and another 13 per cent were actively looking for work. Receipt of the social pension was associated with a 2 per cent higher probability of finding employment and a 2 per cent higher probability of actively looking for work. Alternatively, receipt of the social pension was associated with a 4 per cent lower probability of not participating in the labour force.

The Child Support Grant demonstrates a similar effect. Working age adults that were not participating in the labour force – particularly women – in poor households that receive a Child Support Grant are more likely to look for work and more likely to find employment than comparable adults in households that do not receive it. The matched Labour Force Survey similarly provides a dynamic picture of how labour force participation changes for households receiving and not receiving the child support grant.

Tables 6.2 and 6.3 compare the changes in labour market participation for working age adults and working age women in households with no employed individuals in September 2004. The rows follow the format of Table 6.1, with the first row showing the proportion of adults who were employed in March 2005, broken down by status in terms of household receipt of the Child

Table 6.3 Impact of the child support grant on female labour force participation (corrected data)

Corrected data	Household receives social pension in 2004 (%)	Household does not receive social pension in 2004 (%)	Improvement associated with social pension (%)
Probability that a poor working age adult will:			
Find employment in 2005	15	12	3
Be actively looking for work in 2005	20	14	6
Not participate in the labour force in 2005	65	74	9

Note: Sample includes working age adults (older than 16) in households in the lowest income quintile with older people but with no working individuals in September 2004.
Source: Statistics South Africa Labour Force Surveys and EPRI calculations.

Support Grant. The second row shows the proportion of adults who were actively looking for work but not employed, while the third row shows the proportion of adults who were not participating in the labour force.

In households that received the Child Support Grant, 15 per cent of adults were employed in March 2005 and another 20 per cent were actively looking for work. In households that did not receive the Child Support Grant, only 13 per cent were employed and another 17 per cent were actively looking for work. Receipt of the social pension was associated with a 2 per cent higher probability of finding employment and a 3 per cent higher probability of actively looking for work. Alternatively, receipt of the Child Support Grant was associated with a 5 per cent lower probability of not participating in the labour force.

The effects are even stronger for women, as documented in Table 6.3. In households that received the Child Support Grant, 15 per cent of adults were employed in March 2005 and another 20 per cent were actively looking for work – the same proportions as for all adults. In households that did not receive the Child Support Grant, only 12 per cent were employed and another 14 per cent were actively looking for work. Receipt of the social pension was associated with a 3 per cent higher probability of finding employment and a 6 per cent higher probability of actively looking for work. Alternatively, receipt of the Child Support Grant was associated with a 9 per cent lower probability of not participating in the labour force.

While the magnitudes of these effects are relatively small, it is important to emphasize that social transfers are not intended as employment generating schemes. Their major impact is social protection – with support of labour market participation an ancillary outcome. Nevertheless, this evidence contradicts the misplaced notion that social grants create dependency. On the contrary, social grants support households to participate more actively and successfully in the labour market, assisting workers to break the poverty trap. A more detailed policy discussion and rigorous treatment of the methodology is provided in Samson and Williams (2007) and Williams (2007), including the econometric models that demonstrate the positive and significant impact of social grant receipt on labour force participation using pooled cross-sectional analysis.

The macroeconomic and fiscal effects

Social transfers affect the macroeconomy through two distinct sets of transmission mechanisms. First, they affect the composition of spending – by transferring spending power from upper income groups to the poor. Depending on the labour-intensity and import content of the spending of different income incomes, the redistributive effect of social transfers may reduce imports and increase the demand for labour, supporting job creation. Within a national economy, the increased spending power in remote rural areas holds the potential to revitalize local economies.

Analysis of EPRI's sectoral macro-simulation model demonstrates the positive macroeconomic impact of social transfers. Capacity utilization is low by historical standards, and a significant proportion of excess capacity is attributable to insufficient demand. This suggests that the increase in demand from redistributive transfers is unlikely to have a significant inflationary impact. In addition, the demand of low-income groups is concentrated on sectors in which South Africa produces most of the demanded goods domestically, and in a relatively labour-intensive manner. This suggests that the composition effects of social transfers are likely to improve the trade balance and increase the demand for labour.

For example, the poor spend relatively more of their income on food compared to upper income households (Figure 6.4). South Africa produces domestically most of its food consumption requirements, and the technology is relatively labour-intensive compared to manufactured goods.

Upper income households, on the other hand, spend more on transportation (Figure 6.5), often on automobiles that are imported or include a very high import content. Automobile production in South Africa is relatively capital-intensive compared to food production.

Social transfers shift spending power from upper to lower income households – the composition of spending tends to shift, for example, from automobiles to food grains. On average across all sectors, the composition of spending tends to shift from imports to domestic goods, from capital-intensive to labour-intensive. In general, these effects in any specific country will depend on how different income groups spend.

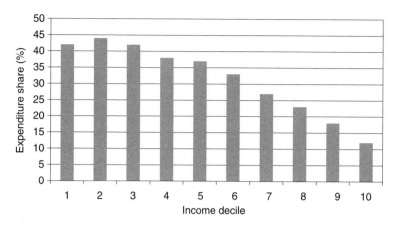

Figure 6.4   Spending on food by income group in South Africa
Source: Statistics South Africa I&E 2000 Survey and EPRI calculations.

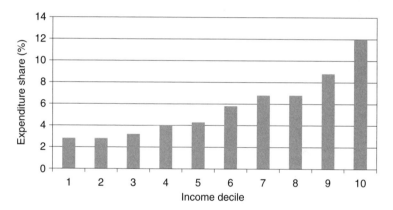

Figure 6.5   Spending on transportation by income group in South Africa
Source: Statistics South Africa I&E 2000 Survey and EPRI calculations.

The second major type of macroeconomic effect stems from investment, which depends on the change in the risk-adjusted return on capital as affected by reduced inequality, better education and improved social stability. The increase in take-up of social grants in South Africa over the past five years has significantly reduced South Africa's Gini coefficient as the income differentials across the income distribution have fallen. The increasingly progressive tax structure that has financed social grants has reinforced the reduction in the Gini coefficient. Using the data provided in the 2000 Income and Expenditure Survey, this study developed a simulation which determined how the Gini coefficient would change under a scenario of full take-up of State Old

Age Pensions, Disability Grants and Child Support Grant. It shows the distribution of household income before full take-up and after the increased take-up. The simulation quantifies a reduction in the Gini coefficient of 3 percentage points, from 63 per cent to 60 per cent, suggesting a shifting up of the Lorenz curve where the straight 45-degree line represents the distribution of income in a perfectly equal society. The curve below this line represents the income distribution before full take-up and the curve above represents the distribution after the increased take-up. The shifting up of the Lorenz curve represents the significant improvement in income distribution resulting from South Africa's social security system.

Social transfers must be financed – either from the government's budget and/or with donor support. In some cases the programmes can cost up to 3 per cent on national income or more. The affordability of social transfers depends in part on their economic impact. Growth expands the country's resources – and usually the revenue available to the government.

Social transfers also conserve fiscal resources in important ways. The infant whose nutrition was funded by a social transfer will grow into a school-age child better able to learn and more likely to succeed in school. Fewer fiscal resources will be wasted on children who have to repeat grades they otherwise would have passed. The child will grow into an adult more likely to find work – and pay taxes. The worker will grow older with a lower chance of contracting a chronic debilitating disease, like diabetes which is a severe problem in South Africa, and so be less likely to unnecessarily burden the public health care system.

Social transfers can support a virtuous circle of growth, greater affordability and sustainability. Social grants represent a transfer of resources to the poor with the direct impact of reducing poverty. Social grants also create a long-term developmental impact by improving nutrition, health, education, labour productivity and social stability. The long-term impact of social grants is cumulative: an investment this year in social grants generates benefits over a multi-year horizon. As a result, social grant transfers build a 'social grant capital stock' that generates real returns – in terms of economic growth, greater tax capacity and fiscal savings – over the long term.

Evidence from other African countries

Much of the evidence discussed in this chapter focused on South Africa's system of social grants. The country's social transfers are the largest in Africa, with take-up rates and coverage that surpass what is encountered in any other developing country. In addition, academic experts have demonstrated a strong interest in South Africa's experience, providing a more comprehensive evidence base than that for any other African country. Other African countries have programmes that offer illuminating lessons for those countries that have yet to adopt social transfer programmes.

Evidence of successful African experiences is important in the context of the African Union's more recent commitments at Livingstone, as well as other long-standing commitments. The African Union's 'Livingstone Declaration' called for African governments to develop costed plans for social transfer programmes that would tackle poverty and provide better national systems of social protection (African Union, 2006). The Organization of African Unity's 'African Charter on the Rights and Welfare of the Child' committed member States to 'ensure, to the maximum extent possible, the survival, protection and development of the child' (1990: 3). Both Lesotho's and Namibia's social transfer programmes provide important case studies of how to meet these obligations.

Evidence from Lesotho

The old age pension represents the most significant social protection programme in Lesotho.[20] Lesotho is one of six African countries and one of only two low-income countries to implement a non-contributory old age pension. The pension is similar to those in Botswana, Namibia and South Africa. Pension eligibility starts at age 70, which is higher than in the other Southern African countries that provide a social grant for older people. In these other countries a social pension is paid from age 60 or 65.[21] Out of a population of around 2 million resident Lesotho citizens[22] about 75,000 are registered to receive the pension.

The level of the pension, initially set at M150, was then slightly above the official national poverty line of M148 estimated for Lesotho in late 2004. Since on average women live longer than men, more women (currently 60 per cent of all pensioners) receive the pension than men.[23] Unlike the social grant paid to older people in South Africa, Lesotho's social pension is not means-tested, although about 5,000 older people are excluded because they already receive a retirement pension paid from the government's Consolidated Fund.

The objective of the old age pension is to relieve the poverty of older people in Lesotho. The debate on the Pensions Bill, and evidence that was gathered for the Poverty Reduction Strategy Paper and for the Vision 2020 strategy recognized that older people are more likely to be financially vulnerable. They also experience declining support from the non-formal social protection networks that have historically tackled poverty.

Although the pension is intended specifically for older people, in practice it often supports the household as a whole. Evidence from the Lesotho Pension Impact Study (LPIS) shows that the typical household containing a pension recipient has an average of four other 'equivalent adults', where children under 16 are counted as half an adult. This means that the M150 translates into an increase in the income of each 'equivalent adult' of only M30. However, this also implies that there are nearly 400,000 direct and indirect beneficiaries from the social pension – almost 20 per cent of the population in Lesotho.

This high benefit dilution does affect the pension's ability to tackle poverty. Nevertheless, even the small amounts made available through the old age pension are beneficial in light of the extreme poverty found in Lesotho. For instance, M30 per adult can make an important contribution to meeting food requirements. On average 61 per cent of the pension is used to supplement spending on food, addressing one of the key characteristics of poverty in Lesotho.

In addition to increasing food consumption, the old age pension has provided older people with more income to spend on health services. Half of the respondents in the LPIS pilot survey said that they were spending more on health services since the implementation of the pension. Spending was mainly on hospital and clinic visits including transportation costs and consultation fees, as well as medicines. Furthermore, pensioners also use some of their pension for contributions towards burial societies and funeral costs in order to take this financial pressure off their relatives.

Sixty per cent of the pensioners covered in the LPIS were in households containing young people attending school or college. Responses show that a significant number of these dependent children have been orphaned by HIV/AIDS. Pension money was being used to increase the support given to these children. Pensioners were buying uniforms, books and stationery. Assuming the respondents in the LPIS survey are representative of pensioners throughout Lesotho, the social pension supports approximately 10,000 school children nationally.

Lesotho's introduction of an old age pension demonstrates that being a poor country does not prevent a nation from implementing a social transfer programme on a significant scale at the national level. Lesotho's experience sends a very strong message about the importance of political will if social protection is to have a widespread impact on the population. One of the most striking features of the old age pension is that it is entirely funded and executed using domestic financial and technical resources.

Lesotho's experience suggests that an old age pension is a good starting point for poor countries wanting to introduce a national social transfer programme. Targeting older people is an effective way of reaching a large number of poor people. The Lesotho experience shows that supporting important vulnerable groups does not require them to be targeted directly by a specific social transfer programme. The social pension addresses poverty by improving nutrition and reducing vulnerability to hunger, supplementing household income in light of falling remittances and meeting the needs of orphans and vulnerable children.

Experience from Namibia

Namibia divides the management of its social transfer programmes between the Ministry of Labour and Social Welfare (MLSW), which administers the old age pension and the disability grant, and the Ministry of Gender and

Child Welfare (MGCW), which oversees all child-related grants.[24] The two ministries have their own administrative and cash payment systems, leading to duplicative bureaucracies which reduce the cost efficiency otherwise enjoyed through economies of scale and other synergies (Morgan, 1991).

Since democratic elections in 1990, the Namibian government has managed to effectively transform the old-age pension, turning it into a widespread and useful tool in reducing poverty for older people and other vulnerable groups. In 1990/91, some regions still had take-up rates as low as 33 per cent, due in large part to the biases of the apartheid-era administration (Morgan, 1991). Unlike in South Africa, where the pensions were equalized at the existing 'white' levels, Namibia set the democratized benefit levels equal to the lowest amount on the scale, citing fiscal and financial constraints.

Today, the unconditional old age pension is by far the most significant social transfer in Namibia. In February 2005 there were 115,824 recipients out of a total number of 128,123 of people over the age of 60, implying a take-up rate of 89 per cent (Ministry of Health and Social Services, 2005). In addition to the social pension, Namibia has a number of other grants that were introduced under South African rule and maintained after independence. However, unlike in South Africa, no major reform to the social protection system has taken place to date,[25] and the levels of the grant have not been increased substantially.

Although Namibia has experienced above-average economic growth in the post-independence era, poverty and inequality continue to affect the majority of Namibians. Social transfer programmes have had some impact on the living standards of the poorest and most vulnerable households. However, relative to other middle-income countries in the region, Namibia spends significantly less on social transfers. There may be room to increase the value of these transfers in a fiscally sustainable manner. This is likely to lead to further reductions in poverty and inequality.

Conclusions

Poverty has many layers, and social transfers tackle them in a comprehensive manner. For countries in Africa, social transfers have demonstrated considerable success in supporting children's health, education and nutrition, helping to break the cycle of inter-generational transmission of disadvantage. In the country studies here they are the most effective government programme for reducing poverty. They support broad household development, and improve labour market participation.

It can be concluded from the evidence analysed here that for most developing countries, more effective social protection is likely to promote economic growth and development. Social transfers significantly reduce inequality – supporting social stability and fostering investment and economic growth. Well-designed social transfers do not automatically create dependency – they can break dependency traps, particularly by nurturing productive high-return risk-taking. At a macro-level they can help restructure the economy to support job creation and economic growth. Social transfers also create fiscal effects that support long-term affordability and economic sustainability.

Notes

1. This adapts DFID's (2005a: 6) and Devereux's (Save the Children et al., 2005: 3) definitions of social transfers and incorporates McCord's (2005: 5) definition of public works programmes.
2. Lustig and McLeod (1997: 63). See also Morley (1992) and de Janvry and Sadoulet (1996).
3. The poverty rates are taken from the United States Census Bureau database, accessed 15 April 2007, available at http://www.census.gov/hhes/www/poverty/histpov/hstpov2.html or from the author. Schmitt and Zipperer (2007) construct the labour union measures using data from the United States National Labor Relations Board (NLRB). Data for the 1970s reflect the time period 1974–9 due to data availability. Data for the 2000s reflect the time period 2000–5 for the same reason.
4. Calculations based on data in Schmitt and Zipperer (2007), cross-tabulated by presidential terms in the United States.
5. Calculations based on United States Census Bureau data, cross-tabulated by presidential terms in the United States.
6. See DFID (2006) for a further discussion.
7. Stefan Dercon (2006), a presentation to the Department of International Development, March.
8. The real cost of not working includes not having any labour income. By choosing not to work, an individual gives up the opportunity to earn labour income (an opportunity cost). Social grants provide income that help to offset this cost. This 'opportunity cost' framework ignores the South African reality that many of those without work have no opportunity to choose employment.
9. This section summarizes results from labour market impact studies by the Economic Policy Research Institute. For more information, see Samson (2002), Samson et al. (2001, 2002, 2003, 2004, 2005) and Samson and Williams (2007). Other studies with corroborating evidence include Posel et al. (2006) and Keswell (2005).
10. Linking the household data from the September 2000 LFS to that of the 2000 IES provides a basis for formalizing this concept of 'earning power', by regressing specifications of household income (including linear and log forms, and excluding social grants) against explanatory variables consisting of household characteristics. These models then can predict an income variable that controls for the simultaneity bias.
11. The cross-sectional model employed a probit regression to predict an individual's probability of participation in the broad labour force. The use of the probit model is preferred to ordinary least squares because the dependent variables are dichotomous, not continuous variables: a given individual either participates in the narrow labour force by meeting the qualifications for that status or does not meet those qualifications and is therefore considered not participating in the narrow labour force. The probit model guarantees that the probabilities it estimates are between zero and one, which are the boundaries for a well-defined probability

measure. In the second stage of the cross-sectional model, the analysis predicts an individual's probability of participation in the narrow labour force, given his or her participation in the broad labour force, using a maximum-likelihood probit estimation with sample selection correction (Heckman, 1979; Van de Ven and Van Pragg, 1981). Finally, using the same MLE probit method, the model predicts an individual's probability of employment, given participation in the narrow labour force.

12. In each step, excluding the first, the study uses the same MLE probit with sample selection used in the individual cross-sectional framework, including dummies for receipt of pension and receipt of remittance income as explanatory variables, and (unlike Klasen and Woolard, 2005) also controlling for the household's pension age eligibility in the regression.

13. The study constructs representative households for each primary sampling unit (PSUs), each comprising an average of 10 households, and creates variables for each PSU's demographic, employment, and social grant receipt characteristics in a given year. Among these variables are the percentage of households in the PSU that received each social grant, the average size of a household, the average number of females per household, and the average number of children within each household. For employment the variables include the percentage of people of working age, the percentage not attending an educational institution, the share of the household in each employment category (employed, in the narrow labour force, in the broad labour force) for each PSU in each year. The study analyses the share of people of working age, non-school population in the broad labour force ('share in the broad labour force'), the share of people in the broad labour force who are also in the narrow labour force ('share of broad in narrow'), and the share of the narrow labour force that is employed ('share of narrow employed'). This has the advantage of being able to determine at what stage social grants have an effect on individuals.

14. Provincial binary (dummy) variables and a variable to capture the rural effect were also included.

15. Ordinary least squares or two-stage least squares.

16. The results from the uncorrected data are not materially different. After September 2004 Statistics South Africa ceased to track social grant status in its Labour Force Survey.

17. The matching methodology utilized for the analysis in this chapter corrects a commonly cited problem with South Africa's Labour Force Survey, in which individual households are not properly linkable with the identifiers reported by Statistics South Africa. The results reported, however, are not sensitive to the specific approach taken to match the records. While there are small differences between these figures and those resulting from the uncorrected data, the magnitudes of the associated improvements are virtually the same with either approach.

18. For example, see Agüero et al. (2006).

19. Baulch and McCulloch (1998) provide a clear explanation of the relationship between transition matrices and probabilities (in the context of poverty): 'A poverty transition matrix shows the number of households in and out of poverty in a particular period, broken down by their poverty status in a previous period. Thus it is easy to see the number of households who have been poor or non-poor in both periods along with the number who have escaped poverty and those who have entered poverty. This approach has been used in a number of studies in both industrialized and developing countries. From any poverty

transition matrix it is straightforward to calculate simple probabilities of entering and exiting poverty between the two periods. For example the simple probability of exiting poverty is simply the number of households exiting poverty divided by the number of households who were poor in the previous period.' Labour market transition matrices work exactly the same way – except that the states are non-participation in the labour market, unemployment and employment rather than 'poor' and 'non-poor'.

20. For more information on the social pension in Lesotho, see Samson et al. (2007) and Croome (2006).
21. For more discussion on this point, see International Labour Organization (2001a).
22. This figure cannot be given exactly because some births and deaths in Lesotho are still not officially registered. Population estimates are extrapolated from census data. The results from the census in April 2006 are not yet available, but it appears that the population may have fallen to below 2 million due to the increased deaths from the high level of HIV and AIDS infection in recent years. Lesotho has the fourth highest level of infection in the world.
23. For more information on the Lesotho Pensions Impact Study (LPIS) pilot survey, see Croome (2006).
24. For more details see Samson (2007) and Haarmann and Haarmann (2007).
25. In South Africa, the maintenance grant was replaced by the Child Support Grant.

7
Investment in Social Security: a Possible UN Model for Child Benefit?

Peter Townsend

We live in a world where children are accorded priority emotionally and politically. Five of the eight Millennium Development Goals (MDGs) of the UN are directed at children: one is to eradicate extreme poverty and hunger, another to drastically reduce under-five mortality, a third to reverse the spread of HIV/AIDS, malaria and other diseases, and the fourth and fifth to ensure full and gender-equal schooling (UN, 2000 and see the Appendix Tables A7.1 and A7.2). Yet international leaders have conceded that declared progress is too slow to meet the goals by 2015.

The policies offered to protect children's welfare have been ineffective (UNICEF, 2004, 2005) – most are over-generalized and indirect or selectively helpful only to very small numbers. Children's social security is not defined precisely but often wrapped up in the 'family' or 'household' benefits to which their parents may or may not be entitled. The scale of their rights to income in developing countries has still to be defined, categorized for different age-groups in different locations, and endorsed by representative government.

Previous chapters have shown the viability and affordability of social security in national economies, and illustrated promising initiatives in middle- and low-income countries to accelerate the growth of social security systems. This chapter aims to take three steps further: (1) to focus on children, who have greater risk of being in poverty than adults and no opportunity to contribute to their own social security; (2) to pin down the nature and causes of child poverty to improve policy-effectiveness; and (3) to demonstrate that international funds have to be found, and can be found quickly, to match national resources to meet child poverty directly. I will discuss:

- the consequences of poverty and multiple deprivation for child survival and health;
- child rights as the appropriate framework for measurement, analysis and the construction of policy;

- the need to reveal the extent of international responsibility for funding anti-poverty strategies;
- the recent disappointing history of international finance; and, as the most practical alternative,
- the use of a currency transfer tax to build up a UN Investment Fund for child benefit.

The consequences of child poverty and multiple deprivation

A special investigation for UNICEF found that 56 per cent of children in developing countries – 1.2 billion – experienced one or more forms of severe deprivation, over half of them (674 million) at least two forms of severe multiple deprivation like total absence of toilet facilities, lack of nearby clean water, malnutrition and extreme overcrowding and poor shelter (Gordon et al., 2003; UNICEF, 2005). This is more potent evidence of child poverty than the (very crude, and unreliable) estimates by the World Bank of the numbers of children in households with less than US$1 per capita per day.[1] Over 10 million children in developing countries die each year, mainly from preventable causes, including malnutrition, pneumonia, diarrhoea, measles and malaria. Poverty, whether measured by household income or multiple material and social deprivation, and early child mortality, are intertwined. The World Health Organization (WHO) found that as many as seven out of every ten childhood deaths can be attributed to these five causes or their combination. Three in every four children seen by health services are suffering from at least one of these conditions. Many of these deaths could be prevented using readily available medical technologies at comparatively little cost and many more by providing resources for shelter, clean water, sanitary facilities, food and fuel. Thus, the free issue of mosquito nets, as illustrated in one initiative in different areas of Kenya (Rice, 2007), can dramatically reduce rates of malaria among children. Again, public provision of shelter, food and sanitary facilities and basic income as well as access to services for those widowed or orphaned by HIV/AIDS can save many from miserable existence and early painful death (Akwanalo Mate, 2006). The number of children in sub-Saharan Africa orphaned by HIV/AIDS is expected to rise to 15.7 million, or a quarter of all children, by 2010 (UNICEF, 2007: 42). Globally, 1,800 children are newly infected every day by HIV/AIDS (UNICEF, 2005: 16).

The accumulating studies of enforced child deprivation are calling sharp attention to mass violations of child rights that for many children maintain, and for some increase, the risks of survival (Pemberton et al., 2007). For health professionals this has led recently to fuller acknowledgement of the positive relationship between human rights and health (Gruskin et al., 2007; R. MacDonald, 2007; T. H. MacDonald, 2007; Pemberton et al., 2005; Singh et al., 2007).

The WHO and other international agencies have been unable until now to distinguish rates of child mortality and malnutrition in richer and poorer

Table 7.1   Child mortality and poor health conditions, three regions (%)

Indicator	India	Sub-Saharan Africa (25 countries)	Latin America (8 countries)
Under-5s stunted for age			
– poorest 20%	58	42	36
– richest 20%	27	24	4
Mortality under-5 years			
– poorest 20%	14	16	9
– richest 20%	5	10	4
1-yr-olds not immunized against measles			
– poorest 20%	72	46	34
– richest 20%	19	22	16

Source: WHO (2007).

households. The use in representative country surveys of questions about assets owned by households has led to a breakthrough.[2] In Table 7.1 I have drawn from the WHO's *World Health Statistics 2007*, in which it has proved possible for the first time to measure ownership of assets, albeit crudely, to compare children in the poorest 20 per cent with the richest 20 per cent of households in the country. In countries where there is mass poverty it should be noted that asset impoverishment may still apply to some among the richest 20 per cent. Table 7.1 shows that 58 per cent of under-fives in the poorest 20 per cent of households in India, compared with 42 per cent in sub-Saharan Africa and 36 per cent in Latin America, are physically stunted for their age, compared with 27 per cent, 23 per cent and 4 per cent, respectively, in the richest 20 per cent of households. Mortality rates of under-fives in the poorest households in these three regions are also disproportionately high, being 14 per cent, 16 per cent and 9 per cent respectively. And, as another indicator, 72 per cent, 46 per cent and 34 per cent of one-year-olds in the poorest households in these three regions have been found not to have been immunized against measles.

Data for individual countries in the three regions are to be found in the Appendix to this chapter. The highest percentages of children found to be stunted in sub-Saharan Africa (50 per cent or more) were in Rwanda, Malawi, Chad, Zambia and Madagascar. The highest percentage in Latin America was 65 in Guatemala. In India this percentage must have been matched or exceeded in some deprived areas.

Using child rights to construct policies to defeat child poverty

Using human rights as a methodology to pin down major patterns of development and assess policy is of growing importance. For the first time *multiple* deprivation as reflected in numerous statements in a number of the human rights treaties can be expressed in precise statistical and empirical terms – using random but coordinated national surveys, namely the Demographic Health Surveys (DHS) and the Multiple Indicator Cluster Surveys (MICS) which have been and are being conducted in countries covering more than 85 per cent of the developing country populations. Beginning in the last decade a practicable method of constructing a measure of the economic and social conditions of small and large populations, so that they can be compared, has evolved. For example, during 2002–8 one research team based at the University of Bristol has been able to produce the first reliable global estimates for children, young people and all adults (Gordon et al., 2003; Gordon et al., 2009; UN, 2009).

The methodology draws on the analytical frameworks of the human rights treaties. Human rights have come to play a central part in discussions about economic and social development, and have been ratified by the great majority of governments in the world. There are rights to income and to social security enshrined in Articles 22 and 25 of the Universal Declaration of Human Rights; 9 and 11 of the International Covenant on Economic, Social and Cultural Rights; and 26 and 27 of the Convention on the Rights of the Child. But in the Convention on the Rights of the Child there are also elaborate injunctions to protect children from malnutrition, maltreatment, neglect, abuse and exploitation and ensure they are not deprived of access to clean water, sanitary facilities, shelter, health care services, education and information: governments are enjoined to 'recognize the right of every child to a standard of living adequate for the child's physical, mental, spiritual, moral and social development' (Article 27 and also see Articles 13, 17, 19, 20, 23, 24, 26, 28, 31, 32, 34, 37 and 39).

The statements, ratified by nearly all of the 191 nation-states in the world, allow single but also multiple measures or indicators of the denial or fulfilment of the specified rights to be devised and tracked. Social science therefore has a considerable role to play in coordinating the collection and analysis of such evidence and evaluating policy impact.

There are two particular arguments in favour of using this methodology in relation to poverty and social security. First, all the human rights treaties allow multiple indicators of violations of those rights to be constructed. The UNCRC, for example, does not contain an explicit human right to freedom from poverty. However, statements about the conditions of material and social deprivation underlying poverty and characterizing ill health, as specified above, occur in a number of different articles of the CRC, and have become the subject of national and international survey investigation. The rights are inter-related, and therefore deliberate action to fulfil a particular right is relevant to the realization of other rights. So the progressive realization of human rights will depend on the prior clustering of rights. Policies designed to implement a particular right have to be tested in relation to the outcomes for other rights. This is the source of scientific confirmation of the problem to be addressed, and of greater public confidence in policies designed to deliver human rights.

Second, human conditions are rarely one thing or the other – either good or bad. For example, there is under-nourishment but also extreme malnutrition. There is poverty but also extreme poverty. Empirical inquiry can trace a continuum from one extreme to the other, and thresholds of severity of conditions experienced by humans found. The advantage of empirical surveys of population conditions is that moderate needs can be distinguished from severe or extreme needs and doubts about over-generalized evidence removed. Another advantage is that by measuring severity as well as multiplicity of condition cause can be more exactly unravelled and priorities for remedial policy demonstrated. There is a gradient or continuum ranging from complete fulfilment to extreme violation of rights – for example on the continuum ranging from 'good health' to 'poor health/death' (see Gordon et al., 2003: 7–8). Courts make judgments in individual cases about this gradient to establish the correct threshold at which rights have been either violated or fulfilled. Correspondingly, scientists and policy-analysts can demonstrate the point on the gradient at which there are severe or extreme violations, so that grey areas of the interpretation of mild or moderate violation can be set aside, and governments and international agencies persuaded that there are grounds for institutional action.

The language of rights therefore changes the analysis of world conditions and the discussion of responsible policies. It shifts the focus of debate from the personal failures of the 'poor' to the failures to resolve poverty of macro-economic structures and policies of nation-states and international bodies (agencies such as the WTO, World Bank, IMF and UN, but also the most powerful trans-national corporations (TNCs) and alliances of groups of governments). Child poverty cannot then be considered as a parental problem or a local community problem but a 'violation of rights' that nation-states, and international agencies, groups of governments and TNCs have a legal and institutional obligation to remedy (Chinkin, 2001). And violations of the rights of children to health, including problems like malaria and HIV/AIDS, would more easily be seen to be socio-structural problems and not only medical or health care problems.

Two 2007 examples may be given. The free issue of mosquito nets to selected populations (as in Kenya) can dramatically reduce rates of malaria among children (Rice, 2007). The problem is the scale of the issue – so that the children's needs are covered universally – rather than a small-scale scheme piloted by NGOs or governments in a few selected areas. Second, public provision of shelter, food and sanitary facilities and basic income as well as access to services for those widowed or orphaned by HIV/AIDS can save many from miserable existence and early painful death. This includes many among the nearly 16 million children orphaned in sub-Saharan Africa by

HIV/AIDS. Resources have to be mobilized for population care and especially material resources that directly reach children (Akwanalo Mate, 2006). Again, the problem is to ensure universal coverage so that children in extreme need do not slip through grudgingly devised nets.

International responsibility for funding

Trans-national corporations

Who is responsible for ensuring these policies are universal? The argument developed here is that trans-national corporations and the international agencies can work wonders by committing a tiny percentage of their growing resources to social security in the low-income countries, and also by moving towards acceptance of minimum standards of monthly or weekly income on the part of wage-earners and those not in paid employment who are entitled to social security.

Both the OECD and ILO have issued guidelines on 'corporate social responsibility' (ILO, 2001c; OECD, 2001a). Both organizations have sought to fill a growing gap left upon the termination by the UN in the early 1990s of substantial monitoring and reporting of the trends in TNC practices. In 2003 the UN produced draft norms on the responsibilities of TNCs and other business enterprises with regard to human rights. It may be the first document to place human rights at the core of its mandate (UN, 2003; Vagts, 2003: 795; and see De Schutter, 2006) but it remains a generalized draft. The guidelines issued by the OECD and ILO are not yet attracting vigorous debate. The desirability of universal rules of practice for TNCs and international agencies is missing from much current commentary and analysis.

The growing bargaining power of the TNCs in headquarter locations in the rich countries is creating social and economic disequilibrium. This 'institutional hierarchy of power' has to be taken seriously. Recent failures of privatization schemes, and of major trans-national corporations such as Enron, WorldCom, ImClone, Credit Suisse First Boston, Hollinger International, Adelphi Communications, Martha Stewart Living Omnimedia and parts of the financial services industry, provide lessons that have to be learned and acted upon internationally to restore structural stability. Recurring reports of instances of corporate corruption have paved the way for calls for collective approaches to be made through law and regulation (for example Hertz, 2001; Hines, 2001; Hudson, 1996; Korten, 1996; Kozul-Wright and Rowthorn, 1998; Lang and Hines, 1993; Madeley, 1999; Scott et al., 1985; Sklair, 2001; Watkins, 2002) that go a lot further than the minimal and highly variable expressions so far of the unenforceable appeals for the observance of 'corporate social responsibility' – as contained in the OECD and ILO guidelines or in the UN's Corporate Citizenship Initiative, 'the Global Compact', launched in June 2000.

Low-income countries are heavily dependent on trade with corporations with far larger resources than they possess. Through subsidiaries and sub-contractors controlled from far away they are restricted in the employment that can be found, the wages that can be charged, the taxes that can be raised and the conditions of life that have to be protected for national populations. The poorest countries have too few resources to make swift headway in reducing poverty and creating real opportunities for enterprise on behalf of the great majority of their populations (see for example Watkins, 2002). The hierarchy of power is illustrated by elaborate stratification of wages, conditions of work and access to social security from the Executive Boards of TNCs in the United States, Japan, Germany and the United Kingdom through to the 70 or 100 countries in which they operate. There has been a huge upsurge in trans-national resources without corresponding modernization of company law to adapt to the new social conditions and responsibilities for economic and social development and impose particular obligations on corporations.

Through its Tripartitite Declaration of Principles concerning Multinational Enterprises and Social Policy, first adopted in 1977, the ILO has sought to encourage governments to reinforce corporate responsibility to pave the way for more specific potentially binding international standards, turning codes of conduct into the seed of customary rules of international law (ILO, 2001c). The problem is that as they stand these guidelines have no teeth and are not routinely publicized and discussed. Observance is voluntary and not dependent on national or international sanctions or law. Some corporations and companies are concerned about their image and good name, and are prepared to moderate their practices, and profits, in consideration of the rights of their workers. Others take advantage of non-existent or inconsistent law.

A starting point might be an agreement about children. One serious and continuing embarrassment for many TNCs are charges that children are involved in extreme forms of labour by sub-contractors and subsidiaries in locations remote from TNC headquarters (ILO, 2005). There is evidence of children as young as 7 who are involved in producing paving stones, foot-balls, clothing and carpets, operating with dangerous pesticides and other chemicals, digging trenches, picking cotton and working in mines – often for 10 or more hours a day. A common corporation plea is that illegal practices, or violations of child rights, along the production line were unintended and unknown, and abhorrence of such practices by headquarters would now be passed down the chain of command. The problem is that the conditions of payment and the standards expected of the finished product are imposed. These inevitably affect incentives and lead to extreme practices. Accountability for such practices could be ensured by legal and other means – particularly through monitored reports and statistics for which headquarter organizations must be held routinely responsible (in the same way as nation-states) and that would have to be submitted for public scrutiny. Agreement reached by the UN and TNCs about their accountability for severe deprivation among children engaged in forms of bonded labour connected with their trade represents one useful future development.

Perhaps the key element in taking such a step would be to concentrate on company responsibility for social security. In the late nineteenth century and throughout the twentieth century employers came to accept provision of a 'social wage' as a condition of making profit. Laws were enacted to provide for temporary and long-term unemployment, and contributions by employers for illness and disability and other dependencies of family members, especially children, were expected. There were insurance payments for specific contingencies and taxes to meet shifts in economic conditions that could not be predicted. The social wage was one of the rules of economic operation that became widely accepted. New global conditions in the twenty-first century have transformed that responsibility and a new legal and social responsibility for impoverished conditions in low-income countries has to be accepted throughout the hierarchy of power exerted by headquarters corporations. The income rights of children could lie at the core of discussions to make globalization work socially.

Employers who were expected or compelled in the OECD countries at early stages of the industrial revolution to make substantial contributions to social protection were national rather than trans-national employers. People with hard-earned professional skills built on minimum standards of living and universal access to public social services were not at that time tempted overseas from national service or careers in the national economy, and neither were they given extensive opportunities to leave chosen countries of domicile. Cross-border social security is one burning question for the twenty-first century, but only one example of the urgent need to develop basic universal social security.

Children have been placed at the centre of this analysis. Trans-national employers can add, or be obliged to add, 1 or 2 per cent of wage costs in different countries for a child benefit to help banish malnutrition, poverty and premature child death, and also encourage more schooling. At the same time, extreme forms of child labour would become less necessary as well as made illegal. Standard contributions towards social insurance for sickness, disability, bereavement and ageing, or represented in new taxes, could follow. The question of social protection or social security in the national interest has become one of social protection in the *international* interest.

International agencies

What cannot be disregarded in this discussion of children's needs is international funding. The responsibility of the UN and other agencies in funding social security, especially child benefit, requires urgent review. What conclusions can be drawn from present international funding, and how much

---

Box 7.1 The current orthodox funding strategy for low-income countries

The strategy has been threefold:

- Broad-based economic growth
- Debt relief
- Overseas aid

Drawing from evidence of the trends over 30 years, the outcome of this strategy can be judged unsuccessful for several reasons:

- 'Trickle-up' growth
- Conditionality policies for loans
- Cost-recovery policies in basic social services
- Cuts in public expenditure
- Lack of social security systems
- Excessive privatization
- Unregulated globalization and unequal terms of trade
- Enhancement of the power of the global 'triumvirate' (G8, TNCs and IFAs)

---

of that funding actually reaches children in extreme poverty? When questions are asked about global, as distinct from national, anti-poverty measures, international agencies stress the importance of three sources of aid – economic growth, debt relief and overseas aid. Box 7.1 summarizes these sources and criticisms of these sources of aid remain largely unanswered. Added lately as a fourth element of international anti-poverty strategy has been fairer trade, through reform of the WTO. In practice all four measures are principally dependent on the big economic powers, including TNCs, in the modern global economy. In working out what this means for children we need to understand that the four types of international funding are relatively indiscriminate and unpredictable in their distributional effect upon populations. Success depends on whether a sufficient share of additional cash income and income in kind from these sources happens to reach the poor and how quickly.

The absence of social security systems in many low-income countries means that 'trickle-down' from economic growth, or indeed most forms of overseas aid and debt relief, does not arise. These forms of funding have 'indirect' social outcomes. They are intended to reach the poorest, but measures of trends in extreme poverty, and not only the lack of investigative precise follow-up, cast doubt on the intended outcome. The over-generalized, and indirect, strategy has contributed to the failure to reduce poverty, especially child poverty.

What different forms of funding have been examined? The scale of resources to be made available has now become an acute problem. In September 2000 the lack of significant progress in reducing poverty, together with severe delays in implementing funding agreements, led the UN General Assembly to ask for 'a rigorous analysis of the advantages, disadvantages and other implications of proposals for developing new and innovative sources of funding'. A panel was set up under the chairmanship of Ernesto Zedillo and its report was issued in 2001 (UN, 2001).

On the question of scale the Zedillo panel estimated conservatively that an additional US$50 billion was required annually to reach the MDGs. The World Bank estimated that additional overseas development aid (ODA) of US$60 billion over 2003 allocations would be needed in 2006, and US$83 billion by 2010 (World Bank, 2005: 162). These estimates were unrealistically low, since they depended on making up the incomes of population below $1 a day and not on the relatively indiscriminate indirect funding provided by economic growth, overseas aid, debt relief and fairer trade. Instead, the necessary increase in ODA was projected as US$20 billion for 2006 and US$50 billion for 2010 – and even these underestimates leave a gap of more than US$30 billion. By that year the total is estimated to reach an average of 0.36 per cent GNI (OECD, 2005b) but 'it is not clear that this is realistic' (Atkinson, 2005: 6). The Netherlands, Denmark, Sweden, Norway and Luxembourg are the only countries to have reached the UN's 0.7 target for ODA. In 2004 the United Kingdom stood at 0.36 per cent and the United States 0.16 per cent.

By 2003 the UN inquiry about alternative funding had lost momentum. A parallel inquiry by the Helsinki-based World Institute for Development and Economic Research (WIDER) was mapping out alternative sources of funding (see Box 7.2). Because the UN process had offered little guidance the alternatives were presented cautiously in 2004 (Atkinson, 2004). The seven alternatives are of course different in scale as well as likely support. The International Finance Facility (IFF) was planned to reach a flow of US$50 billion for 2010–15. Private donations, i.e. from NGOs, totalled US$10 billion in 2003, and might be increased, but on past evidence it is unlikely that in the foreseeable future they will provide the predominant share of the resources needed. They can be expected to fill only a small proportion of the funding gap. The creation by the IMF of Special Drawing Rights has been opposed by the United States and since any new issue has to be approved by an 85 per cent majority, the United States alone can veto progress. The two most promising alternatives for serious examination seem to be a global environment tax and a currency transfer tax (CTT). The former is usually illustrated by a tax on hydrocarbon fuels with high carbon content – or by a tax on

---

Box 7.2 **New sources of development finance**

1. Global environment taxes.
2. Tax in currency flows (for example Tobin).
3. New 'special drawing rights'.
4. International Finance Facility (UK govt.).
5. Private development donations.
6. Global lottery or premium bonds.
7. Increased remittances from emigrants.

Source: Atkinson (2004).

---

airline travel. The 'Tobin' tax alternative is a tax on foreign currency trans-actions (covering different types of transaction – spot, forward, swaps, derivatives and so on).

Both these taxes have been vigorously opposed on economic grounds. As Atkinson has pointed out, both need not necessarily be of a scale to war-rant hostility, and could be reduced even further to produce substantial funds without adverse reactions in different markets. A small-scale initia-tive could of course be criticized, on the one hand, for failing to reduce global warming or pollution, and on the other hand, for failing to reduce currency speculation. But even small-scale taxes could produce substantial sums for international investment in development and the elimination of poverty. Such an investment could also be used to partially fund invest-ments in a social security system by low-income countries. Even a tiny CTT of 0.02 per cent is estimated by Atkinson to raise US$28 billion, and a small energy tax twice this sum – giving figures from three to five times the value of all private donations.

The energies of international bodies were diverted from consideration of the CTT. Two new issues were brought up in 2003. First was the possible creation of an international tax organization. After the United Nations International Conference on Financing for Development in Mexico in March 2003, the Zedillo panel recommended creating within the UN an agency called the International Tax Organization (ITO) and an 'adequate international tax source' for global spending programmes.[3]

Second was to explore how multinational business might promote strong domestic private sectors in the developing world. In June 2003 a Commission on the Private Sector and Development, co-chaired by Ernesto Zedillo, was convened by UNDP at the request of Kofi Annan to recommend 'how to promote strong domestic private sectors in the developing world as a key strategy towards the achievement of the Millennium Development Goals'.[4] There was no reference back to the simplicity and affordability of a single form of international tax in relation to that aim. In particular, the commission looked at how multinational business can become a supportive partner for local entrepreneurs in the developing countries. The discussion of these issues at the world conference in Davos in 2004 was inconclusive. The case for a CTT was effectively kicked into touch.

A currency transfer tax: new resources for child benefit and social security

Since the mid-1990s there has been a groundswell of support for the Tobin tax, particularly in Europe,[5] as a source of international finance for aid and economic stabilization.

James Tobin put forward the idea of such a tax first in 1972 and then it was resurrected in UNDP's Human Development Report for 1994. The rate of tax lately suggested is in the range 0.1 to 0.5 per cent of currency transactions. If applied universally a tax of 0.1 per cent on all currency transactions, including the charge for changing different currencies for travellers, was estimated in 2002 to be likely to raise $400 billion a year (see Townsend and Gordon, 2002: 369) – or five times higher than the low target of debt relief and aid advocated for low-income countries by the international financial agencies and members of the G8.

Eighty per cent of exchange transactions currently involve only eight industrialized countries (with the United Kingdom and the United States accounting for about 50 per cent). Eighty-eight per cent of transactions also take place between five currencies: the dollar, the pound sterling, the euro, the yen and the Swiss franc.[6] Thus, agreement among a bare majority of the G8 countries would be sufficient to ensure large-scale implementation at a first stage.

The key question is taxation for what? In the first years of the millennium progress in implementing international taxation to pump-prime social security systems has made very little progress. In 2002 the General Assembly of the UN considered a report prepared at the instigation of Kofi Annan. The Zedillo panel (the UN High-Level Panel on Financing for Development) had been appointed in 2001, as stated above,[7] to 'recommend strategies for the mobilization of resources required to accelerate equitable and sustainable growth in developing countries as well as economies in transition, and to fulfil the poverty and development commitments enshrined in the UN Millennium Declaration'. The Zedillo panel reported an annual shortfall of US$15 billion for the provision of global public goods, in addition to the extra US$50 billion per year needed to meet the MDG targets. A number of governments had been pressing for consideration of the recommendation by James Tobin of a currency transfer tax. Thus, a 2002 report from the Federal Ministry of Economic Cooperation and Development in Bonn explained that the tax was feasible and could even be introduced right away by the OECD or

EC countries.[8] The European Parliament carried out a feasibility study, with France, Germany and Belgium in favour, and the Vatican coming round to acceptance. Outside the European Union, Canada also offered its active consent. Poor countries saw the Tobin tax as something which rich countries could implement straightaway,[9] a domestic taxation control that had very small financial drawbacks for the donors but large benefits for the potential recipients. At a UN conference on 'Finance for Development' in April 2002 in Monterrey, Mexico, a number of countries pressed for the CTT. The report to be submitted to the General Assembly was signed by 113 countries, but innovative mechanisms of financing were given only one paragraph and were left open for further consideration.

The Zedillo report had described the merits of a CTT as 'highly controversial' and concluded that 'further rigorous study would be needed to resolve the doubts about the feasibility of such a tax'. The Zedillo authors claimed to have examined a range of proposed mechanisms including a carbon tax, a currency transactions tax, and a new allocation of Special Drawing Rights (SDRs), concluding that 'new sources of finance should be considered without prejudice by all parties involved'.

However, there is no evidence that the issues were examined in any depth. Surprisingly the Zedillo panel made no attempt to consider alternative practicable models of the Tobin tax, and to compare them, or to deal with the difficulties said to be involved in implementing such a tax. They did not compare its merits with other methods of raising funds for overseas development, or give persuasive estimates of costs and outcome. The uses to which the tax might be put or what social benefits might be derived were not discussed.

A CTT of 0.2 per cent, compared with a standard fee of 2 or 3 per cent charged by firms for currency exchange at airports, would raise US$280 billion. A start would be feasible for those OECD countries prepared to introduce a CTT for travellers. Compared with an existing charge of 2 or 3 per cent, it seems likely that the travelling public would accept an additional charge for an international investment tax of 0.2 per cent. The social use of such a tax also deserves searching investigation. This has not, hitherto, attracted any attention.

Like a corporation 'tax' of 1 per cent of turnover a currency transfer tax could directly benefit children. The potential use of the tax was not considered by Tobin when introducing his idea in 1972, nor in the 1990s when publicity was again attracted to his proposal and, despite the terms of reference agreed by the Zedillo panel, the idea was not given serious attention in 2001 or subsequently. Interpreted and administered in the name of the world's impoverished children, for example, the tax could have considerably more public appeal and therefore potential acceptance. The proceeds of a tax – introduced severally or collectively by the richest countries – could be used to set up an international investment fund for children. Following its initiative in introducing the MDGs the United Nations would be the obvious international organization to administer the fund. A universal benefit for children, in cash or in kind, would attract worldwide support. It could prove to be not just a salvation for the world's children, but regain public respect for the work of the international agencies on world social development and the fulfilment of the MDGs.

Grants from that fund to governments could be made conditional on, say, payments by each government and by the UN of 50 per cent of the cost of the programme, as well as evidence of payment. The scheme would be monitored by a representative UN committee as well as individual governments.

Conclusion: a universal child benefit

This chapter has pointed up the fragile condition of a fifth of the world's children and has sought to recommend a change of strategy to bring resources directly to children, and to seek substantial funding from international bodies. The current threat to global economic and social development because of the financial downturn obliges the largest economic powers, international agencies and trans-national corporations to reconsider their agreed commitments and obligations to human rights in all parts of the world. The governments of the 'developed' countries have to consider sharing the responsibility for the establishment and emergency reinforcement of social security systems to meet declared goals to eliminate world poverty. It is not just administrative know-how and domestic taxation that count, but also participatory international funding.

The use of a currency transfer tax for universal child benefit would immediately improve the life chances of hundreds of millions of children, and pave the way for the emergence of social security systems in low-income countries on a scale that will eventually compare with that of the OECD countries and therefore radically reduce mass poverty.

The priority recommendation is for an international child benefit that once administratively in place has a direct and immediate effect in bolstering family purchasing power and reducing child poverty. Because the circumstances of countries differ widely a new child benefit would necessarily take a variety of forms and be introduced progressively. It could be a weekly allowance in cash or kind for children under a given age – say 10, or 5, or infants under 2. A low birthweight baby allowance is an example of a measure that could be applied in rich and poor countries alike. The scheme could be phased in, depending on available resources – maybe starting with infants – so long as it is introduced country- or district-wide. Conditional cash transfer schemes that have started in recent years, especially in parts of Latin America and Africa, could be merged or treated as preliminary or complementary stages of a process of rapid extension of entitlement to all children.

A second priority recommendation is a categorical child benefit for severely disabled children. Whether parents are in paid employment or not, the costs of caring for a severely disabled child often account for family poverty. And the market does not recognize this form of dependency. While some forms of congenital or disabling long-term illness may be declining there are the disabling conditions of the major problems of the last two decades, like HIV/AIDS, oil, nuclear and chemical pollution, and armed conflict, including landmines.

Appendix

Table A7.1 Child mortality and poor conditions of health: countries in sub-Saharan Africa

Country (year data collected)	Under-5s stunted for age (per cent)		Mortality under-5s (per cent)		1-year olds not immunized against measles (per cent)	
	Poorest 20%	Richest 20%	Poorest 20%	Richest 20%	Poorest 20%	Richest 20%
Benin (2001)	35	18	20	9	43	17
Burkina Faso (2003)	46	21	21	14	52	29
Central African Republic (1994–5)	42	25	19	10	69	20
Chad (2004)	51	32	18	19	92	62
Comoros (1996)	45	23	13	9	49	14
Eritrea (2002)	45	18	10	6	16	4
Ethiopia (2005)	48	35	13	9	75	48
Gabon (2000)	33	11	9	5	66	29
Ghana (2003)	42	13	13	9	25	11
Guinea (2005)	41	22	22	11	58	43
Kenya (2003)	38	19	15	9	45	12
Madagascar (2003–4)	50	38	14	5	62	16
Malawi (2004)	54	32	18	11	33	12
Mali (2001)	45	20	25	15	60	24
Mauritania (2000–1)	39	24	10	8	58	14
Mozambique (2003)	49	20	20	11	39	4
Namibia (2000)	27	15	5	3	24	14
Niger (1998)	42	32	28	18	77	34
Rwanda (2005)	55	30	21	12	15	12
South Africa (1998)	–	–	9	2	27	16
Togo (1998)	24	15	17	10	66	37
Uganda (2000–1)	40	26	19	11	51	36
United Republic of Tanzania (2004–5)	40	26	14	9	45	9
Zambia (2001–2)	51	37	19	9	19	12
Zimbabwe (1999)	29	21	10	6	20	14

Table A7.2   Child mortality and poor conditions of health: countries in Latin America

Country (year data collected)	Under-5s stunted for age (per cent)		Mortality under-5s (per cent)		1-year olds not immunized against measles (per cent)	
	Poorest 20%	Richest 20%	Poorest 20%	Richest 20%	Poorest 20%	Richest 20%
Bolivia (2003)	42	5	10	3	38	26
Brazil (1996)	23	2	10	3	22	10
Columbia (2005)	20	3	4	2	36	10
Guatemala (1998–9)	65	7	8	4	21	9
Haiti (2000)	31	7	16	11	57	37
Nicaragua (2001)	35	4	6	2	24	6
Paraguay (1990)	22	3	2	2	52	31
Peru (2000)	47	4	9	2	19	8

Source: WHO, *World Health Statistics* (2007: 74–7).

Notes

1. There is good reason to question whether the World Bank had technically achieved accurate updating of its 1985 $1 per person per day poverty line (see for example Kakwani and Son, 2006; Pogge and Reddy, 2003; Wade, 2004) and why the admitted insufficiency of the threshold had not been made good in later research, as promised by the Bank in the early 1990s (see especially Townsend, chapter 14 in Townsend and Gordon, 2002).
2. There are now two principal sources of standardized cross-national survey data – Demographic Health Surveys (DHS) and Multiple Indicator Cluster Surveys (MICS), the latter sponsored by UNICEF.
3. Report of the High-Level Panel on Financing for Development, 28 June 2001, UN Headquarters, New York.
4. Mr Kofi Annan, Secretary-General of the United Nations: Address to the World Economic Forum, Davos, Switzerland, 23 January 2004.
5. For example, a report commissioned by the Federal Ministry for Economic Cooperation and Development, Bonn, concluded that the Tobin tax is feasible and does not need global ratification, but could be started by OECD or EU countries: 'On the Feasibility of a Tax on Foreign Exchange Transactions' (January 2002).
6. Jean-Marie Harribey, Professeur de Sciences Economiques et Sociales at l'Université Montesquieu-Bordeaux IV, France, *The Seven Mistakes of the Opponents to 'the Tax'* (2002), published by the Scientific Committee of ATTAC.
7. Report of the High-Level Panel on Financing for Development, 28 June 2001, UN Headquarters, New York.
8. See Federal Ministry for Economic Cooperation and Development (2002), 'On the Feasibility of a Tax on Foreign Exchange Transactions', Bonn.
9. See *The View from the South on the Tobin Tax*, Afrodad BFA, REPERES, www.ppp.ch for a really good overview of where African countries stand on the Tobin tax.

Part III
Social Protection in Europe and the OECD

8
Three Models of Social Security in the History of the Industrialized Countries

Peter Townsend

If greater priority is given worldwide to social security, as argued in this book, there will be inescapable implications for development planning. The OECD history and current practice of social security illustrates a fundamental problem of development theory. Analysis, planning and action are assumed to be universal. But for too long development has taken little or no explicit account of anti-poverty practices and programmes in high-income countries, except as comparators and implicit models. Development involves convergence or progressively less inequality between nations and also between classes. It also demands identification of best, and worst, policy packages that have common elements and apply in rich as well as poor countries.

Any reformulation of the part to be played in the next stages of economic and social development by social security means that countries with high and low GDP have to be compared, and recent trends in social security expenditure explained. Can national and international agencies find whether development practitioners, donor agencies and developing country governments can learn from the OECD experience with social security?[1] And taking into account the vast disparities in wealth and government finance that exist, does the experience of poverty reduction imply reformulation of the dominant development paradigm in low-income countries?

It is therefore essential to take a closer look at the emergence of modern institutions of social security in the developed countries of the OECD. There was never one standardized model. From time to time systems of social security had common elements and certainly were influenced by schemes adopted by their neighbours. But there were also distinctive features shared with a minority of countries or that applied disproportionately or specially to one nation. The history of social security in four chosen countries/regions, comprising three distinct forms, or models, of the welfare state, will be outlined in particular, to show the nature of the social security/social insurance packages that were developed and why. The Nordic countries (especially Sweden), Germany, the United Kingdom and the United States have been selected to represent those three models. Tables 2.6 and 2.11 in Chapter 2 give illustrations of the scientific reasons for categorizing these regimes. Table 2.6 in fact singles out a fourth type of regime – the South European model, also described by some authors as the 'Catholic', the 'Latin' or the 'rudimentary' model (Leibfried, 1992). However, analysts like Peter Abrahamson argue that this is unnecessarily complex and that the model is 'the discount edition of the Bismarck or Conservative model' (Abrahamson, 1999: 33).

In examining these 'models' it is important to acknowledge the strength of academic work that questions whether they should be distinguished as separate models or sub-categories of the welfare state,[2] and prefers instead to consider each welfare state as separate and having a relatively unique history. However, this preference for analytical fragmentation can, whether consciously or unconsciously, serve entrenched hierarchical power – in particular by ignoring questions of scale or proportion in assessing structure and cause in the distribution of income and other material conditions and opportunities among the population.

The Nordic or social democratic model

The continuing success of the Nordic countries in maintaining their high ranking in measures of both economic and social development has attracted close scrutiny. Is there a Nordic model that others might emulate? The question has been explored intensively. There is first the question of financing public spending in general and social protection in particular. One analyst concluded that 'there is no clear evidence of a unique Nordic model of overall public spending' (Kautto, 1999: 88). Although the Nordic countries were among the top spenders and reasonably similar to each other, they 'differed considerably' in the way financing was shared between government, employers and the insured (ibid.). A shift had occurred during the 1980s and 1990s, however. In Denmark, Finland and Sweden the share of the insured in financing social protection had increased while that of employers in these countries, with the addition of Norway, had fallen. Bismarckian elements in funding were 'gaining ground' (ibid.: 89).

In history 'the early Nordic (pre-) welfare state shared many of the characteristics typical of successful examples of the later developmental state in the global South' (Kuhnle and Hort, 2004: 1). A strong social role for the state was not found to be 'incommensurate with economic development . . . Economic growth and the institutionalization of comprehensive social security could go hand in hand' (ibid.: iii). However, it was not until the emergence of the full employment policies of the 1950s and 1960s 'that a thoroughly coherent developmental perspective on economic prosperity and social change became part and parcel of welfare state philosophy' (ibid.: 1; and see also Kuusi, 1964, and Therborn, 1986). The relative success in the 1930s of the social democratic parties in establishing the welfare state was augmented when a multi-party political structure later emerged with peasant and agrarian representation confirming the early adherence to and support for the principle of universal social security and welfare programmes (Kangas, 1991; Kuhnle and Hort, 2004).

In 1875 child labour was still very common in Norwegian industry. When this question was raised by the trade unions in the 1880s, opinion still concentrated on regulation rather than banning child labour. But as the trade unions gained ground in the 1880s, legislation governing the rights of adult workers also entered the agenda. It was commonly accepted that a law protecting workers was required, including legislation on working hours, overtime and overtime pay. The new arrangements also had to be properly administered and policed. By 1885 there was a decree on work accident cover, and a state pool of money for sick and funeral benefits (Statistisk Sentralbyrå (Norwegian Statistics Office), 2005).

The earliest authority to use the term 'welfare state' was arguably Ebbe Hertzberg, Professor of State Economics, in 1884. This suggests that Norway established a kind of welfare system to rival the Bismarckian model even before social democracy had really entered parliament in force. Although some believe that the Swedish welfare system originated with Bismarck's ideas, others, like Peter Flora and his colleagues (1986), have argued that the German influence was more visible as a preliminary parliamentary initiative than in the actual content of policies devised and measures adopted. Denmark, which they thought had become at the time the Scandinavian welfare leader, was more greatly influenced than Sweden by foreign models. On the other hand, the universal national pension scheme and the early employment programmes can be regarded as specific features of the Swedish system (Olson, 1986: 7). The liberal Sir (later Lord) William Beveridge is sometimes given credit for early welfare state theory, but arguably welfare systems were in place in Scandinavia even before the turn of the century. In Norway, for example, there was the concept of national security (*folkeforsikring*), while in Denmark, the old age pensions law of 1891 was probably not recognized as an element of social protection by its contemporaries (Hatland et al., 2001).

The first major social insurance laws were passed in the course of just three years (1891–4) in Denmark, Norway and Sweden at about the same time as large-scale social insurance laws were introduced in the German Reich (Kuhnle and Hort, 2004: 5).[3] Over the next 50 years universal pension schemes, compulsory work injury insurance, employment programmes and unemployment benefit societies were among the institutions established. In 1891 state subsidies were introduced in Sweden for voluntary sickness benefit societies. In 1909 Norway became the first country in the world to introduce the principle of sickness insurance for the spouse, generally the wife, and children to be insured without the payment of an extra premium. This was universalism in practice. Corresponding schemes were only introduced by other European countries from the 1930s onwards. Thus, public social expenditure in Sweden increased from below 4 per cent GDP in 1913 to over 10 per cent GDP by 1950 (Olson, 1986: 5).

But poor relief continued to play a large part in the social security systems for many more years until the welfare state model, in particular the Swedish welfare state model, was consolidated after the Second World War (Olson, 1986: 4–6).

In the 1950s and early 1960s Nordic schemes were made truly universal, encompassing all citizens – Sweden in 1955, Norway and Iceland in 1956, Denmark in 1960 and Finland in 1963. The exception for different benefits, apart from Norway, was unemployment insurance, which remained voluntary and was complementary to means-tested unemployment assistance. In the war and afterwards the world economist Keynes exerted major influence by treating many of the problems and institutions of social security, especially those of unemployment and benefit support during unemployment as part and parcel of economic policy (Townsend, 2004a).[4]

Post-war stages identified for Sweden in particular and the Nordic countries generally by some observers were (i) the immediate post-war period of 'recovery', characterized by the institutionalization of housing and employment programmes but also universal cover of the population (or relevant category of population) with flat-rate minimum benefits; (ii) protection from a drastic fall in the individual's standard of living by means of the introduction of earnings-related benefits in the second half of the 1950s; (iii) the expansion of public services in the 1960s and early 1970s; (iv) the extension of entitlement and improvement of cash benefit rates in the mid-1970s; and (v) containment and adjustment in the late 1970s and early 1980s (see for example Olson, 1986: 8).

In the 1950s Sweden introduced earnings-related benefits for pensions but also for when adversity, like unemployment or disability, struck. At this time the 'adequacy' of benefits in relation to established living standards at work attracted close attention, partly provoked by increasing public interest in universal human rights. By the 1960s the focus of attention turned from cash benefits to the expansion of public services, particularly health care and education. The county councils became the only health authority, and the final law on the implementation of nine years' compulsory school attendance was passed in 1962 (ibid.: 12). In the 1970s, family-friendly schemes, like paid parental leave, were introduced. These are now the most generous in the world. Special welfare boards and the independent tax-raising power of the three levels of representative government constitute an important part of the Swedish welfare system. This decentralized system is thought in the case at least of Sweden to have facilitated the rise and expansion of social welfare (ibid.: 12).

In general, the Nordic countries were proud to have established 'a universal model of social protection, where benefits and services based on residence are combined with earnings-related social insurance programmes. It has been a successful strategy in terms of combating poverty and social inequalities but also for promoting employment and participation, particularly among women' (Palme, 1999: 7). The decision to include the better off in the systems of social protection had been more successful in reducing social inequalities than strategies more exclusively oriented to the poor. But this had been buttressed by wider and less discriminating employment, promoted by improved incentives, resources and opportunities. At the turn of the millennium much attention was directed to meeting global changes. The strategy had to be overhauled and modernized 'without diluting the socio-political and moral content of the Nordic welfare state model ... and ... maintaining its universal and employment-oriented character' (ibid.: 10–11). Despite cutting back total public social expenditure in the 1990s and acknowledging global trends in orienting schemes to the new labour market, this has turned out for some of the member countries to be temporary. The resilience of Nordic institutions of shared social protection and equality as well as of shared risk and opportunity, established for more than half a century, seems to remain very strong.

The agreement developed between the Nordic countries was 'a project of civilization ... that ... states should redistribute resources so that the poorest persons can also enjoy the degree of civilization which would otherwise be reserved only for the rich' (ibid.: 96; and see also Ferge, 1997). In summary, the model continues to possess three features: 'a comprehensive social policy; a social entitlement principle that has been institutionalized (social rights); and social legislation that is *solidaristic* and *universalist* in character' (Kuhnle and Hort, 2004: 2). All three of these have a bearing on the evolution of human rights in the last 60 years.

The corporatist model

The central value of social cohesion helps to distinguish the Bismarckian or corporatist model of the welfare state. The model has been dominant in Germany and Austria and across the Catholic world. The favoured meaning of social cohesion is not adequately represented by ideas of brotherhood or solidarity, for example. Catholics in Central Europe were concerned with the individual's own community – to integrate the individual within his or her small community, especially the patriarchal family, but also to integrate that small group within larger groups or communities. Each of these nesting groups was 'sovereign in its own realm'. This preoccupation provided an early example of the principle of subsidiarity. The dignity of labour was vital, emphasizing the division of labour and specialization, but not the accompanying competition advocated by many economists and regimes. There had to be cooperation between capital and labour. Broadly speaking, all major groups in society had to agree. Unanimity, rather than the merest voting majority, was the political rule. The basic goal was the preservation of the pre-existing social order.

Those who are poor are not so much groups – because all groups are recognized to have a place at the bargaining table – as individuals. They are unlucky members of groups or have been left out or excluded. They have not been properly 'inserted', or integrated, into the natural economic life of society. From this diagnosis flows the policy response – to integrate people better into groups and to engineer better mutual aid within those groups. Corporatist mutual aid is first and foremost a matter of pooling risks. The role of the state became one of underwriting and facilitating essentially private and self-governing schemes of insurance and assurance but, if needs be, underwriting risks of whole social groups who find themselves collectively in trouble. The basic goal of social policy therefore became one of security and stability. In the German tradition the term 'social policy' was defined to embrace social insurance and labour legislation, broadly excluding education, health and housing. The role of the state was to supplement the market in the best possible allocation of productive resources. This limit to the state originated, as argued above, in the political philosophy of neo-liberalism and the social ethics of Catholicism but should also be understood as a reaction to the extreme bureaucratic control experienced during the Nazi period and the Communist collectivism in East Germany.

In Germany industrialization was late and the challenge perceived by Bismarck was how to protect the emerging working class from its consequences at the same time as creating a strong central state. The government gave serious consideration to social insurance measures in 1878 and by 1884 had created a workers' compensation and sickness insurance programme. The basic premise of his social insurance initiative was *Soldaten der Arbeit*, or social integration and mutual solidarity among employers and workers within the same workplace and ultimately the same industry. At first the older corporate groups, like the feudal Junkers and the guilds of miners, printers and others, defeated parliamentary proposals, as in the case of accident insurance in 1881, but then became strong advocates. The Kaiser led the attempt to persuade the dissidents by referring to the importance of sharing risks so that the weak and the strong each secured benefits as well as sharing new responsibilities. Health insurance was enacted in 1883, accident insurance in 1884, and old age and invalidity insurance in 1889.

The Prussian state had for a long time relied on repression as the best way to react against the mobilization of workers. But once Bismarck had opted for an interventionist economic policy, including high protection tariffs both for agriculture and quickly evolving new industries, he realized that repressive measures would not, and could not, work. Successful fast industrialization depended on the cooperation, not the opposition, of the workers. With the establishment of public social insurance programmes, his goal was to create a tight bond between the state and workers and to split the opposition of the Social Democratic Party and the liberals in Parliament, who were pressing for the creation of a parliamentary government (Alber, 1986: 5–6).

However, education never entered into Bismarck's plans for social reforms. By the 1880s state education was an established fact. The principle of compulsory education was introduced in Prussia as early as 1717, the Prussian state had gained effective control of the education system in 1872 and by 1875 nearly all workers' children attended public primary school. This fact may help to explain why education did not feature prominently as an element of social policy in Germany (ibid.). The consideration of multiple interests during the first parliamentary debates helps to explain the institutional longevity of the German social insurance schemes, whose principles still provide the basis of the modern social insurance scheme in the distribution of administrative powers, the earnings-related character of benefits and the tri-partite character – the employer, the insured and the state – of financing benefits (ibid.: 6).

In 1911 the three compulsory insurance laws (sickness, industrial accident and invalidity or old age) were consolidated in a single uniform National Insurance Code and another law established a pension insurance scheme for salaried employees. Although amended, this legislation is still in force today (ibid.). In addition to social insurance, the German Reich had a fairly developed public assistance scheme. In 1870 the Prussian laws were transformed into a consolidated Public Assistance Law, which had been extended to almost all regions after the unification. However, the federal structure and limited share of revenues accorded to the central government set strict limits to the government's further initiatives in social policy, especially in the public health sector.

After the Second World War and the hardships experienced into the 1950s, corporatist impulses surfaced again in political debates about the future of welfare. Most of the existing social programmes remained intact and only child allowances and some other special schemes developed under Nazi rule were discontinued (ibid.: 11). The subsequent re-establishment of a separate pension scheme for workers and employees signalled the persistence of the disjointed structure of the German social insurance system. Two 1955 laws confirmed the traditional structure of health care provision with its dominance of private suppliers and the limited powers of the public health services. Again, education remained within the authority and supervision of the single states (ibid.: 13).

The Adenauer pension reforms of 1957 may have been accelerated by knowledge of the work of a Labour Party team in the United Kingdom from 1955 before Labour was returned to office, but in scope and generosity the Adenauer scheme was as big and as influential as that of Bismarck in the 1880s. Both contributions and benefits became earnings-related, thus preserving income and status differentials. This maintained inequalities but also public support and cohesion. Pensioners with 50 years of contributions to their credit were entitled to 75 per cent of previous earnings (Esping-Andersen and Korpi, 1984: 198). Pensions were, almost unique to the OECD, linked to earnings in the previous three years and were accordingly regularly updated (Goodin et al., 1999: 75).

The mid-1960s marked the end of the expansion phase and the beginning of a period of transition. The rate of economic growth had declined considerably and the long period of polarization between the bourgeois and social democratic camps had come to an end, making all parties possible coalition partners. Indeed, when a sudden recession in 1966/67 led to conflict between the Federal Democratic Party (FDP) and Christian Democrats over the budget, a grand coalition of Christian Democrats and SPD was formed. For the first time educational issues were given priority: in particular a wider access to higher education was targeted as an investment in human capital; a federal ministry of education was established; and education allowances were introduced for low-income families (Alber, 1986: 14). A new social policy was designed in 1969 when an SPD/FDP coalition was formed and the economic growth provided the federal state with new resources. Special attention was given to the improvement of working conditions, social services were expanded, and education, housing and child allowances were increased and extended. This new social policy was halted by the recession of the mid-1970s, combined with deficits in the pension scheme and a cost explosion in the health sector. The government sought to bring the rate of social expenditure into better conformity with economic growth (ibid.: 15).

In summary, from its early stages the German social policy system came to be characterized by four main features: (i) the *sub-division of programmes* into a large number of uncoordinated and decentralized schemes, both at the level of their design and administration; (ii) the stress on *cash benefits*: most benefits are income maintenance cash payments which leave consumption decisions to the recipient, thus stressing the importance of private provision of services, with the exception of education; (iii) the *centrality of social insurance*: individuals are entitled to income maintenance benefits (usually earnings-related) not as citizens but as members of social insurance programmes, generally financed by the insured and their employers rather than by state taxation; (iv) the insistence on extensive *labour legislation*: all social programmes must be seen in the context of a labour legislation with a high degree of regulation on working conditions, dismissals etc. (ibid.: 4–5).

The liberal or residual model

The third of the welfare regime models in OECD countries is perhaps the most extraordinary. For representative examples it is hard to choose between the United Kingdom – the first country to institutionalize a form of social security – and the United States – one of the last to do so among rich industrialized countries. Each country will therefore be described briefly.

The United Kingdom

The first statute placing responsibility on the government of England for the 'relief' of poverty was enacted in 1536. This endured for three centuries. The population was fewer than 3 million. Beforehand the aim of laws relating to the poor had been repressive with penalties being directed against vagrants (three days and three nights in the stocks) and wandering beggars. Exceptions to repression were gradually found. Punishment was withheld from 'women great with child', and men and women 'in extreme sickness'. In 1516 in his book *Utopia* Thomas More described the desperate conditions of dispossessed farmers – some deprived of husbandry by land enclosure – and the need of the working man for economic security. 'For their daily wage is so little, that it will not suffice for the same day, much less it yieldeth any overplus, that may daily be laid up for the relief of old age' (see Nicholls, 1898: 15). By the end of the sixteenth century, despite the new statute, starvation continued to lead to premature death. Thus, there were numerous contemporary municipal reports, an example of which was of the charges for 'burying 16 poor folks who died for want in the streets' in Newcastle in October 1597.

Even by the start of the nineteenth century relief was grudging, parsimonious and coercive. Opposition to the Poor Laws had gathered momentum but for many years was unsuccessful. The system was held in place by an intransigent ruling class exploiting an imaginative capacity for local social organization. The lives of all members of rural communities were intricately interwoven by custom, ritual and economic necessity. These three formed what can be described as 'a tripartite system' of relationships dominated by the ruling elite. The landed estate provided the focal point and during agricultural distress landlords exercised a paternalistic duty to dole out blankets and firewood while resisting encroachments on their property and wealth by itinerant destitute people as well as by those outside their local fiefdoms. In the early decades of the nineteenth century parish practices were beginning to vary and there were increasing examples of exceptions being made to relatively punitive practices. These applied to outdoor relief in particular. Thus by 1804, for example, 'persons impotent and above the age of 60 years' came to be regarded as more deserving than the able-bodied for relief. In addition to the creeping changes to the Poor Laws, rapid urbanization and industrialization began to throw traditional practices into the melting pot.

Coercive social assistance was established more uniformly by the Poor Law Amendment Act of 1834. This particular year stands out as one of the most significant years in English economic and social history. It confirmed the ambivalent treatment of the poor and marked a new era of coercion. The place of the Amendment Act in the social history of poverty has had mixed historical interpretation, for example being treated by Beatrice and Sidney Webb as a triumph of Benthamite utilitarian centralism over an inert system that had been controlled for generations by the gentry (Webb and Webb, 1929). The Webbs appear to have over-valued what to them seemed rational exercise of administrative and political power, in comparison with achievements in civil rights and in more equal human relationships. Thus within three years 13,264 parishes, 90 per cent of the total, were grouped into 568 unions, and the cost of public assistance cut by a third (De Schweinitz, 1961: 129–30).

The Commissioners took pride in expressing the principle that was to govern administration of relief for the poor in the next 75 years. The situation of the individual relieved was 'not to be made really or apparently so eligible as the situation of the independent labourer of the lowest class'. Every penny of relief additional to this equation with the poorest labourer's wage was 'a bounty on indolence and vice' (quoted from the Commissioners' 1834 report in De Schweinitz, 1961: 123). This principle of less eligibility became famous throughout the world. The report placed the burden of destitution upon the individual and treated that individual's poverty as simply a question of his or her moral fault (ibid.: 126). 'The commissioners were determined to put an end to outdoor relief for the able-bodied, and to do away with, or to curb, parish administration of assistance through the substitution of larger local units combined with a national system of supervision' (ibid.: 126–7).

The deterrent workhouse system was the embodiment of the less eligibility principle. The workhouse remains the abiding social image of nineteenth-century England. Within three years of the passage of the Poor Law Amendment Act, 200 new workhouses and the extension of many existing workhouses was approved. Relief for the able-bodied poor outside the workhouse was ruled out. Admission to the workhouse, with its unremittingly strict discipline and enforced labour, was the test of need. In subsequent decades the Poor Law became more and more callous in its application (ibid.: 139). Less eligibility and the offer of the workhouse became the core of a philosophy and a creed, against which, and for which, conservatives and progressives in the United Kingdom fought repeatedly for generations.

The Act of 1834 and its aftermath led to bitter social divisions that were not resolved until after the reports of a Majority and a Minority of the Royal Commission on the Poor Law 1909, following its appointment in 1905. The Majority report of that Commission referred reluctantly and with qualification to necessary structural changes but the Minority report by Sidney and Beatrice Webb was unambiguous in calling for the abandonment of the Poor Law and for its replacement by public assistance.[5] The total effect 'was to demonstrate that England had at last emancipated herself from the domination of the principles established by the earlier [1834] inquiry' (ibid.: 189).

The stream of enactments during 1905–11 marked the first stage of the establishment of a welfare state – prompted earlier by riots against unemployment in the mid-1880s, widely publicized reports on poverty by Charles Booth and Seebohm Rowntree at the turn of the century, the organization by miners and other working-class groups of friendly societies to mitigate interruptions of wages because of need in sickness and disablement, and the poor physical quality of a large proportion of young men recruited to fight the Boer War. This last factor seems to have brought some members of the ruling class into grudging acceptance of reform. The culmination of a number of measures occurred in 1911. 'In the [National Insurance] Act Britain took a step of profound significance in her efforts to secure social security. In adopting health and unemployment insurance she had applied an innovation only to be compared in importance with the legislation between 1536 and 1601 establishing the responsibility of the state for guaranteeing the individual a protection against starvation' (ibid., 1961: 208).

The second stage of enactments, consolidating the welfare state, had to wait until after the election of a Labour government in 1945, when new schemes for national insurance (1946) and national assistance (1948) as well as a National Health Service (1946) were enacted, partly as a result of decisions taken by the wartime coalition government and the recommendations in the famous Beveridge Report of 1942. Conditional welfare for the few became minimum rights for all. Not until there were independent research investigations in the 1960s of the conditions among large families, low wage-earners, lone mothers, the disabled and the elderly did it become clear that the post-war instruments had not sufficiently disposed of poverty. Universal benefits were largely flat rate and relatively low since they had been restricted to ideas of 'subsistence need'. Partly as a consequence means-tested schemes that were severely administered remained a key feature of organized redistribution to support or provide low income. Decades of attempts to rescue the 'deserving' from the 'undeserving' poor had not turned out to be wholly successful. Successive governments took steps to rename and reorganize the discriminatory and conditional payments that continued to be regarded as stigmatizing (as well as inefficient in their coverage) – first national assistance, which was followed by supplementary benefit, then by income support and later by various tax credit schemes. The emphasis given to selective social assistance – together with the continued refusal to compare conditions of the poor with those of the rich and match their rights – reflected the distrust and lack of acquaintance of leading classes and administrators with the poor that had marked English class attitudes for generations.

Since the 1980s governments have made attempts to divert attention from the strengths of social insurance to those of entrepreneurial private business in an international market economy, and to reduce total public expenditure by decreasing universal benefits and increasing selective social assistance at smaller overall cost. National insurance was used more for funding the NHS than it was earlier and therefore the National Insurance scheme is less clearly a balance struck between individual/employer contributions and guaranteed individual benefit. In the process, a huge under-utilized annual surplus has built up in the National Insurance Fund itself. According to one authority the working balance in the National Insurance Fund over and above the cost of meeting contingencies exceeded by £24.5 billion in 2006 the level recommended by the Government Actuary, and the excess is expected to rise to £48 billion by 2010 (Lynes, 2006: 1).

Writing at the end of the twentieth century social scientists declared that increasing inequality in the labour market, family changes and an ageing population had not led to a decline in social insurance in other industrial countries. The United Kingdom was unique in the extent to which its social insurance scheme had 'withered' in recent years (Clasen and Erskine, 1998: 4). In other EU countries, social protection was seen as relevant to everyone, not only the poor; public insurance contributions were not seen as a tax, but as paid for particular reasons; and social insurance was part of an acceptable notion of social responsibility and social solidarity (Hirsch, 1997).

A year after the Labour government was elected in 1997, the Chancellor of the Exchequer, Gordon Brown, stated, 'Of course, the British idea of National Insurance has changed over time. But no one can deny that by sharing risks among 58 million citizens and by the strong helping the weak it makes us all stronger' (Gordon Brown, *The Guardian*, 12 November 1998). That expression of support has not led to government initiatives to compare the respective roles and potentialities of private and public insurance and promote public discussion to sustain that judgement. According to the government's own research there was strong public support for the contributory principle, for a widening of entitlement, and for a greater degree of risk-pooling to provide good national insurance benefits. The state scheme was preferred to private providers and opposition to means-testing was strong (Social Security Committee, 1999, and for an international review reflecting the same conclusion see van Oorschot, 1991, 2002).[6] A war on child poverty was declared, which was widely approved, but which by 2009 had not yet reduced child poverty in the United Kingdom to average EU dimensions. And measures proposed in that year to restrict disability benefits, even for youngsters severely disabled, reflected the historical preoccupation of the English establishment with the undeserving poor and for all rights and benefits to be conditional on a readiness to work.

The United States

By contrast to England a comprehensive social security system arrived late, but more swiftly, in the United States. The delay was marked in comparison with the United Kingdom and the rest of Europe. Even countries in Latin America, including Chile, Argentina and Uruguay, had established social security systems in the early decades of the twentieth century long before the United States (Hall and Midgeley, 2004: 234).

The catch-up years turned out to be 1935 and 1946. Before 1935 social insurance struggled for legitimacy in a political climate of distrust of centralized state authority and strong belief in private business and local management. The first large system of benefits was restricted to veterans of the Civil War. The next, around 1912, consisted of a variety of work-related compensation for working accidents and social insurance against such risks. Yet the individual states, and private insurance, were invested with responsibility to deliver the actual benefits. The same dependency on state, and even county, government continued with experimentation with survivors' benefits such as means-tested widows' pensions. In the 1920s means-tested old age pensions were fragmentary and reached only a small minority in need (Berkowitz, 1997: 24).

In the early years of the twentieth century Americans became aware of the neglect of poverty by politicians and scientists alike. Writing in 1904 Robert Hunter suggested that more than 10 million Americans were 'under-fed, under-clothed, and poorly housed'. Meticulous studies had been carried out in Europe and especially England 'but we have not made even a beginning in finding out the extent of poverty in America' (Hunter, 1905: v and 19). The figure of 10 million, or over one in six of the population was 'conservative' and built on fragmentary reports and accounts. Four million individuals received poor relief. This was 'a seventeenth century system of relief which degrades all alike without discrimination' (ibid.: 105). Over 2 million working men 'are unemployed from four to six months in the year. About half a million male immigrants arrive yearly and seek work in the very districts where unemployment is greatest ... Over 1.7 million little children are forced to become wage-earners when they should still be in school ... Probably no less than 1 million workers are injured or killed each year ... and about 10 million of those now living will die of ... tuberculosis ... Many workers are overworked and underpaid ... We know of the unsanitary evils of tenements and factories; we know of the neglect of the street child, the aged, the infirm, the crippled' (ibid.: 337). Two years earlier, Jacob Riis published a book full of graphic accounts and photographs of thousands of men, women and children living in New York in sheds in back alleys, starving children, prostitutes, queues outside lodging houses, and shelters erected with money from the city but unconnected to the sewers.

By the 1930s the alternative mechanisms of private life insurance and savings to achieve income security in old age were found wanting. Increasing attention was paid to the need for federal intervention. During the Great Depression more and more elderly were forced to rely on poor relief. The outlook for the younger generations, with mass unemployment, under-employment and the financial losses experienced by many on middle and low incomes seemed bleak. The introduction of a contributory social insurance scheme designed to spread the 'burdens' of an elderly dependent population over a much larger workforce was a logical outcome that attracted growing support. Different generations could share the risks and returns inherent in a market-based economy. The Great Depression had shown how individuals through no fault of their own could experience drastic impoverishment through the economic disadvantages that can arise in the market – of failure and mismanagement of some financial institutions, hard-to-predict falls in the economy, too few assets to permit portfolio diversification, and self-insurance rates that do not and cannot allow for a prematurely shortened work-life because of redundancy, disability and widespread unemployment. During the 1930s there were mass movements calling for change. 'Social insurance ... marked a response to involuntary unemployment. It was a means of harnessing industrial productivity to cushion some of its shocks' (Berkowitz, 1997: 23).

Resistance to unemployment insurance remained strong so help for the able-bodied continued to be sought in poor relief, and its extension into forms of what has become American 'welfare'. By the mid-1930s economists had reached agreement that a valuable stimulus could be injected into the economy by social security payments to elderly and disabled people. President Roosevelt set up a Committee on Economic Security in 1934. By January 1935 the Committee reported and the recommendations in its report were rushed into law by August 1935.

When signing the Social Security Act of 1935 Franklin Delano Roosevelt said: 'We can never insure 100 per cent of the population against 100 per cent of the hazards and vicissitudes of life, but we have tried to frame a law that gives some measure of protection ... against poverty-ridden old age' (Cullinan, 1991: 193).

After the Act was passed, and before it took effect, the need for it was given impetus by a further deep recession in 1937 and, ironically, the minimal provision of help for the immediate needs of the unemployed and aged poor. The Social Security Act came into force for the first wave of elderly beneficiaries in 1940. The programme quickly became a fixture in the American landscape. In that first year 55 per cent of the labour force was covered for benefit. By 1960 numbers reached 86 per cent and by 1990, 95 per cent. Benefits grew faster than either prices or wages. Legislative initiatives enhanced the adequacy of benefits, payroll taxes being levied equally on employers and employees at a rate of 5.7 per cent. As a share of GDP social security costs increased between 1960 and 1980 by 2.1 percentage points, and were expected to remain at GDP 4.5 per cent until numbers of elderly increased faster after 2010. But in the next 30 years, to 2040, the predicted increase needed of another GDP 2 per cent would represent less than the rate of growth from 1960–80, and about the same as the increase in defence spending in the 1980s (Cullinan, 1991: 198–203). Today over 40 million Americans receive benefits from social security and some 140 million pay taxes and contributions to qualify, in their turn, for disability and survivors' insurance protection.

After the 1939–45 war, as in Europe, there was in the United States a determination not to repeat the mistakes of the 1930s and to consolidate social security as part of the new economic enlightenment. The right to social security was included in the Universal Declaration of Human Rights in 1946, and that decision symbolizes the introduction and extension of schemes in different countries in that year and subsequently.

The interpretation of social security concentrated on old age and survivors', and disability, insurance, and there have been tendencies in the United States to define social security to exclude selective or means-tested social assistance. There was political opposition to widening the scope of the legislation beyond elderly and disabled people. Early rates of benefit were low and until an amendment to the law was proposed in 1950 and passed in 1952 the battle between social security and 'welfare' flared and subsided. The survival of social security seemed to be precarious. The delay in making social insurance effective led paradoxically to extension of social assistance measures, despite the variation of administration between states, the bad record of reaching even two-thirds of those eligible for assistance, and considerable waste of administrative costs and energy.

This reluctance to concede the logic of major federal involvement corresponded with a reluctance to accept the fact that the role of private insurance was necessarily restricted. It took much hard argument and accumulating research evidence to persuade opinion that the state had to have a major role in relation to the market. Examples arise in distinguishing the respective roles of market and state:

> Another market failure addressed by a compulsory social insurance programme is the problem of adverse selection. Private or voluntary insurance arrangements face significant difficulties in annuity markets because purchasers are self-selected and they are likely to be those most likely to receive favourable treatment ... Individuals most likely to purchase a life annuity are those who believe they are likely to be long-lived. An actuarially fair premium for the population at risk will attract these individuals, and those with shorter expected lifetimes will choose not to participate ... The suppliers of such annuities would always find these offerings unprofitable.
> (Cullinan, 1991: 197)

Between 1935 and 1950 adherents of the system fought for its survival against Old Age Assistance, a welfare programme that many states favoured and could implement and reorganize easily. But such assistance was deeply flawed, and manifestly unequal and unjust. In 1950 amendments to the 1935 Act were introduced in Congress and were debated for a year and a half (see Berkowitz, 1997). For the first time Democrats and Republicans agreed on the political desirability of an increase in social security. Substantial increases in contributions and benefits were introduced by the law of 1952. When, after being elected in that year, President Eisenhower gave his State of the Union address on 2 February 1953, he recommended that the 'old age and survivors' insurance law should promptly be extended to cover millions of citizens who have been left out of the Social Security system' (Cohen et al., 1954: 16).

There was steady incremental expansion of social security for the next two decades. Wilbur Cohen, an important figure in social security administration, described 1951 as a milestone year, because more people benefited in that year from Old Age Insurance than Old-Age Assistance, and total payments for the former began to exceed those for the latter (Cohen, 1952).

Between 1954 and 1956 attention shifted to the creation of a disability insurance programme and then, from 1956 to 1965, health insurance. There were furious exchanges about health care costs and eventually a restricted insurance scheme for the elderly for hospital costs and supplementary medical costs was accommodated in the Medicare programme enacted in 1965. Substantial expansion of the entire programme continued, but after 1972 persistent efforts to contain growing costs were made. Today, total public expenditure payments are smaller than in other OECD countries, but they have remained as high proportionately, and even increased, in the United States, compared with what they were in the 1970s.

The New Deal of the 1930s had created the social insurance scheme enacted in 1935. It also created the means-tested scheme Aid for Dependent Children in 1936. In its first year there were more than half a million recipients of relief, most of them white, widowed females with children (Miller and Markle, 2002: 86). Later expanded and renamed Aid to Families with Dependent Children (AFDC) this scheme foreshadowed a second stage of 'welfare' in the 1960s and then again another stage towards the end of the century. At its height, in 1994, the AFDC scheme had 14.2 million recipients, or 5.5 per cent of the population. But more and more people were led to believe that 'public assistance without a work requirement promoted indolence as well as childbearing ... Largely spurred by political response to public misperceptions, AFDC slowly began to move towards a work-emphasized approach' (ibid.: 87–8).

In quick succession there was an earned income disregard, a Work Incentive programme, and a Jobs Opportunities and Basic Skills Training programme. Ultimately AFDC was replaced by Temporary Assistance to Needy Families (TANF). A five-year limit was placed on the receipt of benefit. In addition to assistance the objectives were to reduce dependency by promoting work, reduce the number of out-of-wedlock births, and increase the number of stable two-parent families. The right to receive benefit was withdrawn. States were responsible for identifying needy families and providing them with benefits but no person had a right to receive such benefits. This legislative change in 1996 marked the famous shift in the United States from welfare to workfare.

Welfare rolls had already decreased between 1994 and 1996 but by 2000 they decreased by half.

The result is not so much increased self-sufficiency as increased financial need. The current welfare programme is simply not meeting the need of those eligible for assistance. In 1995, approximately 80 per cent of poor families with children received welfare. The figure declined steadily following the 1996 reforms and reached approximately 50 per cent in 1999. Similarly, in 1994, the percentage of poor children receiving AFDC assistance was down to 62 per cent and by 1998 this figure was down to 43 per cent. (Miller and Markle, 2002: 96, quoting Loprest, 1999)

More of the population entered work, but that was at a time of improvement in the economy as a whole. The Earned Income Tax Credit programme and increases in the 1990s in the minimum wage also accounted for part of the fall in the number of recipients of welfare. The cost of the change was in perpetuating poverty for many families, but in work rather than on benefit. The conclusion reached by one research team is that 'the liberal welfare regime succeeds in keeping costs down, but at the cost of allowing poverty to remain comparatively high'. And, 'contrary to liberal hopes, high incomes on average do not translate into adequate incomes for the poor' (Goodin et al., 1999: 244–5).

The Social Security Act of 1935 was critical to American economic and social recovery following the 1929 financial crash and the havoc of the 1930s. Its introduction was a radical departure from traditional US economic and social management. What happened in the years during its implementation after 1935 remains paradoxical in US twentieth- and twenty-first-century history. By introducing unemployment and old age social insurance and other welfare measures the Act transformed social conditions in the US. During the 1940s and 1950s it was eagerly endorsed by successive presidents. Eisenhower, for example, gave speeches reminiscent of the earlier noble declarations of Roosevelt about its importance to Americans worst affected by the years of Depression before the war. Both presidents stated that social security was a necessary institution that would temper many of the worst social effects of any future financial crisis and assist recovery. A reading of the reports prepared for the Committee on Economic Security in 1934–5 shows what a major structural change the Act represented. A break had to be made with the past and schemes developed on the basis of pioneering European schemes. The arguments applied to unemployment compensation, old age security, security for children, provisions for the blind and the extension of public health services. The conclusions for each of these were typified by the argument for unemployment compensation:

The unprecedented extent and duration of unemployment in the United States since 1930 has left no one who is dependent on a wage or salary untouched by the dread of loss of work. Unemployment relief ... is not a solution of the problem. It is expensive to distribute and demoralizing to both donor and recipient. ... [The solution is] income received as a right, [and is] provided by an unemployment insurance or unemployment compensation system. (Social Security Board, 1937: 3)

Conclusion: bringing social security into the twenty-first century: the lessons of the OECD models

Long-standing systems in the OECD countries that are described as 'social security', 'social insurance', 'social assistance' and 'social protection' are being collapsed by some analysts in 2009 into what are described as 'cash transfer schemes' and, in particular, 'conditional cash transfer schemes' for the purposes of discussing developments in low-income countries. If the description takes root it could lead to the even greater isolation of low-income countries from high-income countries. There could be severe losses on both sides, especially in the newly transformed global economy. This is because the description is being restricted in its scope and meaning, and weight given in particular to the ideas of targeting, use of limited available resources, small-scale selection and conditionality (for example International Poverty Centre, 2008, but see the earlier discussion: International Poverty Centre, 2006).

A descriptive term like 'cash transfer schemes' can be newly invented as a title, and may seem innocuous and relatively balanced but when restricted in its meaning or applied only to certain groups of countries can present problems. This is particularly true if 'conditional cash schemes' is treated as the key component. The term can be deployed to draw a veil over the links with the past – especially with long-established systems that exist in the industrialized world. Unmistakable evidence patiently collected about action in one group of countries, like the OECD countries, that is of direct value to possible action today in another group of countries, like the low-income countries, can be ignored. This helps to explain the insistence in this book on the relevance to the elimination of poverty and the achievement of social stability of the continuities and discontinuities of anti-poverty schemes in the history of the industrialized countries.

The action of Roosevelt's administration in the 1930s, extraordinarily relevant to possible action in 2009 across many countries, confirms this theme. The Committee on Economic Security temporarily appointed by President Roosevelt in 1934–5 (Social Security Board, 1937) expressed values about social security in general and made recommendations that suited the needs of the American people. The Committee spelt out the advantages derived in European countries from earlier legislation and reached conclusions that reflected best practice in the countries of Europe and the US.

In the final years of war the Roosevelt administration also played a leading part in framing the Universal Declaration of Human Rights, in which the four freedoms, including freedom from want, were embedded. Mounting acceptance since then throughout the world of human rights, at a time when inequalities of income and wealth have been growing between as well as within countries, puts pressure on all countries to recast development policies and eliminate poverty. Human rights have come to play a central part in discussions about economic and social development, and the great majority of governments in the world have ratified the various instruments. This chapter has traced the divergent historical experience in 'developed' countries of putting into practice the fundamental human rights to social security, including social insurance, and an 'adequate' standard of living.

The results of the study in this chapter of the different OECD models hold special lessons for the international agencies that are advocating entirely different strategies for the developing countries and for the governments of those developing countries themselves. Some of the latter have taken instructive social security initiatives as reported above, despite being relatively small in scale, from which lessons may also be derived by the governments of the OECD countries – for reflection and action applied to their own systems and for them to give much bigger collaborative support for policies to diminish poverty. In the twenty-first century social security in every country will have to become a different mix of (1) international and national funding, (2) tax and social insurance contributions and (3) the direct monetary outcome of such redistribution towards better individual living standards. In 1934 the US Committee on Economic Security showed that a social security system could assist short- and long-term recovery from deep financial crisis and recession. In 2009 their report in 1935 has ironic echoes.

What are the principal conclusions that emerge from our historical analysis?

1. Social security came to be accepted by *all* OECD member countries as one of the major paths to modernization and sustainable growth as well as the principal means to reduce domestic poverty. That path continues to be actively pursued, by and on behalf of the new member States of both the OECD and the EU.
2. The path to social security for low-income countries today will necessarily be different, because of the existence and operation of a global economy, including powerful trans-national corporations, and modern international communications, but cannot be rejected.
3. In all OECD countries a mix of universal (that is, social insurance and tax-financed group schemes) and selective measures (that is, benefits conditional on test of means) came to be developed. The range was from selectively coercive schemes with paltry resources to universally protective low-benefit schemes, and finally to universally positive development schemes, designed to achieve minimally adequate standards of living and social participation and minimally creative collective enterprise.
4. Generally the greatest weight came to be placed on 'universal' contributory social insurance and then tax-financed group benefits. When breaking social security into its three key components it becomes clear

that if they are to be considered for adoption in the developing countries they have to be modernized along the following lines:

(a) contribution-based social insurance depends on revenue willingly provided from wages by employers and employees to earn entitlement to individual and family benefits in adversity, including unemployment, sickness, disability, bereavement and retirement benefits. As employers of huge numbers in their international labour forces transnational companies will be required to make contributions on behalf of sub-contracted labour in countries with which they trade. Individuals will need to be contractually and not informally employed – with beneficial results for the reduction of extensive violations of human rights – especially child labour and other labour violations. Individuals will also require rights when moving to, and/or employed in, other countries. Correspondingly, companies will acquire easier relationships with governments in whose countries they seek to establish production and services;

(b) tax-financed group schemes will be crucial for some groups unable to work, such as children, the severely disabled and the elderly, say over 75. Children have had no opportunity to qualify for benefit through contributory social insurance. Very old people were in paid employment long before social security systems were established. The tax base can no longer be applied only to one country – because of the mobility of labour and the multi-country practices of employers;

(c) tax-financed schemes will also be crucial in countries with extensive informal economies, where social insurance is difficult to organize for substantial sections of the population. By accepting in principle their responsibility for a minimum 'social wage' – as a contribution to national taxation or social insurance – trans-national companies will be able to promote both reliable productivity and social stability;

(d) and, to be effective, selective social assistance will also depend on revenue from trans-national companies, and from all, but especially rich, countries, employing relevant labour and making cross-national profit. One illustration of potential action by high-income countries is of a new application of the 1972 Tobin tax, a currency transfer tax, to raise quickly a sum much larger than current levels of overseas aid and debt relief for a UN Child Investment Fund to develop a system of child benefit in cash and kind in the poorest countries. This was set out in Chapter 7.

5. The path to social security for developing countries has effectively been obstructed or not actively supported, at the same time as social security in the industrialized countries has continued to grow, or has remained at a high level, proportionate to GDP. This has helped to foster the remorseless growth of inequalities between rich and poor countries, and of inequalities

within low-income and middle-income countries, especially those of considerable size and growing economic importance globally, such as Brazil, India and China. The need first for a catching-up exercise and then for a more coherent international development of social security systems in the rich and not only the poor countries have become urgent.

Notes

1. Following a practice paper calling for the strengthening of 'the evidence base on the potential role of social transfers as part of a wider poverty reduction strategy' and giving support to low-income countries to collect and use such data (DFID, 2005c).
2. Among influential analysts are Stephan Leibfried and Paul Pierson (see Pierson and Leibfried, 1995: 32). The diversity of welfare states is a major conclusion, together with what has been more lately described for European history as a whole as 'institutional rigidities and high thresholds of consensus necessary to alter the *status quo . . .* social policy evolution and harmonization is likely, at first, to be more the result of mutual adjustment and incremental accommodation than of central guidance' (Obinger et al., 2005).
3. In Denmark an old age pension law was introduced in 1891; a sickness insurance law in 1892; and an employers' liability act in 1898 (providing compensation to workers injured in industrial accidents). In Norway there was an accident insurance law in 1894, and in Sweden a sickness insurance law in 1891. In the first decade of the twentieth century further laws were introduced, including unemployment insurance as well as sickness insurance and subsidies for various forms of voluntary insurance.
4. Together with the social insurance system, measures to reduce unemployment had been the cornerstone of Swedish social policy from the First World War onwards. However, the crisis in the economy in the 1930s caused Sweden to anticipate Keynes by reformulating unemployment as a problem for economic policy.
5. The 1834 Poor Law was directed to deterrent provision for an undefined pauperism. Paupers included individuals of any age and with every form of ailment and need. Poor Law guardians were responsible for 'the education of pauper children, for the care of the sick and the aged, for the care of the feeble-minded and the insane, and for the employment of the able-bodied'. For those not subject to the Poor Law 'there was care for the sick in public hospitals, there was the Unemployed Workman Act of 1905, there were institutions for the mentally ill and also for the feeble-minded; and in 1908, while the commission was still at work, there had been enacted outside the Poor Law a system of pensions for the aged. Why, asked the Minority, should this duplication of activities and agencies continue?' (De Schweinitz, 1961: 193).
6. 'There is wide evidence that means-tested programmes directed at the poor are generally less supported by the public at large than non-means-tested more universal programmes' (van Oorschot, 2002, quoting several authors from industrialized OECD countries).

9
Social Protection, the European Union and its Member States

Raymond Wagener[1]

Today social protection in Europe is at a crucial moment of its history. With the advances of the integration of the European Union (EU) and the development of the internal market, social protection within the member States of the EU comes under increasing pressure and a new balance has to be found between the four freedoms[2] of the internal market and social justice for all European citizens. A somewhat parallel evolution may be observed at the world level through globalization and promotion of free trade by the World Trade Organization (WTO) which by themselves will not bring about social justice and prosperity for everyone. A new development model based on social justice and solidarity is needed and new initiatives have to be imagined so that growth and development policies will lead to real freedom for all (Sen, 2001).

Common value: the Council of Europe and the European Union

As stated in a recent Resolution of the European Parliament (2005): 'Common European values underpin each of our social models. They are the foundations of our specific European approach to economic and social policies.' In spite of sharing common values the differences between the social models of the EU member States are huge: whereas social protection expenditure is as low as about 15 per cent of GDP in Ireland or Lithuania, it represents up to 30 per cent in France or Sweden.

The European tradition of common social values did not start with the European Communities and the Treaty of Rome in 1957. Indeed in 1949, only four years after the end of the Second World War, the Council of Europe was founded in Strasbourg (Council of Europe, 1950). The Council of Europe considers itself to be a community of 46 European countries based on common values which aims at promoting collaboration between its member states. Already in 1950 the Council adopted the European Convention for the Protection of Human Rights and Fundamental Freedoms, which came into force in 1953 (Council of Europe, 1950). The Convention, which guarantees civil and political human rights, established the European Court of Human Rights in Strasbourg, to which states and individuals may refer alleged violations of human rights by contracting states. Its jurisdiction is compulsory for all contracting parties.

As early as 1953 the Council of Europe started the first attempt to regulate the social security of migrant workers through the European Interim Agreement on Social Security Schemes relating to Old Age, Invalidity and Survivors (Council of Europe, 1953). This pioneering initiative was extended considerably by the work of the European Economic Community (EEC) after its creation in 1957.

In 1961 the Council of Europe completed the Convention on Human Rights by the European Social Charter (Council of Europe, 1996) which guarantees social and economic human rights. In its own words:[3] 'The Council of Europe actively promotes social cohesion ... Improving access to fundamental social rights as laid down in the Revised European Social Charter for all members of society is at the core of the social cohesion strategy.' The rights guaranteed by the Charter revised in 1996 concern housing, health, education, employment, legal and social protection, movement of persons and non-discrimination. These rights are generally described as European 'common values' – discussed in more detail below. The Charter established the European Committee of Social Rights that monitors the implementation of the Charter by the member States by revising national annual reports. Although the Charter did not have much effect on the development of European social models, it is nevertheless an essential pronouncement of a common European social vision (Zacher, 2005).

The European Union is not the child of the Council of Europe, but of the European Coal and Steel Community (ECSC, in French: CECA) created in Paris in 1951 between France, Belgium, Netherlands, Luxembourg, Italy and the Federal Republic of Germany founded only two years earlier. The ECSC resulted from a bold proposal written by Jean Monnet, the head of the French Commissariat du Plan, and announced publicly in 1950 by Robert Schuman, the so-called Schuman Plan. In order to integrate the new Federal Republic of Germany into Western Europe and guarantee peace between Germany and France, the plan proposed to create a de facto solidarity between countries by putting the production of coal and steel of the participating countries under the control of a new supranational 'High Authority', the precursor of the European Commission. By the 1957 Treaty of Rome the ECSC became the European Economic Community (EEC) with the aim to create a common European market. Only in 1992 did the Maastricht Treaty change the EEC into the European Union (EU).

The common social values did not play an important role in the 1951 Treaty of Paris or the 1957 Treaty of Rome. Nevertheless, the Treaty of Paris already stated in Article 2 that the ECSC should contribute not only to the economic expansion of the member States, but also to the development of employment and increasing standards of living, so that the social dimension of the European Union was present from the start in 1951. Discussions about the 'European social model' have become more and more prominent in the last ten years, fuelled by growing worries of European citizens about the direction in which the European Union is heading and the consequences for their personal well-being. To some degree these worries explain the rejection of the 'Treaty establishing a Constitution for Europe' (TCE) in 2005 by the French and Dutch voters.

What specifically are the common values shared by Europeans? The 2005 Treaty (TCE) starts by stating them right at the beginning in Article I-2:

> The Union is founded on the values of respect for human dignity, freedom, democracy, equality, the rule of law and respect for human rights, including the rights of persons belonging to minorities. These values are common to the Member States in a society in which pluralism, non-discrimination, tolerance, justice, solidarity and equality between women and men prevail.

The following Article I-3 of the TCE defines the objectives of the European Union and states in particular that the Union shall work for a 'social market economy' and that 'it shall combat social exclusion and discrimination, and shall promote social justice and protection, equality between women and men, solidarity between generations and protection of the rights of the child'. Further on it states that the Union shall 'contribute to peace, security, the sustainable development of the Earth, solidarity and mutual respect among peoples, free and fair trade, eradication of poverty and the protection of human rights'.

Reading these two Articles of the TCE one may be under the impression that the acceptance of the Treaty by all member States would have helped to rebalance the relation between the rules of the internal market and the promotion of the four fundamental freedoms (free movement of goods, services, capital and people) on one side and the promotion of social protection and social justice at the EU level on the other.

Although the common values, as stated in the TCE, seem to be well accepted by an overwhelming majority of citizens in all member States, there is no common normative understanding today of the concept of a 'European social model' and its importance. The relationship between economic, employment and social protection policies is far from being stable and well balanced, as one can see by observing what happened to the so called 'Lisbon strategy', launched in 2000, after its refocusing in 2006 towards the goal of more growth and more jobs.

The refocusing of the Lisbon strategy did not stop the discussions about common social values and how a common European social model might be further developed. On the contrary, the proposal for a services directive and its possible consequences for the national social policies fuelled new discussions in all member States about the direction towards which the European Union is heading, especially in its social aspects.

Social protection and the member States of the European Union

Today there are at least 27 different social models to be found within the EU member States – at least 27, because regions in some of the federal states, like the United Kingdom, Spain and Belgium, are developing their own social policies according to their social priorities. Even if one agrees that these systems are based on the same social values, there are still plenty of explanations of different systems, in particular the social, economic and political history of these countries. In his famous book *The Three Worlds of Welfare Capitalism* (1990), Esping-Andersen made an attempt to classify the social welfare systems into three types: liberal regimes (for example the United Kingdom), corporatist regimes (for example Germany) and social democratic regimes (for example Sweden). Of course such a classification is not to be understood in a rigid way, because in general one may find in a country classified as for example a corporatist regime some components of social protection belonging to the other two systems.

The social models of the initial six countries of the EEC were basically corporatist regimes, although every country had its particularities.

In Germany[4] social protection was introduced in the first place in order to guarantee decent living conditions to blue-collar workers and their families in case of illness, industrial injuries, disability, old age or death of the breadwinner. The rapid industrialization of Germany in the second half of the nineteenth century, together with the growing strength of the trade unions and of the Social Democratic Party, made it necessary to find a comprehensive solution in order to guarantee the social peace needed for economic development of the country. This led to the creation of social insurances by Bismarck from 1881 onwards with a strong regulation and commitment by the state as asserted by the coordinated law called *Reichsversicherungsordnung* (RVO) introduced in 1911.

Luxembourg (Braun, 1982) followed the same path as Germany for similar reasons, as it became one of the most industrialized countries in Europe between 1871 and 1900 through the development of the iron and steel industry. The different branches of social security were introduced in Luxembourg between 1901 and 1911. In 1925 the coordinated law for all branches of social security, the *Code des Assurances Sociales* (CAS), similar to the German RVO, was introduced. Later the social security was extended to all economically active people: before the Second World War to all wage-earners of the private sector and during the 1950s and 1960s to all self-employed people. As in

Germany, the Luxembourg government has been deeply involved from the beginning in the design, regulation and implementation of social security. Moreover, in both countries the social partners have an extended role in the management of pension and health care insurances. Nevertheless, there are also important differences between the systems in these countries: for example in Luxembourg there is only one compulsory health care insurance fund whereas in Germany health care insurance funds are in competition with each other. Furthermore there is also a stronger co-financing of social security branches by the state budget in Luxembourg than in Germany, including pensions, health care and long-term care.

Italy (Perle, 1998) started already in 1898 to introduce compulsory social security insurances similar to the German Bismarck system. These insurances were extended to all wage-earners after the First World War and during the fascist regime. There were no major reforms after the Second World War until the second half of the 1960s.

In the case of the other three initial members of the EEC the development of social security was strongly influenced by the preparation in London during the Second World War of the post-war reconstruction of these countries. The pre-war history of social security of these countries is very different from the one in Germany and Luxembourg because until the 1940s the dominant thinking in these countries was that the government should intervene as little as possible (Whiteside et al., 2005).

The Belgian state preferred to encourage through legal and financial measures private initiatives to develop social security branches. So health insurance was introduced, and is still managed, by the 'mutuelles' linked mainly to the Christian and socialist trade unions, unemployment insurance through the trade unions and family allowances by the employers. During the Second World War within the country and abroad several work groups worked out projects for the reconstruction of the country after the war. This led to a Social Pact through which the National Office of Social Security was created for the management of the following branches: old age pensions, unemployment insurance, family allowances, sickness insurance and invalidity insurance. The management of yearly holidays was also added to this list of branches. Workers are represented by the trade unions, with the exception of the health care insurance where they are represented by the 'mutuelles'. Contrary to the other five initial member States of the EEC, in Belgium private organizations, especially the trade unions and the 'mutuelles', play an extremely important role in social security and the role of the state is weak. This situation did not change until the 1980s and the introduction of austerity policies.

Until 1945 social assistance was the dominant paradigm of social protection in France (Palier, 2005). Before the Second World War several laws tried to introduce a comprehensive social insurance system, but this was implemented in a comprehensive way only after the war. The 'Action Plan of the Resistance' proposed to introduce a Beveridge type system based on the following 'three U principles': Unity (one system, one institution), Universality (covering all the risks and the whole population) and Uniformity (the same benefits for all). But in fact the system introduced under the leadership of Pierre Laroque in 1945 is a social insurance system sharing similar principles and values with the German and Luxembourg system, for example the strong role of the state and the co-management by the social partners. As in France, Dutch social security was very limited before the Second World War. It was organized at the level of individual firm or industry sectors, not at the national level, with a low degree of redistributive solidarity (van Oorschot, 2006). In 1945 the Van Rhijn Commission presented its report, obviously influenced by Beveridge's report, which stated that 'society, organized in the state, is liable for the social security and protection against want of all its members, on the condition, that citizens themselves do all that can be reasonably expected in order to acquire such security and protection'. The report led to the introduction of 'people's insurances' covering old age, disability and survivors' pensions for all citizens, as well as of social assistance schemes.

When the EEC was founded in 1957 the initial six member States had very different social security systems. Nevertheless these systems shared most of their characteristic elements, so that they may be classified as corporatist systems, according to Esping-Andersen's classification. Therefore the EEC was able to take further the work of the Council of Europe on social security of migrant workers through its Regulation 3 in 1958 and especially through the 1971 Council Regulation 1408/71 encompassing all branches of social security. Freedom of movement of workers is important for the development of the internal market of the EU and the coordination of social security of migrant workers is an important part of it. It is based on four principles:

1. equal treatment of national workers and of citizens of other member States;
2. periods of insurance and employment completed under another member State's legislation are taken into account in order to determine rights on social security benefits;
3. prevention of overlapping of benefits of the same kind;
4. exportability of some types of social security benefits.

The European experience with social security of migrant workers is certainly very interesting and helpful for countries like China or India, or for regional groups of countries which are developing rapidly and need to improve their social protection systems at state or regional level.

The rather homogeneous situation of social security systems throughout the member States disappeared in 1972 when the United Kingdom, Ireland and Denmark became members. Today countries of all three types of Esping-Andersen's classification belong to the EU and there are huge differences between the levels of social protection throughout Europe. For southern

European societies industrialization came later than in Central Europe and economic possibilities were more limited. As to the new member States, with the exception of Cyprus and Malta, their starting points were as socialist systems. In their transition towards a market economy almost all of them were predominantly influenced by the World Bank and the IMF which gave priority to privatization of health care and pensions, as well as to the introduction of means-tested benefits as far as possible. One may wonder if the European Union did not lose a historic opportunity, because it did not establish a deep collaboration with these states immediately after their change of regime. Nevertheless social protection is far from uniform in these new member States. Even when economic and social development are similar and the social values of different societies are similar, there is no compelling reason for choosing the same social protection systems, as one may see in the case of the three Baltic republics which were part of the Soviet Union until 1990 and built their new welfare systems starting from the same Soviet social protection system.

Perhaps one way of explaining these different results can be found by looking at the principles for the reform of the health care system discussed in the book by Kornai and Eggleston (2001: 15–16) on health sector reforms in Eastern Europe. According to these authors, the reforms should be guided by the weighting of nine principles. The first two are ethical principles: sovereignty of the individual and solidarity. The last seven principles are about the involved institutions and coordination mechanisms: competition, incentives for efficiency, the role of the state, transparency, the time requirement of the programme, harmonious growth and sustainable financing. These principles, which according to the authors may also be useful in social policy reforms outside health care, may lead to very different systems according to the weight given, for example, to solidarity or competition.

The common paradigm in Europe is the 'welfare state', which does not reduce itself to the fight against poverty; quite the contrary, as Brian Barry has argued in his article 'The Welfare State versus the Relief of Poverty' (Barry, 1990). The welfare state, as it is conceived in the social protection laws in Germany or in other European countries, aims at designing its policies and programmes in such a way that specific laws for the poor are not required anymore. Social security programmes and benefits should be organized in a comprehensive way, so that social aid is needed only under exceptional circumstances of urgency as the ultimate safety net. Indeed, in the case of the European welfare state most benefits are universal ones and only a small minority of benefits are means-tested.

The welfare state approach is universal and focuses on integrating the whole population through redistributive mechanisms. Its benefits may be index targeted, meaning that they are available according to some indicators. For example, parents may obtain child allowances according to the number of their children without taking into account their income or wealth.

In contrast, the approach of traditional laws on poverty has been selective and individuals are identified as 'persons in need'. Typically a system focusing on limiting benefits to poor people faces the problem of identifying the poor persons 'deserving' a benefit. Furthermore, such targeted benefits may entail that the beneficiaries feel stigmatized and marginalized within society. Universal benefits increase the acceptance and legitimacy of welfare policies and they contribute to national social cohesion (Schefczyk, 2005: 236–7). In the context of developing countries Mkandawire (2005: 7) observes that targeting reflects the point of view that social policy has only the narrow purpose of correcting negative outcomes of macroeconomic policies and that its only purpose is poverty eradication. As shown by the European welfare state, the aims of social protection go far beyond poverty reduction. Social protection is about putting predictability into life: illness, disability, losing a job should not ruin one's life and the life of one's family. Social protection is about social cohesion, equity, 'solidarity – living together in dignity' (Paakjaer Martinussen, 2006) and social justice. In the words of van Parijs (2006) justice 'means real freedom for all, the greatest real freedom for those with least of it'. And he is very explicit: for him 'all' means 'all' and 'justice' means 'global justice'.

Social protection, the European Union and the internal market

In the last ten years the European integration process has become an important factor which the member States of the EU have to take increasingly into account in the design and implementation of their social protection systems. The Economic and Monetary Union, including the Stability and Growth Pact, leads necessarily to the scrutiny of the long-term sustainability of social policies, especially of pension systems. As a consequence of the development of the internal market and of judgements of the European Court of Justice, the balance between social and health policies on one side and the four freedoms of movement of goods, services, persons and capital on the other has been changed to the disadvantage of the former.

In 2004 the European Commission published its proposal for a services directive (the so called Bolkenstein directive) in order to foster the free movement of services.[5] This proposal provoked an extensive discussion throughout Europe, in particular because it included social and health services within its scope, without taking into account the specific objectives of health systems or social protection systems. As a consequence of the discussions and the deliberations of the European Parliament, the proposal was substantially changed and health services as well as some social services were excluded from it. A specific directive on health services will be prepared, but this is far from easy. As to the social services excluded from the directive of services, the text excludes in particular 'social services relating to social housing, childcare and support of families and persons permanently or temporarily in need which are provided by the State, by providers mandated by the State or by charities recognized as such by the State' (European Parliament, 2006, Article 2-2-j). The use of the words 'in need' may suggest that in the future the development of the internal market of services may reduce social policy to the reduction of poverty and inclusion programmes and endanger the universal approach of social protection based on social justice. Nevertheless the recital 28 of the consolidated text of the services directive adopted by the European Parliament at a second reading on 15 November 2006 underlines that 'This Directive does not deal with the funding of, or the system of aids linked to, social services. Nor does it affect the criteria or conditions set by Member States to ensure that social services effectively carry out a function to the benefit of the public interest and social cohesion. In addition, this Directive should not affect the principle of universal service in Member States' social services.' It seems quite obvious that the European Union is at a defining moment: will it develop into a social market economy allowing all its citizens to live in dignity and share the prosperity of the Union, or will it develop into a pure market economy with a residual social policy of poverty reduction?

The development of the globalized market economy and the rules of the World Trade Organization (WTO) are bringing the national social policies in countries outside the EU under similar pressures, although of course the integration of the EU is more far-reaching.

Minimum standards

In the past EU member States did not take many initiatives at the EU level to develop actively a common European social model because, according to the subsidiarity principle, social protection policies are a matter of national sovereignty. But in this way they allowed the EU to gain a growing impact on the national social policies through the development of the internal market and the application of the four freedoms, most prominently through decisions of the European Court of Justice.[6] It is becoming more and more obvious that the common European social values and the development of a European social model need an EU social policy financed at EU level. Today the equilibrium between internal market and national social policies is not a stable one: the EU-wide policy of the four market freedoms will prevail if no new balance is developed through the promotion of an EU social protection system. One may suspect that globalization and the WTO will have a similar impact on national social protection systems throughout the world through the development of the rules of a 'free' and 'more competitive' trade system if there is no similar development of social standards based on values of social justice and equity. One may also think that WTO rules will impact on health care insurance schemes and pension funds. Concerning health care, access to medical drugs and their affordability in developing countries is being discussed in many countries and institutions.

The European Union has to become a social union, as the Luxembourg prime minister Jean-Claude Juncker said in an interview given to the German newspaper *Frankfurter Rundschau*.[7] Otherwise there is a real danger that a majority of European citizens will no longer support the EU project. As the reporter mentioned, Juncker has been for years an active defender of minimum social standards in Europe. He was asked what he thinks is an absolutely necessary minimum EU social standard. In his answer Juncker stressed that it is the introduction of an EU basic income, the right of every citizen living in an EU member State to a minimum income. The level of the minimum income will have to be adapted to the specific conditions of every country, for example according to the purchasing power, but the EU should fix the rules for this basic income to be applied throughout Europe. Philippe van Parijs, the famous defender of the non-means-tested basic income, presented a similar idea at the 2006 Helsinki conference which he called the 'Euro-dividend' (van Parijs, 2006: 7). The basic income should be financed at the EU level, for example through VAT or a 'super-Tobin' tax on all electronic transactions, as van Parijs suggests. It is interesting that he discusses also a gradual introduction of this basic income by age groups, as for example a universal basic pension which exists already in some member States, or as an EU-wide child benefit as suggested by Atkinson (1996, also mentioned in van Parijs, 2006).

Social protection is not only about income but also about health. Some European ministers of health have already started a discussion about minimum health care rights for all EU citizens.

Towards a new development model: social justice and freedom for all

The interpretation of social justice given above by van Parijs is that it means global justice for all. Indeed Europe cannot construct a European social model based on social justice and restrict it to its own citizens. Doing so would be contrary to the meaning of social justice. The EU has to apply the same concept of social justice in its relations with external countries. The EU is linked to the rest of the world by movements of goods, services, capital and persons. In particular, immigration from developing countries, especially from Africa, is becoming more and more of a global human catastrophe. EU firms invest, buy and sell abroad: do they promote the European social values in their relations with their workers and clients? In particular, do they make sure that their workers abroad have the same social protection as in Europe? European pension funds invest in firms within the EU and abroad: do they invest according to criteria promoting social justice? The UNEP Finance

Initiative and the UN Global Compact have developed an interesting initiative called 'Principles for Responsible Investment' in order to incorporate environmental, social and corporate governance (ESG) issues into investment analysis and decision-making processes.[8] Perhaps it would be useful to launch a similar initiative at the EU level in order to promote investment according to ethical criteria of social justice.

The EU member States, the European Commission, the European Investment Bank and European NGOs are also linked to the developing countries by their development projects. What are the development paradigms underpinning the development aid of Europe? It is notable that most social projects are more in line with the poverty reduction approach than with the welfare state approach through universal programmes. And unfortunately EU social ministries and administrations are generally not consulted during the process of identifying social aid projects. Another approach is possible and at least some countries are asking for a change. Indeed at the recent 16th Ibero-American Summit in Montevideo President Néstor Kirchner from Argentina asked Europe to help the countries of the region to fight against poverty not only through relief programmes, but also by supporting structural reforms that these countries have to implement.[9]

By referring to the rich experiences of social protection in its member States and the development of a Europe-wide social model based on social justice, Europe could contribute to a new impetus towards a global human development model built on solidarity and social justice for all.

Notes

1. The author wishes to state that this chapter does not reflect in any way the policy position of the Luxembourg government. His chapter is purely personal.
2. Freedoms of movement of goods, services, persons and capital.
3. For more information, consult www.coe.int
4. On German social security, see Townsend (Chapter 2 in this volume) and Butterwegge (2006).
5. For more information see: http://ec.europa.eu/internal_market/services/services-dir/index_en.htm
6. These facts were discussed extensively at the 2006 conference on 'The Europeanization of Social Protection' organized by the Finnish Presidency of the EU.
7. *Frankfurter Rundschau*, 20 November 2006.
8. For further information see: http://www.unpri.org/
9. *El País*, 5 November 2006.

10
Can the European Welfare Model be Exported?

Peter H. Lindert

Overview

The democratic welfare state – as a defining feature of a societal organization – occupies a small corner of world history. It has happened only in the twentieth and twenty-first centuries, and only in Europe. This raises some immediate historical questions: Why so seldom? What are the trends in their social programmes? Will the welfare state in Europe self-destruct in the face of challenges from ageing and globalization? Or will it prevail? If so, can the model be exported to other countries?

This chapter will argue that the European welfare states are more secure than many have predicted. However, it will also be shown that the spread of the European model of the welfare state to other continents was blocked for a long time by the kind of social transfers that predominated on those other continents. More specifically, it will be argued that:

1. The democratic welfare state is not an endangered species. The number of welfare states has never declined.
2. Nor is there any clear economic reason why the welfare state should wither. OECD experience since 1960 does not show any negative econometric effect of larger tax-financed transfers on national product. There are good economic and institutional reasons for this 'free lunch' puzzle.
3. To judge the new pressures that population ageing will bring to government budgets in this century, we can use OECD pension experience from the 1980s and 1990s. The countries with the oldest populations had already begun to cut the relative generosity of their old age transfers *per elderly person*. They did not, however, cut the average shares of public pensions or other transfers in GDP, nor did they lower the absolute real value of the average pension.
4. Population ageing puts the same pressure on any pension system, whether funded or not, and whether private or public.

5. Some developing countries spend almost as large a share of GDP on transfers as Europe's welfare states today. Indeed, many of them, particularly in Latin America and the Middle East, spend a greater share than the OECD countries did earlier in history, at comparable income levels and population age structure.
6. Yet the incidence of transfers is very different in developing countries. Regressive transfers, especially generous pensions, in favour of high-income government employees have been holding back the potential for a welfare state.

The road to these conclusions needs to start by clarifying the definition of the terms 'social transfers' and 'welfare state' used in this chapter. Social transfers consist of tax-financed government benefits such as:

- basic assistance to poor families, alias 'poor relief' (before 1930), 'family assistance', 'welfare' (in America), or 'supplemental income';
- public aid to unemployed workers (unemployment compensation and help in securing new jobs);
- public pensions, excluding those for government and military employees;[1]
- public health expenditures; and
- housing subsidies.

Such tax-based transfers tend to redistribute income somewhat progressively, as Beveridge and other pioneers had hoped. Their progressivity is not uniform or easily measured, however.

For simplicity's sake the term 'welfare state' is defined here as a country that devotes 20 per cent of GDP or more to social transfers.[2] The welfare state is a tax- and transfer concept, both here and in Beveridge's original 1942 proposals. It does *not* include any direct market controls by government, such as worker protection laws, high minimum wages, import barriers, working hour regulations, or government ownership of industry.

Five features of the definition of social transfers call for immediate emphasis. First, there is no general practical way to add tax rebates and tax credits (alias 'tax expenditures'), that can be conceived as 'imputed' social security expenditure, to the amounts transferred and such implicit subsidies are set aside here. Second, some of the 'transfers' are 'transfers in kind', i.e. in fact purchases of goods and services that are part of national product, as in the case of public health care or public housing construction. Third, public education expenditures are omitted here, as in the conventional reporting of transfers. They are less controversial than true transfers because all sides agree that they are productive to some extent. In addition, the redistributive content of educational spending requires a whole separate analysis, since the incidence varies by level of schooling and level of national development. Fourth, the definition of social transfers excludes output-sector subsidies such as farm or food support programmes. The fifth and final feature is the most noteworthy and perhaps the feature that distinguishes this analysis to some extent from others of a similar nature. I exclude pension and other benefits paid directly to people with public-sector careers. Career-related benefits paid to government officials, civil servants, judges, public teachers, and the military are not 'social' in an egalitarian redistributive sense. Rather, they are part of the salary bargains struck between well-paid employees and employers. Separating public-career benefits from universal or anti-poverty transfers will prove useful in monitoring the social programmes of developing countries, as I will argue later.

Western Europe: no retreat yet

As an economic species, the welfare state has shown strong survival instincts in the countries where it emerged in the twentieth century. Within the expanding OECD, the number of welfare states is stable or expanding. Since 1980, these exits, entries and borderline cases have stood out:

- Ireland definitely left the ranks of welfare states on the 20 per cent yardstick.
- Switzerland took Ireland's place in the late 1990s, quietly becoming a welfare state with major increases in pensions and public health.[3]
- Others are approaching the 20 per cent borderline from above and from below. The Netherlands dropped down to the border, with major cuts in its disability and other programmes after 1995. Japan is approaching welfare state status, now transferring over 17 per cent of national product.
- In Eastern Europe, at least the Czech Republic, Poland and perhaps Hungary are preserving their welfare states, both through the depression of the 1990s and through the subsequent recovery.
- Six other OECD countries continue to hover near the 20 per cent borderline – Australia, Canada, New Zealand, Portugal, Spain and the United Kingdom.

The welfare state's survival over the last quarter century has puzzled many observers. We often suspect that tax and transfers cut the productivity of both the taxed and the subsidized, since both sides face higher marginal tax rates of exerting themselves productively. Many have also suspected that welfare states tend to run bigger government budget deficits.

Yet experience from the late nineteenth century to the early twenty-first fails to support these common suspicions. So says the quantitative evidence, both when you look at crude figures and when you statistically measure the different forces that determine economic growth. There is no international correlation at all between the share of social spending in the economy and either the level or the growth of GDP. However, places differ in other ways than just in their levels of taxes and welfare, so we need an econometric analysis that gives many forces their due. Several economists have performed such tests, and most have found no robust or significant negative effect of higher social transfers on GDP per person.[4] The effect could just as easily be positive, according to the majority of tests, with a zero effect near the centre of the confidence interval. In all the new tests, as in most earlier studies, the welfare shows no clear net costs for the nation as a whole.[5]

A first key to understanding the historical and statistical result is to remember the distinction between imagination and empirical tests. The usual tales about the high incentive costs of the welfare state are based on a compelling microeconomic logic. The logic might have been borne out in the real world if governments had blundered by simply taxing capital and entrepreneurship and effort heavily, while offering young adults the chance to avoid a lifetime of work with a near-wage benefit. Yet the overriding truth about such blunders is that *they never happened*. Only if we extend the econometric estimates out into a world that never happened, a blundering world that taxes 40 per cent of capital and top incomes and pays people who never work, would some of the estimated equations predict those high costs of foolish policy. Within the range of real historical experience, there is no clear net GDP cost of higher social transfers.

The econometric evidence suggests – though it cannot yet quantify – major roles for the following institutional and historical facts:

1. The welfare state tax mix that is better for economic growth puts more emphasis on general consumption taxes and 'sin' taxes (on alcohol, gasoline and tobacco) (Kato, 2003; Lindert, 2004: Chapter 10; Timmons, 2005; Wilensky, 2002).
2. Its work disincentives cost little in terms of GDP (Allard and Lindert, 2006; Lindert, 2004: Chapters 10, 18).
3. The welfare states of Northern (but not Southern) Europe gain in human capital by better supporting continuity in mothers' careers.
4. Health insurance and health care is a particular (huge) sector of the economy where ordinary markets cannot function alone, and the American mixture of private and public performs badly.[6]

If America's Achilles heel is the health care sector, Western European growth and well-being appear to have been dragged down by anti-competitive policies. Through a host of direct market interventions, privileged positions have been protected against competition, with familiar consequences for growth. The most obvious examples have been occupational health and safety laws, high minimum wages, import barriers, government regulation or ownership of industry, restrictions on hours of work and of store openings.[7] Yet, as already emphasized, these protections of privilege are unrelated to the safety nets and égalité of the welfare states.

Ageing gracefully in the twenty-first century

If the welfare state seems innocent of dragging down growth in the twentieth century, might it nonetheless fail in the twenty-first? Daily media coverage emphasizes that a rapidly ageing population may find it harder and harder to keep budgets in balance and to sustain economic growth. Will the welfare state be one of the casualties in this ageing world? For most countries, the budgetary tensions have centred on public pensions. Let us follow the recent debate by focusing on pensions, even though health care poses a bigger budgetary threat.

Three familiar sources of pension trouble

Ageing too fast. The trend towards improved senior longevity and lower fertility is pressuring high-income countries to recalibrate their pension programmes. Actuarial changes are been forced not only on public pensions and health systems, but on private job-based pension schemes as well. If ageing were the only problem, then we could rank different countries' dangers just by looking at the UN projections for population ageing out to, say, the middle of this century. As of 2050 the countries with the highest population shares over age 65 will probably be Italy and Japan, followed by the rest of Europe. North America, Australia and New Zealand face less difficulty here, thanks to their acceptance of immigrants and their generally higher fertility. Most developing countries also face less demographic threat over this half-century. The exceptions tend to be East Asian: China, Taiwan and Singapore are all ageing so rapidly that by mid-century they will face pension problems as severe as those faced by most OECD countries today.

Asking for trouble with early retirement policy. A second source of pension trouble is avoidable, but widespread in Southern and Western Europe. Constrained by their own job-protection laws, several European countries have tried to buy out seniors by subsidizing early retirement of workers in the 50–64 age range. The implicit tax on staying at work peaked at the start of the 1990s. Italy appears to face the biggest problem and is in particularly deep trouble in this respect, yet Italian politics has thus far produced only timid and partial rollbacks of the subsidies to early retirement.

Asking for trouble with overall government deficits. The budget pressures that can crush social programmes need not relate to ageing or to retirement policy alone. They can come from any source. Whatever raises the overall government deficit and national debt relative to annual GDP can force a country to cut back on any kind of spending, including pensions and other social transfers. Even if pensions were ostensibly protected in a special locked-box fund, a desperate government could always raid the box, though governments rarely feel it necessary to consider extreme measures and in history have generally met their enacted commitments.

Within the OECD, the countries with the largest overall deficits have been low-spending countries. Japan's deficits ran at 6–8 per cent of GDP over the decade ending in 2005. The United States was second in the budget deficit ranks from 2001 to 2005. The high spending welfare states have run smaller deficits or even surpluses.

The threat of population ageing is similar for all pension systems

When the population gets older, something has to give. Annual pension benefits simply cannot continue to keep up with annual incomes of the employed. Wage-indexed pensions appear unsustainable, and need to be shifted to price indexation.

Most public pension systems are still financed on a pay-as-you-go (PAYGO) basis. In the aggregate, the current generation of workers pays for the retirement of the currently elderly, and not for its own retirement. Given that PAYGO is the prevailing current system, many have slipped into thinking that PAYGO is doomed and must be replaced with a funded or defined-contribution system. This is not persuasive, however. No pension – no matter how it is financed – is immune to the need to adjust to longevity. Suppose that the only pillar for your retirement structure were individual savings. If a person works and saves for Q years, and draws on savings for an estimated R years of retirement, she must set annual savings and retirement benefits so that the accumulated value of savings just covers retirement needs. For any given rate of return on savings, one cannot enjoy more retirement (raise the ratio R/Q) without cutting your retirement (and earlier) consumption relative to your wage. A public system, like a private pension plan, must adjust the relative retirement benefit to the ratio of years spent in the two phases of adult life.

Just as ageing is a problem in any pension system, so too there is some parametric adjustment in any system that can fix the problem. There are two ways to avoid raising the tax rate and still balance the pension budget, even though we live longer:

1. Slow down the rise of the retired/working ratio, by raising retirement age (or fertility or immigration), and
2. Make benefits rise more slowly than the average income of the employed.

Yet real benefits need not be cut, nor tax rates raised, as long as income grows. Real benefits per retiree could even go on rising slowly, as long as the ageing is less severe than the rapid ageing of Italy or Japan, or the full-benefit retirement age is raised, or both.

The OECD solutions of the 1980s and 1990s

Keeping PAYGO in equilibrium is not purely hypothetical. In fact, several countries of Northern Europe did much of the necessary adjusting in the 1980s and 1990s. It is instructive to see which adjustments their political systems tended to make. By drawing on the underlying econometric estimates of what determines social budgets, we can forecast the likely non-linear effects of population ageing on taxes and transfers (Lindert, 2004: Chapters 7, 8 and appendices). Figure 10.1 gives the revealed policy response to ageing, holding other things equal. When the over-65 share of the population rose from 14 per cent to 18 per cent (a rise of 29 per cent), there was no change in the shares of pensions or other social transfers in GDP. The cost to taxpayers of all social transfers, including pensions, therefore rose hardly at all (a statistically insignificant 0.5 per cent of GDP). Essentially the full burden of the adjustment fell on the elderly themselves. The crude pension support ratio, measured as the ratio of (pensions per elderly) to (GDP per capita), dropped 18 per cent, all other things being equal. It did not show up as a real drop in pension benefits because GDP per capita was growing. Some countries achieved this by encouraging later retirement, others by indexing pensions to indicators that grew more slowly than the growth of earnings. In principle,

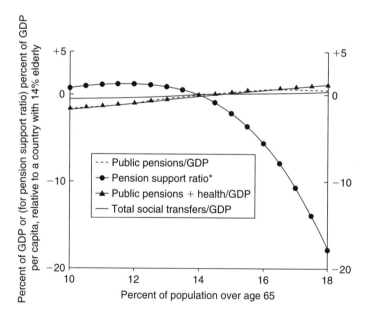

Figure 10.1 How population ageing affected pensions and other social transfers in OECD, 1978–1995

Note: *Pension support ratio = (public pensions/elderly)/(GDP/capita).
Source: Lindert (2004), Appendix Table E3, equations without full fixed effects.

this kind of adjustment in tax-based pensions could continue forever. In the 1980s and 1990s it was part of a larger set of social transfers that did not bring any loss of GDP to those high-budget countries of Northern Europe.

History leads to doubts that reforms bring political pre-commitment

There is no reason to believe that starting a defined-contribution plan has any more permanence than a PAYGO set of benefits. Most countries with PAYGO pensions today had defined-contribution plans earlier, but overthrew them. Consider three famous examples. The original Bismarck social security innovations of the 1880s started as a defined-contribution scheme, but began shifting within a few years to more PAYGO, and more burdens on general taxpayers. The United States Social Security Act of 1935 set up a funded system, not PAYGO. The system was defined-contribution at the aggregate cohort level, though it gave low earners a better rate of return than high earners. Yet political forces gradually abandoned the funded system in favour of PAYGO (Miron and Weil, 1998). Finally, the privatization of Britain's public pensions still exists, but with important modifications is drifting back towards progressive redistribution and PAYGO. While the Blair government retained much of the defined-contribution features of the Thatcher era, it raised minimum income guarantees for pensioners significantly, financed by the general taxpayer (Blundell and Johnson, 1999; Disney, et al., 2004). The political tendency is clear: democracy finds it at least as easy to switch out of funded defined-contribution systems towards PAYGO as vice versa. All pension 'reforms' reflect temporary and reversible shifts in political mood.

Meanwhile, the reforms are regressive. In the process of switching to defined contribution and privatized plans two kinds of elderly poor fall behind – those whose lower lifetime earnings yield less pension support under the less progressive reform designs, and those whose retirement investments turned out worse than predicted. Furthermore, the financial service sector earns a windfall gain if government has compelled households to buy its services. Of all the effects of such compulsory private savings, this is perhaps the clearest. As we shall see, the same might have been true of Chile's famous pensions privatization, once some offsetting effects are weighed.

State and trends in welfare state developments in developing countries

This section tries to sketch out the major typical trends of welfare state developments in developing countries. It will concentrate on the two areas where most innovative developments can be observed from a redistributive point of view: Latin America and India.

It is acknowledged that other experiments, mostly in form of community-based insurance systems, were undertaken during the last decade in many countries, mostly in Africa. Many of these experiments are now – after a first stock-taking – being modified, shifting from stand-alone solutions for communities or occupational groups to federated systems that are supported by central government. With the notable exception of Ghana, which introduced a national health insurance system in 2003 built on district mutual insurance schemes, these schemes have not yet had a major impact in terms of income redistribution. A further major exception to the rule is Thailand where universal access to health care was introduced in 2001 and will have major effects on the income security of the poorer part of the population. This innovation is described in Chapter 16 and does not need to be revisited here.

Aggregate transfer levels in developing countries compared with OECD history

History suggests a straightforward forecast on the prospect for welfare states among today's developing countries: if and when developing countries reach the conditions that Western European welfare states reached in the 1960s, we would predict that they will become welfare states. Past research suggests that the conditions are these:

- full-franchise democracy, with more than 60 per cent of adults actually voting;
- an elderly population, with at least 15 per cent of the population being 65 or older;
- GDP per capita equal to that of (say) Sweden in 1950; and
- a low level of ethnic fractionalization.[8]

This combination has historically distinguished Europe's welfare states from the rest of the world.

To judge whether today's developing countries are approaching these conditions, we can look at their democracy, their population ageing, their incomes, and their ethnic divisions. We can also see whether their social transfers seem to be following a trajectory that reveals as much social spending as the historical paths of the now-rich countries. Since the voting shares and ethnicity divisions are not so easily measured for some countries, let us follow the paths of developing countries in terms of the two more convenient variables, population ageing and GDP per capita. Figures 10.2 and 10.3 do this. The historical paths of Sweden, the United States and Japan are used as standards with which we can compare developing countries in the 1980s and 1990s. Comparing the age shares and income levels of the past and today's developing countries yields a striking perspective. Today's developing countries spend more on social transfers, including pensions, than the advanced OECD countries spent historically at similar age shares and income levels.

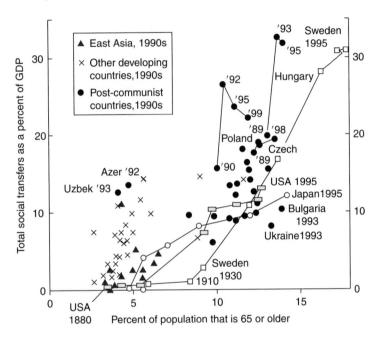

Figure 10.2 Age and total social transfers around the world in the 1990s, versus historical paths, 1880–1995

For example, back in 1930 Sweden spent only 2.6 per cent of GDP on social transfers, at a time when it had a relatively aged population (8 per cent were over the age of 65). Compared to Sweden in 1930, many countries today exceed that 2.6 per cent, despite having younger and poorer populations. Such elevated transfers show up in recent data from many countries in Eastern and Central Europe, and also for Costa Rica, Panama, Tunisia, Sri Lanka, Egypt and Bolivia, among others.

Which developing countries will continue on the path towards being perennial welfare states? The leaders will almost surely be the democracies of Central and Eastern Europe, such as Poland, the Czech Republic and Hungary. These have elderly populations, fair growth prospects, a shift to fuller democracy, and a history of safety nets under communism. While their social transfer shares of GDP have dropped since the depression of the early and mid-1990s, they are still above other countries' historic patterns.

Outside of Europe, two large regions seem to spend more than others. Countries in Latin America, and the Middle East to a lesser extent, generally spend more on the elderly, the disabled, the unemployed and the poor than do South Asia and East Asia. Africa's spending is very low.[9] Among countries that were never part of the Soviet bloc, the early leaders would seem to be

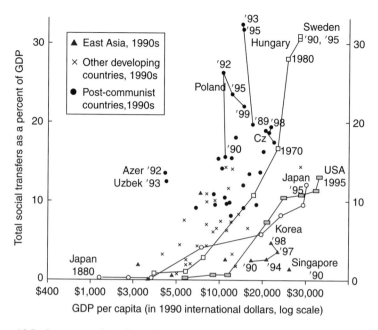

Figure 10.3 Income and total social transfers around the world in the 1990s, versus historical paths, 1880–1995

Israel, Uruguay and Brazil. At face value, the numbers imply that Uruguay has joined the welfare state 20 per cent club as of 1998 (transfers = 23.5 per cent of GDP), and Lula's Brazil was close as of 2004 (19.3 per cent).[10]

What kinds of transfers? Robin Hood in reverse?

The aggregate numbers can deceive, however. Before we can identify the developing countries likely to become welfare states, we must look behind the numbers on their social transfers. Who is actually getting those transfers, and who is paying for them?

In fact, throughout the developing world, the social transfers seemed – for a long time – to flow mainly to well-paid government officials. Public pensions in particular flow to civil servants, teachers and the military, and seldom to agricultural or any informal sector in large amounts per household.[11] That is true even in East Asia, where the widespread reluctance to launch anti-poverty transfers contrasted with curiously generous pensions and other payments for officials (Gough, 2004). It is also true of Latin America, the set of developing countries for which these issues have been studied in most detail.[12] Let us also draw on this relatively rich Latin American literature, turning first to the good news before confronting the profound elements of regressivity.

Truly progressive anti-poverty programmes have expanded in a few Latin American countries over the last dozen years. The programmes range in size. Brazil's *Bolsa Familia*, which evolved from *Bolsa Escola* and other programmes launched in the mid-1990s, is now the largest in the region, covering 11 million families (46 million people, or close to a fifth of its population). Mexico's *Oportunidades*, launched as *Progresa*, now covers 5 million families. Chile's *Solidario* programme, launched in 2002, covers over 200,000 families, and Colombia's *Familias en Acción* programme covers about 400,000 families.

The progressivity of such programmes, as measured by a World Bank team, is illustrated for Brazil, Chile and Mexico in Figure 10.4. The Bank's chosen measure is a 'concentration index' summarizing the extent to which poorer income ranks receive more (negative concentration signals progressiveness) or less than higher income ranks.[13] Progressive redistribution, in the Robin Hood direction, characterizes the large anti-poverty programmes just mentioned, and also several other programmes, especially in Chile.

Yet these recent advances in anti-poverty programmes are offset by long-standing regressivity in other transfers. Latin American behaviour combines the world's greatest income inequalities with regressive transfers, producing what has become known as the Latin American 'truncated welfare state'.[14] While these programmes are not as unequally distributed as are the original incomes represented by Figure 10.4's Gini coefficients, they are regressive nonetheless. The privileged recipients here are those employed in the formal sectors, especially civil servants, judges and the military. Formal sector jobs are so well paid relative to the median member of the labour force that even unemployment benefits are regressive, because the top 40 per cent of households get more than 40 per cent of the benefits, as Figure 10.4 shows for Brazil, Chile and Mexico.

Latin America's most consistent offender is its set of public pension systems, which redistribute from poor to rich even after deducting each income group's own contributions to calculate the net pension subsidy from general government revenues.[15] While some might argue that the use of general revenues for the pensions is just a different way of paying public-sector wages in lieu of straight pay, the fact that government and military straight pay is well above private sector alternatives, with little competition, suggests that the pensions are more akin to redistribution, i.e. a source of rents.

The regressiveness of public-sector pensions is well illustrated by the best-documented case, the public pension system of Brazil. In its defence, one can say that Brazil's system has recently begun to provide pensions for the poorest groups. Yet these safety nets provide less than $1,000 a year for those poor who receive them. By contrast, Brazil's civil servants receive a huge subsidy even if that subsidy has been curbed by recent reforms.

(A)

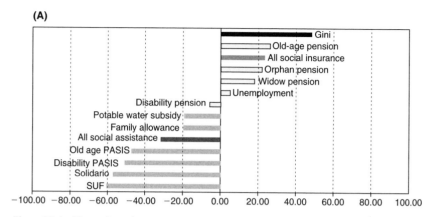

Figure 10.4 How selected government programmes in Latin America allocate transfers 'progressively' and 'regressively'
Panel A. Brazil 2002–2003
Panel B. Chile 2003
Panel C. Mexico 2002

Notes: (1) Horizontal axis = 'concentration coefficient', measuring the Lorenz-curve impact of a unit of transfer benefits. Note that the measures shown here are not yet weighted by programme size. (2) Gini = the Gini coefficient of original income. (3) The public pension receipts are net of public employee contributions on a pay-as-you-go basis. (4) In Panel A for Brazil: Seguro deemprego = a main programme of unemployment compensation for the formal sector; Renda minima = minimum income programmes offered by some sub-national governments; Bolsa Escola = conditional cash transfers to poor families, conditional on the child's attending school and receiving health services. Starting mid-1990s, absorbed into Bolsa Familia in 2003, Auxilio gas = transfers managed by the Ministry of Mines and Energy, providing small bi-monthly cash transfers to low-income families in lieu of price subsidies on cooking gas (which were phased out in 2001). PETI = conditional cash transfers under the Programme for the Eradication of Child Labour, conditional on the child's remaining in school and not at work. (5) In Panel B for Chile: PASIS = Pensiones Asistenciales de Ancianidad y de Invalidez, also known as the assistance pension programme, created in 1975. It grants pensions to persons over 65 years of age and to the disabled, provided that their income is lower than 50 per cent of the minimum pension; Solidario = Sistema Chile Solidario, builds on the Puente ('Bridge') programme piloted in early 2002, and acts as the entry point to the Chilean social protection system. Participating households identified as poor receive both a conditional cash transfer and health services; SUF = Unified Family Subsidy, an income-support programme for indigent households with children under 18 years of age and not covered by social insurance, initiated in 1981. Eligibility is based on a proxy means test. (6) In Panel C for Mexico: PROCAMPO = since 1993, an agricultural income-support programme offering fixed monetary payments to low-income farmers per-hectare of basic crops, independent of production levels; Oportunidades, formerly Progresa = since 1997, transfers to poor rural households conditional on children's participation in basic education and health services, rural only, 1997–2000, and then extended to cities.
Source: K. Lindert et al. (2006). See also De Ferranti et al. (2004).

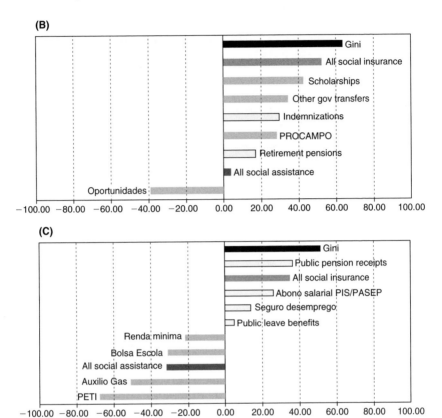

Figure 10.4   (Continued)

Here are some parameters of a typical Latin American civil service system:[16]

(a) It is mostly paid out of general taxes, and not by contributions from the civil servants themselves or even from their employing units. The subsidy from the general budget can reach 100 per cent. The general budget revenues come largely from the sales and excise taxes paid by people further down the income ranks.

(b) A retiring civil servant can often count *all* his or her years of work, even in the private sector, as service years. He or she may need only one year of employment as a civil servant to earn pensions entitlement based on a high civil service salary.

(c) In many countries civil servants can still retire at a very early age, receive benefits calculated on the basis of the peak salary, and still take another job.

Such systems are not easily reformed. The valiant efforts of Presidents Cardoso and Lula in Brazil, for example, were restrained for a long time by the 1988 Constitution's legal protection of civil service and military pensions. Only recently has the government of President Lula made progress in curbing expenditure and creating fiscal space for the financing of urban and rural basic pensions.

The regressiveness extends to other countries under left-of-centre administrations, including high-spending Uruguay. Even Mexico's effective anti-poverty programme *Oportunidades* is not yet covering the elderly poor. So for Latin America an obvious route towards establishing progressive welfare-state pensions will be to scale down the powerfully defended pension subsidies to the high-income public-sector elite.

Reinterpreting Chile's 'privatization' of social security

Chile's pension system serves as a world-famous model of privatization. In 1981 the Pinochet dictatorship abolished social security pensions that were a soaring public budget burden, and replaced them with compulsory individual savings schemes. A widely accepted interpretation of the results of that reform is that Chile's privatized system transfers nothing to the poor, restores the old inequalities, and raises national saving.

This consensual story is wrong, as one can discover by reading the works of Carmelo Mesa-Lago and others, including World Bank economists, who have analysed Chilean pension history in detail.[17]

The first correction to the consensus story is to note that Pinochet did not abolish Chile's social security system, because Chile did not have a true social security system that covered most of the people in the first place. As in other Latin American countries, Chile's pension system covered only those occupational groups holding power and privilege. In Chile's case, this extended down towards the middle class, including not only the military and government elite but also the private sector industries that were under the influence of the most powerful labour unions. Even Allende did little to change this. While promising to support the whole society someday, he de facto extended pension coverage only to small groups of self-employed merchants. Most of Chile's high-end occupational pensions were paid out of contributions by the employees and their direct employers, but the system faced financial problems in the 1970s and a rising share of those in the privileged occupations began to receive pensions that were subsidized by the general government budget.

The effect of the reforms of 1979–81 was more complex than often quoted in the international debate. First, Pinochet left the generous military pensions alone, and they remain essentially untouched to this day. Second, he used general tax funds to buy out the employers' contributions to the occupational pensions. This was a gift to employers paid by the general taxpayers. Finally, he gave the elderly poor of the countryside and the informal sector their first pension safety net. Not a generous safety net, but the first of its kind in Chile. The state budget thus shouldered a considerable part of the costs of the reforms.

Since 1981 – that is, since the 'privatization' of Chile's pensions – the social security attributed budget deficit has slowly risen to about 4.5 per cent of GDP. Chile's total social security expenditures under Pinochet became the second highest in Latin America, second only to Castro's Cuba. The consensus story of Chilean 'privatization' is convenient for both the right and the left. One side can benefit from and applaud Chile's privatization through earning handling fees and access to investment resources, and the other side (the left) can deplore it based on the uncertainty of pension levels and still deficient population coverage.

The true relevance of Chile's experience for today's privatization debate is quite different. Pinochet's Chile, like Thatcher's Britain, found that the budgetary cost of the transition to privatization in any form turns out to be large. It causes government to dis-save a sizeable share of GDP, in the name of promoting national savings. In the end, the main justification for privatization of pensions in certain developing countries might be an extreme second-best argument. It could be that privatization brings equity and efficiency gains in cases where the only alternative to privatization is an even less equitable elite-pension system. This second-best argument, however, does not apply to OECD democracies.

It has to be noted here that the new Bachelet government in Chile has just adopted a social assistance tier for the national pension system that will cover 60 per cent of the poorest population in old age and will thus address some of the lacunae of the Pinochet system.

The public health system and social security in India

While the Latin American literature is the most developed, economists have also begun to identify and publicize the distributional patterns of social transfers in developing countries on other continents as well. The next case of regressive transfers arose in a surprising place. Surely the world's greatest democracy should have egalitarian social transfers. Yet India's health and education policies transfer income from the poor to the rich. Let us focus on health care here.[18]

On the health front, the World Bank has put it bluntly. India's 'publicly financed curative care services are unambiguously pro-rich'.[19] For efficiency, it would be good to distribute public aid to health care so as to maximize national life expectancy. Evidence shows that the actual distribution of expenditures departs from this by under-investing in the health of the poor, even more so in India than in the United States. In either country, an extra tax dollar put into basic rudimentary care saves more years of life than an extra tax dollar put into high-end care.

Here are some clues that show the Indian public health system – or the system in most states to be correct – is inefficient and inequitable:

(a) in hospitals, the rich get more frequent and higher-quality care than the poor, in the public facilities as well as in the private;

(b) public hospitals offer so little quality care to the poor that 39 per cent of poor patients pay the eight-times-higher private hospital rates rather than enter the public hospitals that are available to them. Such imbalances are not restricted to hospital care, though that is the illustration chosen here;

(c) these imbalances are greatest in the states of India that have the greatest poverty and inequality. They are greatest in the poor heartland states, like Bihar and Uttar Pradesh. The more efficient and equitable states are the richer ones, like Kerala, Tamil Nadu, Gujarat and Punjab.

Following a national debate on poverty and working and living conditions in the informal sector the government appointed a national Commission for Enterprises in the Unorganized Sector. The Commission issued its report in May 2006. It contains *inter alia* suggestions to introduce a set of basic social security provisions for the informal economy consisting of an insurance approach to basic health care, maternity protection and disability and old age pensions. A bill reflecting similar provisions is presently (June 2008) being discussed in Parliament. The potential population coverage of the new schemes could be between 300 and 360 million people, a major step forward. In 2005 the government promulgated the Rural Employment Guarantee Act, which guarantees 100 days of work paid at the minimum wage level to all poor rural households. In modern terminology this scheme would qualify as a conditional cash transfer; in a more antiquated language one could describe it as social assistance or workfare. After initial piloting it was rolled out in 2008 to the entire country and is supposed to reach between 80 and 100 million people. Both schemes combined will not cost nearly as much as the present expenditure on classical social security transfers and hence the overall regressive nature of the Indian social security and health systems will not be fully corrected. However, the fact is that just as in many countries in Latin America the Indian government is actively addressing the regressive nature of its overall social transfer system as well as the gaps in coverage.

A tentative conclusion

Clearly, social transfers have different, even opposing, redistributive effects in different climates. Rich democracies have relatively egalitarian programmes, some of which are universal and some of which are targeted at the poorest income ranks. In developing countries relatively regressive, or even elitist, programmes still prevail. I have argued before that differences in political voice were and are the main reason for this great divide (Lindert, 2003, 2004). Interestingly, the Latin American and the Indian examples prove the point. These are the two major regions of the world where vibrant democracies are changing the weight of the voice of the poor and disenfranchised. The welfare states in these regions are far from qualifying – with respect to their redistributive dimension – as European style welfare states, but giving greater weight to the voice of the poor could make them more progressive and even explicitly pro-poor – at least in part. In Thailand an explicitly pro-poor health system was used to harness the votes of the poor. The European model of welfare may never be fully emulated in developing countries, but the fact that it is resilient in Europe and continues to stabilize societies – despite the fashionable shorted-sighted criticism that it faces in many countries – still provides a useful reference for welfare state reformers and protagonists in the developing world. It is too early to say how far welfare reforms in the developing world will go, in aiming at greater income security and more equality. However, what we can observe is a positive gradient.

Notes

1. It is desirable to exclude the contributory amounts paid by oneself or one's employer. They are not a controversial redistribution of resources between major social groups, but rather just part of one's employment contract. It is not easy, however, to remove all employer and employee contributions from the expenditure data. As a smaller step towards isolating non-contributory payments, I have tried to exclude government employee, and military, pensions from the OECD measures used here.

2. As of 1995, the welfare states, ranked by the share of total social transfers in GDP, included Sweden, Finland, Denmark, Norway, Belgium, France, the Netherlands, Germany and Italy. Also included for 1995, but only slightly above the 20 per cent line, were the United Kingdom, Austria and Spain (Lindert, 2004, Vol. 1: 177). Ireland was above the line only in 1985–7. When Switzerland became a welfare state depends on which OECD series one uses. It could have been a welfare state at the start of the 1990s (latest OECD estimates, with a bothersome series break at 1990) or not until the end of the 1990s (OECD earlier estimates).

3. It is not clear why OECD data show such a strong rise in Swiss pensions and health expenditures, as a percentage of GDP, since the early 1990s. The elderly share of the population has not risen much, and is low by OECD standards. One might have suspected a role for relatively sluggish growth of the GDP denominator, but Switzerland's growth has been relatively poor since 1975, well before the rise in the shares of pensions and health care in GDP.

4. The literature is rich, even when we focus just on studies explaining the determinants of GDP per capita, and set aside the determinants of employment. Much of the literature is surveyed in Atkinson (1999), Lindert (2004, Vol. 2: Chapters 18 and 19) and Slemrod (1995). Perhaps the most plausibly specified set of econometric tests finding a significant and sizeable cost of larger government is Fölster and Henrekson (1999, with a rebuttal by Agell et al., 1999). Its relevance to the issue of social transfers is limited, however, by its focus on the effects of total taxes. These taxes go to finance all government consumption and investment, not just social transfers.

5. Lindert (2004: Vol. I, Chapter 10, Vol. II, Chapters 18 and 19, and the sources cited there). The underlying data sets are available at http://www.econ.ucdavis.edu/faculty/fzlinder

6. Americans die younger than people in countries having a greater share of their health expenses paid for by taxes. The United States ranks 19th out of 20 rich countries in life expectancy. Not all of this is due to the health care system. Americans have worse health habits and slightly more pollution exposure. Yet when you weigh all the separate effects statistically, the nature of the United States health

care system seems to account for a significant part of United States mortality (Or, 2000). And the more private system costs much more. Part of the extra expense of American health care is a justifiable purchase of higher-quality care, a tendency that the rest of the world will soon emulate. Part of it, though, consists of higher bureaucratic costs. Contrary to the usual rhetoric assuming that bureaucracy means government bureaucracy, the private health insurance sector in the United States imposes greater administrative costs trying to keep people insured and compensated than other countries spend administratively on providing public care to all. Obviously, Americans have the world's best cutting-edge medical care. But few can afford it.

7. See, for example, OECD (1994). Allard and Lindert (2006); Blanchard and Portugal (2001); Lindert (2004: Vol. II, Chapter 19 and Appendix E). There are many signs that the European Union countries have begun to improve their competition policies since 1992. See Blanchard (2004).
8. See Lindert (2004: Vol. I, Chapter 7, Vol. II, Chapters 16 and 17) and, for similar perspectives on international differences, Alesina and Glaeser (2004).
9. The ILO figures for sub-Saharan Africa, not shown here, imply that social security transfers were below 2 per cent of GDP in all data-supplying countries.
10. World Bank data underlying Lindert et al. (2006). A dark horse gaining on these leaders is President Hugo Chavez's Venezuela. In 2000, at the dawn the Chavez era, Venezuela was still a low spender (6.1 per cent). Yet if Chavez ramps up the oil dividends for the masses, and if the country somehow remained democratic, it could become a welfare state.
11. On the restrictive coverage of public pensions around the globe, see Sala-i-Martin (1996: 281–6).
12. The regressivity of Latin American social transfers may have worsened in the 1980s and 1990s, to judge from shares of the labour force covered by social insurance (Barrientos, 2004: 147–51).
13. The concentration index of the Bank's study does not examine the way in which taxes or contributions used to fund transfers are collected – or the redistributive impact of these financing sources. Rather, it compares the existing distribution of the transfer benefits with the implicit norm of equal benefits for all, i.e. a poll subsidy.
14. Barreto (1994); De Ferranti et al. (2004); Filquiera and Moraes (1999); Kay (2000); Mitchell (1996); Palacios and Pallarès-Miralles (2000).
15. Ideally, the 'net pension subsidy' for each individual should be based on the net present value of the pension income received by a pensioner over his or her whole life, minus the value of the contributions to the pension plan made over his or her working life. The main shortcoming of this approach is the absence of data on an individual's (historical) pension contributions. In the absence of such data, one can adopt the alternative, albeit imperfect, pay-as-you-go approach of just subtracting current-year contributions received from benefits paid out. This was done in the World Bank study.
16. On Brazil's runaway public-sector pensions, see *The Wall Street Journal*, 9 September 1999: 1; Paes de Barros and Foguel (2002); De Ferranti et al. (2004: Chapter 9); Medici (2004); World Bank (2004b); and again Lindert et al. (2006).
17. Bertranou et al. (2004); Borzutsky (2002); Cruz-Saco et al. (1998); Gill et al. (2004); Madrid (2003); Mesa-Lago (1978, 1994, 2005); World Bank (2001).
18. On the regressivity of Indian education policy, especially in the poorer heartland states, see Lindert (2003; 2004: Volume 2, Chapter 15, and the studies cited there).
19. Peters et al. (2002: 218); see also Misra et al. (2003); World Bank (2003).

11

The Poverty Effects of Social Protection in Europe: EU Enlargement and its Lessons for Developing Countries

Bea Cantillon

It is by no means evident that conclusions drawn from European experiences with social protection may be transposed to the developing countries. There are, after all, very substantial economic, demographic and cultural differences to take into account. One way of bridging the divide between the two groups of countries is to look at the history of the now-rich powers and to ascertain the extent to which their responses to protests against poverty and injustice remain relevant to the situations of low-income populations today. Through trial and error, and measured responses to movements protesting hardship and injustice, the governments of the then-emerging welfare states were slowly able to develop effective anti-poverty policies. Social security systems were gradually brought into being. This long history undoubtedly holds fascinating lessons for the poor countries that are going through sometimes unspeakable hardships today. However, the diversity of outcomes in terms of social protection in the now-rich powers is equally fascinating. Present-day European systems vary greatly. Identifying quite what their effects are in terms of reducing poverty and enhancing or obstructing economic growth is crucially important.

The present chapter is rather descriptive in nature. It explores what we know about social security, poverty and income inequality in the rich welfare states. I will not dwell upon the historical development of the social security systems, nor discuss the various social models that exist in Europe today. Instead, I will restrict my argument to a reading of the European social indicators on poverty, employment and welfare and how they relate to the so-called welfare effort, i.e. the volume of public spending on social security. Although this approach does not allow conclusions to be drawn on possible causal relationships, it will indicate whether and to what extent poverty in rich nations is related to their economic base, employment and social protection.

The chapter starts with a short elucidation of the indicators applied, which is especially significant given the different meanings that can be attributed to the notion of poverty in relation to the affluent West on the one hand and the poor South on the other. In the second and third sections, the scope of poverty and inequality in Europe is discussed. The following three sections deal with the relationship between poverty indicators and GDP, employment and social expenditures. In the seventh section the focus is on the relationship between the generosity of social assistance programmes and poverty. The final section examines the general relationship between economic growth, social and demographic change, on the one hand, and the maturation of social security systems in post-war Europe on the other, and concludes the chapter.

The EU social indicators and the concept of 'relative poverty'

The official EU indicator for income poverty is defined as 60 per cent of national median income using the OECD modified equivalence scale (Atkinson et al., 2002). I will not review the problems of definitions and measurement and the resolutions that have been offered in the rich literature on this topic. I will, however, briefly consider the meaning of this indicator, particularly in the context of worldwide comparisons.

In the European Council of Ministers' decision of 1975, the poor are defined as 'individuals or families whose resources are so small as to exclude them from the minimal acceptable way of life of the Member State where they live'. This and similar definitions (see for example Atkinson, 1998; Room, 1995; Townsend, 1979) imply that poverty cannot be defined in an absolute way, as it is essentially a *relative* notion, i.e. relative to the society under study. Poverty is defined in relation to the general level of prosperity in a country at a given point in time. What is regarded as a minimally acceptable way of life depends largely on the prevailing lifestyle in the community concerned and thus on its level of social and economic development and constructed needs. The idea is thus that it is senseless to search for an absolute standard, whereby the context of poverty can be determined accurately for all countries and for every moment in time. Relative poverty indicators must therefore be understood as indicators of 'low income' in a country or countries at a particular time rather than as unvarying and timeless measures of absolute deprivation or living standard.

In a global perspective, this notion is far from self-evident. Even within the EU, it has emerged after the accession of six Eastern European nations that the application of a relative poverty indicator yields counter-intuitive results. After all, many of the poorer new member States (with an average GDP amounting to around 47 per cent that of the rich 'old' member States) rather remarkably display a lower poverty risk. The Czech Republic and Slovenia even rank among Europe's best-performing countries (see below).

Drawing from the 1995 World Summit for Social Development in Copenhagen and the ensuing report, the United Nations defines 'absolute poverty'
as 'a condition characterized by severe deprivation of basic human needs,
including food, safe drinking water, sanitation facilities, health, shelter, education and information. It depends not only on income but also on access to
services', and overall poverty is considered to take various forms, including:

lack of income and productive resources to ensure sustainable livelihoods;
hunger and malnutrition; ill health; limited or lack of access to education and other basic services; increased morbidity and mortality from
illness; homelessness and inadequate housing; unsafe environments and
social discrimination and exclusion. It is also characterized by lack of
participation in decision-making and in civil, social and cultural life.

Although it is absolutely true that poverty 'occurs in all countries: as mass
poverty in many developing countries, pockets of poverty amid wealth in
developed countries', it is equally the case that poverty in rich nations is
relatively different from poverty in the poorest nations of the world. This
should be kept in mind when reading the next pages on poverty and social
protection in Europe.

Poverty in Europe

Figure 11.1 shows the relative at-risk-of-poverty rates for Europe. For the EU
as a whole, the percentage of people whose income is below 60 per cent of the
national median is 16 per cent. The best-performing countries, with a poverty
risk of around 10 per cent, are the Netherlands, Hungary, Sweden, Finland,
Luxembourg, Denmark, Slovenia and the Czech Republic. Countries where
a large proportion of the population is below the threshold are Slovakia,
Portugal, Ireland, Spain and Greece, exhibiting a poverty risk of around 20
per cent. Countries with a poverty risk between 17 per cent and 19 per cent
are Italy, the United Kingdom, Estonia and Poland. Germany and Latvia are at
the EU-25 average. In Malta, Lithuania, Cyprus, Belgium, France and Austria
the rate is 13 to 15 per cent.

Compared with the United States, Europe, as a whole, performs
substantially better. Using the 50 per cent threshold at state level, the median
across the EU-25 amounts to 9 per cent, compared with 16.5 per cent across
states for the United States. The figure for the best-performing EU member
State (Czech Republic) is 4 per cent, compared with 11 per cent for the best-
performing federal state of the United States (Hawaii) (Jesuit et al., 2002).
Likewise, if one compares the scores of the worst performers, Europe comes
out on top: the poverty risk in Ireland is 15 per cent compared with 22 per cent
in Washington, DC. However, not unimportantly, the dispersion within the
EU-25 is much greater than that within the United States. In Europe, the

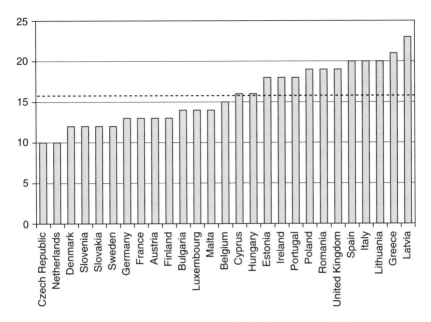

Figure 11.1   Population at risk of poverty for EU-27 (income year 2005)
Source: Eurostat, EU-SILC.
Notes: - - - - EU-25 average. The at-risk-of-poverty rate is the proportion of the population that has
an equivalized income below 60 per cent of the median equivalized income of the member State.
Malta (MT) and Portugal (PT) provisional values.

difference between the best performers and the worst is a factor of almost 2
to 1 (Marlier et al., 2007).

Poverty thresholds and well-being

The rather counter-intuitive consequence of the choice for a poverty line
that is set relative to current income is that poverty in the new member
States (where GDP amounts to 47 per cent of the level achieved in the EU-15)
appears on average to be the same as poverty in the 'old' Europe. Therefore,
we need to complete the picture by adding information about the meaning
of the different national poverty lines in terms of purchasing power in each
individual member State. On this basis, we may conclude that the purchasing
power of the poverty line[1] in the three poorest EU member States, i.e. Estonia,
Latvia and Lithuania, is four times lower than that in the richest member
States (after Luxembourg), namely Denmark, Germany and Austria.

The meaning of the various values of the poverty lines in terms of well-
being becomes visible in Figure 11.2, in which poverty thresholds have been
plotted against life expectancies for all females and males (panels a and b).

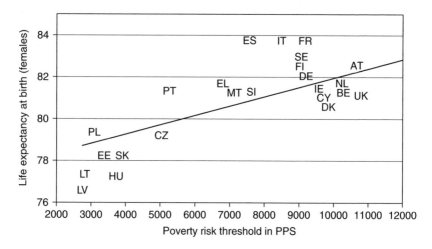

Figure 11.2a Life expectancies at birth for females (2005) and poverty risk threshold (income year 2005)

Source: Eurostat, EU-SILC.

Notes: Risk of poverty threshold is 60 per cent of the median equivalized income of the member State, for a single person household, expressed in purchasing power parities. Luxembourg (LU) is outlier with a poverty threshold of 17208. Life expectancy at birth in Luxembourg is 76,7 for males and 82,3 for females. Life expectancy data for Italy (IT) refer to 2004; poverty risk thresholds for Portugal (PT) and Malta (MT) are provisional.

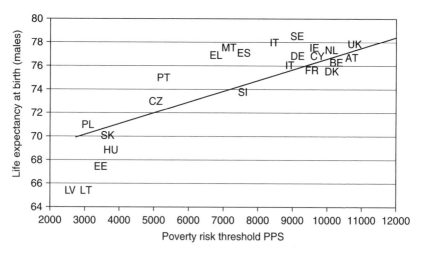

Figure 11.2b Life expectancies at birth for males (2005) and poverty risk threshold (income year 2005)

Source: Eurostat, EU-SILC.

Notes: Luxembourg is outlier with a poverty threshold of 17208. Life expectancy at birth in Luxembourg (LU) is 76,7 for males and 82,3 for females. Life expectancy data for Italy (IT) refer to 2004; poverty risk thresholds for Portugal (PT) and Malta (MT) are provisional.

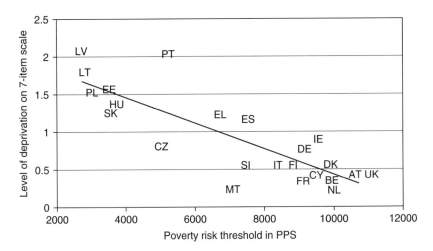

Figure 11.3 Deprivation index and the poverty risk threshold (income year 2005)
Source: European Foundation for the Improvement of Living Conditions (2004): 'Low Income and Deprivation in an Enlarged Europe'. Luxembourg: Office for Official Publications of the European Communities and Eurostat, EU-SILC.
Notes: Luxembourg is outlier with a poverty threshold of 17208. In Luxembourg the deprivation index is 0,26. Poverty risk thresholds for Portugal (PT) and Malta (MT) are provisional.

To eliminate the differences in price levels between countries the poverty thresholds are converted using purchasing power parities. The thresholds for one-person households are used as a proxy for the thresholds for all family types. The value of this threshold correlates strongly with per capita GDP. The strongly positive linear correlation indicates how greatly the life-chances of Europeans differ and how these differences correspond with the varying poverty thresholds and GDP levels. An average Latvian man lives for 65 years, 14 years less than a Swedish man. In all former communist countries, life expectancy is below the EU average. In the rest of Europe, life expectancies are much more homogeneous, ranging from 74 years for Portuguese men to 78 for Swedish men (80 years for Danish women and 84 years for Spanish women).

The divergence of living conditions within the European Union also becomes apparent when poverty thresholds are plotted against indicators of life satisfaction and material deprivation (Figures 11.3 and 11.4). These data come from the European Commission report on 'Perceptions of Living Conditions in an Enlarged Europe' (2004). Both graphs suggest a strong relationship between the purchasing power of the poverty line on the one hand and levels of life satisfaction and deprivation on the other.[2] Again, we see that most former communist states (with the exception of the Czech Republic and Slovenia) form a cluster with a very low score on life satisfaction and

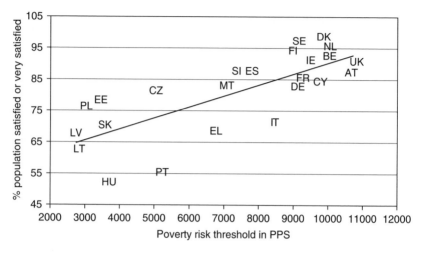

Figure 11.4 Life satisfaction (2007) and poverty risk threshold (income year 2005)
Source: Eurobarometer 68 and Eurostat, EU-SILC.
Notes: Luxembourg is outlier with a poverty threshold of 17208. In Luxembourg, 94 per cent of the population report that they are satisfied or very satisfied. Poverty risk thresholds for Portugal (PT) and Malta (MT) are provisional.

a relatively high degree of material deprivation. Greece, Portugal and, as far as deprivation is concerned, Spain are also included in this cluster. The rich countries of the 'old' Europe score well on both indicators, as do the Czech Republic, Slovenia, Cyprus and Malta. The latter four countries belong to the cluster of poor egalitarian countries (see below).

I must emphasize that this statistical correlation represents the first step in the analysis and later steps are to be explored. The correlation depends on all-population data, not distributional data concerned to distinguish, say, life expectancy of the richest and poorest 10 per cent or 20 per cent, or of the professional and managerial occupational classes, compared with the unskilled and semi-skilled manual class. The correlation will be stronger if inequality of living standards *between* populations is reinforced by inequality *within* populations.

Poverty, inequality and general level of income

Figure 11.5 plots income inequality as measured by the S80/S20 ratio (net income of the poorest 80 per cent over the net income of the richest 20 per cent) and GDP per capita in 26 European member States. We notice that, actually, all four combinations of income level and income distribution occur within Europe: the countries in North and continental Europe belong to the cluster of rich egalitarian countries (I); the rich inegalitarian cluster (II)

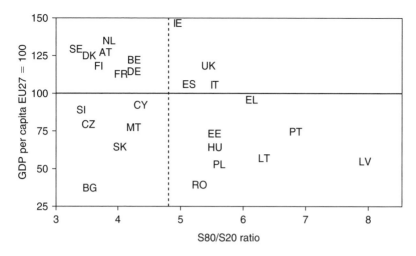

Figure 11.5 Income inequality (S80/S20 income year 2005) and GDP per capita (2006)
Source: Eurostat and EU-SILC.
Notes: - - - EU-25 average, EU-27 average. GDP per capita is expressed in purchasing power parities; RO is forecast. Luxembourg is outlier with a GDP per capita of 278.9 per cent of EU-27 average. In Luxembourg, the S80/S20 ratio is 4.2. S80/S20 ratios for Portugal (PT) and Malta (MT) are provisional.

is represented by the United Kingdom, Ireland, Italy and Spain; the cluster of poor egalitarian countries (III) are Malta, Cyprus, the Czech Republic, Slovenia, Slovakia and Bulgaria; the cluster of poor inegalitarian countries (IV) is composed of the Baltic States, Romania, Greece, Hungary and Poland.

The great diversity that exists in Europe in terms of income, income distribution and poverty provides three important insights. First, a relatively equal income distribution and a low poverty rate do not seem to be an impediment to high GDP levels. On the contrary, most rich countries also attain the lowest number of relative income poor and the lowest income inequality. Only in the United Kingdom, Ireland and to some extent Italy and Spain does a high level of GDP coexist with a relatively high income inequality. Second, enlargement has added a new cluster to Europe. With the exception of the Baltic States six out of the new member States are poor but egalitarian countries. Third, the dimensions 'income' and 'income distribution' do not seem to suggest the existence of one so-called European social model. Nine of the present 27 member States combine high income level with a fairly equal distribution.

Figure 11.6 plots poverty thresholds in the countries of the EU-25 against poverty risks in each of those countries. The poverty threshold is defined as 60 per cent of standardized national median income. The value of this threshold correlates strongly with per capita GDP. Therefore the relationship between poverty thresholds in PPS and the poverty risk may be interpreted

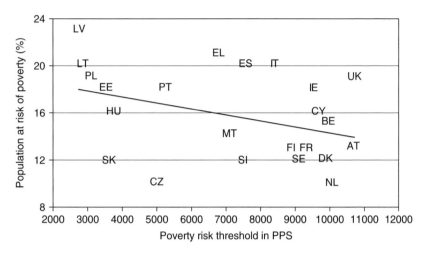

Figure 11.6 Population at risk of poverty (income year 2005) and poverty risk threshold (income year 2005)
Source: Eurostat and EU-SILC. Data for Portugal (PT) and Malta (MT) are provisional.

as follows. Poverty risks tend to be lower in countries where median (standardized) income is higher, but the correlation is far from perfect. Thus, the European indicators confirm that there is a positive relationship between the welfare level in a country – treated here as standardized national median income level – on the one hand and the level of (relative) income poverty on the other. Within the EU-15, poverty falls as we move from poorer to richer countries. However, the relationship is not very strong. Ireland and Denmark are at the same income level, but relative poverty risk in Ireland is much higher as in Denmark. The same holds – albeit to a lesser degree – for the United Kingdom and Austria, countries which combine a similar income level with a very different poverty rate. Moreover, not unimportantly, in the new member States poverty is generally lower than predicted by their level of income. With the exception of the Baltic States and Poland (low income and high poverty), the new member States combine a relatively low level of income with a low poverty risk.

Poverty, social protection and social expenditures

There are indeed substantial differences between Europe's welfare states. Building on Esping-Andersen's typology, four groups may be distinguished: the Anglo-Saxon countries (United Kingdom, Ireland), continental Europe (the Netherlands, Belgium, France, Germany, Austria and Luxemburg), the Nordic countries (Denmark, Sweden, Norway, Finland) and Southern Europe (Italy, Spain, Portugal, Greece). The former communist states, Malta

Table 11.1 Social protection spending in the EU-10, as a percentage of GDP, 2003

	Social protection expenditures
EU-25	27.4
EU-15	27.8
Cyprus	18.4
Czech Republic	20.2
Estonia	12.6
Latvia	13.8
Lithuania	13.6
Hungary	21.1
Malta	17.9
Poland	21.0
Slovenia	24.1
Slovakia	18.2

Source: Eurostat based on ESPROSS.

and Cyprus have as yet not been subsumed under a typology. In the liberal, Anglo-Saxon welfare states, the market is the dominant factor. Welfare state provisions are of a residual nature and often involve means-testing. Private insurance and social assistance play an important role. The role of the social partners in decision-making and implementation is limited.

The countries belonging to the conservative-corporatist type (continental Europe) have strongly developed social insurance systems, often organized per professional category. Social policy in these countries is based on multi-governance in which the social partners are strong and institutionally involved.

The social democratic type (the Nordic countries) is characterized by universal social provisions, which in principle are aimed at all citizens. These regimes offer generous social benefits, and not only to the poor.

The Southern European welfare states are the least developed. Here, social protection is directed strongly towards pensions, while traditional family structures are attributed a significant supporting role in dealing with social risks.

The various welfare state architectures are reflected in the levels of social spending. High expenditures on social security of more than 25 per cent of GDP are observed in the Nordic countries and in most continental welfare states. In the Southern European welfare states, the level of social spending is generally much lower.

There are also great differences in expenditures among the newly acceded EU member States. In the Baltic countries, as Table 8.1 shows, total public social expenditure amounts to less than 15 per cent of GDP, compared with almost 25 per cent in Slovenia, and some 20 per cent in Poland, the

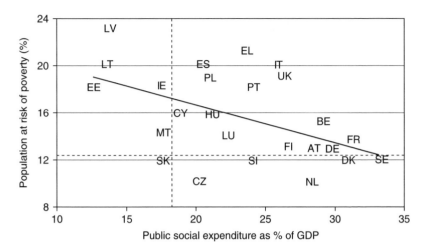

Figure 11.7   Social expenditure as percentage of GDP (2003) and population at risk of poverty (income year 2005)
Source: Eurostat based on ESSPROS and EU-SILC. Population at risk of poverty is provisional for Portugal (PT) and Malta (MT).

Czech Republic and Hungary. For the longer-established EU-15 the average expenditure is 28 per cent.

Figure 11.7 expresses social protection expenditures as a percentage of GDP in relation to poverty rates for the EU-25. Although the various countries are scattered around the diagram, there seems to be a negative correlation between the level of social expenditures and relative poverty. With the possible exception of Slovakia all countries with a poverty risk beyond the limit of the first quartile are represented in the quadrant below the first quartile of social expenditures. In Estonia, Latvia and Lithuania poverty rates range from 17 to over 20 per cent. In all these countries social expenditures are far below 20 per cent of GDP.

The analysis of the relationship between poverty risks and overall social protection expenditures can be refined a little further. Using EUROSTAT's breakdown of such expenditures, poverty risks for pensioners, for households with children and the risk faced by the unemployed are plotted against expenditures on pensions, families and children and the unemployed (Figures 11.8, 11.9 and 11.10). The correlation between expenditures on pensions and old-age poverty is weak. This can be explained in part by the rather heterogeneous composition of elderly people's incomes across the Union: in some countries, pensioners' income consists almost entirely of public pensions, while in others it is made up of compulsory or voluntary occupational pensions and private pensions.

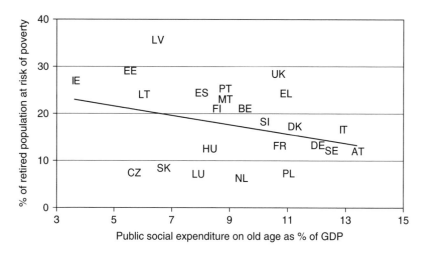

Figure 11.8   Social expenditure on pensions as percentage of GDP (2003) and poverty risk of the retired (income year 2005)

Source: Eurostat, ESSPROS and EU-SILC.

Notes: Retired population refers to population that indicates 'retirement' as main activity. At risk of poverty rate is percentage of population that has an equivalized income below 60 per cent of the median equivalized income of the member State. Cyprus is outlier with a poverty risk for retired persons of 51 per cent and public social expenditure on old age pensions representing 8.1 per cent of GDP. Population at risk of poverty is provisional for Portugal (PT) and Malta (MT).

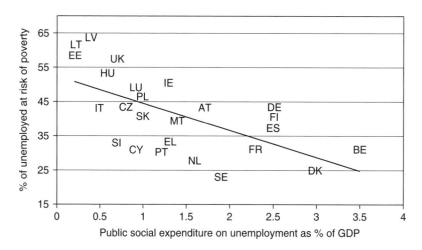

Figure 11.9   Social expenditure on unemployment as percentage of GDP (2003) and poverty risk of the unemployed (income year 2005)

Source: Eurostat, ESSPROS and EU-SILC.

Notes: Unemployed population refers to population that indicates 'unemployment' as main activity. At risk of poverty rate is percentage of population that has an equivalized income below 60 per cent of the median equivalized income of the member State. Population at risk of poverty is provisional for Portugal (PT) and Malta (MT).

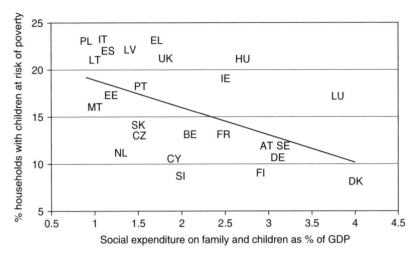

Figure 11.10 Social expenditure on families and children as percentage of GDP (2003) and poverty risk of families with children (income year 2005)
Source: Eurostat, ESSPROS and EU-SILC.
Notes: At risk of poverty rate is percentage of households with dependent children that has an equivalized income below 60 per cent of the median equivalized income of the member State. Population at risk of poverty is provisional for Portugal (PT) and Malta (MT).

The relationship between public spending on unemployment and the poverty risk that the unemployed face is much stronger: the higher the level of expenditure, the lower the level of poverty. Surprisingly, this correlation seems unaffected by the scale of unemployment. In low-unemployment countries where expenditure on the unemployed is also low (Luxembourg, United Kingdom and Ireland), poverty among the unemployed is very high, whereas in countries with high unemployment and high expenditures (Belgium, Germany and France), poverty among the unemployed is relatively low. In Denmark, Finland and to a lesser extent Sweden, unemployment is low, but expenditure on the unemployed is relatively high, resulting in the lowest risk of poverty among the unemployed in the EU-15.

The relationship between public spending on families with children and child poverty confirms previous findings by, among others, Bradbury and Jäntti (2001) that low risk of child poverty requires high levels of public spending on families with children.

The negative relationship between social expenditures and relative poverty has now been well established in empirical studies. Although simple correlations do not necessarily indicate causality, the conclusion is that if it is at all possible to attain low or moderate poverty rates in Europe without significant social spending, then it has yet to be demonstrated (see Marlier et al., 2007).

It is true that, in the new member States (except Poland), the same level of spending on social protection (in percentage of GDP) is associated with a poverty risk that is (sometimes much) lower than that in the EU-15. However, in those new member States displaying a poverty risk below the EU-25 average, social protection expenditure amounts to 20 per cent of GDP or more. This is the case in the Czech Republic, Slovenia and Hungary. The most recent figures for Slovakia suggest that this country combines a below-average public spending (18.2 per cent) and below-average relative poverty. This is an interesting case that should be studied in greater detail.

It is equally true that, within the EU-15, some countries end up with higher poverty than others, even though they display the same level of social protection expenditure. This suggests that other variables are to be considered in explaining cross-country differences in poverty risk. Here, the importance of the institutional structure of social protection expenditure (efficiency) and the pre-transfer poverty risks (i.e. the distribution of primary or pre-tax income) should be stressed.

Evidently, welfare states differ in more respects than the scale of total public social expenditure. Social democratic welfare states seem to be the most successful in terms of poverty alleviation. Compared with the corporatist welfare states of Belgium and France, they attain a lower poverty rate at lower (Finland) or the same (Denmark) social expenditure levels. Social expenditures seem to be most efficient in the Netherlands: with expenditures that are (far) lower than in Belgium, Denmark, Germany, France and Austria a much lower poverty level is attained. Conversely, in the UK and Italy, poverty is significantly higher than it is in Finland, even though these countries exhibit very similar expenditure levels.

Simulations by Van den Bosch (2002) using Luxembourg Income Study data suggest that expanding welfare state expenditures within the existing social transfer systems will not necessarily have a strong impact on poverty rates. His simulations confirmed the general proposition that more social spending generates less poverty. Nevertheless, the response of poverty statistics to increased expenditures was in some countries smaller than expected, indicating that poverty risks in developed welfare states are sometimes less sensitive to increases in social transfers than the cross-country pattern would suggest. This is due to various institutional factors. In Italy for instance – where poverty was found to increase with higher social spending – a large portion of the social budget is accounted for by retirement pensions. In this country, to increase pensions would have only a marginal impact on old age poverty, and the households of those in the economically active ages would be dragged into poverty by the increase in taxes and social contributions.

Poverty, unemployment and jobs

Within any country, poverty among those in paid work is far smaller than among those who are not – certainly if one considers the non-elderly only. Across countries, however, the link between employment and poverty is

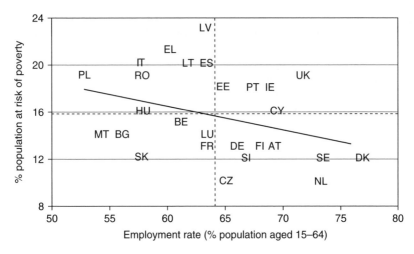

Figure 11.11   Employment rate (2005) and poverty risk (income year 2005)
Source: Eurostat, EU-SILC.
Notes: - - - EU-25 average. At risk of poverty rate is percentage of population that has an equivalized income below 60 per cent of the median equivalized income of the member State. Population at risk of poverty is provisional for Portugal (PT) and Malta (MT).

much less strong, as shown in Figure 11.11, which plots poverty rates for the working-age population[3] against employment rates. The relationship is weakly negative in the EU-15 and non-existent within the EU-10 (Marlier et al., 2007).

Although the greatest number of countries is found either in the quadrant indicating 'below-average employment – above-average poverty' or in that indicating 'above-average employment – below-average poverty', there are also countries such as Belgium, Slovakia and Malta that combine low employment with low poverty. Ireland, Portugal and the United Kingdom, on the other hand, combine high poverty with high employment.

Why is the relationship between employment and poverty so weak? A first reason is that job growth does not always benefit jobless households. In a number of countries, employment growth over the past decades has not been to the benefit of workless households. Most remarkably, in the Netherlands, the United Kingdom and Ireland, massive employment growth in the 1990s did not lead to comparable employment growth at the household level. A common feature has been the increase in two- or three-worker households.

A second reason why the connection between high employment rates and poverty is not as strong as is often assumed has to do with the level of low wages and the relatively high incidence of in-work poverty in some high-employment countries. Although in-work poverty is the highest in Greece, Spain and Portugal, high-employment countries such as the United Kingdom have in-work poverty risks that are up to twice as high as in low-employment countries like Belgium and Germany. Features here seem to be the existence of a statutory minimum wage, and/or low wages paid and accepted by non-contracted, especially migrant, workers, in some countries.

The third factor to weaken the positive relationship between employment and poverty is the degree of social protection that is provided for those out of work. There is a negative relationship between employment rates and the poverty risks faced by the unemployed, suggesting that social protection against unemployment tends to be more successful in high-employment countries. However, in some high-employment countries, social protection appears to be rather inadequate. Typically in the United Kingdom and Ireland, poverty rates among the unemployed are much higher than the average for the unemployed in the EU-15. While this may be attributable in part to differences in household composition of the unemployed, it is probably also indicative of a less-effective social protection system for the jobless in some high-employment countries.

The conclusion is that jobs are important in raising households above the poverty threshold but, in order to have a significant further effect, job growth should include workless households and should be accompanied by adequate minimum wages and social protection for those who remain without work.

Poverty, generosity and social assistance

In a large majority of EU-countries minimum income provisions for the poor have been introduced as general safety nets for the poor. Contrary to social insurance schemes which cover social risks (unemployment, old age, sickness, disability) social assistance provides benefits only conditionally to persons of small means in amounts sufficient to meet minimum standards of need.

Categorical assistance schemes for groups like the elderly and the disabled originated historically earlier than social insurance. However, the guaranteed universal safety nets constituted the final piece of the social protection systems in the Western as well as in the Eastern European member States (Lødemel and Schulte, 1992). In the 'old' member States this finalization process began about three decades earlier than in the new member States. In most 'old' EU member States, general rather than varying local social assistance schemes were usually introduced in the 1970s and the 1980s. Only the German, Dutch and British safety nets date back to the 1960s. In Eastern Europe basic social safety nets to supplement social insurance were developed only recently.

The existing general social assistance schemes in Europe display substantial variation, in eligibility rules, organization and administration (Cantillon et al., 2008). Likewise, generosity of the benefits varies considerably from country to country. For lone-person households the net social assistance,

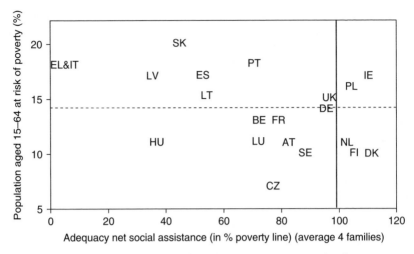

Figure 11.12 Net disposable income of social assistance recipients (working-age, average of four family types) (2004) as percentage of poverty line and poverty risk of working age population, 2004

Source: Cantillon et al. (2008).

for example, is about 54 euros a month in Latvia and 1000 euros in the Netherlands. Although there are very large differences across the Union, in most European countries social assistance is much less important than social insurance. However, in some countries such as the United Kingdom and Ireland, social assistance is an important part of the social protection system. In most European countries expenditures for means-tested benefits make up 10 per cent or less of total social expenditures. In countries such as Estonia, Belgium and Sweden the means-tested benefits constitute even less than 5 per cent of social expenditures. In the United Kingdom and Ireland, on the other hand, 26 per cent and 16 per cent respectively of social expenditures are spent on means-tested benefits (ESPROSS, 2004). This is less the case in continental Europe where social protection relies much more on social insurance. The Scandinavian social model is made up primarily of universal social benefits and services.

In Figure 11.12 average benefit levels for four family types are plotted against poverty risks of the working age population as measured by the EU poverty threshold. The pattern of the relationship shows that most countries with below-average poverty risks indeed provide rather generous benefits, but some do not. Although in Belgium, Luxembourg and France assistance benefits are more than 20 per cent lower than the poverty line these countries display below-average poverty risks. It is equally true that poverty is not always low in countries with 'adequate' levels of benefit. Only three of the five countries with benefit levels above the poverty line display a below-average risk of poverty (the Netherlands, Finland, Denmark). Despite relatively generous social assistance in Poland and Ireland poverty in these countries is well above average. Conversely, in Hungary, Belgium, France, Austria and Sweden poverty is below average despite low social assistance. Generous social assistance benefits on their own do not guarantee low risk of poverty, while less generous social assistance schemes do not necessarily lead to high risk of poverty.

The reason is simple: the effectiveness of social assistance on poverty reduction depends not only on generosity but also on eligibility rules and take-up. And in most European countries social assistance accounts for much less poverty alleviation than social insurance. Figure 11.12 suggests that the Irish and Polish social assistance schemes are not very effective although the benefit levels seem to be adequate. In the case of France, Belgium and Luxembourg social assistance forms only a small (although rising) part of the social protection system. In these countries social assistance is only a complement of social insurance. These countries show that low social assistance benefits do not necessarily result in high poverty risks. If other income arrangements such as social insurance schemes that compensate for disability, sickness, old age and unemployment are very effective, then poverty risks might be modest or small despite low social assistance benefits. This explains why the relationship between social expenditures and poverty is much stronger than the relationship between poverty and generosity of social assistance.

Social security in Europe and its economic and political base

Castles (1982), Flora (1986), Swank and Hicks (1985) and Wilensky (2002) have investigated the relationship in the affluent welfare states between the volumes of social expenditure on the one hand and GDP, employment, demography and power on the other. These studies put forward three key determinants of the development of social expenditures in postwar welfare states: economic growth, socio-demographic change (population ageing, individualization of households) and the specific nature of political decision-making in the welfare state concerned.

First and foremost, it should be noted that, after the Second World War, economic growth in Europe reached an unprecedented level. Over a period of 35 years, GDP increased threefold in real terms. This growth constituted a necessary condition for the achievement of social progress. High social expenditure in Europe was thus an aspect of high welfare. Conversely, however, the strong positive relationship between economic growth and growth of social expenditure in the 1950s and 1960s also implies that high social expenditures contributed to economic growth or at least did not present an obstacle to growth.

Table 11.2   Social expenditures as a percentage of GDP, 1950–1997

	1950 ILO	1960 OECD	1980 OECD	1997 OECD
Australia	4.7	7.71	11.7	17.9
Austria	12.4	16.47	22.3	25.3
Belgium	11.6	14.46	25.6	23.5
Canada	6.2	8.63	13.3	16.6
Denmark	7.9	12.40	27.6	30.8
Finland	7.4	7.96	18.9	28.7
France	11.5	14.34	23.5	29.4
Germany	14.8	17.51	25.0	26.2
Ireland	7.2	8.98	19.4	17.6
Italy	8.4	13.32	18.2	26.4
Japan	3.5	4.68	11.1	14.3
Netherlands	8.0	11.31	28.7	24.2
New Zealand	9.7	10.72	18.2	20.9
Norway	6.2	7.88	18.9	25.1
Sweden	9.7	10.29	30.4	31.9
Switzerland	5.9	4.98	14.1	22.4
UK	10.0	9.81	18.3	21.4
US	4.0	7.13	12.4	14.5
Average	8.28	10.48	19.9	23.2

Source: 1950–1960: Schmidt, 1997; OECD, Economic Outlook, June 2000.

Moreover, in the early 1950s – before the golden years of economic growth – social expenditure levels in the six countries of the European Community already amounted to more than 10 per cent of GDP (in Germany even 15 per cent, i.e. the present expenditure level in the United States). More or less generalized systems of child benefit, old age and invalidity pensions and health care were already in place at that time (Table 11.2). In Europe, economic growth was thus firmly based upon a substantial level of social redistribution and social security. Increasing income in the 1960s meant that a larger proportion of that income could be spent on the further elaboration of collective goods and services, in the fields of education, health care and income support through social security. Conversely, these social transfers, goods and services ensured a healthy and qualified working population and an inclusive society which in turn enhanced economic growth.

A second explanation for the growth of social expenditures in Europe since the Second World War is the fundamental change that has occurred in the composition of the population in general and the working population in particular: the maturation of formal labour markets and the feminization of the labour force, as a result of which the number of protected persons and the number of social risks to be covered under the social insurance system has increased; the ageing of the population, implying that more individuals now require pensions and health care; and finally the individualization of households, as a result of which the burden of care has shifted somewhat from the family to public authorities.

These explanations seem to suggest, then, that the rise in social spending and the development of social security systems is attributable primarily to the evolution of economic and societal structures (industrialization, growth, maturation of formal labour markets, medical technology, population ageing and individualization). Social security should then be regarded as a rational and functional response to societal issues and growing needs in consequence of modernization and industrialization. Research into the autonomous influence of governments has indeed shown that, irrespective of those governments' political leaning, the social sector was further developed.

Still, within the world of the welfare states, we observe considerable differences. The architecture of social market economies varies considerably as does the level of social redistribution and expenditures between welfare states. These differences are partly the result of path-dependency, as the development of all social systems was incrementally based on existing small-scale initiatives of mutual assistance and charity. However, the impact of differential politico-democratic processes on the emergence of social protection systems should not be underestimated. Political science research, for example, has found liberal welfare states in countries with a majoritarian electoral system. Social democratic generous welfare states in the Nordic countries have been the result of coalitions between Social Democratic parties and parties of agrarian defence while on Europe's continent, in turn, welfare states are the product of coalitions between social and Christian democracy (Manow and Van Kersbergen, 2008). According to Iverson and Soskice (2008), the reason why the liberal welfare states are less developed than the Nordic and continental welfare states is that the left more often governs in countries with proportional representation systems (where welfare state regimes are more developed), whereas the right more often governs in countries with majoritarian systems (where welfare state systems tend to be less generous). Likewise, differences in interest group formation explain the great variety of welfare states (for a discussion see Galston, 2006).

Conclusion

Poverty in Europe is correlated with relatively low GDP, low rate of employment and low level of public social expenditure. The relationship between low social expenditure and poverty in particular is of importance. The European social indicators confirm that – with the possible exception of Slovakia – no European country has succeeded in achieving below-average poverty with below-average social spending.

The Nordic countries where the risks of poverty are lowest combine a high level of social spending with high GDP as well as high employment rates. Some countries (such as France, Germany and Belgium) where the employment rate is low did succeed in keeping poverty (relatively) low, thanks to a high level of social spending. Likewise, some poor countries succeed in attaining below-average poverty thanks to social spending. In other words, an unfavourable position in terms of employment or GDP is compensated for through high social expenditure in certain EU member States. It is, however, difficult to find a country that succeeded in compensating too low a level of social spending merely through economic growth or high employment. Rich, high employment countries where social spending is low end up with high poverty. This leads to the conclusion that, if it is possible to attain a low risk of poverty without substantial public spending, it has not yet been demonstrated.

The high economic growth attained in post-war Western Europe was a necessary condition for achieving social progress. Conversely, however, rising social expenditures also contributed to economic growth. The successful combination of economic growth and greater social redistribution in the post-war era was built on social security systems that had gradually evolved since the end of the nineteenth century and were generalized and institutionalized immediately after the Second World War. In Western Europe, economic growth was thus firmly based upon social redistribution and vice versa.

The experience of enlargement seems to suggest that also in the new member States low poverty is associated with relatively high social expenditures. It is true that, in most new member States, the same level of spending on social protection (in percentage of GDP) is associated with a poverty risk that is lower than that in the EU-15. However, in those new member States displaying a poverty risk below the EU-25 average, social expenditure levels amount to 20 per cent of GDP or more. This is the case in the Czech Republic, Slovenia and Hungary. Conversely, in all those countries where social expenditures are below average poverty is typically high. Slovakia seems to be an exception.

Of course, welfare states differ in more respects than the size of social expenditures. The importance of the structure and the efficiency of social protection should obviously not be underestimated. In Estonia and Poland poverty seems to be high despite relatively generous expenditure levels. This suggests a rather inefficient social protection system in these countries.

Not unimportantly, in Europe the correlation between the generosity of benefits targeted to the poor and poverty is surprisingly weak. In most European countries expenditures for means-tested benefits make up 10 per cent or less of total social expenditures. Although in a large majority of EU countries means-tested minimum income provisions have been introduced as general safety nets for the poor, only in five EU countries do these benefits equal the poverty threshold. Most countries with below-average poverty risks provide inadequate benefits (by this standard) while in two out of the five countries with adequate benefits overall poverty is high. This suggests that in most European countries universal social insurance programmes are much more important in the fight against poverty than means-tested social assistance systems of social protection.

There is a great diversity in Europe in terms of both social architecture and poverty outcomes, and this diversity has undoubtedly been further increased with enlargement. The newly acceded member States will most likely develop various new models of welfare democracies. Europe's diversity demonstrates that there are many paths towards attaining a social welfare democracy, depending on the socio-economic, demographic and cultural particularities and social practices that can vary strongly from country to country.

Notes

1. Purchasing power parity (PPP) is a currency conversion rate that converts monetary indicators expressed in a national currency to an artificial common currency that equalizes the purchasing power of different national currencies. In other words, PPP is both a price deflator and a currency converter; it eliminates the differences in price levels between countries in the process of conversion to an artificial common currency, called the purchasing power standard (PPS).
2. Life satisfaction is measured on the basis of the following question: 'Please tell me whether you are very satisfied, fairly satisfied, not very satisfied or not at all satisfied with your life in general'. The data originate from the Eurobarometer surveys. 'Deprivation' is measured in terms of possession of seven consumer goods, namely television, video recorder, telephone, dishwasher, microwave, car or van, and PC.
3. The working-age population comprises all individuals aged between 16 and 64.

Part IV
Experiences from Low-Income Countries

12
Social Security in Developing Countries: a Brief Overview

Peter Townsend

The history of social security in the OECD countries holds particular implications for anti-poverty action and social and economic stability in the developing countries. Before drawing these together one prior question requires an answer. How does the historical and current account of systems in the OECD countries in this book relate to the policies currently being followed in the developing countries?

One implication of the historical analysis in Chapters 2 and 8 is the value to governments of using 'direct' measures to reduce poverty. For example, contributory social insurance schemes for those of working age who may become sick, disabled, unemployed or bereaved, and non-contributory tax-based benefit schemes, especially for children, disabled people and the elderly, have been shown to have an early but also lasting impact.

Existing social security schemes in developing countries are desperately under-resourced, as Table 2.4 in Chapter 2 graphically illustrates. Expenditure on such schemes in the low-income countries is generally around 1 per cent of GDP and rarely as much as 2 per cent, compared with the nearly 14 per cent of GDP on average in the industrialized countries. The schemes in the poorest countries present a diverse picture (see, for example, ILO, 2001a; van Ginneken, 2003). A semblance of a system had been introduced by colonial authorities in most of Asia, Africa and the Caribbean a hundred or more years ago. They were extended in the first instance to civil servants and employees of large enterprises. There were benefits for relatively small percentages of population that included health care, maternity leave, disability allowances and pensions. In general they neglected the poor, and especially rural poor.

In the last decades there has been mounting concern about slow progress in developing social security in the poorest countries. In 2005 the ILO reported a modelling exercise – applying three models of very basic social protection packages. Costs turned out to be 'within reasonable affordable limits' if countries were committed to reducing poverty (Pal et al., 2005: i; see also Behrendt and Hagemejer, in this volume). But the 'mobilization of international resources will be needed in order to make this an achievable target'

(Pal et al., 2005: xii). In an early page of that report the large gap between rich and poor countries in GDP and in percentage of GDP devoted to redistributive social services and social security is clearly revealed (ibid.: 13).

India

Today there are a number of examples of new as well as previous initiatives taken in developing countries themselves to establish social protection schemes. For example, in India there are schemes in different states intended for large numbers as well as a range of schemes for small categories of population such as middle- and high-ranking civil servants. Cash allowance schemes for children, the disabled and elderly are, however, few and far between. Allowances for children seem likely to develop only as a by-product of other social protection schemes. In 1995 the Government of India introduced an all-India social protection scheme – the National Social Assistance Programme (NSAP). Social assistance benefits are intended to become gradually available to poor households in the case of old age, death of the breadwinner and maternity. Thus there are three types of benefit: the National Old Age Pension Scheme, the National Family Benefit Scheme and the National Maternity Benefit Scheme. Along with expenditure on education, health, public health, labour welfare and family welfare, total 'social security' expenditure per person grew very slowly at constant 1980–1 prices from 128 rupees in 1973 to 142 rupees in 1999, or by 11 per cent. 'Although this increase is not large, it is nonetheless likely to have contributed towards the sharp decrease of poverty in India in recent years' (Justino, 2003: 16).

One current national initiative, also relevant to children, is the National Rural Employment Guarantee Act of 2005 (NEGRA), launched by Prime Minister Manmohan Singh in February 2006. The Act seeks to guarantee employment for 100 days a year at the minimum wage to one person from every poor household to improve rural infrastructure – roads, school buildings and village water supply and to regenerate the land while reducing soil erosion (Mehrotra, 2006: 13). A major problem in developing a social security system for those who cannot be employed, or are unlikely to be employed in the foreseeable future, and especially in considering child allowances, is that the government collects only 8–9 per cent of GDP in taxes, compared with 22 per cent (2003) in China and 14 per cent generally in low-income countries (1990–2001). And tax revenues from the richest sections of the population have actually fallen in the last two decades (ibid.).

Latin America

In Latin America some countries introduced social insurance and other schemes before the Second World War, and other countries followed suit after the war. In that continent there is already more of an established system of social security on which to build. However, benefits tend to be limited in range and coverage. In earlier decades they were not administered by one central government agency. There were multiple schemes for different occupational groups (Hall and Midgeley, 2004: 241). Social insurance had to be greatly extended. And in the informal sector of the economy non-contributory schemes, or schemes with minimal contributions, were needed.

A good start has been made by individual governments in the twenty-first century, including Brazil, especially in schemes for children, for example, the *Bolsa Escola* programme. Relatively local 'conditional cash transfer' (CCT) schemes preceded this programme, which was launched in 2001. In less than a year 5 million households with children between the ages of 6 and 15 were receiving a cash benefit. Transfers were limited to US$15 a month per family, conditional on school attendance. In 2003 the programme was absorbed with other federal CCTs into *Bolsa Familia* (Britto, 2006a: 15). Early research showed positive effects on schooling and nutrition but longer-term effects on rates of poverty and child labour remained unclear (ibid.: 15–16).[1] The enlarged *Bolsa Familia* programme now reaches 11 million households. Mexico was in fact the first country in Latin America to introduce a nation-wide CCT programme – *Progresa*, in 1997. This was expanded and renamed *Oportunidades* in 2002. This confers cash or in-kind allowances to the household (up to US$60 a month) on condition the children attend school and health check-ups are arranged for all members of the household (ibid.: 15).

Less publicized than the *Bolsa Familia* programme in Brazil has been the 'Continuous Cash Benefit Programme', or *Beneficio de Prestacao Continuada* (BPC) in Portugese. After 1993 people aged 65 and over and people with a severe disability whose household per capita income is less than a quarter of the minimum wage (approximately US$1 a day in March 2006) became eligible for a transfer equivalent to the monthly minimum wage (approximately US$4 a month). In December 1996, after its first year of operation, as many as 346,000 benefited. At the end of 2005 2.1 million benefited, just over half being disabled and under the age of 65 (Medeiros et al., 2006: 15). There are other cash transfer mechanisms, including one of invalid pensions, a contributory scheme for workers in the formal market which benefited 2.6 million in 2005.

This illustration shows that programmes to gradually increase public expenditure so that categories of the extreme poor start to benefit offer a realistic, affordable and successful alternative. Under President Lula da Silva, the Brazilian government's Zero Hunger Programme was planned to provide quantity, quality and regularity of food to all Brazilians in conjunction with accelerated social security reform (Suplicy, 2003). The Zero Hunger Programme includes food banks, popular restaurants, food cards, distribution of emergency food baskets, strengthening of family agriculture and a variety of other measures to fight malnutrition. The social security reform programme includes social assistance for low-income 15–17-year-olds; assistance for 7–14-year-olds who are enabled to go to school and avoid the exacting toll of the worst conditions of child labour; minimum income and food scholarships for pregnant and nursing mothers with incomes less than half the minimum wage or who are HIV positive; benefits for elderly disabled with special needs; and a range of other transfer programmes for the elderly, widowed, sick and industrially injured and unemployed that are being enlarged year by year (Suplicy, 2003).

The social security programmes being developed in Mexico, Chile, Costa Rica and especially Brazil are useful models for poorer countries in Africa and South Asia. They provide a parallel set of evidence to that for social security in the OECD countries, and can help governments and international financial agencies to avoid making mistakes in their plans to reduce poverty and improve social and economic well-being.

Africa

Africa presents a more varied picture of measures taken to counter poverty than is often appreciated. In some countries new social insurance schemes have been introduced – for example a maternity and sickness scheme in Namibia. Mauritius and the Seychelles have universal benefit programmes (and relatively low poverty rates). Means-tested cash benefits are found in Botswana and Mozambique. Zambia has successfully piloted a social cash transfer scheme targeted to the poorest tenth of households (Gassmann and Behrendt, 2006). But social security expenditure in countries like Burundi, Cameroon, Ethiopia, Ghana, Kenya, Madagascar, Mauritania and Nigeria has declined or remains at a tiny level compared with GDP (ILO, 2002a).

South Africa has high rates of poverty, labour migration and unemployment, and the problem of HIV/AIDS has become acute. Nonetheless, since the fall of apartheid in 1994 strong attempts have been made to begin to introduce a comprehensive social security system. In 1998 a Child Support Grant was started, worth R100 for each child below the age of 7 whose carer had an income of less than R800–R1,100, depending on composition of family and other factors. The 1998 figure of R100 has been increased regularly in line with inflation, reaching R180 in 2006. By early 2003 there were 2.5 million beneficiaries. By late 2005 the age limit had been increased gradually to 13, and the number of beneficiaries reached over 6 million (and the number of adults 4 million). There are criticisms of coverage. While there is good evidence that the grant reaches some of the poorest of children (Case et al., 2003) the increasingly large numbers of orphans, street children and child-headed households, in many cases the consequence of the spread of HIV/AIDS, remain largely ineligible (Barrientos and DeJong, 2004, and see the initiatives in measuring child poverty by Noble et al., 2008). Despite the difficulties, many South Africans regard the development as the 'road to universality' and give the example of the Child Support Grant when illustrating the significance of the incorporation by South Africa of the principle of the 'progressive realization' of economic and social human rights into their common law jurisdiction. The idea of a staged programme towards comprehensive coverage was a feature of a major commissioned report (Committee of Inquiry into a Comprehensive System of Social Security for South Africa, 2002). There is a new cash grant in South Africa. But everywhere wider non-contributory schemes for children are urgently needed, preferably schemes that are categorical and not means-tested or otherwise conditional (as shown above in Chapter 11).

China

China has the largest population in the world (though India is rapidly catching up). Information about social security is improving rapidly and social surveys in particular are providing data about poverty and policy measures – particularly for urban areas – that were previously inaccessible. For example, one survey draws on 1998 urban household survey data covering 17,000 households in 31 provinces, conducted by the National Statistics Bureau (see Hussain, 2002). The research team, made up of experts from China and from other countries, including the United Kingdom, decided to distinguish between a 'food poverty line' – defined by the average cost in different provinces for people among the poorest 20 per cent of just buying enough food to provide the minimum necessary average of 2,100 calories per person per day – and a (higher) poverty line. The cost of meeting the poverty line was the cost of meeting the 'food poverty line' plus the cost of meeting other basic non-food needs. These were worked out using a regression exercise on the urban data and, just as food needs were calculated on the basis of an average of 2,100 calories per person, non-food needs were calibrated for different households in accordance with basic non-food expenditure of households just satisfying the criterion of spending on food to ensure a minimum of 2,100 calories.

The national average food poverty line of 1,392 yuan per month was estimated to be 32 per cent lower in the province of Qinghai, at one extreme among the 31 provinces, and 69 per cent higher in the province of Shanghai, at the other extreme. The general poverty line is lower than the purchasing power parity equivalent of the World Bank's poverty standard of $1 per day. It produces an estimate for the whole of China of 4.7 per cent, or 15 million in poverty, when income is the standard, and 11.9 per cent, or 37 million in poverty, when expenditure is the standard. Where the exact poverty line is drawn matters in China because a large proportion of the population have very low incomes. Thus, if the poverty line were drawn 50 per cent higher than the very stringent threshold in fact adopted, the figure of 4.7 per cent in poverty becomes 20 per cent or nearly 90 million in urban areas. It would be even higher if it measured the costs of subsistence, like the study undertaken by the Institute of Forecasting of the Chinese Academy of Sciences and even that by the National Statistics Bureau and the Ministry of Civil Affairs.

The key policies for the urban poor in China are the Minimum Living Standard Scheme (MLSS), a recent addition, and a longer-established social security package that includes social insurance. The MLSS began as a local initiative that was gradually extended to regions and then all urban areas. With the disappearance of the living allowance for laid-off employees by the end of 2003, the MLSS and unemployment insurance will be the 'two last lines of defence against urban poverty'. By the end of the 1990s, 3.3 million registered unemployed, or 55 per cent, were receiving unemployment benefit; and 3 million of the 460 million urban population were recipients of the MLSS. Eligibility is restricted and special investigation of particular cities found that only about a quarter of those in poverty were receiving assistance.

For China to make improvements in anti-poverty policies many authorities seem to agree that publicly provided social assistance and social insurance need to be extended and benefits raised; the administrative infrastructure greatly strengthened; poverty monitored more successfully; and the methods of financing benefits overhauled. Certainly different models of social security in both rich and poor countries are being scrutinized closely.

According to the ILO, 'One of the key problems facing social security today is the fact that more than half of the world's population are excluded from any type of statutory social security protection' (van Ginneken, 2003: 1; see also Cichon and Hagemejer, 2006; Cichon and Scholz, 2004; ILO, 1984; Midgeley, 1984; Reynaud, 2001; Rodgers, 1995; van Ginneken, 1999). In South Asia and sub-Saharan Africa approximately 90 per cent and in middle-income countries between 20 and 60 per cent lack such protection. 'Social security has become more necessary than ever due to globalization and structural adjustment policies ... The challenge for governments, social partners and civil societies is to create such conditions that the large majority of the population contributes to basic social insurance schemes' (van Ginneken, 2003: 66).

The ILO Social Security (Minimum Standards) Convention (No. 102) 1952 laid down minimum income requirements per child, of either 3 per cent of the ordinary manual labourer's wage, for the economically active, or 1.5 per cent of that wage for all other families. In families with four children the benefit would amount to 12 per cent (or 6 per cent in the case of those not in work). The ILO Convention was signed by 40 countries – including Niger, Senegal and Mauritius. It became part of the European Code of Social Security and the blueprint for such instruments as the European Social Charter, the Treaty of Amsterdam of the European Union and regional agreements in

Africa and Latin America (Kulke et al., 2006: 4). If the World Bank had sought policies to enforce this Convention rather than develop the neo-liberal anti-poverty strategy that has turned out to be so counter-productive there would have been a dramatic fall in world poverty.

A serious obstacle to the extension of social security schemes in developing countries to reduce poverty has been the difficulty of reaching agreements on trade (see, for example, Held, 1995; Kanbur, 2000; Offenheiser and Holcombe, 2003; Watkins 2002) and therefore the exact needs and rights to income of people to be employed directly and indirectly by trans-national corporations. Discussions about the nature, still less the legal enforceability, of 'corporate social responsibility' (ILO, 1998; OECD, 2001c) have not been resolved – in particular the question of employing trans-national corporations making contributions to the extension of social security in developing countries in which they have a substantial interest and where many workers are employed on their behalf. Another serious obstacle has been the difficulty of rebuilding and/or strengthening tax administration. Taxation and contributory insurance systems can be introduced or strengthened to raise national revenue to match international tax or aid revenues both for the protection of children and families, but also to be fully answerable to representatives of national electorates as well as participating overseas governments, with independent powers to monitor policies and outcomes.

Because of mounting criticism of the insufficient powers and therefore the policies of nation-states to resolve poverty in the global economy of the twenty-first century joint funding of social security between countries is likely to evolve (see, for example, Townsend, 2004b, for an illustration of joint funding of child benefit). Demands for joint action, including action to build and enforce tax and contribution revenues, will necessarily lead to the introduction of new forms of international taxation and accompanying independent international inspectorates.

Conclusion

The end of the first decade of the twenty-first century marks an emerging and increasingly disputed choice between two alternative grand strategies for the developing countries: (1) staged progress towards a major public system of social security for the population as a whole, and particularly those unable to participate in ordinary economic activity, such as children, sick and disabled people and the elderly, costing substantially more than 10 per cent of GDP; or (2) conditional public cash transfer schemes targeting the extreme poor and costing less than 3 per cent of GDP. The debate about the difficulties of fulfilling the Millennium Development Goals by 2015, the global financial recession of 2008–9 and the attention now being given to the long arm of social security in OECD history is becoming intense.

Notes

1. 'Initial evaluations have shown positive effects of CCTs on schooling and nutrition. The evidence regarding the impact on child labour is not conclusive, since school attendance can be frequently combined with work and requires broader interventions. The impact on poverty is still not so clear ... In the long run, the translation of higher educational attainment into higher earnings cannot be taken for granted. It depends on the quality of education, rates of employment, absorption of skilled labour in the economy and general rates of return to education' (Britto, 2006a: 15–16). See also Britto (2006b).

13
Introducing Basic Social Protection in Low-Income Countries: Lessons from Existing Programmes

Armando Barrientos[1]

Social protection is scarce in low-income countries, but there are encouraging signs that this situation is rapidly changing. There is growing recognition that social protection is an essential component of an effective development strategy, especially in the context of supporting and facilitating rapid social and economic transformation (Fouarge, 2003; ILO, 2005). A wide rage of evidence emerging from the evaluation of large-scale social protection programmes in middle-income developing countries underscores the large potential gains from these programmes in terms of poverty and vulnerability reduction and human capital accumulation (Barrientos and Lloyd-Sherlock, 2003; Morley and Coady, 2003). This raises the important issue of whether introducing or extending social protection programmes in low-income countries could secure similar gains. This chapter addresses this issue by drawing out the main lessons emerging from existing social protection programmes in low-income countries.

There is a diversity of views on the scope of social protection, but for our purposes in this chapter it will be helpful to define some key parameters. Social protection is commonly taken to include social insurance, social assistance and labour market regulation. Social insurance normally covers schemes financed by contributions from employees, employers and the state; and protecting contributors and their dependants from contingencies associated with the life course, employment and health. Social assistance is predominantly tax-financed and aims to support those in poverty. Labour market regulation enhances security and protection of workers and ensures rights to participation and voice. I believe that a focus on low-income countries inevitably invites us to concentrate mainly on the second of these three, and therefore in this chapter I will be concerned to elaborate on social assistance.[2] Our concern is not with safety nets, involving short-term support in emergencies, but with stable and reliable forms of support for poor and vulnerable households and communities.[3] The chapter examines social protection programmes and policies which focus on poor households and help reduce deficient consumption, facilitate investment in human and physical assets, and strengthen the agency of the poor for example by empowering them to overcome social exclusion. This applies to a range of social protection instruments, but especially to transfers in kind or cash – i.e. social assistance. A key implication of defining social protection in this way is that it necessarily involves, at the same time, redistribution, insurance and learning.

It is taken for granted that the challenges of establishing and developing social protection are that much harder in low-income countries. There are several dimensions to this issue. The demand for formal social protection instruments is weaker in economies that are predominantly rural. Informal support systems and social norms are commonly in place to ensure a measure of protection. Economic development and urbanization strengthen the demand for more extensive social protection institutions. Present-day low-income countries generally have weaker, and perhaps fragmented, political systems and labour organizations, with the implication that wider social contracts and solidarity are very limited in scope. In most cases, low-income countries have large deficiencies in state capacity to collect taxes and to design, as well as support and deliver, social protection. The list of dimensions could be usefully extended, but these factors – underdevelopment, politics, finance and administration – are key constraints in establishing effective social protection instruments in low-income countries.

It would be wrong to take the factors above as preconditions for a successful introduction of social protection. There is an argument, less prominent now, that low-income countries should concentrate on growth fundamentals before tackling more directly issues of poverty and inequality. It is pleasing to note that this approach has been replaced by a broader perspective on growth and development, backed by a considerable weight of evidence, taking social protection as an integral component of a successful growth and development strategy. This perspective reflects more accurately the experience of developed economies, in which the establishment and extension of social protection was an important factor in facilitating development, nurturing strong solidarity values, and strengthening state financial and administrative capacity. The issue then is how to generate these synergies in low-income countries. In consequence, the factors listed above should more appropriately be seen as constraints rather than preconditions.

Even if we accept the view that growth and social protection policies are mutually reinforcing, it would still be possible that the nature of their dynamics could retard the establishment of social protection. It could be argued that 'low income–low social protection' traps apply to low-income countries. The term 'trap' indicates that low-income countries with marginal levels of social protection will remain in that situation, in the absence of externally induced change. Another possibility is that social protection is retarded by policy path dependence, in which existing, informal or formal, social protection arrangements weigh down the chances of reform and expansion. It is important therefore to consider the qualitative nature of the constraints, as it signals qualitative differences in the nature of the policy responses likely to be successful.

The chapter is organized as follows. The first part provides summary information on selected social protection programmes in low-income countries. The second discusses whether 'low income–low social protection' traps, or alternatively, path dependence, are helpful in explaining the strength of constraints in the introduction of basic social protection in developing countries. The following parts tackle separately the main constraints. One focuses on the politics of developing social protection. Another deals with issues of design and delivery. The next covers financing issues, followed by one dealing with the issue of the 'productivist' qualities of social protection in low-income countries. A final part of the chapter summarizes the main conclusions.

Social protection programmes in low-income countries

It will be useful to begin by considering summary information on selected social protection programmes in low-income countries. This will provide the necessary empirical background. The programmes in the list were selected to show the scope of social protection initiatives in low-income countries.[4]

Each of the programmes contributes some information of interest to the discussion below. Table 13.1 includes conditional and unconditional transfer programmes,[5] and a single example of an integrated anti-poverty programme.

The fact that Table 13.1 provides a selection of programmes should not be taken to imply that social assistance programmes abound in low-income countries, although it is likely that many small-scale, localized projects, pilots or programmes exist.[6] The list includes two programmes from lower-middle income countries, Bolivia and Nicaragua.[7] They illustrate universal non-contributory pension and conditional human development programmes respectively. Bolivia's programme is interesting from a political economy perspective, as will be explained below. All other examples are taken from low-income countries.

There are many social protection initiatives underway in low-income countries. As noted above, there is growing interest in social protection among African countries (Beales and German, 2006). Countries in East Africa are currently developing social protection strategies which could lead to the establishment of relevant programmes in Uganda, Kenya, Rwanda, Tanzania and Malawi. The development of social protection is slower in West Africa, but Nigeria is planning the introduction of an education-based conditional cash transfer programme, and Ghana is at the earliest stages of planning a similar initiative. New and large-scale social protection initiatives in South Asia are planned for India, with the National Rural Employment Bill, and for Pakistan.

Table 13.1 Summary of selected social protection programmes in low(er)-income countries

Programme title	Description	Politics	Financing	Delivery
Bangladesh's Targeting the Ultra Poor	Integrated asset and cash transfers/learning/health and micro-credit	Introduced and managed by BRAC (poverty reduction NGO) in response to operational lessons	Donor consortium	Targets poorest, through geographic and wealth ranking/delivery through local committees; 110,000 beneficiary households in 2006
Bangladesh's Old Age Allowance scheme and assistance programme for widowed and destitute women	Unconditional cash transfer; US$2 per month	Introduced in National Plan; managed by Ministry of Social Welfare and local committees	Tax-financed; cost around 0.03 per cent GDP	Targets fixed number of poorest and oldest beneficiaries in each ward, then selection by local committees; 1.4 million beneficiaries
Bolivia's *Bono Solidario*	Unconditional cash transfer of US$248 annually	Introduced to ease privatization of utilities; entitlement for cohort aged 21 and over in 1995	Privatization proceeds fund; cost is 0.25 per cent of GDP	Paid to those aged 65 and over; public agency manages bond paid through banking system; approx. 250,000 beneficiaries
Ethiopia's Productive Safety Net programme	Conditional transfers in cash or food to chronically food insecure households with available labour (US$3–5.5 per month), and unconditional transfers to households ineligible for work (US$1–5 per month)	Adopted by government after protracted discussions with donors over shift from emergency food aid to social protection	Mix of tax financed and joint donor group support; five-year window	Geographic selection of food insecure districts, then community identification of vulnerable households; 1.6 million beneficiary households

India's Employment Guarantee Scheme – Maharashtra State	Conditional cash transfer; public works employment	Statutory programme developed in 1970s; about to scale up nationally	Tax financed	Geographic targeting then self-selection; in 1990s supported 100 m person days; reaching 20 million beneficiaries
Nicaragua's *Red de Protección Social*	Conditional cash transfer programme; transfer is US$18 per household plus US$5 per child of school age per month	Converted from a social fund set up to address conflict emergency	Inter-American Development Bank and social fund FISE; cost is around 0.02 per cent of GDP; five-year window	Geographic targeting selects poorest municipalities with available infrastructure, then proxy means test; managed by social fund; 10,000 beneficiary households
Zambia's Kalomo District social transfer pilot scheme	Unconditional cash transfer programme, transfer is US$8–10 per month	Piloted by GTZ as an alternative to recurrent emergency food aid; managed by Public Welfare Assistance Scheme	Financed by GTZ, four-year window; cost of scaling up nationally is 0.4 per cent of GDP	Community targeting of 10 per cent poorest and economically inactive households; 1,200 beneficiary households

Source: Data from Barrientos and Holmes (2007), available from www.chronicpoverty.org.

Is there a low income–low social protection trap?

Some have suggested low-income countries face a 'low income–low social protection' trap (Fritzen, 2003). This argument borrows from the poverty trap literature, in which countries are said to be unable to break out from the hard constraints of their underdevelopment (Bowles et al., 2006). The key point about this being a 'trap' is the fact that these conditions are more or less permanent, the product of self-reinforcing mechanisms. There are many different poverty trap models, but it will be useful to focus on a simplified two-sector model to fix the essentials of the discussion (Azariades and Stachurski, forthcoming). Assume an economy with an informal sector, in which agents receive a constant return for their labour w_{inf}, normalized to zero (w_{inf}^*). Agents in the formal sector receive a return for their labour equal to w_f which is dependent on the share of the labour force employed in the formal sector, that is $w_f = f(h)$ where h is the fraction of the labour force employed in the formal sector. The intuition behind this simplified model is that the informal sector is essentially a subsistence economy sector, while the formal sector is a knowledge-intensive sector in which aggregate output enjoys increasing returns to scale dependent on the size of the sector.

Figure 13.1 shows the rates of return to the two sectors according to the share of the labour force in the formal sector. Note that there is a threshold h' at which the returns to the formal sector and the informal sector are the same. To the left of h', the returns to the informal sector dominate and agents will transfer from the formal to the informal sector until there is only an informal sector ($h = 0$). To the right of h', the rates of return to the formal sector dominate, and informal workers will shift to the formal sector until

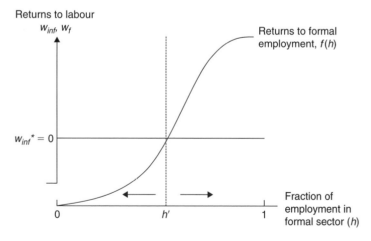

Figure 13.1   Rates of return to formal and informal sectors according to the share of the labour force in the formal sector

everyone is in the formal sector ($h = 1$). There are three points at which the dynamic adjustment will come to rest – $h = 0$, h' and $h = 1$ – and the first one represents a poverty trap. Admittedly, this is a highly simplified and unrealistic model, but it helps us to fix on the potential meaning of a 'low income–low social protection' trap.

In fact, it is possible to read a low social protection trap directly from the figure. Informality is synonymous with lack of social protection: informal workers are those without access to it. Their productivity would rise significantly if they were to work in knowledge-intensity employment, with large gains for the economy and their welfare. There are also wider gains from social protection in terms of a strengthening of solidarity, state capacity and political stability. However, unless and until employment in the formal sector achieves critical mass, informality will continue to dominate.[8] Put differently, social protection will only take off when a critical mass of formal employment is reached, but there are no forces pushing an economy dominated by informality towards this point.

This kind of argumentation could provide an explanation of why employment-based social protection remains extremely limited in sub-Saharan Africa. The coverage of social insurance pension plans or health insurance is, in those countries where it exists, limited to civil servants and the military, and a scattering of highly paid private sector workers. Not only has it proved extremely difficult to expand the coverage of these schemes, but recent public sector retrenchment and fiscal restrictions have actually led to stagnant or declining coverage. This is related to evidence in the recent years of growing inequality of household income in developing countries (for example, Cornia, 1999). The size of informal employment places strong constraints on the development of employment-based social protection in low-income countries, especially as it reduces the tax base, and therefore the capacity for governments to finance social protection interventions (Auriol and Warlters, 2002; Tanzi, 2000). The substantial role of development aid in low-income countries, and the focus on poverty and vulnerability reduction associated with the Millennium Development Goals, might be crucial in helping low-income countries break out of 'low income–low social protection' traps.

In the context of tax-financed social protection focused on the poor, a political economy approach would be needed to flesh out the substance of the processes of decision-making at work. A political economy approach would seek to model the conditions under which taxpayers, including workers making payroll contributions, would be willing to support anti-poverty programmes, for example through transfers of some kind (Besley, 1997). Taxpayers have preferences over their own consumption, but also over the consumption of the poor. There are different ways in which the consumption of the poor affects taxpayers. Altruistic taxpayers will see direct benefit in reducing poverty, while self-interested taxpayers might be concerned with the extent to which poverty feeds social unrest and criminality. Taxpayers would also need to take into account the potential costs of anti-poverty programmes, and, of course, their effectiveness. Modelling the different elements in the taxpayer's decision is beyond the scope of this chapter, and there are no straightforward leads from the literature (Pritchett, 2005; Snyder and Yackovlev, 2000). For example, we could interpret $f(h)$ as the returns to taxpayers' support for social protection focused on those in poverty as a function of the fraction of the population covered by social protection. However, for most plausible conditions it would be hard to envisage low social protection traps in the sense described in Figure 13.1. It is likely that the schedule of costs and benefits for taxpayers associated with anti-poverty programmes could exhibit some discontinuities over some ranges of coverage,[9] and it is even possible to generate thresholds beyond which the coverage of anti-poverty programmes rises rapidly, but it is hard to conceive of plausible conditions under which minimal or zero coverage constitutes a stable point.

It would make more sense to consider path dependence as a source of constraints on the establishment and development of social protection in low-income countries. There are at least two levels on which path dependence operates. At a macro-level, path dependence reflects the particular configuration of policy responses to social risk in a country, or groups of countries. In the welfare regime literature as applied to developed countries, these are grouped according to the specific configuration of welfare-producing institutions: state, markets, and households (Esping-Andersen, 1999; Gough and Wood, 2004). This is the welfare mix. Scandinavian countries favour the state as the dominant provider, while Anglo-Saxon countries rely to an important extent on the market, and conservative countries make the family the central welfare-providing institution. The welfare mix generates both institutions and expectations among the populations of these countries which reinforce the welfare mix. These in turn generate strong path dependence in welfare regimes. But it is hard to find such well-formed welfare regimes in low-income countries. In fact many of the welfare institutions observed in developed countries are missing, and family and informal social protection dominate (Gough and Wood, 2004). It could be argued that it is precisely the lack of consolidation of welfare regimes in developing countries that facilitates rapid and far-reaching changes in welfare institutions, for example the reforms of pension schemes in Latin American countries (Barrientos, 2004a). It is unlikely that macro-level path dependence is the main constraint on the development of social protection in low-income developing countries.

There is also path dependence at a micro level, associated with the presence of fragmented programmes with attached constituencies. The constraints on shifting from emergency food relief to regular transfers in cash or kind in low-income countries in Africa is well documented (DFID, 2005c). These constituencies include, for example, local and national politicians and beneficiary groups, national and international NGOs, faith organizations and donors engaged in specific interventions on target groups, and public agencies serving specific groups or communities. They constitute an important source of constraints on the development of larger scale social protection programmes.

In sum, I have attempted to shed some light on the strength of the constraints on introducing and developing social protection in low-income countries. We began by considering the conditions in which 'low income–low social protection' traps could arise. The discussion suggested that simplified models of formal/informal poverty traps could throw light on the difficulties involved in expanding employment-based social protection in low-income countries, for example in the context of generating resources for social protection through the tax system. We concluded that it is hard to envisage similar traps in the context of tax-financed social protection focused on the poorest. We then moved on to consider whether the constraints on the establishment and development of social protection can be said to arise from policy path dependence. In discussion we found that micro-, as opposed to macro-, level path dependence is likely to be a stronger source of constraints. The strengths of the constraints vary across different types of social protection, employment-based and tax-financed based, but these seem to be less pronounced for tax-financed social protection focused on the poor.

Getting the politics right?

The sustainability of social protection programmes requires a measure of political support or at least the absence of significant opposition. Getting the politics right is essential for the establishment of social protection programmes. Public choice models of policy processes are perhaps not very helpful in the context of low-income countries. They rely on assumptions about the presence of a competitive political system in which voters signal preferences over different policy alternatives to which politicians respond. On the assumption that the preferences of voters over a single issue, say social protection for the poor, would show a single peaked distribution, public choice would confidently predict that the preferences of the median voter will prevail. In the context of low-income countries, with high poverty incidence, the median voter is likely to be fairly close to the poverty line and should favour social protection programmes. The reality is very different from the predictions of public choice models.

In developing countries, but especially low-income ones, the shortcomings of these models are apparent. Voters are ill-informed about the relative advantages of policy options, and regard the promises of politicians as having little credibility (Keefer and Khemani, 2003).[10] Patronage, clientelism and corruption undermine the basis for competitive politics. The political system is as a result less effective in aggregating voter preferences, than in protecting and nurturing patron–client relationships. This underscores the importance of factors exogenous to the political system, such as major disasters or crises, or the intervention of donors and NGOs, in forcing social protection on to the political agenda. The experience of low-income countries suggests that the following factors are influential in the adoption of social protection programmes.

Cross-national policy transfers

Low-income countries are to an important extent aid-dependent and as a consequence are exposed to donor-led policy transfers. Regional bodies are another significant mechanism supporting policy transfers. Rational policy transfers involve the voluntary adoption in one country of social protection policies which have been shown to be effective in other countries (Banks et al., 2005). Rational policy transfers invoke a virtuous process of learning across countries, with clear programme objectives and strong evaluation in the country of origin and careful learning and adaptation in the destination country, typically malaria prevention measures. It is also possible to envisage more coercive cross-national policy transfers, in which a third party enforces the adoption of a social protection programme, typically structural adjustment programmes. In between these two extremes, there is a range of possible permutations, with degrees of rationality and coercion.

There is no doubt that the more recent adoption of social protection programmes in low-income developing countries reflects strong cross-national policy transfers at work.[11] Most of these are at the rational end of the spectrum. There are extensive cross-country policy networks in operation around social protection, and concerted efforts are made by many international organizations, regional bodies and national governments to learn from the international experience. Many international organizations also seek to influence the type of social protection considered for adoption in some countries. At the same time, it could be argued that elements of coercion[12] can be detected, although these also reflect the influence of the MDGs in providing targets and benchmarks.

Domestic policy learning

Learning about the outcomes of domestic policies has been an important factor in persuading policy-makers of the need to adopt social protection. There is, in many cases, a deep understanding among researchers and policy-makers within low-income countries of the deficiencies of anti-poverty programmes implemented in the past, and this provides a strong motivation for considering potential alternatives. In many cases, this understanding fails to translate into policy reform, in part because of path dependence but also because of the perceived risks from policy reform. Bangladesh's Ultra-Poor Programme is a good example of the adoption of social protection targeted on the poorest following from an assessment of the limited success of existing interventions in reaching the very poorest.[13]

Perceived opposition to government policies or social unrest

It is no surprise that the adoption of social protection programmes often reflects a desire on the part of policy-makers to counteract real or perceived opposition to government policy, and the threat of social unrest. A good example is the introduction of Bolivia's *Bono Solidario*. The government used the pension programme as a means to ensure political support for the privatization of utilities, by promising to use the proceeds from privatization to fund a pension for every citizen aged 21 or over at the time of privatization (Gray-Molina, 1999). Interestingly, the government suspended the pension entitlement after successfully completing the privatization process, reinstated it later under public pressure but at a reduced level of benefits, and renewed public pressure led a new government to reinstate the pension in full (Barrientos, 2006).

The political conditions needed to make social protection programmes sustainable are less demanding. This is especially the case where programmes are felt to be effective. Political fragmentation also imposes conflictive restrictions on the size of the programme and the opportunities for scaling up. Small-scale interventions, perhaps localized in certain areas, are easier to get off the ground if they fit in with local or regional political elites and their constituencies. It is much harder to scale these up, even when they are evidently successful. On the other hand, programmes with national coverage can overcome political fragmentation providing they allow for decentralized management and to some extent design. Scaling up local programmes or introducing centralized national coverage programmes is that much more difficult in the context of fragmented, clientelist, political systems.[14]

In this part of the chapter the political constraints in establishing social protection programmes in low-income countries, where the absence of competitive political systems work to enhance the role of exogenous events and actors, have been noted. The main factors explaining political support for the adoption of existing social protection programmes in low-income countries are cross-national policy transfers, lessons learned from domestic policy, and the perceived need to counteract opposition to policy or social unrest. The political sustainability of established programmes can be secured where programmes are perceived to be effective, but political fragmentation poses difficulties for scaling up programmes.

Design and delivery

The programmes in Table 13.1 cover a range of different types of interventions, from cash transfer programmes to integrated anti-poverty programmes, although the majority are cash transfer programmes. There are several issues associated with cash transfers which could be reasonably raised in the context of low-income countries. An important concern is whether cash transfers could lead to higher prices in conditions of inelastic supply, thus reducing their effectiveness in reducing poverty. There is little or no evidence that cash transfers have produced this effect. This is most probably due to the very low level and population coverage of the transfers. It is more likely that in communities starved of cash and credit, small injections of cash could generate local economy multipliers, but there is only limited evidence for this effect in low-income countries.[15] A second concern relates to the opportunities for corruption, and especially skimming of the benefits along the distribution chain. However, this applies to all transfers, and it could be argued that cash is easier to track than food. The experience of low-income countries does not suggest that cash transfers are especially affected by corruption.[16] The potential for generating dependency among beneficiaries also affects all transfers, whether in kind or in cash. Short-term or unpredictable transfers are less likely to generate dependency. At the same time, they are much less likely to lead to sustained investment by poor households in human and physical capital, a necessary condition for long-term poverty reduction. At the very least, the selected programmes demonstrate that transfers, and especially cash transfers, are feasible in low-income countries.

The majority of the programmes select the poorest and most vulnerable households for participation, and for this range of programmes targeting appears to be the norm. The programmes in Table 13.1 show the use of a range of selection methods: geographic targeting of marginalized communities; fixed benefit quotas; selection of beneficiary households through local committees and proxy means tests; selection by household characteristics; and self-selection. These suggest that there are many options for selection available to low-income countries, and also some efforts directed at finding the types of selection methods that can deliver programme objectives and overcome operational capacity constraints.[17]

For our purposes it is important to consider the reasons for the selection of beneficiaries. Firstly, financing constraints in low-income countries with high incidence of poverty makes the selection of a sub-group of beneficiaries a necessity. As discussed below, the potential for rapid escalation of transfers is an understandable concern for national governments. Secondly, and this is perhaps the more interesting reason, selection is needed to identify those to whom the programme is directed. Ethiopia's PSNP seeks to identify households that are vulnerable to food deficits, and then distinguish those that can provide work from those that are not able to do so. The former could be supported through public works, but not the latter. In this case, selection follows from the need to achieve the objectives of the programme. Bangladesh's Targeting the Ultra Poor programme seeks to reach households without assets that are otherwise excluded from alternative anti-poverty programmes. Nicaragua's *Red de Protección Social* targets poor households in the poorest communities with health and education infrastructure because of the human development objectives built into the programme. Most social protection programmes in low-income countries aim to reach the poorest.[18]

A binding constraint for the development of social protection programmes in low-income countries has to do with operational capacity, the capacity to deliver the entitlements promised by the programme. Administrative and delivery capacity is problematic at all levels of government in low-income countries, but even by these standards public agencies responsible for social welfare programmes are relatively weak and under-resourced. In most cases, they lack the capacity for needs assessment, policy formulation and design, and programme implementation and evaluation. An area of great concern is evaluation, which has been shown to be central in exploiting the public goods characteristics of social protection programmes and mustering political support in similar programme in Latin America (Coady, 2003). Quasi public agencies, such as Bangladesh's BRAC or Nicaragua's FISE can do better, partly because of their relative autonomy which enables them to resource and remunerate their staff appropriately.[19] Information systems are essential to the delivery and monitoring of social protection programmes.

In this part of the chapter we have considered three main design and delivery issues, directly related to state capacity to introduce social protection programmes in low-income countries. We noted the increasing use of cash transfers. In selecting beneficiaries we picked up on two issues: first, the fact that there is a wide range of selection methods in use suggesting that there are many options available to low-income countries; and second, the relative importance of delivering programme objectives, rather than financial constraints, as the main rationale for targeting. In delivering programmes we underlined, third, the considerable constraints imposed by public and quasi public agencies.

Financing

Financing is a key constraint on the development of social protection (Barrientos, 2008b). This is despite the fact that well-targeted social protection programmes, such as conditional cash transfers, have overall budget costs typically well below 1 per cent of GDP. Low-income countries have large numbers in poverty and a very limited capacity for raising domestic revenue. It is not surprising, therefore, that the majority of social protection programmes in low-income countries are financed off budget, mainly through donor support.

We have to consider the 'mix' of social protection financing. Social protection in the wider meaning given at the start of this chapter (social insurance and employment regulation as well as social assistance) normally draws on several sources of finance: public expenditure by national governments; donors; private, community and NGO financing; and household financing, through out-of-pocket expenditures or saving. Within private as well as public financing of social protection, employer contributions are very important for workers in formal employment. The full mix of financing is sometimes overlooked. For example, social protection programmes with community targeting involve a measure of support from communities, usually by supporting the administration and delivery of the programme with labour time. In the case of conditional transfer programmes, the costs to beneficiaries of complying with conditionalities could be usefully looked upon as co-financing. Household activities to reduce the likelihood of experiencing predictable as well as unpredictable income hazards are also an important source of financing social protection programmes. Table 13.1 illustrates the main sources of explicit funding of selected social protection programmes, but it is important to keep in mind that implicit co-funding is an important component in many social protection programmes.

Few of the social protection programmes in the table are financed from domestic tax revenues, although many are financed by taxpayers in a different jurisdiction, again underscoring the political constraints involved in developing social protection in low-income countries. The issue is less to do with affordability, especially as the entries in the table show the low absolute cost of well-targeted social protection programmes. Concerns around issues of financing social protection among national governments in low-income countries usually focus on medium and longer-term fiscal liabilities and/or strategic positioning vis-à-vis donors over sectoral or programme support.[20] These concerns are justified. In low-income countries, high poverty incidence implies a potentially large number of beneficiaries, with the implication that even if social protection initiatives are initially well-targeted on the poorest and set low-level transfers, political pressures could rapidly escalate the programmes and consequently the programme budget. Take Zambia, for example, where the official poverty headcount in 2000 was 76 per cent of the population, with another 10 per cent of the population just above the poverty line. A proposal to scale up the Kalomo social transfer pilot scheme, which targets the 10 per cent poorest households, estimated the costs of a scaling up to a nationwide programme at 0.4 per cent of GDP (Schubert, 2005). Government concerns focused not on the immediate affordability of the proposal (in fact donors offered assistance over the medium term) but instead on the likely escalation of the programme.

The adoption of tax-financed social protection is more likely where selection or other design features in the programme set clear parameters to manage future fiscal liabilities. For example, Bangladesh programmes for poorest widows and older persons provide a fixed level benefit to a fixed number of beneficiaries per ward. Such 'categorical' selection is also helpful to a strategy of progressive realization because by focusing on the oldest and poorer as the beneficiary group, the design and implementation of a scheme involves natural exit points.[21] This illuminates the important trade-off in public financing of social assistance programmes. It is possible to manage future fiscal liabilities by paying close attention to selection and design parameters, but only at the cost of reducing the insurance capabilities of the programme. In developed countries, the expansion of social insurance schemes in the past provided the financing required for the expansion of social protection, while extending insurance to cover a range of contingencies.

The scope for switching other forms of government expenditure as a means of financing social protection programmes is probably very limited in low-income countries (Smith and Subbarao, 2003). This is particularly the case for social expenditures. Moreover, an explicit feature of conditional cash transfer programmes is to increase demand for health and education by the poorest. Therefore these programmes may well result in complementary increases in public expenditure on health and education to ensure overall effectiveness (Rawlings and Rubio, 2005). And path dependence suggests it will be difficult to switch resources from underperforming anti-poverty programmes, especially where they have developed support constituencies.[22]

In many low-income countries, donors have taken a very supportive approach to social protection. Table 13.1 shows that many of the social protection programmes listed are financed by them. In addition, donors are providing most of the funding for the policy and technical studies leading to the adoption of social protection programmes. Donors have an important role in financing the set up, or reform, costs of social protection. In this context, the ILO's Social Trust financial support model which covers initial technical and capacity building support and support for the recurrent costs of social protection schemes with a gradual withdrawal after a long lag, has many advantages (ILO, 2002a).

One key issue is the short- or long-term structure of aid. Social protection interventions are most effective in the medium and long run. Social protection programmes require longer time windows for piloting and design, and a sustained run to generate the desired effects on poverty and vulnerability. This is in contrast to the shorter time preferences of donors, with the implication that the optimal length of time of social protection programmes may extend beyond the maximum period to which donors may be willing to commit themselves. In Table 13.1, Ethiopia's PSNP has a five-year window, Nicaragua's RED has a five-year window, and Zambia's pilot scheme a four-year window. The relatively short number of years of aid favoured by donors is a limiting factor in the development of social protection in low-income countries.

The shift to budget support among some donors (for example DFID) could provide the framework within which longer-term support for social protection programmes could be secured. The expectation is that budget support will provide a partnership-based, predictable and transparent aid modality. This could have the effect of lifting the short-term constraint and at the same time reduce the incentives for strategic bargaining by national governments over the sectoral focus of aid. Some issues will still need to be resolved (Barrientos, 2008a, 2008b). Budget support reflects a move away from aid conditionalities, to be replaced by the identification of shared objectives, strategies and targets across donors and national governments. But, other things being equal, this could make it more difficult to establish social protection initiatives in countries in which governments remain unpersuaded of the merits of social protection.

To date, few NGOs or private organizations have established large-scale social protection programmes in low-income countries. The few examples available, as listed illustratively in Table 13.1, suggest that NGOs have comparative advantage and preferences for small, localized, shorter-term, and community-based social protection initiatives (Save the Children Fund et al., 2005). They have an important contribution to make in managing and delivering social protection programmes of this type. As the literature has long acknowledged, there are significant constraints in scaling up these programmes – by comparison with resources, and potential resources, available to governments and other public sector institutions.

Household and community co-financing of social protection programmes is commonly overlooked, but can be essential to the effectiveness of a programme. Co-financing is explicit in conditional transfer programmes, whether conditional on labour supply or human development activities. One reason why household and community financing of social protection is commonly overlooked is that it makes very little sense when the redistributive functions of social protection dominate. It makes a great deal of sense in the context of the insurance function of social protection (in standard insurance models co-financing performs an effective role in reducing the hazards of sudden, or long-expected, loss of income), but could also be important in strengthening the agency of the poor.

In this part of the chapter we have confirmed that financing is a major constraint in establishing social protection initiatives in low-income countries, where the majority of selected social protection programmes listed in Table 13.1 are financed off budget, and mainly by donors. The core issue relates less to concerns over immediate affordability than with concerns over the medium- to longer-term implications for public finances of these programmes which could potentially escalate due to political pressures. Donors have an important role to play in financing pilot, transition and reform costs of social protection programmes, but their preference for short-term aid is a limiting factor. It is important not to overlook the element of co-financing by households and communities. Their qualitative significance in ensuring the effectiveness of programmes and the example they can set for the government or public sector easily outstrips their quantitative significance. Lifting the financing constraints on the extension of social protection in low-income developing countries means giving close attention to the entire 'mix' of funding. Donors have an important role in facilitating the research, pilot and transition costs associated with the introduction of social protection programmes. In the medium and longer run the sustainability of these programmes will come to rely on strengthening the tax collection capacity of domestic governments.

'Productivist' social protection

It was noted in the introduction that social protection is an important component of a growth and development strategy. This is especially true of social protection in low-income countries, where the need for all public policy to maximize the development potential is paramount. This implies that social protection must be 'productivist', in the sense of demonstrating that it can contribute to the development process. Social protection contributes to the development process in several ways: through reducing poverty and associated costs; helping overcome inefficiencies associated with missing or imperfect markets; facilitating investment in human capital; lifting cash and credit constraints; and protecting people and assets against sudden or random hazards.

There is limited evidence from existing social protection programmes in low-income countries regarding the quality and strength of these effects. Many of the selected programmes in Table 13.1 have been implemented only recently, yet the evidence of their value is building up. Evaluations of Bangladesh's Targeting the Ultra Poor programme indicate that the transfer of assets and the protection of asset accumulation among poorest and excluded households has been effective.[23] Bolivia's *Bono Solidario* appears to have been successful in stimulating agricultural production in rural areas where the poor have access to land but are traditionally cash strapped (Martinez, 2004). Nicaragua's *Red de Protección Social* proved to be effective in protecting beneficiary households' asset accumulation against an unexpected drop in coffee prices, demonstrating that transfers can be effective against unexpected and expected hazards that can have idiosyncratic and covariate effects (Maluccio, 2005). Current research efforts, and a longer run of the programmes, will ensure a stronger body of evidence demonstrating the contribution of social protection to the development process.

There are two issues for future research. First, there is a need to clarify the extent to which the impact of social protection programmes combine and compound over time to relieve poverty and promote development. Critics of social protection might argue that alternative interventions could show greater local effectiveness, for example, than cash transfers for the poor and poorest in lifting credit constraints. They might argue that micro-credit programmes would more effective. However, compared with micro-credit programmes, cash transfers are more likely to reach the poorest, can help to accumulate *and* protect assets, and are less likely to contribute to the incidence of child labour. The combined effects of social protection programmes help maximize their developmental impact. The point is that the strength of the 'productivist' nature of social protection could well be in the combination and compounding of its positive effects.

The second issue concerns the impact of social protection on incentives. Remarkably, there is little evidence that social protection programmes have observable adverse effects on work incentives. This is probably associated with the fact that social protection programmes in low-income countries are focused on the poorest, as in the unconditional components of the Ethiopia PSNP or the Kalomo pilot. It is also likely to follow from the low level of benefits, especially when measured as a fraction of household consumption. Transfer programmes conditional on work ordinarily set wages below market rates, and are therefore unlikely to have adverse incentives effects. At the same time, it could be argued that wider social protection programmes have the effect of propelling those in poverty towards more productive employment and lives, especially as these programmes strengthen their productive capacity, and facilitate their social integration. Nevertheless it is important for work incentives in relation to social protection programmes to be investigated as thoroughly as they have been in the industrialized countries.

In this part of the chapter we have noted that social protection in low-income countries ought to be 'productivist' in the sense of contributing to growth and development. There is accumulating evidence to the effect that social protection in low-income countries could make a contribution to economic development without involving significant adverse effects on incentives.

Conclusion

This chapter has sought to draw out the main lessons from existing social protection programmes in low-income countries. Many assume that establishing social protection is that much harder in low-income countries because of underdevelopment, fragmented political and policy processes, poor revenue raising capacity, and deficiencies in operational capacity. It is important therefore to learn from the experience of the handful of social protection initiatives in those countries.

We began by examining whether there are structural constraints to the development of social protection in low-income countries, associated with the dynamics of the development processes, for example, 'low income–low social protection' traps, or strong policy path dependence, that make the task of establishing social protection in these countries unfeasible. We found, admittedly more on the basis of intuition than systematic analysis, that low levels of social protection may hinder the development of employment-based social insurance, and perhaps also hinder schemes to raise substantial amounts of domestic revenue. However, it was difficult to envisage how tax-financed social protection focused on the poor could hinder the latter. Either way, empirical information on this issue is very limited. In the chapter we found that micro policy path dependence was a more likely structural brake on the development of social protection in low-income countries.

The chapter went on to consider the main perceived constraints: the political and policy processes, financing, and design and delivery, in existing programmes in low-income countries. The broad conclusions boil down to two: first, the experience of low-income countries with social protection demonstrates that there are many options available to them in establishing such programmes, and perhaps more options than pessimists allow; and second, that financing and delivery constraints are much less tractable in scaling up programmes to a sufficient extent.

The rapid expansion of social protection programmes focused on those in poverty in developing countries demonstrates that a commitment to reducing global poverty and strong partnerships between national governments, international donors, NGOs and researchers can work effectively to lift the financing and capacity constraints. Donors have a role to play in facilitating the expansion of social protection in these countries by reducing the initial costs associated with setting up appropriate programmes and policies, and national governments need to work on guaranteeing their sustainability by strengthening the domestic mobilization of resources and by strengthening capacity with support from NGOs and researchers. This investment will bring large rewards from the significant contribution social protection can make to social and economic transformation.

Notes

1. The chapter benefited from comments and suggestions by the editor which greatly improved it. The errors that remain are mine.
2. In European countries, social assistance is residual, given the strength of social insurance, labour market regulation and basic services. In many developing countries, and especially low-income countries, social insurance is limited in its coverage to workers in formal employment, labour market regulation is poorly enforced, and basic services are insufficient and highly unequally distributed. There, social assistance can be the most significant component of social protection, and far from residual (Barrientos, 2007a).
3. Programmes supporting vulnerable groups, such as old age or disability pensions, will be included. In low-income countries, these programmes have a strong poverty reduction orientation.
4. A regularly updated database of social assistance in developing countries can be accessed at www.chronicpoverty.org (Barrientos and Holmes, 2007).
5. Conditional transfer programmes require some activity on the part of beneficiaries as condition for continued receipt, for example that children in beneficiary households attend school regularly or that adult members of the households provide a specified amount of labour. Unconditional transfer programmes do not require any counterpart activity, for example disability pensions. All transfer programmes have some requirement for entitlement, for example a level of disability as a requirement for entitlement to a disability pension, or low household income

as a requirement for a child schooling subsidy. These are requisites or conditions for entitlement.

6. India's National Social Assistance Programme which includes an old age pension, a family benefit scheme, and a maternity benefit scheme was one of the larger programmes left out (Dev 2004). A recent study trawled the presence of cash transfer schemes in Eastern and Southern Africa, including small-scale and localized programmes. It found 43 such programmes in 15 countries. These include, for example, the Meket Livelihoods Development Project in Ethiopia which provides transfers in cash of around US$17 per household per months conditional on work to 46,000 beneficiary households; and the Food Subsidy Programme in Mozambique which provides US$2.8–5.6 per month to destitute households (Save the Children Fund et al., 2005).

7. The UN classification of countries according to per capita gross national income for 2006 identifies 54 low-income countries at or below US$875. Lower middle-income countries, including 58 entries, have per capita incomes between US$876 and US$3465. Bolivia and Nicaragua are at the lower margins of this group. The chapter leaves out of the discussion transition countries from the former Soviet Union.

8. In practice, there are several factors which explain the persistence of informality, for example, low earnings and insecurity in informal employment may push workers into informality, inadequate provision of basic services and security undermines incentives for paying taxes, lack of trust in the governance and financial returns of social insurance institutions, etc.

9. We could envisage that for taxpayers benefits will rise with coverage, both because of the reduction in the probability of social unrest and the rising likelihood of personally receiving a transfer. Operational costs, on the other hand, will probably fall with coverage but rise with the number of beneficiaries.

10. This applies with some force to social protection programmes because of the complexity of associated terms and technical features (Beales and German, 2006). There are no studies on public attitudes to redistribution and insurance in low-income countries that the author is aware of. Graham approaches this issue for Latin America and the United States (Graham, 2002).

11. This is despite concerns about the strong voice of donors in low-income countries in Africa.

12. Coercion is perhaps too strong a term in the context of social protection policy transfers, although perhaps appropriate in the context of structural adjustment or trade policies.

13. At face value, this assessment of the influence of domestic learning from unsuccessful anti-poverty programmes would appear too optimistic. There are, of course, plenty of examples of development policies adopted without the benefit of lessons from domestic experiences, for example structural adjustment, or pension reform in the area of social protection (for example, Townsend and Gordon, 2002: Chapters 8 and 10). My point is that, in the context of poverty and poverty reduction policies, most low-income countries have a knowledge base, albeit one shared by perhaps too few researchers.

14. This is a slightly separate point, but the fragmentation of social protection into employment-based and tax-financed programmes implies that it is possible to improve the protection of the minority in the former without addressing the needs of the majority. Note also that in many developing countries employment-based

social insurance programmes, for example civil servant pensions, are in reality financed by general taxation.

15. This is discussed in more detail in section six below.

16. However, benefit skimming has been regularly observed in programmes in India and Bangladesh.

17. More information on this for a wide range of anti-poverty programmes is available (Coady et al., 2004).

18. Whether this is due to a Rawlsian concern with the least advantaged, a concern to limit future fiscal liabilities, or a growing understanding of the kind of programmes that could lift households from extreme poverty, is a very interesting question but beyond the scope of this chapter.

19. There is a note of caution to be made here. Reflecting on the experience with social funds in Latin America, largely introduced in response to the acute deficiencies in public agencies responsible for dealing with the consequences of the 1980s crises, Graham writes: 'programmes that operate outside the mainstream public sector institutions and allocate expenditures according to demand-based criteria, while having a number of advantages, have limited capacity to target and a great deal of heterogeneity in outcomes. In addition such programmes usually are not part of a broader social contract, and cannot replace broadly based social assistance and insurance systems in the long term' (Graham, 2002: 22). Of course, the issue before us is how to establish social protection institutions in the absence of social assistance and insurance institutions.

20. The point here is that public money is highly fungible, with the implication that governments able to attract donors' support for social protection may be in a position to allocate resources to other areas of the budget which donors are less likely to support.

21. This is also a concern for middle-income countries. Chile's assistential pension programme PASIS has hard ceilings for annual budget expenditures, so that newly eligible beneficiaries have to queue until new places become available (Barrientos, 2006).

22. Free or subsidized school meals are a case in point. These tend to have many positive effects when introduced but are hard to change once conditions make them less effective, especially as they support supply and distribution networks (Tabor, 2002).

23. See the papers posted on the BRAC website at www.bracresearch.org

14

Social Protection, Rural Livelihoods and Economic Growth: the Case of Cash Transfers in Malawi, Ethiopia and Bangladesh

Rachel Slater, John Farrington, Rebecca Holmes and Paul Harvey

Policies and activities that promote rural livelihoods and rural growth are conventionally developed and implemented in institutions and departments differing from those responsible for protecting poor households via social assistance and social transfers. Among both governments and donors there is a widespread view that initiatives to reduce risk and vulnerability are a drain on public funds and limit levels of public investment in the productive sectors – including agriculture. However, emerging research is showing that there can be positive synergies between social protection and agricultural growth policies whereby social protection interventions reduce the risks faced by poor rural households who are dependent on the agriculture sector for their livelihood or where growth in agriculture – especially that permitting access to cheaper, more plentiful food or increased incomes – is itself socially protecting.

This chapter reviews evidence from three programmes — in Malawi, Ethiopia and Bangladesh – where objectives of livelihood protection and livelihood promotion have been linked together. It explores both the positive and negative effects of linking multiple objectives and considers what the institutional implications might be – especially in rural areas where investments in livelihoods and poverty reduction are threatened by serious shocks and stresses. The chapter suggests what lessons can be learnt about the design of social protection programmes that facilitate pro-poor growth, and what the implications of linking social protection more closely to agricultural growth policy are for institutional and financing arrangements. Finally the chapter assesses the evidence on whether cash transfer programmes might be a particularly effective way to link the protection and promotion of rural livelihoods.

Risk, vulnerability and rural livelihoods

This chapter is based on an emerging stream of policy work linking agricultural and rural development with the establishment of long-term social protection programmes in the developing world (Dorward et al., 2006; Farrington et al., 2004a, 2004b). The focus on social protection in rural areas is driven by concerns that investments in rural livelihoods and poverty reduction are threatened by serious shocks and stresses. Most of the world's poor people continue to live in rural areas and are heavily dependent, often with limited success, on agricultural production. In 2001, IFAD's *Rural Poverty Report* stated that three-quarters of the world's 1.2 billion extremely poor people lived and worked in rural areas and depended on agriculture for their survival (IFAD, 2001). Whilst the 1990s saw a very heavy focus on non-farm or off-farm rural livelihoods as potential routes out of poverty for poor people (see for example Ashley and Maxwell, 2001; Barrett et al., 2001; Reardon et al., 2001; Start, 2001), more recently the pendulum has swung back to agriculture. Evidence of this is found in recent and forthcoming policy statements on agricultural growth and poverty reduction from DFID, OECD POVNET and the EU (see, for example, DFID, 2005b). The *World Development Report 2008* also focuses on agriculture.

Whilst there is renewed interest in agriculture, it is also recognized that risk and vulnerability may prevent the poor from taking up new opportunities in the agricultural and wider rural economy. As a result, social protection research, policies and programmes in the developing world, particularly in Africa, are focusing on rural areas.

Concepts and approach

Social protection is defined as an encompassing sub-set of public actions – carried out by the state or privately – that address risk, vulnerability and chronic poverty (DFID, 2005c: 6). This includes:

- Social insurance where individuals pool resources by paying contributions to the state or a private provider so that, if they suffer a 'shock' or permanent change in their circumstances, they are able to receive financial support. Examples include unemployment insurance, contributory pensions and health insurance.
- Social assistance where transfers are made on a non-contributory basis to those deemed eligible by society on the basis of their vulnerability or poverty. Examples include social transfers and initiatives such as fee waivers for education and health, and school meals.
- Setting and enforcing minimum standards to protect citizens within the workplace, although this is difficult to achieve within the informal economy (DFID, 2005c: 6).

In the developing world, policy-makers and implementers tend to use the term 'safety nets' to refer to the range of activities above, though frequently the focus is more narrow – mainly social assistance – and related to humanitarian emergencies or post-emergency responses. Wider policies including food subsidies or inputs transfers are often seen as part of the safety nets response (see section two).

We define risk as the likelihood of shocks and stresses, which can be either endogenous or exogenous to the household, and can be either idiosyncratic (affecting one person or household at a time) or covariant (affecting many simultaneously). 'Risk' here reflects the use of terms by policy-makers and practitioners in the countries in question, rather than traditional and strict economic definitions that are used in insurance and financial service industries. Shocks are usually unpredictable and rapid onset and include drought, floods and accidents leading to illness or death. Stresses tend to be slow onset and include chronic illness (particularly from HIV/AIDS), declining soil fertility or indebtedness due to high marriage costs. Vulnerability is the degree of exposure of communities, households or individuals to adverse events, and their capacity to deal with them.[1] Vulnerability is increasingly recognized as being related to the assets that households own or can access – hence vulnerability is a function of risk plus poverty.

There are many types of risk – health, social, environmental, political and economic/market-based. Risks manifest themselves in different ways and can be complex. The kinds of risks that rural households face are described in Table 14.1, along with potential responses. With some risks it is easy to identify and understand their impacts. With others – for example longer-term trends and cycles – it is more difficult to understand causation and impact. When risks are intertwined they are also more difficult to understand – for example, when long-term downward trends in soil fertility due to poor soil and water management increase the likelihood of floods, or when poor nutrition leads to increased illness. There are implications for the different methodologies that are suitable for understanding the different dimensions of risk and vulnerability.[2]

Why are we so concerned with risk and vulnerability? We know that poor households are risk averse and, as a result, they tend to get trapped in low input–low output activities, especially in agriculture. But moving out of poverty requires that households take risks – whether that is investing in fertilizer even though the rains might fail, or spending scarce resources to travel to small towns to seek work. More remunerative livelihoods require some kind of risk-taking. For as long as households stay risk averse, they are also likely to stay poor. Addressing risk and vulnerability is, therefore, not just about reducing the risks – for example, the use of drought resistant seed or improved irrigation to avoid drought – but also about mitigating their impact or enabling households to cope better with them. This is where there is serious potential for social protection to support pro-poor growth.

Table 14.1 Managing shocks and stresses in relation to the agriculture sector

Types of rural household		Domestic	Production-related
Established farmers	Types of shock and stress	Illness Injury Disability Death Costs of weddings and other rituals	Collapse in prices resulting from globalization Extreme weather events (drought, hail, flooding) Degradation of soil, water and other natural resources Inadequate access to input, finance and output markets owing in part to failed liberalization
	Types of response	Promote private sector insurance schemes	Promote private sector input supply and marketing, and insurance schemes (which may require public start-up and regulatory controls); develop new types of crop insurance and price hedging (Hess, 2003); public/private partnerships to control soil erosion
Marginal farmers	Types of shock and stress	Illness Injury Disability Death Costs of weddings and other rituals	Extreme weather events (drought, hail, flooding) Degradation of soil, water and other natural resources Inadequate access to input, finance and output markets owing in part to failed liberalization (Possibly) collapse in prices resulting from globalization
	Types of response	Promote micro-savings, micro-credit, micro-insurance	Promotion of private sector inputs supply and marketing may have to be accompanied by measures to reduce market segmentation and interlocking Insurance and savings schemes may require a strong public or community-based leadership

(Continued)

Table 14.1 Continued

Types of rural household		Domestic	Production-related
Labourers	Types of shock and stress	Illness Injury Disability Death Costs of weddings and other rituals	Loss of rural employment opportunities and/or reduction in real wages attributable to the above Loss of opportunities for seasonal/permanent migration attributable to same or other causes
	Types of response	Promote micro-savings, micro-credit, micro-insurance Investigate possibilities of occupation-linked insurance and pensions	Public works programmes Support for seasonal migration through improved information, accommodation, education provision for children, easier means of making remittances, etc.
Those unable to engage fully in productive activity	Types of shock and stress	Illness Injury Disability Death Costs of weddings and other rituals	Reduction in informal intra-household transfers resulting from above shocks/stresses in agriculture Reduction in opportunities for gathering fodder/fuel from commons owing to natural resource degradation
	Types of response	Social pensions for the elderly, widows and disabled; school feeding programmes; promotion of infant health and nutrition; distribution of free or subsidized food	Social pensions for the elderly, widows and disabled; school feeding programmes; promotion of infant health and nutrition; distribution of free or subsidized food Schemes to rehabilitate the commons and ensure equitable access

Table 14.1 shows the risks that different types of rural households face and the importance of identifying interventions to manage shocks and stresses that are appropriate for different kinds of households. The focus of conceptual frameworks for understanding risk and vulnerability has often been on how to make households more resilient and better able to 'bounce back' after a specific shock or stress (see, for example, Holzmann and Jorgensen, 2000). In such frameworks, households that are unlikely to ever be productive tend to be ignored and, importantly, the impact that any increased demand for farm produce that would result from income transfers to them is also ignored.

Whilst policy thinking on both pro-poor agricultural growth and social protection is evolving rapidly in many parts of the developing world, the links between the two remain poorly conceptualized in both policy and practice. Often it is assumed that expenditures on social protection are 'non-productive' and that there are trade-offs between these and expenditure on agricultural growth programmes (Farrington et al., 2004a). Debates continue about what the appropriate balance of public expenditure should be – more for growth or more for social protection? Where the potential synergies between the two are not seen, governments tend to introduce *agriculture* policies that exhibit sub-optimal combinations of efficiency enhancement and social protection, and/or introduce *social protection* policies that either do much less than they could to support pro-poor growth or actually hamper growth.

However, there are examples from governments in the developing world where something different is taking place. The next three sections of the chapter review the evidence from the implementation of Starter Packs and targeted inputs programmes in Malawi, experiences with Ethiopia's Productive Safety Net Programme (PSNP) and lessons from the Bangladesh Income Generation for Vulnerable Group Development Programme (IGVGD). Linkages between growth and social protection in each case have implications for the ways in which programmes are designed, financed and implemented.

Malawi: from Starter Pack and targeted inputs programmes to cash transfer pilots

For more than a decade, Malawi has been characterized by growing chronic food insecurity, high levels of rural poverty and stagnating smallholder productivity and growth. Emergency appeals have been required to meet the food needs of millions of Malawians every year since 2002, more than half of the population live in poverty,[3] whilst any growth in agriculture has been outside the smallholder sector where most poor households are located. It was in response to these problems that the government of Malawi began the implementation of a free inputs distribution programme known as the Starter Pack. The pack contained enough fertilizer, maize seed and legume seed to cultivate about 0.1 ha of land (Levy, 2005). In the first few years, the Starter Pack provided near universal benefits to smallholders and, it is argued, avoided the costs of fertilizer subsidies which would be more regressive and benefit estate farmers and 'graduated smallholders'. In subsequent years, from 2000 onwards, the Starter Pack was scaled back in coverage and became known as the Targeted Inputs Programme (TIP). Both Starter Pack and TIP were implemented via the Ministry of Agriculture and Irrigation (subsequently Ministry of Agriculture, Irrigation and Food Security) with funding from donors, particularly DFID. In 2003/4 the TIP cost about 1,285 million Kwacha, or about US$12 million.

The impacts of the Starter Pack and TIP are contested. Whilst it has been argued that the Starter Pack and TIP have had a significant impact on national level production in Malawi, volatility of both production and prices remains a significant problem. Levy (2005) estimates that the pack increased maize production on average by between 125 kg and 150 kg and suggests that the Starter Pack increased the supply of maize to the market, thereby keeping prices low. In contrast, Dana et al. (2005) show that annual fluctuations of output in Malawi, unrelated to the Starter Pack/TIP, regularly result in price variations of 50 per cent or more from one year to the next.

Part of the dispute about the success of the Starter Pack and TIP results from the fact that whilst the programme began with a relatively simple objective – to make available the agricultural technology (seed and fertilizer) to enable small farmers to make productivity gains in maize production – over time, the policy objectives of the Starter Pack and TIP became more complex. Levy notes that 'different stakeholders have different expectations of free inputs programmes: for agricultural economists they should boost agricultural growth and reduce poverty in the medium term; social protection specialists see them as part of a safety net for the most vulnerable; and politicians hope they will eliminate food insecurity, thereby boosting their popularity with voters' (Levy, 2004: 2).

The Malawi experience has provided some important lessons and raised some challenges for linking social protection and pro-poor growth[4] in programme design. First, if too many objectives are expected to be achieved through a single simple programme, the programme is likely to fall short of all of those objectives. Expecting the Starter Pack/TIP to kick-start smallholder maize production, achieve national level food security and provide social protection to the poorest households was unrealistic. But these issues raise a difficult question for policy-makers and programme designers who are trying to create synergies between social protection and rural growth: Table 14.1 suggests that poor labour-constrained households are unlikely to require the same kind of support as smallholders with more labour and greater potential but does that mean that a large number of different programmes each tailored to meet the needs of a small group of households would be better? Whilst on the one hand, targeting different kinds of smallholders through a single programme may not be the best way to meet their different needs, on the other hand it is not feasible in countries with low capacity to have a wide range of programmes.

Second, in a complex situation like Malawi, the outcomes from a programme like the Starter Pack/TIP are numerous, and linking growth and social protection objectives are not necessarily direct or intuitive. Where programmes have social protection and growth objectives, it is not easy to know what outcomes and indicators to use to understand the impact of the programme. If the programme increases maize production on smallholdings but has a negligible effect on the food balance sheet (or vice versa) is it a success or failure? If the pack stimulates investments in private fertilizer markets by some smallholder farmers, but is sold at below market prices by those who cannot use it, is it a success or failure? What remains unclear is where the sensible middle ground between these two positions lies and whether cash transfers can overcome this problem because cash provides more fungible benefits that different types of households can use in the way that best suits their specific needs.

Third, because there are concerns over the appropriateness of the Starter Pack and TIP approach for the poorest households and for market development, there may be scope for cash transfers as an alternative. The government of Malawi and some donors and NGOs are already exploring and piloting cash transfer and other safety net programmes as alternatives to the Starter Pack and TIP (Devereux et al., 2006; Harrigan, 2005; Harvey and Savage, 2006).

The Starter Pack/TIP experience offers rather less illumination into financing issues. In 2003/4 the programme cost 1,285 million Malawi Kwacha (MK) with about 80 per cent of this being fertilizer, maize and legume seed costs (including importation costs where required) and the rest being transport, warehousing, bagging, administration, etc. Comparisons of cost-effectiveness of the Starter Pack/TIP and other interventions including safety nets (cash transfers or public works programmes) and food aid distributions are difficult where the objectives of the programmes are different and we are not comparing like with like. There is evidence to suggest that targeting has been unsuccessful and has not brought programme costs down. Chisinga (2005: 141) notes that 'the main lesson emerging from the Malawi experiment is that community targeting is complex and difficult to do, especially in circumstances where poverty data is either crude or non-existent. It is achievable with the help of external facilitation, but the human and financial resource demands of such facilitation are too great for large-scale input distribution programmes.'

In terms of institutional capacity, Malawi's experience with the Starter Pack/TIP distribution means that the system has become more efficient. Evaluation of early implementation found several problems including beneficiaries not receiving packs and the lack of dedicated personnel within the Ministry of Agriculture to ensure efficient implementation. This situation improved over time and delivery of fertilizer improved. However, in common with other kinds of transfers, including cash, for the Starter Pack/TIP to be effective it requires additional investments – especially in agricultural extension – to ensure that beneficiaries have the knowledge and skills to make the most of the packs.

Overall the Malawi experience shows the difficulties of implementing, managing and evaluating the performance of programmes that have multiple objectives.

From food to cash: Ethiopia's Productive Safety Net Programme[5]

Ethiopia has a per capita income of only 20 per cent of the African average and very high poverty rates are combined with a poor record of agricultural growth (Diao et al., 2005). In every year since 1984, an emergency appeal has been issued to address hunger. However, Ethiopia's Productive Safety Net Programme (PSNP) represents a significant change in the response to hunger in Ethiopia. In the last few years there has been an increasing recognition that food insecurity in Ethiopia is predictable and chronic and that, rather than addressing it through emergency appeals, it would make more sense to treat it as a predictable problem requiring predictable resources (WFP, 2005; World Bank, 2004a). At the same time the government, recognizing the damaging effect that food aid distribution has had on local markets and incentives to farmers to invest in agricultural production, has sought to move away from a food-first to a cash-first approach. As a result the government of Ethiopia, with support from a wide range of donors, developed the PSNP, a programme providing six months of support on an annual basis to households in designated food insecure *woredas* (districts). Payments are made either as cash or food or a combination of cash and food. About 80 per cent of beneficiary households can only gain their entitlement if they participate in public works, whilst about 20 per cent (households with no labour, lactating women, etc.) receive direct support with no work requirement.

The programme began in January 2005 and in the first year experienced significant implementation challenges (Sharp et al., 2006). The most serious of these was inclusion in the programme of household beneficiaries that were not the poorest or most food insecure, and the exclusion of some of the poorest. In most cases these inclusion and exclusion errors resulted from the pressure on regional governments and *woreda* authorities to demonstrate that households could 'graduate' from the programme and into food security within three years. As a result, *woredas* targeted households that they thought would be most likely to graduate (Kebede, 2006). Other implementation problems included poorly organized public works and delays of the payment to beneficiaries.

There are four main findings about the extent to which the Productive Safety Net Programme can support rural livelihoods and growth. First, where it is implemented efficiently and payments are made in a timely way, the programme can make significant improvements to household consumption.

In many cases PSNP income was used not only to buy food but also for medical costs, school fees and equipment and savings (this was more prevalent in cash payment *woredas* than food payment *woredas*). A large number of the households interviewed as part of the study also reported that the PSNP enabled them to avoid both distress sales of their physical assets (cattle, sheep, goats) to meet household needs and helped them avoid having to participate in uncertain casual labour markets thereby freeing up their labour to work on their own or sharecropped land. The avoidance of distress sales was equally the case for cash and food payment *woredas*.

Second, by securing household income, the PSNP encourages households that were previously very risk averse, to take credit packages under the Government Food Security Programme or other donor and NGO implemented programmes. The policy of the government to target agricultural credit packages on PSNP beneficiary households appears logical – it enables the combination of the two programmes to achieve consumption smoothing, asset protection and asset building objectives. Households made investments in productive assets including small ruminants, dairy cattle and beekeeping. Some households were able to put their PSNP income into savings, either to buy more assets or to enable them to pay back the loan, even if they lost their assets at a later date (for example, cattle dying due to drought or disease). Of particular note is the fact that these effects were far more prevalent in *woredas* where beneficiaries received cash than where they received food.

Third, PSNP public works had both positive and negative impacts on rural livelihoods and growth. On the positive side, public works created some important community assets. Soil and water conservation and road building and maintenance were seen as the most important assets created. Conservation efforts in some places were having benefits in a short period of time – for example in Amhara where flooding due to soil erosion had been stemmed by the planting of grasses and the fencing of areas of communal land. Roads made villages more accessible so that households could get to markets more easily, children spent less time walking to and from school and health care facilities became easier to access. However, the PSNP work requirements appeared to undermine the logic of linking the PSNP with wider programmes. Some households spent very large amounts of time doing public works at the expense of working on their own land. To some extent this was an implementation failure: public works were supposed to take place during the agricultural slack season but in many *woredas* they continued during the ploughing, planting and weeding times. Even when public works were better timed, households were then prevented from doing other non-agricultural activities by public works requirements. In some households the problem was especially acute. Five days of public works were required for each PSNP beneficiary – so getting benefits in a single parent household with four children would require the parent to work for 25 days each month for six months. Ironically, whilst public works were put in place to avoid 'dependency', the public works were actually doing the opposite – creating dependency on the programme. Households were unable to make the most of agricultural credit because they had so little time to spend on their investments.

Fourth, many households expressed a preference for receiving food and not cash and argued that cash often bought them much less than the 15 kg of grain plus vegetable oil and corn soya blend that was distributed as payment in food *woredas*. They argued that prices had risen in the *woreda* as a result of the cash payments. Tracking of food price data in local markets by Save the Children UK suggests that this is a problem in other *woredas* too (Kebede, 2006). In the first year and a half of PSNP implementation, the injection of cash into the local economy had created inflationary effects and had not, as hoped, triggered a supply response in the local agriculture sector.

Some of the lessons from the early experience of the PSNP for programme design, financing and implementation are as follows:

- Safety nets that secure household consumption and protect households from distress sales or distress migration during times of shock or stress provide a critical base for households to build assets. However, whilst there are isolated examples of saving or investments from PSNP income, safety nets themselves will not result in asset building unless the amounts of money are much larger than is the case in the PSNP.
- In practice cash transfers have additional costs. They will only work if investments are made in local marketing infrastructure to ensure that there is supply into markets. One possible approach would be the timely release of government stocks for commercial sale in local markets where cash is distributed. Without it cash transfers will simply create inflationary pressure on food prices.
- Cash transfers and other types of safety net programmes need to free up and not absorb labour so that households can invest in their own livelihoods and graduate to a sustainable and independent livelihood.
- Beyond fundamental contradictions in the programme – such as counter-productive labour requirements – implementation problems in the PSNP suggest that the transition from food to cash is not as simple as is often made out. The different skills and expertise that are required for delivering cash are often not present at *woreda* level where there are significant capacity constraints and where the sheer size of the PSNP compared to *woreda* budgets creates an administrative burden and has distorting effects on strategic operations.

Vulnerable group development in Bangladesh: sequencing protection and promotion

In contrast to Ethiopia's PSNP which targeted better off households in its first year, the Bangladesh Rural Advancement Committee's (BRAC) Income

Generation for Vulnerable Group Development Programme (IGVGD) was initiated to reach Bangladesh's 'hardcore poor' (Matin and Hulme, 2003). Bangladesh has made only modest progress with poverty reduction with estimates showing a 10 per cent reduction in poverty in the 1990s but increasing inequality (Government of the People's Republic of Bangladesh, 2005). Thus, IGVGD seeks to address the needs of households unable to escape extreme poverty that are currently supported through protective measures and have little or no support to enable them to engage in productive activities or to build productive assets and resources. The programme works through collaboration with the World Food Programme (WFP) and local government to couple a monthly wheat ration (for two years) with training and credit provided by BRAC. Whilst the wheat ration smoothes consumption and protects assets in the face of shocks and stresses, credit is used to set up income-generating activities, such as poultry, livestock and sericulture. IGVGD targets widowed or abandoned female heads of household, households owning less than 0.5 acres, and earning less than 300 Taka/month. In developing the programme 'BRAC understood that wheat donations provided a "breathing space" for the poorest, and created a strong incentive for them to interact with development agencies, but it doubted the capacity of such handouts to remove chronic poverty' (Matin and Hulme, 2003: 653).

Matin and Hulme go on to argue that IGVGD has been successful in reaching the very poor and increasing the economic position of beneficiary households. Average incomes have risen significantly and ownership of homestead plots, land, beds and blankets increased. In 1994, before the programme was established, monthly income averaged 74 Taka (less than US$2). The income of beneficiaries leaving the programme in 1996 rose almost tenfold to 717 Taka (around US$17). After two years, when wheat distribution ends, many participants experience a drop in income and consumption but the income-generating activities founded on the micro-credit intervention kept many incomes above pre-programme levels. The programme has been impressive in successfully 'graduating' households of such low-income and low-asset holdings to access regular micro-finance programmes.

In spite of these successes, there remain several challenges facing IGVGD. One is the trade-off between the 'correct' implementation of the programme and flexibility. On the one hand, it is argued that implementation gaps resulting from a lack of administrative capacity lead to manipulation and elite capture by powerful individuals and groups and to the pursuit of organizational needs over programme goals. At the same time though, Matin and Hulme (2003) suggest that where plans are modified to better reflect local conditions, the poor are then able to substitute programme resources and put them to better use. A second major challenge regards the question of capacity of field staff working for the programme. There are concerns that fieldworkers who are concerned with, for example, agricultural extension are overloaded with responsibilities if they are then mandated and retrained to also provide social protection expertise. In a similar way there are questions about whether social workers can be trained to provide advice relating to the productive sectors. If this proves impossible, can the costs of running two parallel services be sustained? The third challenge is that of reaching those who have most difficulty in becoming upwardly mobile, and those who cannot raise their levels of economic activity. Evidence from the programme showed that some households could not recover from loss of food subsidy and had to mortgage assets and use the loan for consumption.

Additional issues emerging from IGVGD are that:

- Access to IGVGD is not seen as 'fair' by villagers and local government officials can use VGD cards for patronage.
- The provision of food aid, skills training, savings schemes and micro-credit is not sufficient to assist some/many very poor households to improve their situation.
- Having BRAC's rural development programme staff take on training and microfinance for IGVGD did not provide clients with the incentive and customized support that they needed.
- Providing training (and loans) only in sectors where BRAC had pre-existing course modules presented too narrow a range of activities.
- Not all IGVGD clients can be rapidly assimilated into village organizations according to a rigid timetable. Some clients will fall behind and require additional support (Matin and Hulme, 2003).

The lessons learnt from IGVGD influenced the subsequent design of their new programme 'Challenging the Frontiers of Poverty Reduction' (CFPR). Matin and Hulme (2003) conclude that, whilst the combination of protection and promotion, where protection acts as a base for productivity, can be a successful ladder for households able to seize economic opportunity, other households need additional inputs such as social development/social mobilization (activities to increase the social capital assets of poor households), or asset transfers. Thus, elements of social protection programmes must be well-sequenced, if social protection is to ultimately promote growth and livelihoods, as well as being protective.

Conclusions and policy recommendations

The experiences of Malawi, Ethiopia and Bangladesh with programmes that combine social protection and pro-poor growth objectives raise a set of general issues about the design of social protection programmes and their institutional and financing arrangements.

With reference to design, it is clear that social protection needs to free labour and not absorb it. This has implications for public works that can reduce risk and enable productivity gains by farmers but may mean that households become dependent on low but stable incomes from public works at the expense of (what are perceived as) riskier investments in agriculture, rural non-farm livelihoods and migration. It is also clear that linking the protection and promotion of livelihoods can lead to a confusing plethora of potentially competing objectives that make it difficult to assess the real impact of programmes and leave programmes susceptible to becoming political rather than a poverty reduction tool. The final main finding around programme design is the need to combine two actions: first, to meet the diverse needs of different types of rural households; and second, to introduce a simple programme instrument that is patently 'universal, fair and comprehensible'. What this means for programme design will vary from one context to another.

It is clear that transfer programmes, especially cash transfer programmes, can enable consumption smoothing and asset protection but are much less likely to lead to the creation of assets at household level. In many developing countries the size of transfer is simply too small to move households beyond meeting their basic needs and avoiding distress sales of assets. Larger cash transfers, in development contexts at least, are unlikely to be seen in the developing world in the near future, though in emergency contexts (for example, post-conflict) there may be scope for making significantly larger one-off payments (see, for example, Doocy, 2006). Given these fiscal constraints, the Bangladesh and Ethiopia experiences show how a combination of well-sequenced interventions, those that link together instruments that both protect and promote livelihoods, can help households take small steps on a ladder out of poverty. There is considerable scope for countries to learn about better sequencing of programmes to capture the synergies between protecting and promoting livelihoods.

However, there are hidden costs with cash transfer programmes that have implications for the financing and budgeting of safety nets. It is clear that anecdotes about the low cost of cash transfers compared to in-kind transfers (such as food or seeds and fertilizers) are failing to recognize the additional investments that are required if cash transfers are to both protect and promote rural livelihoods. The Ethiopia experience shows clearly how, particularly in the early implementation of cash transfer programmes, without investments in markets to ensure supply, cash transfers are likely to cause increases in the price of food and inflationary effects.

Cash transfers and other social protection programmes also raise questions about the institutional arrangements for programme financing. There is reluctance on the part of many governments in the developing world to commit to the recurrent spending that long-term welfare payments imply. However, where the growth impacts of these programmes can be demonstrated, there may be an increased incentive to support social protection spending, even in the long term. Similarly, donors tend to focus on a fixed-term programme of project spending (especially in fragile states where direct budget support may be inappropriate). If cash transfers and other instruments are to have the optimum impact of pro-poor growth, both governments and donors will need to commit to them in medium-term expenditure frameworks and long-term plans.

Finally, the evidence from all three programmes demonstrates that cash may provide a good alternative to food and inputs transfers. Cash enables greater choice on the part of beneficiaries and can stimulate wider economic growth. However, the evidence from Ethiopia shows that cash is not an institutional quick fix. It is just as complicated and difficult to implement as food or other in-kind transfers, particularly where the implementing agencies have little experience with cash. Linking programme objectives creates a significant burden of work and the need for additional training and skills for programme staff at all levels. In developing countries this may be unrealistic given the capacity challenges that countries like Malawi, Ethiopia and Bangladesh already face, especially at district and village level. The link between protecting and promoting livelihoods also raises questions about where programmes should be housed. Are ministries of agriculture and rural development the best institutional home for social protection programmes that aim to have positive pro-poor growth effects, or should they be housed in ministries of labour, welfare and social affairs? By what mechanisms can different institutions best coordinate their roles?

Whilst there are many remaining knowledge and policy gaps regarding social protection and rural growth linkages, the good news is that as thinking on new programmes emerges and pilot programmes are implemented, they are increasingly complemented by a commitment to well-planned and well-resourced monitoring and evaluation systems to ensure that lessons are generated and some of the outstanding questions can be answered.

Notes

1. The definitions here are those developed and used in two ODI programmes, one on Linking Agricultural Growth and Social Protection, and one on the Role of Cash Transfers in Development and Emergencies. They draw on work by the World Bank on Social Risk Management (SRM); see for example, Holzmann and Jorgensen (2000).
2. There are a number of different methodologies employed for measuring the dimensions of vulnerability. For example, see the Vulnerability Assessment Committees in Southern Africa which draw on household economy approaches (see www.sahims.net/vac/default.htm) and the WFP VAM framework. Many are good at providing information on food gaps to inform developmental and humanitarian responses, but are rarely used to explore and measure wider dimensions of vulnerability over different timeframes.
3. This is based on the government poverty line. The dollar-a-day poverty line is significantly higher.
4. Pro-poor growth can be measured absolutely – how poor the incomes of the poor are growing – or relatively – if poor people's incomes grow faster than those of the

population as a whole. Many countries can achieve absolute pro-poor growth but in very few cases do reductions in inequality accompany growth in poor people's incomes. Social protection is viewed as one mechanism to enhance relative pro-poor growth (DFID, 2004).

5. This case study is based on fieldwork at federal, regional, *woreda*, village and household level in eight *woreda*s in four of Ethiopia's regional states (Tigray, Amhara, Oromia and Southern Nations). For more information see Slater et al. (2006).

15
Welfare, Development and Growth: Lessons from South Africa

Francie Lund

This volume has presented evidence from OECD countries that there can be a coexistence of social spending, economic growth and stability. A recurring theme is: If this combination is appropriate for the north, why should it be inappropriate for the south? And is there evidence from the south that it is indeed possible and appropriate? This chapter focuses on South Africa, which contains both the affluence of the north, and the unacceptable scale of poverty in sub-Saharan Africa.

The transition to democracy in 1994 brought to power the African National Congress (ANC) with its commitment to a non-racial and unified South Africa, and a resolve to share the country's wealth more equitably. However, as with increasing numbers of countries globally, inequality endures. The new government inherited an extensive system of social security. Despite the generally conservative macroeconomic policy introduced in 1996, spending on the social pensions and grants, which are the main subject of this chapter, has increased sharply. The non-contributory cash transfers that were racially equalized by 1993 presently reach about 11 million people, just about one-quarter of the population of 44 million. This is a significant fiscal intervention, constituting about 17 per cent of government expenditure in 2006/7. Most of the recent growth in numbers of beneficiaries has been driven by the introduction in 1998 of a new cash benefit for young children.

Visitors to South Africa from neighbouring Southern African Development Community (SADC) countries are surprised by the extent of state welfare provision for children, people with disabilities, and elderly people. Visitors from countries with well-established welfare systems are appalled that a country where there is so much wealth has a welfare system that is so uneven and patchy. There is little coverage for the unemployed, while the unemployment rate is about 26 per cent according to the narrow definition, and 40 per cent by the broader, which includes discouraged workers. There is little support at all if one is not the caregiver of a young child, and not disabled, and not elderly. The support for children that exists is not tied to any objective level of need. Thus within the social sector itself, there is paradoxically much to be admired yet much still to be done to ensure that all South Africans are guaranteed basic forms of security. There is a need to move away from the idea of 'short-term safety nets', towards a situation where social security is a permanent feature of the landscape of economic and social development. In this chapter I will draw out lessons and implications from the South African social transfer programmes for the development of social security for other developing countries, and especially for those poorer than South Africa. The following section sketches the main socio-economic characteristics at the time of transition, and a broad outline of early policy responses in economic and social terrains. I then turn to address the social security system, with a special focus on the social assistance component. A brief history of the development of the system of cash transfers is followed by details of the main categories of grant. The chapter then summarizes what is known to date with respect to the outreach and impact of this form of income support, drawing on a rich and diverse set of empirical studies done over the last two decades on *inter alia* targeting and the role in poverty reduction and in household security. Findings on economic effects at the local level are also presented, as well as the known effects on the labour market.

I then turn from the primarily state-supported system of social assistance, to another pillar of provision required for comprehensive social security – occupation-related social security. Changing trends in employment mean that fewer and fewer people worldwide are in jobs that provide the 'social wage' benefits of the past, while in many southern countries, formal employment was never the norm.

The following section attempts to draw out implications for other developing countries, especially bearing in mind countries that are poorer than South Africa both in economic terms and in terms of the infrastructure necessary for delivery. The section tries to build a bridge between aspects of South Africa that unusually gave rise to this relatively extensive system and other countries. The chapter concludes with some ideas of likely barriers to the adoption of what can, for many countries, be an effective, affordable and developmental plan to address poverty.

The inheritance at 1994 and the early years of the new South Africa

In the centuries of colonial and then apartheid rule, the white minority developed a complex set of policies and laws, which led to racially determined patterns of poverty and inequality. In 1994 about half of all South Africans were in poverty. The essential patterns of political disenfranchisement, confiscation of land, control of labour, and denial of access to education were laid down in the colonial period. The Nationalist Party took power in 1948, and during the 1950s introduced the key legislation which formalized apartheid: classification of every citizen into one of four racial groups, criminalizing of inter-racial sexual relationships and the prohibition of marriages between people of different race groups, and increasingly the banning and criminalizing of political opposition. Legislation also determined the racial segregation of urban residential areas, and the creation of the ten different 'countries' within South Africa for Africans who were not in urban areas. Millions of South Africans were extruded into these Bantustan areas. South African capital colluded with the state in moulding policies which ensured white privilege on the one hand, and African, coloured and Indian exclusion and poverty on the other.

The classification of race determined every aspect of a person's life – i.e. where one could live, access to education and the kind of curriculum one would be taught. Health and welfare services were also racially segregated. Regulation of the movement of labour, primarily through the migrant labour system and the restriction of access to cities by those who were not working, meant that over a period of a hundred years, families were torn apart, while access to the labour market and labour mobility were severely constrained.

The outcome of this inexorable creation of racially determined structural poverty was evident in all the main socio-economic indicators. South Africa is classified as a low middle income country yet many of its poverty indicators are far worse than those of countries that are poorer in income levels. In 1994 the infant mortality rate (IMR) for the total population was 49 per 1,000 live births, but it was 54.3 for Africans compared to 7.3 for whites, 9.9 for Indian people and 36.3 for coloured people (Health Systems Trust data). The poverty and inequality can be seen in income shares: in 1995 the poorest 40 per cent of households comprised 50 per cent of the population, and earned only 11 per cent of national income; the richest 10 per cent of households comprised 7 per cent of the population and accrued 40 per cent of income (1995 Income and Expenditure Survey). The health and wealth of the white population was underpinned by extensive social spending on whites:

> South Africa's spending on health, education and welfare, which was approximately 10 per cent of GDP in the late 1980s, was a little higher than had been achieved by most of the now developed countries when they were at levels of per capita income comparable to those of South Africa today. (Moll, 1991)

The problem, as Moll, points out, is that the *distribution* of the social spending was racially discriminatory and regionally uneven (ibid.).

The new government had to take over the reins of a weak economy, high unemployment rates, and high popular expectations of immediate redistributive reforms, across a wide range of policies. The situation was aggravated by the HIV/AIDS pandemic, with prevalence rates that are now among the highest in the world, which has far-reaching implications for the society and the economy with disproportionate effects on vulnerable groups, and on the need for care.

The climate for policy reform changed rapidly. The Freedom Charter, adopted in 1955, had expressed a vision of the South Africa that was hoped for in future, when the shackles of apartheid were broken. It advocated a strong role for the state, and this was expressed in the 1993 version of the Reconstruction and Development Programme (RDP). This document, developed by the government that was about to come to power, did express the need for a balance between economic growth and redistribution. A short four years later, the macroeconomic policy GEAR – Growth, Employment and Redistribution – shifted the discourse more towards fiscal constraint. The economic reforms – industrial policy, changes in the trade regime, competition and privatization policy – were embedded in a framework of liberalization and incorporation into the global economy. The pro-poor and redistribution policies, while remaining evident in the land reform policy, took a more residual status, reflected in infrastructural development policies, and in the major components of the social cluster, which in South Africa are health, education, social welfare and housing.

After the first decade of democracy, a flurry of studies sought to measure progress in addressing poverty and inequality. While there is a contentious debate, in general it can be said that studies, including those based on data collected by the official statistics council (StatsSA), agree that *both* poverty and inequality, as measured by income, have increased (Hemson and Owusu-Ampomah, 2005). A greater share of the African population is even poorer – but the number of very wealthy Africans has also grown.

Most observers would agree that the new government's most important failure was the lack of creation of employment. Land reform has proceeded very slowly, and many would argue that progress on this front is the critical underpinning to both basic security and livelihood creation for the poor population. There has, however, been extensive investment in infrastructure, in the form of water to homes, electricity and communication technology. According to the government's 2006 fiscal review, 1.9 million low-cost houses have been built since 1994, with uneven provision between provinces, and between years (National Treasury, 2006). The backlog, however, continues to grow, especially in cities such as Durban, where internal and cross-border migrants seek economic opportunities in the city. Both rural and urban areas are characterized by densely crowded informal settlements.

A policy of free primary health care for everyone using public health sector facilities was introduced early. In fact, health care had been free for poor people in the apartheid era, but was generally of very poor quality in urban areas and very limited in rural areas for those who were not white. Reforms in education included free schooling for eight years, and no child is supposed to be excluded from schooling because of its costs. The system still works poorly, as government subsidies to schools are not sufficient to cover even basic costs. Hence school governing bodies, who should implement fee exemptions, have to raise the fees from parents to keep schools open. In addition, schools attended by poorer children (most of whom are African and coloured) are of very poor quality.

Other anti-poverty programmes and policies include the housing subsidy for first time low-income owners. The primary school nutrition programme aims to ensure that all poor children have one free meal a day (Kallmann, 2005). The welfare policy objective was to move towards a social development model with more emphasis on social and economic integration of vulnerable groups, and a move away from the expensive institutional care and an urban bias that had characterized much of the welfare provision under apartheid. There has been growing appreciation that one of the most effective programmes in addressing poverty and inequality has been social security, the main focus of this chapter.

State social security in South Africa

In 2007, about 11.8 million South Africans were in receipt of the state cash transfers, more than 2 million were receiving the pension for elderly people (the oldest grant) and 8 million were receiving the child support grant (the latest grant). In the 2007 financial year, estimated overall government state expenditure was R529 billion and total social expenditure (of which more than 90 per cent is allocated to social security) received some R81 billion.

A brief history of social security

There is a common misperception that the new government is responsible for the social security system. In fact, the first elements of it were introduced in the first half of the twentieth century. Non-contributory pensions went first to white people, and then these and other grants were gradually extended to the whole population, in a racially determined and spatial form – first to Indian and coloured people, and only in urban areas, and then gradually including the African population, to be subsequently rolled out to rural areas. The grant levels and the procedures for receipt were racially discriminatory. By the mid-1980s, the first signs of 'upward harmonization' began to be seen, in a move by the former government to both broaden coverage and racially equalize the system.

In 1990, the total government spending on the non-contributory cash transfers amounted to R3.9 billion. In that year, 67 per cent of the old age pension allocation went to the African population. Of the total disability allocation of R827.8 million, 55 per cent went to Africans. Of all expenditure for family and child grants (total of R38 million), a tiny 11 per cent went to the African population – contrasting with their 72 per cent share of their total in the population. By 1993, with the exception of the State Maintenance

Grant, all the major racially discriminatory aspects of the system had been addressed. In that year, 89 per cent of the pensions for elderly people were received by African beneficiaries, and about a quarter of African households had at least one resident pension recipient.

The 1992 Social Assistance Act introduced a number of improvements, and by 1994 the only significant part of the system that still had to be reformed was the State Maintenance Grant. This grant, important to those 400,000 women and children who received it, was exceptionally poorly targeted in racial terms, and went largely to coloured, Indian and white people in urban areas. It was replaced by the new child benefit, the Child Support Grant, which was implemented in 1998, and this has led to a significant shift in the overall welfare budget; a greater proportion now being allocated to young African children.

The cash transfers

As in the OECD countries, support for the three principal most vulnerable groups of children, disabled and elderly are 'the bedrock' measures of state social assistance. The main grants are non-contributory, payable from general revenue, means-tested on income and assets, and take the form of a monthly cash transfer, payable into a bank or post office account, or most commonly in cash through a mobile delivery system.

Three of the grants depicted in Table 15.1 are targeted at children, and each originally had a different purpose. The Child Support Grant (CSG) is a poverty-oriented grant. It is targeted at children up to the age of 14, payable to the primary caregiver (who need not be the biological parent). The vast majority of caregivers who apply are women, and about 90 per cent declare themselves to be the biological mother of the child being applied for. The rapid increase in the number of CSGs shown above is simply a maturation effect of a new form of support. It was introduced in 1998 for children up to their seventh birthdays, and the government has incrementally extended the

Table 15.1 Cash transfers: numbers of beneficiaries, and monthly level of grant

Type of grant	April 03 ('000s)	April 05 ('000s)	April 07 ('000s)	Monthly individual transfer value
Child Support Grant	2 631	5 126	7 880	R200
Foster Care Grant	139	249	381	R620
Care Dependency Grant	58	85	104	R870
Disability Grant	954	1 292	1 438	R870
Old Age Pension	2 009	2 067	2 186	R870
War Veteran's Pension	5	3	2	R890
TOTAL	5 796	8 822	11 991	

Source: National Treasury.

age of eligibility. The amount of R200 is not based on any objective measure of need. When introduced it was related to the cost of providing food for a child for a month, but since then, the level of the grant has only been adjusted slowly compared to increases in other grants, and the means test has not been revised. This means that, as earnings and incomes generally rise, more children are excluded (see Budlender et al., 2005 for estimates of the costs of applying the means test).

The Foster Care Grant (FCG) is for foster parents of children who are orphaned, abandoned, or otherwise in need of care. It was not originally poverty-oriented, and was designed for the protection of children who required adult carers. The third child-oriented transfer is the Care Dependency Grant (CDG). It was poverty-oriented in origin, and designed to go to caregivers of children below 18 who are profoundly physically and mentally impaired. It is meant to compensate for the costs of the institutional care when the child cannot to be cared for at home. Now, the AIDS pandemic has led to far greater numbers of children who are disabled for a period of time, though estimates are not very reliable.

There is a private parental maintenance system whereby a parent, usually the mother, can claim income maintenance from the other parent. Many men are unemployed, or earn very low wages, such that many women cannot secure reliable support of meaningful value.

The Disability Grant (DG) is for people over 18 years of age who are disabled and cannot work. It has recently been extended to people with AIDS-related disability, and this is likely one of the factors driving up the growth in numbers of the permanent DG. A study (Delaney et al., 2005) showed that there was a significant decrease in the average age of applicants between 2001 and 2004, from 46.2 to 42.9 years. There was also an increase in the proportion of female applicants over the same period – from 45 per cent in 2001 to 57 per cent in 2004. The amount of the Disability Grant covers only a small part of the overall financial needs of those with disabilities.

The state pension for the elderly (OAP) is received by just over 2 million of the approximately 5 million South Africans of retirement age, with the age of eligibility being 60 for women and 65 for men. The War Veterans Pension (WVP) is a small top-up to the Old Age Pension for older people (mostly men) who fought in certain wars. These grants for elderly people were widely accessible to all population groups before the new government came to power, and the race discriminatory practices were addressed since the mid-1980s, with race parity reached in 1993. The OAP is the grant that has garnered most research attention.

Evidence of outreach and impact

The numbers of beneficiaries of the various cash transfers are shown in Table 15.1. The take-up rate for the pension for elderly people is relatively easy to establish, and is estimated to be at around 85 per cent. The take-up of the disability grant for adults is less easy to capture, as it depends on the extent of the disability required to qualify for a grant. The FCG and CDG grants reach relatively few needy children. The age of eligibility for the new Child Support Grant has been increased over the few years since its introduction, hence take-up rates are again difficult to establish.[1]

Targeting

The grants are well-targeted racially and for poverty (Ardington and Lund, 1995; Case and Deaton, 1998; Case et al., 2005; van der Berg and Bredenkamp, 2002). These two criteria are associated with each other. In the past the grants have not reached households in the bottom income decile – since many of them were young family households that did not have a disabled person or an elderly person (Ardington and Lund, 1995; Department of Social Development, 2002). This is now changing with the increasing allocation to the CSG. Demographically, there are more children, in more poor households, than there are elderly people in poor households. Thus, there will be an effect even though the CSG amount is so much smaller than the OAP (or DG) amount. There is conclusive evidence of lower rates of poverty as a consequence of the cash transfers. They are also well targeted to women, and to rural areas.

Household level consumption benefits

The numbers in Table 15.1 pertain to the number of direct beneficiaries of cash transfers, or in the case of child-oriented grants, to the caregivers of the targeted children. A crucial question is whether the transfers also benefit other members of the households in which beneficiaries reside. South Africa's history of apartheid, racialized poverty, and the regulation of residential and labour mobility contributed to the situation where large numbers of poor people in both urban and especially in rural areas live in households containing three generations or more. Data from national household surveys in 1995 and 1998 showed that about half of poorer African households contained three generations or more (Møller and Devey, 2003). A number of studies have found that the majority of elderly people pool their pensions (Ardington and Lund, 1995; Case and Deaton, 1998). Most pension income is spent on food, and health and educational expenses incurred by other household members.[2] A study in the Langeberg district in the Western Cape Province by Case (2003) found that pensions are pooled, and especially when women receive them there are measurable effects on the nutritional status of other household members. Case and Menendez analyse results from a rural area where it was possible to compare households with and without male or female pensioners. Households with pensioners were less likely to miss meals; girls living with a female pensioner were significantly more likely to be enrolled in school (Case and Menendez, 2007). An early assessment of the impact of the CSG showed that it extends the time children spend in school. This is particularly significant if the primary caregiver is the biological mother (Case et al., 2005).

Agency and empowerment benefits

The effects of the transfers on household income and on spending patterns, and on access to education, have been captured in a number of studies. The effect of transfers on people's own sense of self-esteem, dignity, and on their status in the household is much more difficult to assess. However, a number of qualitative studies, for example that of Møller and Søtshongaye (1996), reveal how older people talk about their enhanced sense of worth and dignity attributed to pension receipt. An analysis of a national data set which included subjective quality of life indicators shows that respondents in African pension-receiving older households reported more satisfaction (Møller and Devey, 2003) than African households with older members that receive no pension. Case and Menendez (2007) suggest that the receipt of the pension might increase the bargaining power of the pensioners with regard to all kinds of decisions made within households.

Creation of markets and of enterprises

Anyone who does field research in South Africa, or who has happened to witness events around a monthly pension paypoint, will understand that pension day is economically the most important day of the month. Local traders set up their stalls adjacent to the paypoints, as described in the following description from a field site in which there was a pension day in rural KwaZulu-Natal in 2001:

> Over the years, and especially since the mid 1980s when the pension amount to African people rose significantly, informal markets have grown up around this important day in local economic life. In the situation described by Ardington and Lund, 1995, the main transactions on pensions days were between pensioners (or their household members) and vendors. In 2001, the (research) team observed that the periodic pension market now involved the entire community. It was the one day of the month when retailers brought goods in bulk into the rural areas; it was a day of intense social interaction as well. During the field visit to Ntumbane, no household interviews could be done at all on 'pension day', as all households were involved in the market, doing their general household shopping. There is a great deal of tension in the air at that time, because of the amount of money involved, and there is suspicion of outsiders. Nevertheless, the research team observed that there were traders from at least two other countries present (nearby Swaziland and remote Botswana) who

came to sell new and second-hand clothes. Local people on the other hand sold goods they had produced or procured locally. We noticed vegetables from household plots as well as from the communal gardens, livestock that had been raised on a project supported by the department of agriculture, and natural resources such as honey and indigenous herbs.

In this same research site, there was a noticeably better-off area, where houses were large and solid. A knowledgeable local informant [was asked] how the owners of the large houses had accumulated their wealth. In all cases, the answer was the same: either a household member had a job in government employment, or someone had started with small retailing at the pension market, and grown the enterprise from there. In two of the latter cases, people had grown their enterprises to substantial fixed shops.

As suggested elsewhere (Lund, 2002a: 686) the pension payout has given rise to a sort of periodic market which addresses the distorted underdevelopment of markets created by apartheid in rural areas: 'It is surely unusual that this market is stimulated by cash state transfers. It is surely important to local economic development.' (Adato et al., 2003)

This important example illustrates the potential of social security transfers in poor countries, which clearly contribute to the buoyancy of local markets. They are a particular stimulus to informal employment creation and the sustainability of rural production and consumption because – according to substantial historical and contemporary evidence – the poor spend a much higher proportion of available income on food and other basic goods than middle- and high-income groups, and the money transfers create local supply of goods and services.

Labour market effects

South Africa has an exceptionally high unemployment rate, and the question might reasonably be asked, should the money being spent on social assistance rather be diverted to employment creation? Furthermore, does the pension have an effect on entry to and exit from the labour market?, The South African government, even with its conservative economic policy, has answered the first question: enjoying the present period of relatively modest economic growth, with improved revenues since 1994, the first budget surplus in 2007 is being used largely to improve the social security system, in particular its contributory component.

With regard to the entry to and exit from the labour market, Bertrand et al. (2003) presented findings which showed that prime age men voluntarily left work when a pension came into their household (most likely to one of their parents). Bertrand and her colleagues had, however, excluded from the data non-resident household members – the majority of whom were not at home as they had gone in search of work. Posel et al. (2006) reanalysed the same data set, including the data on migrants, and found that there was indeed a labour market effect, but in a different direction: when a pension was received by a woman, younger women with a child left the household, and migrated, presumably in order to look for work. Job and poverty effects of the introduction or extension of social security payments therefore must take account of split-family migrant labour.

Klasen and Woolard (2005), in a careful study of the association between unemployment and pensions, found that rural households receiving a pension were more likely to have unemployed younger people. They suggest that since South African rural areas lack employment opportunities, younger people stay close to a pensioner rather than seek uncertain employment prospects in other areas.

Political solidarity

The social assistance programme has been declared by the government and others as being one of the most effective anti-poverty measures. There are critical gaps in the system, and there remain bureaucratic obstacles in many procedures, which are costly to the poor, and sometimes breed hostility and contempt between the administrators of benefits beneficiaries. Nevertheless on a monthly basis a substantial sum of transfer resources is received by one-quarter of all South Africans, most of whom are very poor.

In the 2007 Budget Speech, Finance Minister Trevor Manuel announced the intention to reform social security. He specifically noted that he was using the first budget surplus to support the poor as well as on increased infrastructural spending to sustain economic growth. He invoked a number of proverbs from indigenous official languages as mantras, all of which mean more or less that all 'human life has equal worth'. A 2007 policy document of the ANC says that the model of the South African state should be based on a combination of the best traditions of social democracy (as in Sweden) and a successful developing economy (such as Malaysia).

However, one should not overlook the possibility that as successful and effective as the cash transfers are, their receipt could become a mechanism for exclusion. With regard to the grants for elderly people, the focus on the cash transfer tends to detract attention from other health and social services needed by elderly people. Under the old regime, white and to a lesser extent Indian and coloured elderly South Africans had access to some institutional care, and some community-based services. Some of the old subsidized institutions have lost their subsidies and have been closed or privatized without replacing capacities. Cash transfers need to be combined with other social services like health, welfare and education. Funding cash transfers should not crowd out the provision of social services.

The same is true for people with disabilities. Severe disablement can affect anyone and drive individuals into severe penury. Mitigation does not just consist of income relief or compensation but also depends on the availability of long-term nursing care. There is anecdotal evidence that the entitlement to a disability grant may create tensions between grant recipients and people without impairments. The vast majority of disabled people say that they want to work, rather than receive a grant. Poorer people with disabilities are constrained in their choice of employment, and many have to become traders in public municipal spaces. In eThekwini (Durban) there is a conflict between informal traders and the municipality over the allocations of scarce trading sites in the central city. The municipality included a quota for people with disabilities in its allocation policy. Traders without disabilities complained that this was not fair, as the disabled traders already received a grant income.

For disabled people the right to a minimal basic grant can enable them to afford the transport to access work sites in the city, and can cover at least part of their additional basic income needs which are incurred by the disability. For some, the grant itself is a necessary (though not sufficient) condition for their participation in disability networks.

Social insurance, risk and the labour market

The primary focus of this chapter has thus far been on state provision for those who are not working, or who work for very low incomes. This is only one of the pillars of social security. There are a number of programmes such as those commonly found in OECD countries, for those in formal employment (Lund, 2002b; van der Berg and Bredenkamp, 2002).

To cover the risk of work-related disability and death, formally employed people have access to a contributory scheme (contributors are workers and employers) generally known as 'workers compensation'. This gives access to benefits for occupation-related disease, disability and death. Formal workers also have access to an unemployment insurance fund, which includes also maternity benefits. For retirement savings, there are about 14,000 private pension schemes through which individuals (as individuals and as workers) can save for their retirement. These schemes have some 10 million members (some individuals belong to more than one scheme), and many are too small to be viable over the long term. They cover mostly people who are in formal employment, and those who can afford to buy private provision as individuals.

The informal economy is expanding, both in terms of the number of workers, as well as the number of enterprises. In 2002, the ILO estimated that informal employment as a proportion of non-agricultural employment is 72 per cent in sub-Saharan Africa, 65 per cent in Asia and 51 per cent in Latin America. The informal economy in South Africa amounts to 40 per cent of the workforce and is smaller than in other countries of the region, that have a rate of informality of over 70 per cent in countries such as Malawi, Kenya and Ghana (ILO, 2002b). There is debate about the root causes of the persistence of the informal economy in different regions of the world. Some hold that in Africa it is simply 'normal', and that there was never an extensive formal economy. In some Asian and Latin American countries, the growth is more likely explained in terms of responses to the severe financial crises of the 1990s. However, Chen et al. (2005) point out that those who work in the informal economy are likely to have less access to basic infrastructure and social services, face greater exposure to contingencies such as illness and disability, have less access to the means to cope with these contingencies, have fewer rights and benefits of employment, and face greater exclusion from the state, market and political institutions. There are also disadvantages for employers to recruit and then maintain a skilled workforce that would enable them to minimize the costs of staff turnover. In general, however, workers and their families bear the risks of informality.

South Africa faces two contradictory trends. On the one hand, some labour legislation has been extended to cover more categories of workers for certain work-related benefits. For example, the nearly 1 million domestic workers, the vast majority of whom are women, are now covered by the unemployment insurance fund. Thus their work has become formalized. On the other hand, there is a trend towards 'contractualizing' formal jobs. Workers in formal employment continue to do the same work, for the same firm or company, but their status is changed to 'contract workers'. Due to that change, access to major social benefits – for example, paid leave, sick leave, compensation for disability at work – is lost.

Poor informal workers know that they will receive the pension for elderly people in time; many also earn so little that they qualify for the Child Support Grant. Cash transfers received by others in the household may mitigate some income risk, but there remain enormous gaps in covering work-related risks for informal sector workers. The access to benefits for unemployed workers in the informal economy is also incomplete. There is a need to extend and conjugate residence-related and work-related social security benefit properly.

It is intended that South Africa will have a new mandatory, contributory earnings-related social security fund by 2010 that will be the vehicle for retirement savings, unemployment insurance, and disability and death benefits. It is aimed at those who fall outside the scope of the current unemployment insurance and worker compensation schemes, and who cannot afford to buy private insurance. It is specifically proposed as a bridge between the social assistance type cash transfers discussed above, and the occupation and private individual pension provisions that are beyond the financial reach of many workers and citizens. This will be a major step towards a more comprehensive scheme – but coverage will still be incomplete. A voluntary scheme aimed at informal workers, such as that introduced successfully in Costa Rica, would possibly extend coverage to some, albeit limited, extent.

Large national and multi-national companies 'outsource' more and more components of the production process to labour brokers, who in turn arrange for piece rate production of such components, for example in the garment industry. The producers – thousands of very poor men and women often working from their own homes – do not know who they are working for. They know only the broker who delivers material inputs and collects finished products, which they produce under the disguise of being 'self-employed'. Where contracts exist (and most often they do not) these abolish the responsibilities of the owners of capital for regular payment, compensation in the case of accidents caused in the production process, sick leave, and so forth. The Bretton Woods institutions are now allowing back on to the development agenda a more active role for state intervention, but remain relatively silent on the roles and responsibilities of private capital for employment conditions and the general well-being of workers that are not directly employed by them.

Extending social security – bridging to poorer countries

Barrientos (Chapter 13, this volume) states that active social policy is needed which meets three requirements: reduces deficiencies in consumption (reduces income poverty), helps investment in human and physical assets, and strengthens the agency of the poor. A growing body of research demonstrates that the South African cash transfers meet all these requirements, and more. In South Africa, social security is beginning to be recognized as one central element in an overall development approach, and the evidence of its effectiveness is clear. The cash transfers are affordable and managed by the Treasury and the newly established South African Social Security Agency. The levels of the benefits are the outcome of ongoing dialogue and negotiations between government and civil society.

South Africa is a lower middle income country, which has now had five years of continuous though modest economic growth. What lessons can be drawn for other countries with less stable economies? Different authors have examined the issue. Behrendt and Hagemejer (see Chapter 5) consider that social security, at least at low basic benefit levels, is affordable in poorer countries; Townsend gives historical reasons and evidence from the effects of contemporary redistribution in the industrialized countries that low-income countries can reasonably explore the expansion of their social security systems, although different options for financing those systems nationally and internationally have to be explored; and yet Barrientos suggests that sustainable financing can be an intractable problem.

It is assumed that the benefits of cash transfers are widely accepted. It is also assumed that investing in social security is morally right, as we know that a modest basic entitlement brings basic security and access to a range of fundamental rights, such as the ability to participate in the society. The conclusion is then drawn that there is no need to 'pilot' this to produce more evidence: in cash-based societies, the lack of cash is a binding constraint (though not the only one) to psychological and material well-being. Social security has then to be sensibly designed with regard top priority objectives and diligently delivered. Design decisions have consequences for exclusion and inclusion. Delivery has costs that reduce the fiscal space for benefits. What about countries with fewer resources than South Africa? In this section, we draw on the experience of South Africa and address the question: if one was arguing for the introduction of a modest cash transfer for children in the first years of their lives, what would be the main considerations for countries with relatively fewer resources and relatively limited institutional capacity?

Complementarity and synergy between economic and social policies

In mainstream economic thinking, economic policy and social policy are held to be completely separate, and social policy is the residual add-on that is introduced to offset negative impacts of economic policies. This is vastly different from the philosophy that governs the development of the welfare state, which perceives the provision of income, nutritional support and investing in children as prerequisites to long-term sustainable economic and social development.

While social spending is an investment, leading to longer-term security and productivity gains, it needs to be complemented in the short and long term by economic programmes of support that can assist poorer people to escape poverty. Such programmes, belonging to the category of overall macroeconomic policy, would include industrial and trade policies. They would also include enterprise support programmes, which are built on an understanding of the way that poor people work and employ others in micro-enterprises. In countries where there are large informal economies, employment creation includes ways to assist poorer people to create their own employment and stopping those already formally employed from losing any social benefits.

Complementarity and synergy among social policies

There are many reasons for advocating cash transfers, and some of the main arguments are given here and in the chapters by Samson, Barrientos and others. We know, however, that cash transfers are one part of a required overall set of policies for poverty reduction. Earlier the post-apartheid programmes intended to address poverty – free health and education, a housing subsidy, nutrition in schools – were sketched out as necessary complements to cash transfers. In the absence of such complementarity and synergy, each programme may be less effective.

In South Africa, for example, 'free' education has remained expensive for poor people, with two costly items being transportation and school uniforms (especially those for boys). Some advocates for age extension of the CSG argue for it on the grounds of the high costs of education. The CSG paid from the welfare budget is used to pay for expensive and often inappropriate uniforms. Similarly, we know that the pension for elderly people is often used to pay for educational and health expenses of younger household members. As suggested earlier, one cannot exclude the possibility that the focus on cash transfers for elderly people 'crowd out' resources for other services required by elderly people themselves.

Conditionality

Many cash transfer programmes, such as those found in Latin America (see Barrientos, Chapter 13), are conditional – that is, the beneficiary has to ensure that someone in the household engages in some prescribed behaviour that the programme designers (the government or international agency) considers 'socially responsible'.[3] Typical examples are that a child must be enrolled in school, or all household members must attend medical check-ups a certain number of times. The South African cash transfers are formally unconditional benefits: if you are entitled to a grant, and you pass the means test, you are entitled to it. However, there are multiple ways in which informal conditions are placed on access (Goldblatt, 2005).

Conditionalities impose costs on the administration and people trying to access the benefit system. It thus is important to ensure that the imposition of conditionality is compatible with local needs, and is likely to result in valued outcomes. In South Africa, for example, enrolment in primary school is extremely high, both for girls and for boys. Hence, it may make little sense to impose school enrolment as a condition.

Typically, and sometimes as a matter of policy design, the benefit will go to women, and it is women who ensure the fulfilment of the conditionality. Women may feel that the value of the benefit justifies the efforts. Yet, women are already doing most of the unpaid care work that is being caused by caring for people affected by HIV/AIDS (Akintola, 2004).

Universalism versus means testing

In South Africa it has been argued for years that imposing a means test on the pension for elderly people is a waste of resources. The vast majority of elderly people are very poor (take-up is in excess of 80 per cent). Pension payments to the rich are partially taxed back.

It could be argued that imposing a targeting mechanism such as a means test in countries poorer and with less administrative capacity than South Africa would be even more costly in administrative terms. Where a large fraction of the population is poor enough to qualify, it makes little sense to say 'target the 20 per cent of the very poorest'. The delivery of such a system becomes too costly and is not likely to work effectively.

Objective level of need

The level of a benefit should be set to meet some objective level of need, even if at the beginning only a portion of that need can be met. It could be linked to a measure of the real costs of a child's nutrition, for example, or nutrition and clothing, or nutrition and clothing and material for personal hygiene. Linking it to a measure provides justification for increasing the grant in line with inflation.

Development of other needed services

The South African system was built up over a period of decades, initially targeted just at whites, and at other groups in urban areas, and was then gradually extended to cover everyone in the population. By about 1960 almost the total population was eligible for the grants to the elderly and to people with disabilities. There were seventeen 'national' social security offices. Social security offices were set up in the capitals of all the homelands and 'independent states'. Procedures were archaic, technology outdated and transport systems limited – but the officials and the procedures were in place. Though many were formerly excluded, it was a system that could be improved rapidly after the political change.

Given that geographical distribution of the population in a typical developing country is often clustered in one or two major cities and a few regional towns, the delivery of benefits can pose a major logistical problem. However, the South African experience shows that there are significant areas for administrative synergy.

The first area is the need for citizen identification and birth registration. No social security system can be properly managed without a system of citizen identification, and if it is child-oriented, there has to be a system of birth registration. Development interventions can only be properly planned for, managed and monitored if there are good basic demographic data. Part of the reason for the rapid take-up of the CSG in South Africa was that millions of adults had registered for the first time in order to vote in the 1994 elections. One argument to be made for the introduction of a cash transfer is that it provides an incentive for the poorest to come forward and register births, and receive adult identification numbers. This could also be used attract pregnant women to antenatal clinics, and/or to a follow-up visit for immunization at the crucial time when the child is around 30 months old.

The second area for synergy is information communication technology and infrastructure. The information system needed for planning and monitoring cash transfers has to be transparent, efficiently managed and accountable. The move to an electronic system of payment through individually held smart cards has enormous potential to route the cash transfer directly from the state to the pockets of the poor, even if this can first only be done in urban areas. In South Africa this technology is tied into the private financial sector and to retailers. Many poorer countries need an 'injection' of technology and communications. The introduction of wide-coverage cash transfers could be one way of kick-starting innovation – for example, extending banking technology to rural areas.

The third potential synergy area is developing public–private partnerships. Social security systems need to be immune against government changes. Social security systems worldwide are susceptible to patronage and clientelism, which when taken to extremes become forms of corruption. There is no doubt that some corruption exists within the South Africa social security system. The introduction of more transparent forms of local government has the potential to address this problem. The controversial outsourcing of the delivery function to the private sector (which is making substantial profits through this) can, if properly regulated, control the corruption, contingent on the ability and willingness of government to regulate this public/private relationship.

Conclusion

The post-apartheid government inherited a substantial system of social assistance, and has built on it since 1994. Positive hallmarks of the last decade have been the introduction and rapid implementation of the Child Support Grant, improvements in many aspects of the delivery of other grants, and enhanced transparency through publicly accessible data. Importantly, the benefits of the system have been subject to substantial research which has increased their acceptance by the government. The cash transfers have been shown to be compatible with development and growth, and a highly effective intervention when planned and managed well. With the Child Support Grant, the government managed to switch some of the social spending more directly towards vulnerable younger children, without dismantling the cash transfers for elderly people and people with disabilities.

More broadly, the government's plan to introduce a mandatory earnings-related fund by 2010 shows that it is now turning to longer-term improvements in strengthening the private pillar of the social security system. And it is of interest to note that South Africa was one of the first 80 countries to sign the United Nations Convention on the Rights of Persons with Disabilities, in March 1997.

Much remains to be done, however. Despite strong advocacy for the introduction of a basic income grant (BIG), the government has not accepted this main policy recommendation of the Taylor Committee, which was mandated to investigate a comprehensive system of social security (Department of Social Development, 2002). The BIG is a highly complex issue, and its acceptance would have implications for the rest of the social security system. Despite some endorsement by the welfare minister of the idea of the BIG, the Treasury has consistently opposed the idea, and the government has been pursuing piecemeal reforms of the existing transfer system.

There has, moreover, been no coherent or comprehensive social assistance policy in the face of the HIV/AIDS epidemic. There is still confusion about the conditions under which people with AIDS can get access to the Disability Grant. There are few special measures in place to protect the millions of children affected and infected by HIV/AIDS. The impact of HIV/AIDS on mostly unpaid care work by women is not yet properly appreciated (Akintola, 2004; Ogden et al., 2004). There is too little awareness of the 'chains of care', which exist in the Southern Africa situation (Chen et al., 2005).

As is common in poverty debates, the focus on the poverty alleviation impact of cash transfers detracts attention from the patterns of inequality in society, and South Africa is an example of a country where the accumulation of vast assets by a minority is related to the increasing impoverishment of the vast majority. The barriers to building a more comprehensive and affordable transfer system, in the interests of all South Africans, seem to be the mental barriers of the rich, rather than 'perverse incentives' attributed to the poor. One of the key messages of this chapter is that in all countries, not just poorer and less developed ones, mental barriers of those who control society are instrumental and pivotal for the persistence of the residual nature of social policies in these societies. These attitudes can be changed by rigorous and careful research, such as in the South African case. Research studies can be used to support the call to rethink social policy and move it away from its conception as a residual category of a 'safety net' that merely counteracts policy failures or development disasters. Social policy should be conceived as a means of development policy that works in tandem with economic policy (Mkandawire, 2004).

South Africa can draw on a wealth of indigenous evidence showing the advantages of specific forms of redistribution of cash to poor people. Political, business and social leadership is required to ensure that resources are immediately available to children in dire poverty, with special additional measures for children affected by HIV/AIDS.

South Africa has been lauded as a leader in the field of international human rights, and has been positioning itself as keeper-of-the-peace on the African continent and further afield. Starting within the African continent, and taking into account lessons already learned by countries such as Lesotho, Mozambique and Zambia, which have introduced elements of cash transfer systems, South Africa could become an effective champion – achieving in parallel social justice and economic development – of the extension of cash transfers as a crucial component of social and economic policies.

Notes

1. See van der Berg and Bredenkamp (2002) for an interesting and detailed discussion of take-up issues.
2. Budlender and Woolard (2006) summarize the evidence.
3. Such behavioural conditionalities are here distinguished from administrative requirements for eligibility, such as age, or place of residence.

16

From Targeting to Universality: Lessons from the Health System in Thailand

Viroj Tangcharoensathien, Phusit Prakongsai, Supon Limwattananon,
Walaiporn Patcharanarumol and Pongpisut Jongudomsuk

In May 2005, the World Health Assembly endorsed Resolution WHA 58.33 (WHO, 2005b) urging member States to move towards universal coverage (UC) and to ensure that the population has access to health care without facing risk of catastrophic expenses. The core guiding principles include enhancing pre-payment, risk pooling, contributions according to ability to pay and the right to use of services according to health needs (WHO, 2000, 2005b).

Paradoxically, out of pocket payments by poor households are the major source of financing health care in most developing countries; such payment at times results in disaster. Worldwide some 150 million individuals are facing catastrophic health care expenditures annually. Of these, about 100 million people are pushed into poverty after paying medical bills (Xu et al., 2007).

In developed countries with a large formal sector, the move towards UC took several decades (Carrin and James, 2004). The transition period, measured by intervals between the first law on health insurance and the final law on implementing such coverage, averaged seven decades. For example, it took 127 years for Germany to reach universal coverage, 118 for Belgium, 84 for Israel, 79 for Austria, 72 for Luxembourg, 36 for Japan, 26 for the Republic of Korea and 20 for Costa Rica.

Efforts in these countries were incremental, through systematic expansion of population coverage over the transition period, with a range of organizational arrangements and different combinations of sources of financing. The two – most often used – parallel financing approaches were payroll taxes for the formal sector employees and general tax financed schemes focused on the poor. The coverage of the informal sector is the most difficult challenge. The two parallel approaches were described as 'squeezing the middle' at a recent conference (PhilHealth, 2007), the middle layer referring to the non- or not-so-poor informal sector, while the top layer consists of formal sector employees and the bottom layer comprises the poor. Crucial determining factors in achieving UC in these countries have been income levels, the structure of the economy, the demographic structure and the geographical distribution of the population, the national ability to administer social health insurance (SHI), and the degree of solidarity within a society (WHO, 2005a). The wide range of international experience can be used as policy leverage in other developing countries.

The history of coverage extension in Thailand[1]

By early 2002, Thailand had achieved UC for the whole population. It was the final stage of a long march. It took 27 years from the first public social protection scheme for the poor (the Low-Income Scheme) in 1975 until the introduction of the now famous 30-Baht scheme.

For a long time Thailand applied the 'squeeze the middle' approach. In addition to the tax-financed medical benefit for low-income households (the bottom layer), successive governments applied a 'piecemeal' approach (Tangcharoensathien et al., 2005) of gradually extending insurance coverage to the non-poor (the middle layer) by a subsidized voluntary public insurance scheme (Health Card Scheme) in 1983[2] (Tangcharoensathien, 1990).

In 1990, a Social Security Act was promulgated for formal private sector employees (the top layer). They are covered under mandatory tripartite payroll tax- (contribution) financed SHI. SHI gradually extended from larger enterprises of more than 20 employees in 1990 to the smallest firms of more than one employee in 2002.

The formal sector public employees (the top layer) and retired officials and their dependants (generously including parents, spouse and children under 18 years of age) were covered by the non-contributory tax-financed Civil Servant Medical Benefit Scheme (CSMBS).

As shown in Table 16.1, more than two-thirds of the population were uninsured in 1991, reducing to over half by 1996, and around 30 per cent by 2001 despite government efforts to extend coverage quickly.

The best scheme in terms of coverage was the Social Welfare scheme for the poor, which later was extended to cover the elderly (>60 years), and children less than 12 years old.

The voluntary Health Card Scheme was also relatively successful, covering 1.4 per cent in 1991 and 20.8 per cent in 2001. The rapid increase in coverage from 1996 to 2001 was due to the 50 per cent government subsidy of the premium to households.

As a result of downsizing the government sector, the population coverage of the CSMBS stagnated and then shrank, down from 15.3 per cent in 1991 to 8.5 per cent in 2001.

Table 16.1 Trend in the population coverage of health insurance (per cent) prior to UC

Scheme	1991	1996	2001
Social Welfare for the poor, elderly and social disadvantage groups	12.7	12.6	32.4
Civil Servant Medical Benefit Scheme	15.3	10.2	8.5
Social Health Insurance	–	5.6	7.2
Voluntary Health Card	1.4	15.3	20.8
Private health insurance	4.0	1.8	2.1
Total insured	33.4	45.5	71.0
Total uninsured	66.6	54.5	29.0

Sources: Health and Welfare Surveys in various years – National Statistical Office (NSO).

System deficiencies

Despite gradual improvements in the objective criteria and local community participatory processes in identifying the poor, two decades of experience with means testing to identify the poor demonstrated deficiencies, especially in effective coverage of the 'real poor' and preventing the affiliation of the non-poor. In some villages the poor could join the scheme due to nepotism in some village committees who conducted the primary screening of the poor.

The prospects of extending SHI were limited, as the formal employment sector was still small. The vast majority of labour was engaged in agriculture, self-employment and other informal sectors. The government lacked a clear policy and the Social Security Office (SSO) the institutional capacity and willingness to extend coverage to the informal sector. In addition, the 1990 Social Security Act does not cover dependants of the employee (except for maternity). This coverage gap was not addressed by political efforts to extend coverage to family members by SSO despite strong recommendations by the ILO and others in the country.

Due to the voluntary nature of the subsidized Health Card Scheme, it faced adverse selection when the sick and frequent users perceived the benefits and subscribed in increasing numbers every year. Healthy members of the population opted out because they foresaw no benefit. Understandably, the scheme therefore became financially non-viable and could not play the expected role as a major tool to achieve UC.

The uninsured 30 per cent of the population in 2001 were left responsible for their own medical bills. They faced difficulties in accessing needed health care; medical expenditure often turned into financial catastrophes for the household and large medical bills impoverished them.

As a result of the piecemeal approach to health insurance coverage, there was a great discrepancy in efficiency and equity in access to health services as well as the quality of care. This was reflected in different levels of financing and government budget subsidies, gaps in benefit packages, and variations in provider payment methods. For example, the CSMBS was the most generous and well funded non-contributory scheme, which applied a conventional fee-for-service reimbursement model that resulted in a cost containment problem. The Low-Income Scheme was always underfunded by the annual budget allocation. Hospitals had to cross-subsidize the Low-Income Scheme by overcharging the CSMBS (the so-called 'Robin Hood' behaviour). The CSMBS and the SHI provided the most generous benefit package including, for example, renal dialysis, while this was excluded from the Low-Income Scheme.

Before the implementation of UC, the quality of governance of insurance funds differed widely. The Ministry of Finance's Comptroller General Department, which is responsible for the CSMBS, performed poorly as a third party payer or 'insurance' agency. For example, there was no beneficiary database, no system of effective claims audit, no mechanism for filtering and rejecting false claims, not to mention the capacity to review unnecessary diagnostics and treatments, and no check on the magnitude of supplier-induced demand. By contrast, the SSO has developed a good up-to-date beneficiary database and individual records of hospitalization. Its high-performing purchasing function is a result of the adoption of the capitation contracting model and its ability to contain health care cost.

Objectives

In the context of global advocacy for UC, the lessons to be drawn from Thailand would be useful for other developing countries that may decide to follow similar or different trajectories of health insurance development in their efforts to establish an equitable health system.

In view of the achievement of UC in 2002 and the remaining system deficiencies, this chapter describes and analyses the policy processes of reforms towards UC including the reform content, the role of policy actors and the contextual environment. The chapter further describes the systems design, which addresses deficiencies in order to ensure equity, efficiency and long-term financial sustainability. This chapter, however, does not cover the favourable outcomes of the reform in terms of equity and efficiency achievements. They have been published elsewhere.[3]

The reform processes: context, actors and contents

The authors[4] had first-hand experience in health care provision in Thailand prior, during and after the reforms. This included exposure to key historical

events, the contextual environment, engagement with key actors and dia-
logues, involvement in the design of downstream implementation processes,
and the development of information systems for monitoring progress and
the achievement of UC (Tangcharoensathien et al., 2004; Towse et al.,
2004). Some of the factors that critically contributed to the reform process
are listed below. Some of the observations and analyses have been documented before, and some are published for the first time as evidence of
eyewitnesses.

The state of the health system prior to the achievement of UC

As said earlier, there were large-scale investments by successive governments
in public health service infrastructure at district and sub-district levels during
the past two decades (Wibulpolprasert, 2005). Explicit pro-poor and pro-rural
policies were adopted to achieve geographical coverage of health services at
sub-district health centres and district hospitals in all locations.

Policy was not only well intentioned, but implemented in practice by
means of adequate capital and operational budget allocation. The extension
of the health infrastructure was fully supported by long-term manpower production plans and actions. The Ministry of Public Health (MOPH) Nursing
Colleges played the most important roles in the production and distribution
of professional nursing and midwifery staff. High capital investments were
possible due to favourable consistent economic growth from the mid-1980s
to the mid-1990s.

As a result, there was extensive geographical coverage of health services
up to the very periphery of the country. A typical health centre and district hospital covers 5,000 and 50,000 population respectively. A health
centre is staffed by a team of 3–5 nurses and paramedics while a 30-bed district hospital is staffed by 3–4 general physicians, approximately 30 nurses,
2–3 pharmacists and 1–2 dentists, including all other paramedics. There is
a lean but adequate number of qualified staff at health centres and district
hospitals to provide health services. This increasingly gained the confidence
of the rural population and utilization increased over time (Wibulpolprasert,
2005).

In addition, public health programmes (disease prevention and health
promotion) were introduced at all levels of care. The programmes included
immunization, mother and child health services, prevention and treatment
of TB, and HIV and other sexually transmitted diseases. During the past two
decades, while MOPH focused on public health infrastructure extension, the
private sector delivery system grew significantly in urban areas, provided services mostly to the middle classes and the better-off, and played a significant
role in providing services to SHI members under the capitation contractual
arrangement with the SSO.

Since 1972, all public health and medical students have graduated from publicly funded health and medical colleges, the students being heavily subsidized by the government. In return, the new medical graduates (including nurses, dentists and pharmacists) serve a period of mandatory rural service for three years. They play a significant role in the functioning of district hospitals.

The economic context

The 1997 Asian financial crisis was experienced also by Thailand, but Thailand managed to transform crisis into an opportunity. The crisis was a catalyst for political reform guiding the newly promulgated 1999 Constitution, which focuses on good corporate and public governance. A check-and-balance mechanism has been written into the Constitution.

After the economy showed signs of early recovery in 2001 the plans for UC were introduced. Expensive schemes like the CSMBS which had adopted a fee-for-service reimbursement model and is currently facing huge cost escalation and system inefficiency had to be reconstructed.

In view of favourable SHI experiences, the capitation contract model was adopted by consensus for the UC scheme. The political context during the 2001 general election did not favour a contributory scheme for the 29 per cent uninsured (Table 16.1) who were mostly engaged in the informal sector. There would be difficulties of enforcement and a long administrative lead time would be needed to achieve UC. Political promises in the election campaign were made to reach UC immediately, and a tax-financed scheme seemed to be the only option.

An assessment of financial requirement and fiscal capacity by the authors indicated high feasibility – provided there could be some additional budget allocation. The principle was to categorize the whole population into two groups, the CSMBS and SHI in one group that was already covered, the other group consisting of the rest of the population, either currently covered by the Low-Income Scheme and the Health Card Scheme or uninsured.

The decision to adopt a tax-financed UC scheme was not taken in relation to the progressivity of various financing sources. However, subsequent studies indicated that the general tax is more progressive than the SHI contribution. The Concentration Indices (CI) for the direct tax, indirect tax and SHI contribution are 0.822, 0.559 and 0.498, respectively, in 2002; 0.816, 0.596 and 0.456, respectively, in 2004; and 0.769, 0.551 and 0.449, respectively, in 2006 (Prakongsai et al., forthcoming). The larger the CI value (close to 1), the more progressive the respective tax system is, i.e. the rich contribute more than the poor. On the expenditure side the application of capitation payment[5] for outpatient visits and case-based payment under global budget for inpatient admissions has a favourable capacity to contain cost in the long term.

The institutional capacity to generate evidence and manage knowledge

Melgaard (2004) described a strong in-country technical skill and research capacity to back up reforms and to guide effective policy formulation. The effective interface of research communities and policy-makers is the key input for the evidence-based policy development on not only UC scheme design but other public health initiatives also.

The UC agenda-setting took place under the leadership of the former Prime Minister Thaksin Shinawatra of the Thai Rak Thai (TRT) Party, who won a landslide victory in the 6 January 2001 general election. With regards to policy formulation, the evidence indicates that reformists and researchers generated evidence and proposed policy options that were influential. For example, the Health Systems Research Institute (HSRI) supported the development of National Health Accounts (NHA), a tool for monitoring financing flows since 1994, and researchers were able to maintain and continuously update the NHA system (Tangcharoensathien et al., 1999a). The mapping of various health insurance schemes and their performance also served as a strong foundation for policy analysis implying reform (Tangcharoensathien et al., 2003). The in-country institutional capacity to generate evidence on systems deficiencies is a foundation for the continuous monitoring and evaluation of policy interventions in a changing environment.

The escalating costs of CSMBS prompted the HSRI to support provider payment reform by replacing an open-ended, fee-for-service model by the close-ended capitation and global budget model. This proposal failed, however, due to resistance from the CSMBS beneficiaries who feared a reduction in their entitlement to the benefits.

The role of politics

The plan for UC was much talked about, but did not receive sufficient support to reach the political agenda, until the TRT saw it as an opportunity to boost its political campaign in the 2001 general election (Pitayarangsarit, 2005).

The power was vested in the new Prime Minister and bureaucrats to influence the process of UC agenda setting, before and after the general election, which also provided the opportunity for these actors to pool their resources.

Although there was considerable discussion among policy-makers, ultimately the decision rested with the party leader. The UC plan was obviously chosen for three reasons: legitimacy, congruence with the TRT's principles and the needs of the general public (as it eases financial burden from medical bills) and feasibility. It was considered an opportune moment to promote UC as the solution to health care problems.

Bringing researchers and political actors together

We observed a close relationship between the reformists and politicians – who made difficult decisions based on advice from the reformists and researchers – who generated knowledge and evidence. An evidence-based political culture developed. The technical capacity to produce evidence is a sound foundation for any reform, coupled with strong political will and overwhelming public support.

The development of a strategic approach towards UC

There was extensive debate on three possible approaches to achieving UC. These are the conservative, the progressive and the big bang approaches.

The *conservative* approach is to maintain the status quo, by extending to more people the fragmented insurance schemes, and thus perpetuating a degree of existing inequity. The examples are the expansion of SHI coverage to small establishments of more than one worker, and extending coverage to non-working spouses and children; extending the Social Welfare Scheme to the real poor and the needy; and expanding the voluntary Health Card Scheme. There is no legislative requirement, as this strategy simply would have developed existing administrative instruments. However, UC was unlikely to be reached in the nearer future.

The *progressive* approach was developed among the reformists and researchers, with the purpose of functionally integrating[6] the three major public schemes. This allowed a dual system for (1) the formal sector group and (2) the rest of the population. This required legislation for a merger between the CSMBS and SHI. UC would be achieved quickly without much resistance. This approach envisaged, for example, the pooling of the management of CSMBS (7 million beneficiaries) and SHI (7 million beneficiaries), and extending cover to dependants (spouses and children). The rest of the population (the informal sector employees and their dependants and the poor) would be managed by a newly established agency (the National Health Security Office – NHSO). In addition, both schemes would share a similar core package and provider payment methods. This de facto would become a virtual single scheme, if harmonization could be achieved at a later date.

The *big bang* approach would be a major change, through physical integration of all health financing sub-systems into a single fund – to be managed by the NHSO – in order to purchase health care for the whole population. It would require legislation and would achieve UC instantaneously, but with a foreseeable strong resistance from stakeholders in the CSMBS and SHI. Through a single fund, perfect or near-perfect equity might be achieved across the whole population.

Pros and cons of the three strategies were discussed among reformists. Eventually the decision was taken to discard the conservative approach, and to *adopt a progressive functional integration* approach rather than the big bang approach. Legislation was prepared accordingly. The functional integration includes the convergence of benefit packages (UC applies SHI benefit packages, though CSMBS is the most affluent package) and levels of payment across the three schemes. A provision in the National Health Security Act

Table 16.2   Characteristics of three public insurance schemes, 2002

Insurance scheme	Population coverage		Financing source	Mode of provider payment	Access to service
Social Health Insurance (SHI)	Private sector employees, excluding dependants	16%	Tripartite contribution, equally shared by employer, employee and the government	Inclusive capitation for outpatient and inpatient services	Registered public and private competing contractors
Civil Servant Medical Benefit Scheme (CSMBS)	Government employees plus dependants (parents, spouse and up to two children age <20 years)	9%	General tax, non-contributory scheme	Fee for service, direct disbursement to mostly public providers	Free choice of providers, no registration required
Universal coverage	The rest of the population not covered by SHI or CSMBS	75%	General tax	Capitation for outpatients and global budget plus DRG for inpatients	Registered providers, notably district health system

Source: Authors' synthesis.

allows the physical merger of the three schemes in the longer-term future, if the functional merger is considered to be successful and all concerned parties agree. The future merger will be done through a Royal Decree.

As a result, by early 2002 there were three public insurance schemes. The CSMBS covers 9 per cent of the population, the SHI covers 16 per cent of the population and the UC scheme covers the rest of the population, 75 per cent in total (see Table 16.2). Payment of health care providers is dominated by the close-end method in SHI and UC schemes. At the other extreme, CSMBS still applies a fee-for-service reimbursement model.

Reform content

As described above, reformists sought to redesign the schemes with a view to their harmonization, especially by developing a benefit package for UC members similar to that for SHI members.

There are several policy statements that reflect the reform objectives. The first objective is to improve health systems' *efficiency* through a rational use of health services with respect to care levels. The scheme beneficiaries are bound to use primary care first and are then ensured a proper referral to the secondary and tertiary levels of care. The UC scheme applied a capitation contract model, with its merits of cost containment as evidenced in the SHI (Mills et al., 2000; Tangcharoensathien et al., 1999b). Beneficiaries have to register with a network of health care providers in health centres and district hospitals in their domicile district.

Second, *equity* is ensured progressively across all schemes through a standardized benefit package, equal access to care by beneficiaries and standardization of level of resource use.

Third, good *governance* and minimization of conflicts of interest is pursued through splitting purchaser and provider functions. While the NHSO serves as the purchaser, the MOPH and other public and private entities serve as health care providers and service contractors. The National Health Security Board has an inclusive participation by all partners, ex-officio representatives from government agencies, non-government organizations and experts to ensure that all stakeholder concerns are taken into account.

Fourth, to ensure the *quality of care* an accreditation system and utilization reviews are used. The Hospital Accreditation Institute performs this function. It has been functioning for the last six years, though the accreditation of health care facilities is still on a voluntary basis. It is not a condition for contracting. The District Health System (DHS) is a typical contractor unit of primary care for the NHSO. Due to geographical monopoly of the DHS, it is the sole provider in the district. It is not possible to apply quality standards as a qualifying condition for contracting in such circumstances. The NHSO needs a new mechanism for the quality improvement of the DHS system.

A comprehensive benefit package was designed to cover outpatient and inpatient services, accidents and emergencies, and other high cost but effective interventions, for example, bone marrow transplantation, and open-heart surgery. At point of service, there was a 30 Baht nominal co-payment, but this was abolished in November 2006 when a new government came into power. The design provides both breadth and depth in risk protection. Subsequent studies indicate a consistent reduction in the incidence of catastrophic expenditure and impoverishment after the reform (Limwattananon et al., 2007).

Legislation of the UC scheme

The government policy was introduced by law at the end of 2001. By November 2002, the National Health Security Act was promulgated by the House of Representatives and finally endorsed by the Senate. The NHSO was set up as an autonomous body with its own Governing Board. The Board was chaired by the Minister of Public Health and Dr Sanguan Nittayaramphong became the first Secretary General of the NHSO.

The UC Scheme came into operation prior to the completion of the legislative processes, with the continuing involvement of all policy stakeholders through the parliamentary processes, with discussions taking place between stakeholders and representatives in the House of Representatives and the Senate.

Conclusion: lessons learned

Evidence generation

Human resources and institutional capacity to generate evidence to guide policy formulation prior to and after the implementation of the UC scheme in 2002 were key determinants of the success in Thailand.

Lessons from various health insurance schemes were the foundation for policy formulation. The capitation contract model was adopted by SHI in 1991, and had been proven during 1991–2001 to be the model that can work effectively and efficiently while maintaining a decent level of quality of care, cost containment and social acceptability. The SHI served as a predecessor for the UC scheme system design. At the same time, evidence from the fee-for-service CSMBS model serves as a 'no-go comparator model' for the UC scheme.

Thai reformers and researchers do not favour a contributory scheme, especially because of the very large size of the informal self-employed sector in the country. Law enforcement or compliance in the informal sector, and the collection of premiums, is deemed difficult and expensive. Neither is the political climate in favour of the contributory scheme due to the long lead time to achieve UC.

Reformers played an important bridging role between researchers and policy-makers. Evidence-based decisions have played an important role in the policy formulation of UC, while agenda setting and commitment has been vested in the political leadership. Hard evidence provides a strong foundation for reforms. The integral relationship between researchers, reformers and politicians is recognized.

Health system infrastructure

The commitment of successive governments in investing in the health of the population together with consistent and favourable economic growth were two main determinants of the development of the health system infrastructure.

The extension of the geographical coverage of health care facilities in the last two decades, the mandatory service in rural areas by new medical graduates, and clear budget support for the DHS have resulted in a strong and functioning health service delivery system. This is reflected in many health outcome indicators, such as a 98 per cent coverage of antenatal care (facilitated by rapid nationwide scaling up of the Prevention of Mother-to-Child Transmission of HIV Programme within a year in 2001), a 73 per cent prevalence of modern contraceptive use, and a 98 per cent immunization coverage of DTP3.

Without the extensive DHS, the policy on UC would be merely a rhetorical statement: citizen rights would be ensured only on paper and the poor would be unable to access and use services. Health care would be enjoyed only by the urban elite minority.

System design and implementation capacity

The resilience of the health system during the rapid nationwide scaling-up of UC within six months demonstrated its institutional capacity. The credit goes to staff in the provincial health offices, district health offices and district hospitals throughout the country.

Learning from the SHI experience, the government has taken further advanced steps towards UC, for example, by improving efficiency through primary care contractors to ensure the proper referral and better use of primary care. Cost containment is achieved through the application of capitation charges for outpatient visits, and a global budget with case-based payment for inpatient admissions.

Through contracting with the DHS the role of primary health care is emphasized and the rational use of low-cost integrated services, while ensuring proper referral, is fostered. The use of the DHS ensures client proximity notably for the rural population. The DHS is a major conduit for fostering the pro-poor subsidies on public health spending.

Data availability

A recent study (Tangcharoensathien et al., 2006) illustrates the availability of extensive national representative data sets that facilitate health equity monitoring and evaluation. The household survey databases regularly produced by the National Statistics Office provide maximum capacity in the analysis of equity outcomes. The Health Welfare Survey and the Socio-Economic Survey are very comprehensive in terms of a range of health dimensions, from health care use and payments to health status and risks. In addition, variations can be analysed across population sub-groups with respect to inequity in terms of geographic, demographic, social and economic variations of access and in terms of third party payment arrangements.

In the past decade there has been a genuine institutional relationship between the statistical community, that generates information, and the health constituency, that uses the information for their policy-making and system monitoring. Nationally representative household surveys are applied to monitor and evaluate impacts of health policy at household level. This is another strong foundation for evidence-based decision-making. Institutional capacity to improve the survey questionnaires and to maximize the use of these national surveys for policy decisions is also at hand.

Notes

1. We wish to acknowledge the contributions by various partners to the development of policy concepts and institutional capacities, notably, international partners including ILO (for peer review of the capitation rate for universal coverage in 2002

and for the long-term financing forecast for 2005–20); the WHO country office that provided financial support for an estimation of the UC capitation in 2003; and the EU-funded Equity in Financing, Health Utilization and Public Subsidies in Asia Pacific Region (EQUITAP) Project. The following national partners are recognized: Thailand Research Fund (TRF) for institutional grants to IHPP; the National Statistics Office (NSO) for their national household surveys for UC programme evaluations; the National Health Security Office (NHSO) and other partners who initiated, designed and steered the UC scheme; and finally the Ministry of Public Health (MOPH), the major health care provider in Thailand.

2. The Health Card project was initiated by the Ministry of Public Health in 1983 as a community health financing scheme focusing on mother and child health (MCH) services and managed by village committees. Later in 1984, MCH was extended to cover additional health care services for family members. In 1991 the community health financing (or community-based health insurance – CBHI) nature of the scheme was transformed to a formal voluntary health insurance and finally in 1994, the government decided to subsidize 50 per cent of the total premium.

3. See Limwattananon et al. (2005, 2007) and Prakongsai et al. (2007) for in-country evaluation and O'Donnell et al. (2007) and Van Doorslaer et al. (2006, 2007) for cross-country comparison of the financial outcomes.

4. One of the authors of this chapter, Viroj Tangcharoensathien, was involved with the design of SHI in 1991, proposing a capitation contract model as against fee-for-service reimbursement model, estimating the first capitation rate for the SSO, proposing the minimum data set for monitoring and evaluation of SHI, and proposing new rates for maternity benefit in 1993. The same author was also involved in proposing the government subsidies to the Voluntary Health Card Scheme in 1995, and proposing reforms of CSMBS during the period 1994–2000.

5. The authors' estimate capitation for UC scheme for 2002–4 and the first capitation rate was peer reviewed by ILO for scientific soundness.

6. Functional integration means maintaining the institutional identity of SSO, which handles SHI, and the Comptroller General Department, which handles CSMBS, but introducing similar benefit packages, public budget subsidies and provider payment methods.

Part V
Conclusions

17
Rethinking the Role of Social Security in Development

Christina Behrendt, Michael Cichon, Krzysztof Hagemejer, Stephen Kidd, Rüdiger Krech and Peter Townsend[1]

Countries which have been the most successful in achieving long-term sustainable growth and poverty reduction have achieved this – to a greater or lesser extent – by putting in place extensive systems of social security. Clearly, social security has only been one factor among many and, of course, one might ask whether there is a potential chicken and egg dilemma: what came first, growth or social security? In reality, though, evidence suggests that growth and social security have been mutually interdependent and have together contributed to the long-term success of these countries. There is no doubt that OECD countries have made the conscious decision to invest heavily in social security – often at more than 15 per cent of GDP – as part of their long-term growth and poverty reduction strategies.

Paradoxically, however, investments in social security have not been part of OECD donor governments' development strategies in low-income countries. There is a range of reasons for this. Some development practitioners, for example, have been driven by ideologies about deregulation, privatization and the free market, the case for which in 2008–9 has now collapsed, while many others have assumed that there is insufficient fiscal space in low-income countries to finance social security benefits and hence social security is not affordable in very poor countries. Yet, this latter assumption looks increasingly mistaken as evidence emerges that the costs of a minimum package of social security costs a relatively small proportion of GDP which is not out of the reach of even the poorest countries if transitional external support is being taken into account (cf. ILO, 2008a; Mizunoya et al., 2006; Pal et al., 2005).

Increasing numbers of middle-income countries are putting in place more extensive systems of social security. A number of national social pension schemes have been established, for example, in countries such as Brazil, Argentina, South Africa and Namibia; other types of social transfer schemes have been established, such as conditional cash transfers in Latin America and child benefits in South Africa; and free access to health and education services is becoming more common in some countries. And there are even some low-income countries that have also put in place limited social security support for the poor and vulnerable – even when this goes against the advice of the international community (for instance, Lesotho's recent implementation of a universal social pension scheme).

Nonetheless, overall government spending on social security in low-income countries, in particular in sub-Saharan Africa and South Asia, remains minimal. The correlation between a lack of progress on the Millennium Development Goals (MDGs) and levels of spending on social security is certainly not coincidental.

The question at the centre of this book is whether development practitioners, donor agencies and developing country governments can learn anything from the OECD experience with social security. Does the experience of poverty reduction in OECD countries provide a challenge to the dominant development paradigm in low-income countries? Can a case be built for putting in place low-cost social security systems within low-income countries based on experiences within OECD and middle-income countries? Eighty per cent of people worldwide still do not have access to adequate social security yet 2 per cent of *global* GDP is sufficient to provide all the world's poor with a minimum standard of social security.

The moment is opportune to consider these questions since a number of international donors and agencies are giving greater consideration to the role of social security in development: the United Kingdom developed a White Paper on International Development (DFID, 2006), Germany has been moving forward its thinking on the role of social protection and in January 2008 the parliament requested the government to make social security one focus of its development policy, and the new EU development policy highlights social security as a priority area. And, for a number of years, the ILO has been campaigning to extend social security to all and has developed a strategy to take this campaign forward. Within a number of low-income countries, there are signs of increasing interest in considering social security as a poverty reduction tool, although to date there is little indication of this influencing government spending plans.

Support is gathering for the policy position that countries can grow with equity, i.e. providing some form of social protection from the early stages of their development. The ILO Director-General's report to the International Labour Conference of 2004 initiated the ILO's increased efforts to test the financial feasibility and deliverability of basic non-contributory pensions, basic health services and access to basic education (ILO, 2004). The United Kingdom-based initiative 'Grow Up Free From Poverty' (2006), a coalition of 21 leading NGOs, promotes a 'social minimum' benefit package consisting of a basic set of cash transfers similar to the one listed by the ILO as a crucial tool in the combat against poverty in developing countries. This position is fully endorsed by the recent White Paper on development policy of the United Kingdom government (DFID, 2006: 85–6). The governments of Belgium,

France and Portugal have, for several years now, supported the extension of health security through a combination of community-based and central government approaches (see, for example, ILO, 2006c). The government of France launched a health insurance initiative for developing countries during the G8 meeting in St Petersburg and is actively following up on this initiative. What we observe is a real shift in development policy paradigms. The 'grow first–distribute later' policies appear to be consigned to history. The Rt Hon. Hilary Benn, then Secretary (Minister) for Overseas Development in the government of the United Kingdom, described the new development policy with the statement 'Our agenda is about growth with equity, not either or' (Benn, 2006). We are witnessing a growing awareness of the potential value of social transfers in development policies as was recognized in the G8 Labour Ministers' Meeting in Dresden[2] as well as the 2006 ECOSOC High Level Segment Ministerial Declaration that stated explicitly, 'countries need to devise policies that enable them to pursue both economic efficiency and social security and develop systems of social protection with broader and effective coverage'.[3] The ILO further developed the issue during an informal meeting of the Ministers of Labour and Social Affairs during the Labour Conference 2007[4] where a possible new approach to a policy for balanced and inclusive growth was presented by the office.

It is against this background of changing paradigms in development policy that this book has aimed at facilitating an exchange of opinions on current thinking, to stimulate debate on these issues and to help clarify the direction of future efforts. The intention of this book therefore has been:

1. to take stock of and discuss the knowledge that we have on the principal relationship between the economic and social development of nations and the build-up of national social security systems, and to consider whether this can provide a challenge to the prevailing development paradigm for low-income countries;
2. to draw conclusions that should influence development policy debates; and
3. to identify knowledge gaps and suggest a research agenda for the three institutions.

In the following, selected issues discussed in the book will be highlighted and reflected with a view to drawing lessons for the further development of social security policies in a development context.

Lessons from the development of social security in today's industrialized countries

In industrialized countries, social security has been an important factor in facilitating economic development, nurturing solidarity values and strengthening states' financial and administrative capacity. The low levels of poverty in those countries are closely related to social security policies. Today's challenge is how to create such synergies between economic and social development in developing countries.

Development of social security in today's OECD countries

Being aware of the difficulties in transferring lessons from one context to another, there is a rich historical experience from which lessons can be learned. It is important to identify best practices of social insurance and group-based schemes in developed countries from which lessons could be learned for today's developing countries.

The emergence of social security schemes in Western Europe and North America was closely linked to demographic change, industrialization, urbanization and democratization. Yet, whereas some of the social security pioneers in today's OECD world have introduced social security schemes before their full democratization (yet responding to pressures of democratization), others have introduced the first programmes on rather low levels of industrialization (cf. Pierson, 2004). In general terms, the conditions under which most of today's OECD member States expanded their social protection schemes, were the following: democracy (full suffrage), openness to trade, ageing of population and ethnic homogeneity.

An important step in the development of social security in OECD countries was the move from coercive social assistance to more universal schemes based on clear social rights. Social security thus is an important building block of social citizenship and social cohesion.

The success of social security in today's OECD countries has been described as a means to marry capitalism and democracy. Social security has facilitated and supported the process of economic development. This is also of utmost importance to today's developing countries, as economic development and the progress of emerging markets are often accompanied by social tensions. It is no coincidence that many Asian countries extended their social protection schemes as a response to the Asian financial crisis of 1997–8 (Kwon, 2005; Park, 2008).

The economic development of today's industrialized countries has shown that economic growth is compatible with high levels of social security expenditure. There is inconclusive evidence on the effect of social security expenditure and economic growth, but there is at least no clear evidence supporting the hypothesis of a negative effect. However, there is clear evidence that extensive welfare states and strong economic performance can coexist. There is furthermore strong evidence that, if well-organized, social security systems do help to cushion the effects of structural change in the economy, smooth consumption and do help to safeguard and promote human capital. Therefore, social protection is a key instrument in managing economic change.

The role of social assistance

When discussing the role for social assistance (or safety nets) in developing countries, it is often forgotten that, in most industrialized countries, such schemes play only a residual role in addition to non-means-tested programmes. In most OECD countries, social insurance and non-selective group benefits are by far the largest programmes, not only in terms of expenditure, but also in terms of coverage of the population. As such, they play a key role in preventing and reducing poverty while a much smaller role is left for means-tested social assistance programmes. It is the interplay between social insurance, universal non-contributory benefits and social assistance which has made some of the OECD countries so successful in reducing poverty. These programmes cater for those who – for one reason or another – cannot make ends meet from income from work or other market income, or non-means-tested benefits. Typical examples of social assistance beneficiaries are first-time job seekers, long-term unemployed who have exhausted their benefit entitlements and single parents.

In many low-income countries, the situation is different. Social insurance and non-selective group benefits presently cover only a minority of the population, that is, those who are (or were) in formal employment. The large majority of the population, mainly those working in the informal economy, would usually be considered as potential beneficiaries of social assistance benefits.

In some countries, social insurance benefits would not be considered as contributing to poverty reduction, and are often not even mentioned in national poverty reduction strategies. However, it has to be acknowledged that, even if these benefits cater for only a minority of the population in the current situation, these play an important role in preventing poverty for those groups of the population. They are also an important means of participating in the funding as well as benefit of schemes and, by designating entitlement as well as contribution, quickly acquire public approval. It is therefore important to include these benefits in comprehensive national poverty reduction and social protection strategies, and to maximize their contribution to the prevention and reduction of poverty. One of the lessons of pension reforms in some Latin American countries, where the role of social insurance in the prevention of poverty has recently been reconsidered and strengthened, is that younger members of families have acquired a share in the additional income (see for example Kay and Sinha, 2008).

Designing appropriate targeting mechanisms for social assistance programmes in the developed and developing world is a particular challenge. The experience with means-tests in many parts of the world shows that these are not easy to handle, especially in a development context (cf. Coady et al., 2004). In a situation where the majority of the population lives in poverty, it is difficult to discriminate between those who should be eligible for benefits and those who should not. This is exacerbated by the difficulty of assessing the level of resources if incomes are often non-cash and very irregular. Both inclusion and exclusion errors are favoured by fears of stigmatization, lack of information, difficulty of accessing benefits and administrative discretion. On balance, although the perfect targeting suggested by many quantitative targeting models might sound seductive, real-world experience suggests that means-tested programmes may not be the most effective and efficient type of programmes in a particular context (see, for example, Lloyd-Sherlock, 2008).

Given these difficulties, non-means-tested categorical programmes certainly have clear advantages over means-tested programmes in a development context. One prominent example is a social pension programme for older persons. If resources can efficiently be channelled into poor households through older persons, the situation of many needy households will improve considerably.[5] Existing evaluations show that a large proportion of social pension in fact benefits children with significant effects on their school attendance and physical development.[6]

Fears that the provision of social pension would weaken inter-generational support networks within families and communities are not supported by conclusive empirical evidence. On the contrary, there is strong evidence from developing countries that social pensions lead to the empowerment of older persons, but also to the sharing of resources within the family, mostly towards children (see for example Barrientos and Lloyd-Sherlock, 2003). Similar results on inter-generational support networks have been found for industrialized countries (Attias-Donfut and Arber, 2000).

Social expenditure

Countries on the same level of development have different levels of social expenditure. There is no conclusive empirical evidence that high levels of social expenditure would hamper economic development. On the contrary, in many countries we find both high productivity and high social expenditure. This illustrates that countries are rather using their political choice in determining public spending. This political space is filled based on underlying values and beliefs on solidarity, equity and fair distribution of resources.

At the same time, there is a close link between economic openness and social spending. Open economies tend to be the ones with the highest levels of spending. This underpins the role that social security plays in maintaining a healthy and productive workforce and in supporting economic change.

Lessons for the extension of social protection in developing countries

Social security and economic growth

For a long time, the relationship between economic and social development was ignored in developing countries. During the era of structural adjustment policies, public expenditure was drastically cut down, which had devastating effects on public services in health, education and other social services in many countries. According to the underlying beliefs of these policies, this should have led to more economic growth which would have eventually trickled down to the poor. This did not happen, however.

The recent shift of attention towards 'pro-poor growth' has eventually recognized that sustainable economic development can only be achieved if the social foundations of development are being taken into account. One of the essential mechanisms of pro-poor growth is social protection (OECD, 2006b) which helps to channel resources to those who cannot directly benefit from economic development due to their own low productive capacities. In addition to its redistributive function, social protection also plays a critical role in enhancing productivity of the workforce. Social protection has a positive impact on productivity by maintaining a healthy and productive workforce. By this token, social protection not only tackles income poverty but effectively supports broader development objectives. In other words, there is a virtuous circle between social protection and growth in a development context.

Social protection has not only an essential contribution to make to economic growth by smoothing consumption, but it also enhances the predictability in people's lives, so that people can plan ahead and invest in more productive income generating activities. It also serves as an automatic stabilizer of aggregate demand in times of economic crises, a role that is more important than it has been for a long time, now that the world is facing the deepest depression since the 1930s. Just as Franklin Roosevelt used social security to contain the social and economic fall out of the last dramatic crisis in the 1930s national social security systems should again today play an important role in global crisis management.

Role of employers

More attention should be given to the role of employers. Employers have played a two-fold role in the extension of social protection. On the one hand, employers traditionally have been concerned about labour costs, especially in view of international competition. In some industrialized countries, employers have perceived social spending as excessive and have used both voice and exit options.

On the other hand, employers have a strong interest in externalizing certain responsibilities for their employees into common risk pools. One obvious example is a maternity insurance scheme. If the 'risk' of maternity can be covered by a larger risk pool, employers are insured against the risk of having to cover the costs of paying the new mothers' salaries during maternity leave. This mechanism benefits in particular smaller enterprises, and contributes to create a level playing field of labour costs for employers. In addition, it addresses one of the causes of discrimination against women in the labour market, and supports women entering and remaining in the formal labour market. Similar arguments apply to other groups and illustrate the arguments in earlier chapters for early consideration of schemes that may involve indirect and sub-contracted employees in the countries in which global corporations operate.

Social security as a right

The right to social security, as pronounced in the Universal Declaration of Human Rights, is not a reality for the majority of today's population in many parts of the world. In order for it to be so, it is necessary to translate this right into national constitutions and legislations, and to make sure that it is implemented on the ground, which also includes sufficient financial resources and administrative capacities (cf. ILO, 2008b; Kulke and López Morales, 2007). This is the only way to fill the right to social security with life.

The role of international labour standards in social security has long been neglected. A review of the existing international labour standards in social security and their role for developing countries would help to pave the way for a better understanding and use of these standards to promote the extension of social security in low and middle income countries.

The role of the state

It is essential to acknowledge the responsibility of the state in ensuring the right to social security. This does not necessarily imply that social security benefits have to be provided directly by the state; they may well be provided by private sector institutions (cf. ILO, 2006a) or indirectly by international organizations and corporations. Independently of the nature of provision, a pluralistic approach to the provision of social security requires an effective regulatory role for the state. In countries with weak institutional capacities, strong efforts in terms of capacity-building and technical assistance are needed to ensure that the state can indeed fully assume this role in a responsible way. In countries where public attitudes toward the state are rather negative, this might help to increase confidence in public institutions.

Particularly in countries with weak institutional capacity, it is important to look for social security champions which assume ownership for these policies and are able to promote these policies at the national level. In many countries, national or international NGOs may assume this role. In failed states, these might actually crowd out the state as a provider of social protection. In these contexts, it is a particular challenge for development organizations to effectively implement programmes through these organizations while at the same time ensuring that the responsibilities of the state are not further undermined.

Finding fiscal space for social protection policies is certainly one important policy issue and major challenge in many countries. It is important to acknowledge that fiscal space is not a given factor, but is dependent on political priorities and political will.

Governance

Governance is critical to create and sustain trust. Effective governance structures are essential for sustainable policies. Clear and transparent rules are one cornerstone of effective governance, a guarantee for securing entitlements and an important safeguard against corruption. Such rules are easier to communicate than complex procedures, and this will help to inform people about their entitlements, to claim their rights and to appeal against decisions if necessary.

If social protection policies are to be successful in the medium and long term, it is essential to take political aspects into account. Timing is an important issue. There is a certain time lag between the political decision on a certain programme and its tangible effects on the lives of the population. This implies that some politicians prefer quick political returns over sustainable long-term programmes.

Sustainable social policies need to be firmly integrated in national policies and national institutional structures. If this is not the case, social protection programmes are short-lived, and are prone to die at the next change of minister on the national level, the end of project funds or a change in donor priorities.

Path dependence

There is some evidence that the development of social policies assumes a certain path dependence, with existing programmes and institutions influencing future policy reform and expansion. It is important to acknowledge the significance of existing institutions and to be aware that reforms tend to be much easier to implement if they follow the same pathway. In turn, deviating from the pathway entails high transition costs.

This point on path dependency also raises some issues on pilot programmes, which play an important role in testing new approaches to social protection, but which at the same time create expectations which are hard to achieve. Too much tampering with pilot programmes might lead to weakening public support and confidence.

Linking social security and rural development

Social protection policies need to be linked to broader rural development policies in order to achieve the maximum impact on the local level. More efforts are needed to assess the impact of cash transfers on the functioning of local markets, especially in rural areas. There have been concerns that the inflow of cash into local communities would lead to inflationary pressures, yet there is no systematic evidence for this so far. More research is necessary to scrutinize the effects of food and cash transfers on local markets.

Some countries, such as Ethiopia and India, have established large public works programmes, yet with mixed results. The experience with these programmes shows that it is important to make sure that the labour force is not greatly distracted from working for their own livelihood.

If cash transfers are linked to strong conditions in terms of school attendance or health check-ups, it is important to consider supply-side restrictions. These problems arise if the necessary infrastructure and human resources in the health and education sectors are not available, or if their utilization imposes prohibitively high cost in terms of time and money on families, affecting mostly mothers. The introduction of such conditionalities therefore needs a careful assessment of such supply-side restrictions. Such constraints are also important to consider when it comes to maximizing the impact of conditional or non-conditional social protection programmes on child labour, particularly in rural settings (see ILO, 2006b; Tabatabai, 2006).

Promoting employment and social protection

Greater attention should be placed on the interaction between employment patterns and social protection in developing countries. The relative weakness of social protection in many developing countries is essentially linked to the small size of the formal economy. This is compounded by the changing nature of the employment relationship in many countries, which has profound implications for the provision of social security.

One critical question is whether the formal sector needs to achieve a critical mass in order to trigger large-scale social protection. However, this should not become an excuse for not thinking about alternative options for the extension of social security. There are contributory and non-contributory forms of social protection which are compatible with a large informal economy. These avenues need to be further explored. There are also advantages to government when social security schemes are introduced because they tend to prompt enlargement of the formal economy.

Greater efforts are needed to analyse the linkages between receipt of social transfers in the household, labour force participation and quality of employment/economic activity. For this purpose, greater attention is needed when it comes to building the statistical database for such analysis through regular surveys. Labour force surveys as well as household income and budget surveys constitute a very useful source of data if information on social security is included. Essential variables for labour force surveys include the coverage by social protection schemes (active contributor or member of scheme and benefits received, by scheme or function). Household income and budget surveys can include questions on the amount of specific transfers received or paid. In some countries, panel surveys might even be feasible.

Strengthening families and communities

In many developing countries, families and communities are the main – and often only – agents of social protection. These networks play an essential role in providing support. However, there is a certain danger of romanticizing these traditional support networks, and of overestimating their potential. Migration, HIV/AIDS and other diseases, widespread underemployment and poverty take their toll on these support networks and weaken their self-help capacities.

Likewise, well-designed policies strengthen families and communities and replenish their self-help capacities. This can be exemplified by social pension programmes which have transformed older persons, often perceived as a burden to their families, into agents of change in their families.

Given the limitations of small support networks, it is essential to explore the potential for larger solidarity networks at the national level. This would not only provide a larger risk pool, but also increase the potential for redistribution, which is obviously limited in smaller, more homogeneous support networks. Larger solidarity networks, for example at the national level, provide a larger and therefore more reliable risk pool with greater scope for horizontal and vertical redistribution.

Moreover, such nationwide solidarity networks may also contribute to nation-building in countries with a troubled history of colonialism, conflict and war. Such networks help to bridge national social and economic cleavages and foster social inclusion. It is no coincidence that the extension of social security in developed countries often took place during or after major crises. One prominent example is the Beveridge Report in the United Kingdom which can only be understood against the background of the Second World War. A similar role could be assumed by social policies in today's developing countries.

The role of social security in development

The discussions at the seminar on which this book is based showed that it is time to place a greater emphasis on social security in a development context. There is now growing consensus within the development community that social transfers and social services not only tackle income poverty but effectively support broader developmental objectives (cf. for example OECD, 2006b). This consensus is supported by encouraging results from well-functioning social protection programmes in low-income countries. The programmes implemented there have shown that a substantial reduction of poverty can be effectively achieved by such means.

The conventional development strategy that has been promoted for most developing countries was trade growth and aid. This strategy, however, is very different from what has been successful in many OECD countries, where economic growth has been underpinned by social policies.

It is very clear that economic growth alone is not sufficient to achieve sustainable social development, but that sustainable economic and social development needs mechanisms to deliver the fruits of economic growth to the population and to protect individuals from social and economic risks. Social security, together with social services in health and education, is thus key to achieving sustainable and equitable growth and development.

The issue of social protection has become more prominent in recent development policies. However, current development policies often follow a piecemeal approach that might lead to a verticalization of social rights based according to issues, projects or programmes. This goes together with a growing number of pilot projects. Both trends are a reflection of funding trends and internal structures of the donor community. Development policies have to be coordinated and integrated in larger development frameworks in order to make sure that they respond to the needs and priorities of the population. A mix of universal and selective measures would be promising, with greater weight placed on universal measures. A good mix between access to social services and cash benefits is important to responding to people's needs.

In furthering the debate on the role of social protection in development, it is essential to strike a balance between idealism and pragmatism. There is conclusive evidence from a wide range of social protection programmes and pilot projects which underline the value and importance of social protection in a development context. It is now time to pull the evidence together and use it to move on to policy formulation on a larger scale in order to make sure that social protection can play its role in poverty reduction, and social and economic development.

A key recommendation

Growing with equity is not possible without guaranteeing at least a minimum level of social security for the world's population. It is therefore imperative to promote a social security floor as a catalyst for the role of social security in development polices, which should comprise a minimum set of four essential basic social security guarantees (a basic benefit package) that could constitute a social security floor:

- all residents should have access to basic/essential health care benefits, where the state accepts the general responsibility for ensuring the adequacy of the delivery system and financing of the scheme;
- all children should enjoy income security at least at the poverty level: through family/child benefits aimed to facilitate access to nutrition, education and care;

- there should be some targeted income support for the poor and unemployed in active age groups; all residents in old age and disability should enjoy income security through pensions granted at least at the poverty-line level.

The floor thus consists essentially of a guaranteed set of basic social transfers in cash or in kind to all. It is formulated as a set of guarantees rather than a set of defined benefits. This leaves the option open to individual countries to realize these guarantees by way of means-tested, conditional or universal transfers. The essential fact is that everybody in a given society can access these essential transfers. The ILO considers this concept as a potentially central instrument to give effect to the human right to social security (ILO, 2008b). An informal coalition of international agencies, donor agencies and international NGOs is emerging that promotes the concept.

While the construction of such a basic social floor is the overriding priority for low- and middle-income countries, it is important not to end at this point, but to use this recommendation to establish a basic social floor as a solid grounding for more extensive social security systems in line with economic development and subsequently widening fiscal space. During the agonies of cross-national planning for recovery in the aftermath of the financial crash of 2008–9 there is more reason than ever to believe that the early introduction of social security as a means to build decent societies will become a widely accepted development policy paradigm.

Notes

1. The authors wish to stress that the views expressed in this chapter do not necessarily reflect the positions of their organizations.
2. See the G8 Labour Ministers' Conference: Shaping the Social Dimensions of Globalization, Dresden, 6–8 May 2007, Chair's conclusions.
3. See United Nations, Economic and Social Council (E/2006)/L.8, para 19.
4. The ILO tabled and presented a discussion paper entitled 'Growth, Employment and Social Protection: a Strategy for Balanced Growth in a Global Market Economy'.
5. For micro-simulations in two low-income countries, see Gassmann and Behrendt (2006).
6. See Barrientos and Lloyd-Sherlock (2003) for an overview.

References

Abrahamson, P. 1999. 'The Scandinavian Model of Welfare', in MIRE-DREES, pp. 31–60.
Adamchak, D. 1995. 'Pensions and the Household Structure of Older Persons in Nambia', *Southern African Journal of Gerontology*, 4(2): 11–15.
Adato, M., Lund, F. and Mhlongo, P. 2003. 'Capturing "Work" in South Africa: Evidence from a Study of Poverty and Well-being in KwaZulu-Natal', paper presented at Policy Conference on Socially Embedded Inequality and Economic Mobility: Livelihoods, Social Networks and Exclusion in Peru and South Africa, Washington, DC, 4 December 2003.
Adema, W. and Ladaique, M. 2005. *Net Social Expenditure*, 2005 edition, Social, Employment and Migration Working Papers, No. 29 (Paris: OECD).
African Union. 2006. *Livingstone Call for Action on Social Protection*, Livingstone, Zambia.
Agell, J., Lindh, T. and Ohlsson, H. 1999. 'Growth and the Public Sector: a Reply', *European Journal of Political Economy*, 15: 359–66.
Agüero, J., Carter, M. R. and May, J. 2006. *Poverty and Inequality in the First Decade of South Africa's Democracy: What Can be Learned from Panel Data?* Department of Agricultural & Applied Economics, Staff Paper No. 493 (University of Wisconsin-Madison).
Akintola, O. 2004. *A Gendered Analysis of the Burden of Care on Family and Volunteer Caregivers in Uganda and South Africa*, Durban, Health Economics and HIV/AIDS Research Division (University of KwaZulu-Natal).
Akwanalo Mate, F. 2006. *Children's Property and Inheritance Rights: Experience of Orphans Affected by HIV/AIDS and Other Vulnerable Orphans in Africa*, Department of Social Policy (London: London School of Economics).
Alber, J. 1986. 'Germany', in P. Flora (ed.), *Growth to Limits: the Western European Welfare States Since World War II*. Vol. 2: *Germany, United Kingdom, Ireland and Italy* (Berlin: Walter de Gruyter).
Alderman, H., Hoddinott, J. and Kinsey, B. 2003. *Long-term Consequences of Early Childhood Malnutrition*, Food Consumption and Nutrition Division Discussion Paper No. 168 (Washington, DC: International Food Policy Research Institute).
Alesina, A. and Glaeser, E. 2004. *Fighting Poverty in the US and Europe: a World of Difference* (Oxford: Oxford University Press).
Alesina, A. and Spolaore, E. 2003. *The Size of Nations* (Cambridge, MA: MIT Press).
Allard, G. 2003. 'Jobs and Labor Market Institutions in the OECD', PhD dissertation (University of California-Davis).
Allard, G. and Lindert, P. 2006. *Euro-Productivity and Euro-Jobs since 1960: Which Institutions Really Matter?* NBER Working Paper 12460 (National Bureau of Economic Research).
Amin, S. 1997. *Capitalism in the Age of Globalization* (London and New York: Earthscan).
Ardington, E. and Lund, F. 1995. 'Pensions and Development: Social Security as Complementary to Programmes of Reconstruction and Development', *Development Southern Africa*, 12(4): 557–77.
Ashley, C. and Maxwell, S. 2001. 'Overview: Rethinking Rural Development', *Development Policy Review*, 19(4): 395–426.

Asian Development Bank. 2003. *Education: Our Framework, Policies and Strategies* (Manila: Asian Development Bank).

Åslund, A. 1997. 'Social Problems and Policy in Postcommunist Russia', in E. B. Kapstein and M. Mandelbaum (eds), *Sustaining the Transition: the Social Safety Net in Postcommunist Europe* (New York: Council on Foreign Relations), pp. 124–46.

Atkinson, A. B. 1991. 'A National Minimum? A History of Ambiguity in the Determination of Benefit Scales in Britain', in T. Wilson and D. Wilson (eds), *The State and Social Welfare* (Harlow: Longman).

Atkinson, A. B. 1995. 'Is the Welfare State Necessarily an Obstacle to Economic Growth?' *European Economic Review*, 39: 46–96.

Atkinson, A. B. 1996. 'The Distribution of Income: Evidence, Theories and Policy', *The Economist*, 144: 1–21.

Atkinson, A. B. 1998. *Poverty in Europe* (Oxford: Basil Blackwell).

Atkinson, A. B. 1999. *The Economic Consequences of Rolling Back the Welfare State* (Cambridge, MA: MIT Press).

Atkinson, A. B. 2002. *Income Inequality and the Welfare State in a Global Era*, The J. Douglas Gibson Lecture (New York, Queen's University).

Atkinson, A. B. (ed.) 2004. *New Sources of Development Finance*, UNU-WIDER (Oxford: Oxford University Press).

Atkinson, A. B. 2005. *Global Public Finance and Funding the Millennium Development Goals*, Jelle Zijlstra Lecture 4, Wassenaar, Netherlands Institute for Advanced Study in the Humanities and Social Sciences (NIAS).

Atkinson, T., Cantillon, B., Marlier, E. and Nolan, B. 2002. *Social Indicators: the EU and Social Inclusion* (Oxford: Oxford University Press).

Attias-Donfut, C. and Arber, S. 2000. 'Equity and Solidarity across the Generations', in S. Arber and C. Attias-Donfut (eds), *The Myth of Generational Conflict: the Family and State in Ageing Societies* (London: Routledge), pp. 1–21.

Auriol, E. and Warlters, M. 2002. *Taxation Base in Developing Countries*, mimeo (Toulouse, ARQADE).

Azariades, C. and Stachurski, J. forthcoming. 'Poverty Traps', in P. Aghion and S. N. Durlauf (eds), *Handbook of Economic Growth* (London: North Holland).

Banks, J., Disney, R., Duncan, A. and Van Reenen, J. 2005. 'The Internationalisation of Public Welfare Policy', *Economic Journal*, 115(502): C62–C81.

Barreto, F. E. (ed.) 1994. *Social Security Systems in Latin America* (Washington, DC: Inter-American Development Bank).

Barrett, C., Reardon, T. and Patrick, W. 2001. 'Non-farm Income Diversification and Household Livelihood Strategies in Rural Africa: Concepts, Dynamics and Policy Implications', *Food Policy*, 26(4): 315–32.

Barrientos, A. 2004. 'Latin America: Toward a Liberal-Informal Welfare Regime', in I. Gough, G. Wood, A. Barrientos, P. Bevan, P. David and G. Room (eds), *Insecurity and Welfare Regimes in Asia, Africa and Latin America* (Cambridge: Cambridge University Press), pp. 121–68.

Barrientos, A. 2006. 'The Missing Piece of Pension Reform in Latin America: Poverty Reduction', *Social Policy and Administration*, 40(4): 369–84.

Barrientos, A. 2007a. 'Modernizing Social Assistance to Promote Social Inclusion', in ILO (ed.), *Social Protection and Social Exclusion: Converging Efforts from a Global Perspective*, Conference Proceedings, Geneva: ILO–EU–Government of Portugal.

Barrientos, A. 2007b. 'Tax-financed Social Security', *International Social Security Review*, 60(2–3): 99–117.

Barrientos, A. 2008a. 'Cash Transfers for Older People Reduce Poverty and Inequality', in A. J. Bebbington, A. A. Dani, A. De Haan and M. Walton (eds), *Institutional Pathways to Equity: Addressing Inequality Traps* (Washington, DC: World Bank), pp. 169–92.

Barrientos, A. 2008b. 'Financing Social Protection', in A. Barrientos and D. Hulme (eds), *Social Protection for the Poor and Poorest: Concepts, Policies and Politics* (Basingstoke: Palgrave Macmillan).

Barrientos, A. and De Jong, J. 2004. *Child Poverty and Cash Transfers*, Childhood Poverty Research and Policy Centre CHIP, Working Paper 2, available from the Institute for Development Policy and Management, University of Manchester (also available from www.childpoverty.org).

Barrientos, A. and Holmes. R. 2007. Social Assistance in Developing Countries Database version 3.0 (Manchester, Brooks World Poverty Institute, University of Manchester).

Barrientos, A. and Lloyd-Sherlock, P. 2002. *Non-contributory Pensions and Social Protection*, Issues in Social Protection Discussion Paper 12 (Geneva: ILO).

Barrientos, A. and Lloyd-Sherlock, P. 2003. *Non-contributory Pensions and Poverty Prevention: a Comparative Study of Brazil and South Africa* (Manchester: IDPM and HelpAge International).

Barro, R. J. 1997. *Determinants of Economic Growth: a Cross-Country Empirical Study* (Cambridge, MA: MIT Press).

Barro, R. J. and Jong-Wha, L. 1993. 'Winners and Losers in Economic Growth', in *Proceedings of the World Bank Annual Conference on Development Economics* (Washington, DC: World Bank), pp. 267–314.

Barry, B. M. 1990. 'The Welfare State versus the Relief of Poverty', *Ethics*, 100(3): 503–29.

Baulch, B. and McCulloch, N. 1998. *Being Poor and Becoming Poor: Poverty Status and Poverty Transitions in Rural Pakistan*, Institute of Development Studies Working Paper 79 (Brighton, IDS, University of Sussex).

Beales, S. and German, T. 2006. *Situation Analysis of Social Protection and Cash Transfers in Africa Report* (London: Development Initiatives and HelpAge International).

Beckman, M. 2006. 'Resilient Society, Vulnerable People: a Study of Disaster Response and Recovery from Floods in Central Vietnam', PhD dissertation (Uppsala, Swedish University of Agricultural Sciences).

Benn, H. 2006. *First White Paper Speech of the Secretary of State for International Development*, 19 January (London: New Economics Foundation).

Berkowitz, E. D. 1997. 'The Historical Development of Social Security in the United States', in E. R. Kingson and J. H. Schulz (eds), *Social Security in the 21st Century* (New York and Oxford: Oxford University Press).

Bertrand, M., Mullainathan, S. and Miller, D. 2003. 'Public Policy and Extended Families: Evidence from Pensions in South Africa', *The World Bank Economic Review*, 17(1): 27–50.

Bertranou, F. M. and Grushka, C. O. 2002. *The Non-Contributory Pension Programme in Argentina: Assessing the Impact on Poverty Reduction*, ESS Paper 5 (Geneva: ILO).

Bertranou, F. M., van Ginneken, W. and Solorio, C. 2004. 'The Impact of Tax-Financed Pensions on Poverty Reduction in Latin America: Evidence from Argentina, Brazil, Chile, Costa Rica, and Uruguay', *International Social Security Review*, 57(4): 3–18.

Besley, T. 1997. 'Political Economy of Alleviating Poverty', in *Annual World Bank Conference on Development Economics 1996* (Washington, DC: World Bank), pp. 117–34.

Beveridge Report. 1942. *Social Insurance and Allied Services*, Cmd 6404 (London: HMSO).

Bhorat, H., Leibbrandt, M. and Woolard, I. 1999. *Understanding Contemporary Household Inequality in South Africa*, DPRU Working Paper 99 (Cape Town: University of Cape Town).

Blanchard, O. 2004. 'The Economic Future of Europe', *Journal of Economic Perspectives*, 18(4): 3–26.

Blanchard, O. and Portugal, P. 2001. 'What Hides Behind an Unemployment Rate: Comparing Portuguese and US Unemployment', *American Economic Review*, 91(1): 187–207.

Blanchard, O. and Wolfers, W. 2000. 'The Role of Shocks and Institutions in the Rise of European Unemployment: the Aggregate Evidence', *Economic Journal*, 110(462): C1–C33.

Blundell, R. and Johnson, P. 1999. 'Pensions and Retirement in the United Kingdom', in J. Gruber and D. Wise (eds), *Social Security Programs and Retirement around the World* (Chicago: University of Chicago Press), pp. 403–36.

Bolton, P. and Roland, G. 1997. 'The Break-up of Nations: a Political Economy Analysis', *Quarterly Journal of Economics*, 112(4): 1057–80.

Borzutsky, S. 2002. *Vital Connections: Politics, Social Security, and Inequality in Chile* (Notre Dame: University of Notre Dame Press).

Bowles, S., Durlauf, S. N. and Hoff, K. (eds) 2006. *Poverty Traps* (New York: Russell Sage Foundation and Princeton University Press).

Bradbury, B. and Jäntti, M. 2001. 'Child Poverty across the Industrialized World: Evidence from the Luxembourg Income Study', in K. Vleminckx and T. Smeeding (eds), *Child Well-being, Child Poverty and Child Policy in Modern Nations* (Bristol: The Policy Press), pp. 11–32.

Braithwaite, J., Grootaert, C. and Milanovic, B. 2000. *Poverty and Social Assistance in Transition Countries* (Basingstoke: Palgrave Macmillan).

Braun, M. 1982. *Die luxemburgische Sozialversicherung bis zum Zweiten Weltkrieg* (Stuttgart: Klett-Cotta).

Britto, T. 2006a. 'Conditional Cash Transfers in Latin America', in *Social Protection: the Role of Cash Transfers, Poverty in Focus* (Brasilia: UNDP, International Poverty Centre).

Britto, T. 2006b. 'Recent Trends in the Development Agenda of Latin America: an Analysis of Conditional Cash Transfers' (Brazil: Ministry of Social Development).

Brown, G. and Wolfensohn, J. 2004. 'A New Deal for the World's Poor', *The Guardian*, 16 February.

Budlender, B. and Woolard, I. 2006. *The Impact of the South African Child Support and Old Age Grants on Children's Schooling and Work* (Geneva: ILO).

Butterwegge, C. 2006. *Krise und Zukunft des Sozialstaates* (Wiesbaden: VS, Verl. für Sozialwissenschaften).

Cantillon, B., Marx, I., Rottiers, S. and Van Rie, T. 2007. *Een vergelijking van België binnen de Europese kopgroep: Postremus inter pares* (Antwerpen, Berichten/UA: Centrum voor Sociaal Beleid Herman Deleeck).

Cantillon, B., Van Mechelen, N. and Schulte, B. 2008. 'Minimum Income Policies in Old and New Member States', in J. Alber, T. Fahey and C. Saraceno (eds), *Handbook of Quality of Life in the Enlarged European Union* (Milton Park: Routledge), pp. 218–34.

Carrin, G. 2005. 'Social Health Insurance: Key Factors Affecting the Transition towards Universal Coverage', *International Social Security Review*, 58(1).

Carrin, G. and James, C. 2004. *Reaching Universal Coverage via Social Health Insurance*, Health System Financing, Expenditure and Resource Allocation Discussion Paper No. 2 (Geneva: WHO).

Carvalho, I. 2000. *Elderly Women and their Living Arrangements*, mimeo (Cambridge, MA: MIT Press).

Case, A. 2003. *Does Money Protect Health Status? Evidence from South Africa Pensions*, NBER Working Paper 8495 (Cambridge, MA: National Bureau of Economic Research).

Case, A. and Deaton, A. 1998. 'Large Cash Transfers to the Elderly in South Africa', *Economic Journal*, 108: 1330–61.

Case, A. and Menendez, A. 2007. 'Does Money Empower the Elderly? Evidence from the Agincourt Demographic Surveillance Area', *Scandinavian Journal of Public Health*, 35(S69): 157–64.

Case, A., Hosegood, V. and Lund, F. 2003. *The Reach of the South African Child Support Grant: Evidence from KwaZulu-Natal*, Working Paper 38, Centre for Social and Development Studies (Durban: University of Natal).

Case, A., Hosegood, V. and Lund, F. 2005. 'The Reach and Impact of the Child Support Grant in South Africa: Evidence from KwaZulu-Natal', *Development Southern Africa*, 22(4): 467–82.

Castles, F. G. 1982. 'The Impact of Parties on Public Expenditure', in F. G. Castles, *The Impact of Parties: Politics and Policies in Democratic Capitalist States* (London: Sage), pp. 21–96.

Castles, F. G. and Mitchell, D. 1993. 'Worlds of Welfare and Families of Nations', in F. G. Castles (ed.), *Families of Nations: Patterns of Public Policy in Western Democracies* (Aldershot: Dartmouth).

Chang, H.-J. 2003. *Kicking Away the Ladder: Development Strategy in Historical Perspective* (London: Anthem Press).

Charlton, R. and McKinnon, R. 2001. *Pensions in Development* (Aldershot: Ashgate).

Chen, M., Vanek, J., Lund, F. and Heintz, J., with Jhabvala, R. and Bonner, C. 2005. *Progress of the World's Women: Women, Work and Poverty* (New York: UNIFEM).

Chen, S. and Ravallion, M. 2001. 'How Did the World's Poorest Fare in the 1990s?' Development Research Group, *Review of Income and Wealth* (Washington, DC: World Bank), pp. 1–33.

Chen, S. and Ravallion, M. 2008. *The Developing World is Poorer Than We Thought, but No Less Successful in the Fight Against Poverty*, Policy Research Working Paper 4703 (Washington, DC: World Bank).

Chen, W.-H. and Corak, M. 2005. *Child Poverty and Changes in Child Poverty in Rich Countries since 1900*, LIS Working Paper No. 405 (Luxembourg: LIS).

Chinkin, C. 2001. 'The United Nations Decade for the Elimination of Poverty: What Role for International Law?' *Current Legal Problems*, 54: 553–89.

Chinkin, C. 2002. 'The United Nations Decade for the Elimination of Poverty: What Role for International Law?' in *Current Legal Problems 2001* (Oxford: Oxford University Press).

Chisinga, B. 2005. 'Practical and Policy Dilemmas of Targeting Free Inputs', in S. Levy (ed.), *Starter Packs: a Strategy to Fight Hunger in Developing Countries* (Wallingford: CABI Publishing), pp. 141–54.

Chossudovsky, M. 1998. *The Globalization of Poverty: Impacts of World Bank Reforms* (London and New Jersey: Zed Books).

Cichon, M. and Hagemejer, K. 2006. *Social Security for All: Investing in Global Social and Economic Development: a Consultation*, Issues in Social Protection Discussion Paper No. 16 (Geneva: ILO).

Cichon, M., Scholz, W., van de Meerendonk, A., Hagemejer, K., Bertranou, F. and Plamondon, P. 2004. *Financing Social Protection* (Geneva: ILO and ISSA).

Clasen, J. (ed.) 1997. *Social Insurance in Europe* (Bristol: Policy Press).

Clasen, J. and Erskine, A. 1998. 'Meltdown Inevitable? National Insurance in Britain', *Benefits*, 23: 1–4.

Coady, D. 2003. *Alleviating Structural Poverty in Developing Countries: the Approach of Progresa in Mexico*, mimeo (Washington, DC: International Food Policy Research Institute).

Coady, D., Grosh, M. and Hoddinott, J. 2004. *Targeting of Transfers in Developing Countries: Review of Lessons and Experience*, World Bank Regional and Sectoral Studies (Washington, DC: World Bank)

Cohen, W. 1952. 'Income Maintenance for the Aged', *Annals of the American Academy of Political and Social Science*, 154.

Cohen, W., Ball, R. M. and Myers, R. J. 1954. 'Social Security Act Amendments of 1954: a Summary and Legislative History', *Social Security Bulletin*, 16.

Commission for Africa. 2005. *Our Common Interest: Report of the Commission for Africa* (London: Commission for Africa).

Commission on Macroeconomics and Health. 2001. *Macroeconomics and Health: Investing in Health for Economic Development* (Geneva: World Health Organization).

Committee on Economic, Social and Cultural Rights (CESCR). 2006. *General Comment No. 20, The Right to Social Security Article 9* (Geneva).

Committee of Inquiry into a Comprehensive System of Social Security for South Africa. 2002. *Transforming the Present. Protecting the Future*, Draft Consolidated Report (Pretoria: Committee of Inquiry into a Comprehensive System of Social Security for South Africa).

Commonwealth Human Rights Initiative. 2001. *Human Rights and Poverty Eradication* (New Delhi).

Conseil d'Etat. 2006. *Le Conseil d'Etat face à l'évolution de la société luxembourgeoise* (Luxembourg: Conseil d'Etat).

Corak, M. 2005. *Principles and Practicalities for Measuring Child Poverty in Rich Countries*, LIS Working Paper No. 406 (Luxembourg: LIS).

Cornia, G. A. 1999. *Liberalisation, Globalisation and Income Distribution*, WIDER Working Paper 157 (Helsinki: UNU-World Institute for Development Economic Research).

Cornia, G. A. (ed.) 2002. *Harnessing Globalization for Children* (Florence: UNICEF Innocenti Research Centre).

Council of Europe. 1950. *European Convention for the Protection of Human Rights and Fundamental Freedoms* (Strasbourg).

Council of Europe. 1953. *European Interim Agreement on Social Security Schemes Relating to Old Age, Invalidity and Survivors* (Strasbourg).

Council of Europe. 1996. *European Social Charter (revised)* (Strasbourg).

CPRC (Chronic Poverty Research Centre). 2005. *The Chronic Poverty Report 2004–05* (Manchester: CPRC, Institute for Development Policy and Management, University of Manchester).

Croome, D. 2006. *Lesotho Pensions Impact Project*, background paper submitted to the Economic Policy Research Institute, Cape Town.

Cruz-Saco, Oyague M. A. and Mesa-Lago, C. (eds) 1998. *Do Options Exist? The Reform of Pension and Health Care System in Latin America* (Pittsburgh: Pittsburgh University Press).

Cullinan, P. R. 1991. 'Social Security and Income Distribution', in L. Osberg (ed.), *Economic Inequality and Poverty: International Perspectives* (New York and London: M. E. Sharpe).

Dagdeviren, H., van der Hoeven, R. and Weeks, J. 2001. *Redistribution Matters: Growth for Poverty Reduction*, Employment Paper 2001/2010 (Geneva: ILO).

Dana, J., Gilbert, C. L. and Shim, E. 2005. 'Hedging Grain Price Risk in SADC: Case Studies of Malawi and Zambia', paper presented at World Bank–DFID workshop Managing Food Price Risk and Instability, Washington, DC, 28 February–1 March.

Daniel, J., Southall, R. and Lutchman, J. (eds) 2005. *State of the Nation: South Africa 2004–2005* (Cape Town: HSRC Press).

De Ferranti, D., Perry, G. E., Ferreira, F. H. G. and Walton, M. 2004. *Inequality in Latin America: Breaking With History?* (Washington, DC: World Bank).

de Janvry, A. and Sadoulet, E. 1996. *Growth, Poverty and Inequality in Latin America: a Causal Analysis, 1970–94*, Working Paper (Berkeley: University of California).

De Kam, F. and Owens, J. 1999. 'Financing Social Protection in the 21st Century', in Ministry of Social Affairs and Health, *Financing Social Protection in Europe* (Helsinki).

de la Brière, B. and Rawlings, L. 2006. 'Examining Conditional Cash Transfer Programmes: a Role for Increased Social Inclusion?', in ILO, *Social Protection and Inclusion: Experiences and Policy Issues* (Geneva), pp. 9–32.

de Neubourg, C. 2002. *Institutional Design and Institutional Incentives in Social Safety Nets*, Social Protection Discussion Paper No. 0226 (Washington, DC: World Bank).

de Neubourg, C. 2006. 'New Worlds of Welfare Capitalism', paper presented at the conference New Worlds of Welfare Capitalism, Maastricht, April.

de Neubourg, C. and Castonguay, J. 2006. 'Enhancing Productivity: Social Policy as Investment Policy', in W. Mitchell, J. Muysken and T. van Veen (eds), *Growth and Cohesion in the European Union* (Cheltenham: Edward Elgar), pp. 181–206.

de Neubourg, C., Castonguay, J. and Roelen, K. 2007. *Social Safety Nets and Targeted Social Assistance: Lessons from the European Experience*, Social Protection Discussion Paper No. 0718 (Washington, DC: World Bank).

De Schutter, O. (ed.) 2006. *Transnational Corporations and Human Rights* (Oxford: Hart).

De Schweinitz, K. 1961. *England's Road to Social Security* (New York: A. S. Barnes).

De Swaan, A. 1988. *Care of the State: Health Care, Education and Welfare in Europe and the USA in the Modern Era* (New York and Cambridge: Oxford University Press and Polity Press).

Deacon, A. and Bradshaw, J. 1983. *Reserved for the Poor: the Means-Test in British Social Policy* (Oxford: Basil Blackwell).

Deacon, B. 2005. 'From "Safety Nets" Back to "Universal Social Provision": Is the Global Tide Turning?' *Global Social Policy*, 5(1): 19–28.

Delaney, A., Budlender, D., Moultrie, T., Schneider, M. and Kimmie, Z. 2005. *Investigation into the Increase in Uptake of Disability and Care Dependency Grants since December 2001*, Braamfontein: Community Agency for Social Enquiry (CASE).

DeLong, J. Bradford. 2002. *Macroeconomics* (New York: McGraw-Hill).

Department of Social Development, South Africa. 2002. *Transforming the Present – Protecting the Future*, Consolidated Report of the Committee of Inquiry into a Comprehensive System of Social Security for South Africa.

Dercon, S. 2005. 'Risk, Vulnerability and Poverty in Africa', *Journal of African Economies*, 14: 483–8.

Dercon, S. 2006. 'Risk, Poverty and Growth', paper presented to the Department for International Development, London (March).

Dercon, S. and Hoddinott, J. 2003. *Health Shocks and Poverty Persistence*, WIDER Discussion Paper No. 2003/08 (January).

Dercon, S., Hoddinott, J. and Woldehanna, T. 2005. 'Shocks and Consumption in 15 Ethiopian Villages, 1999–2004', *Journal of African Economies*, 14: 559–85.

Dev, M. S. 2004. *Safety Nets for Chronic Poor in India: an Overview*, Working Paper 19 (New Delhi: Chronic Poverty Research Centre and the Indian Institute of Public Administration).

Devereux, S. 2001. 'Livelihood Insecurity and Social Protection: Re-emerging Issues in Rural Development', *Development Policy Review*, 19(4): 507–19.

Devereux, S., Mvula, P. and Solomon, C. 2006. *After the FACT: an Evaluation of Concern Worldwide's Food and Cash Transfers Project in Three Districts of Malawi*, a report for Concern Worldwide by the Institute for Development Studies (Concern Worldwide).

DFID. 2004. 'How to Accelerate Pro-Poor Growth: a Basic Framework for Policy Analysis', DFID Pro-Poor Growth Briefing Note 2 (September).

DFID. 2005a. *The Choice of Aid Instruments for Government-to-Government Aid*, DFID Issues Paper (London).

DFID. 2005b. *Growth and Poverty Reduction: the Role of Agriculture*, DFID Policy Paper (London).

DFID. 2005c. *Social Transfers and Chronic Poverty: Emerging Evidence and the Challenge Ahead*, DFID Practice Paper (London).

DFID. 2006. *Eliminating World Poverty: Making Governance Work for the Poor*, DFID White Paper (London).

Diao, X. and Nin Pratt, A. with Gautam, M., Keough, M., Chamberlin, J., You, L., Puetz, D., Resnick, D. and Yu, B. 2005. *Growth Options and Poverty Reduction in Ethiopia: a Spatial, Economy-wide Model Analysis for 2004–15*, DSGD Discussion Paper No. 20 (Washington, DC: IFPRI).

Disney, R., Emmerson, C. and Smith, S. 2004. 'Pension Reform and Economic Performance in Britain in the 1980s and 1990s', in D. Card, R. Blundell and R. B. Freeman (eds), *Seeking a Premier Economy: the Economic Effects of British Economic Reforms, 1980–2000* (Chicago: Chicago University Press), pp. 233–73.

Dollar, D. and Kray, A. 2000. *Growth is Good for the Poor* (Washington, DC: World Bank).

Doocy, S. 2006. 'Implementing Cash for Work Programmes in post-Tsunami Aceh', *Disasters*, 30(3): 277–96.

Dorward, A., Sabates-Wheeler, R., MacAuslan, I., Buckley, C., Kydd, J. and Chirwa, E. 2006. *Promoting Agriculture for Social Protection or Social Protection for Agriculture?* Future Agricultures Briefing (available at: http://www.future-agricultures.org/pdf%20files/Briefing_SP_1.pdf).

Duflo, E. 2000. *Grandmothers and Granddaughters: Old Age Pension and Intra-household Allocation in South Africa*, Massachusetts Institute of Technology, Department of Economics Working Paper (Massachusetts: MIT).

Duncan, O. D. 1984. *Notes on Social Measurement, Historical and Critical* (New York: Russell Sage Foundation).

Eardley, T., Bradshaw, J., Ditch, J., Gough, I. and Whiteford, P. 1996a. *Social Assistance in OECD Countries: Country Reports* (London: HMSO).

Eardley, T., Bradshaw, J., Ditch, J., Gough, I. and Whiteford, P. 1996b. *Social Assistance in OECD Countries: Synthesis Report* (London: HMSO).

Edwards, K. C. 1944. *Luxembourg*, Geographical Handbook Series (London: Naval Intelligence Division).

Esping-Andersen, G. 1990. *The Three Worlds of Welfare Capitalism* (Cambridge: Polity Press).

Esping-Andersen, G. 1999. *Social Foundations of Postindustrial Economies* (Oxford: Oxford University Press).

Esping-Andersen, G. and Korpi, W. 1987. 'From Poor Relief to Institutional Welfare States: the Development of Scandinavian Social Policy', in R. Erikson, E. J. Hansen, S. Ringen and H. Uusitalo (eds), *The Scandinavian Model: Welfare States and Welfare Research* (New York: M. E. Sharpe).

ESPROSS. 2004. *European System of Integretated Social Protection Indicators* (Luxembourg: Eurostat).

European Parliament. 2005. *Resolution on a European Social Model for the Future* (2005/2248(INI)).

European Parliament. 2006. *Legislative Resolution on the Council Common Position for Adopting a Directive of the European Parliament and of the Council on Services in the Internal Market* (10003/4/2006 – C6-0270/2006 – 2004/0001(COD)).

Eurostat. 1996. *Social Protection Expenditure and Receipts 1980–94* (Brussels: Statistical Office of the European Communities).

Eurostat. 1999. *Annual Statistical Handbook of the European Union* (Brussels: Statistical Office of the European Communities)

Farrington, J., Slater, R. and Holmes, R. 2004a. *The Search for Synergies between Social Protection and the Productive Sectors: the Agriculture Case*, Working Paper 232 (London: Overseas Development Institute).

Farrington, J., Slater, R. and Holmes, R. 2004b. *Social Protection and Pro-poor Agricultural Growth: What Scope for Synergies*, Natural Resource Perspectives 91 (London: Overseas Development Institute).

Ferge, Z. 1997. 'And What if the State Fades Away? The Civilizing Process and the State', paper presented at the conference of the European Sociological Association, 27–30 August, Wivenhoe, Essex University.

Ferrera, M. 1986. 'Italy', in P. Flora (ed.), *Growth to Limits: the Western European Welfare States Since World War II*. Vol. 2: *Germany, United Kingdom, Ireland and Italy* (Berlin: Walter de Gruyter).

Filquiera, F. and Moraes, J. A. 1999. *Political Environments, Sector Specific Configurations, and Strategic Devices: Understanding Institutional Reform in Uruguay*, Working Paper R-351 (Inter-American Development Bank).

Fisher, G. M. 1976. 'Poverty among the Aged and Social Security Benefits', in F. E. Waddell (ed.), *The Elderly Consumer* (Columbia, Maryland: The Human Ecology Center, Antioch College), pp. 54–64.

Flora, P. 1981. 'Stein Rokkans MakroModell des politischen Entwicklung Europas: Ein Rekonstruktionsversuch', *Kölner Zeitschrift für Soziologie und Sozialpsychologie*, 33(3): 397–436.

Flora, P. (ed.) 1986. *Growth to Limits: the Western European Welfare States since World War II*, 2 vols, Vol. 1: *Sweden, Norway, Finland, Denmark*; Vol. 2: *Germany, United Kingdom, Ireland and Italy* (Berlin: Walter de Gruyter).

Flora, P. and Heidenheimer, A. J. (eds) 1981. *The Development of Welfare States in Europe and America* (New Brunswick and London: Transaction Books).

Fölster, S. and Henrekson, M. 1999. 'Growth and the Public Sector: a Critique of the Critics', *European Journal of Political Economy*, 15: 3337–58.

Foster, J. and Székely, M. 2001. 'Is Economic Growth Good for the Poor?' paper presented at the WIDER Development Conference on Growth and Poverty, Helsinki, 25–26 May.

Fouarge, D. 2003. *Costs of Non-social Policy: Towards an Economic Framework of Quality Social Policies and the Costs of Not Having Them* (Brussels: Employment and Social Affairs DG, European Union).

Frenkel, M. and Rimbert-Hemmer, H. 1999. *Grundlagen der Wachstumstheorie* (Vahlen München).

Fritzen, S. 2003. 'Escaping the Low Income–Low Social Protection Trap in Developing Countries: What are the Options?' *Indian Journal of Social Development*, 3(2).

Galston, W. A. 2006. 'Political Feasibility: Interests and Power', in M. Moran, M. Rein and R. E. Goodin (eds), *The Oxford Handbook of Public Policy* (Oxford: Oxford University Press), pp. 543–56.

Gassmann, F. and Behrendt, C. 2006. *Cash Benefits in Low-Income Countries: Simulating the Effect on Poverty Reduction for Tanzania and Senegal*, Issues in Social Protection Discussion Paper 15 (Geneva: ILO).

George, V. and Wilding, P. 1976. *Ideology and Social Welfare* (London: Routledge & Kegan Paul).

Ghai, D. 2001. *Social Security for All*, Technical Commissions, Leo Wildman Symposium, Stockholm (Geneva: International Social Security Association).

Gilbert, B. 1966. *The Evolution of National Insurance in Great Britain: the Origins of the Welfare State* (London: Michael Joseph).

Gill, I., Packard, T. and Yermo, J. 2004. *Keeping the Promise of Social Security in Latin America* (Stanford: Stanford University Press).

Gilson, L., Russell, S. et al. 1998. *Exempting the Poor: a Review and Evaluation of the Low-income Card Scheme in Thailand* (London: London School of Hygiene and Tropical Medicine).

Goldblatt, B. 2005. 'Gender and Social Assistance in the First Decade of Democracy: a Case Study of South Africa's Child Support Grant', *Politikon*, 32(2): 239–57.

Goodin, R. E., Heady, B., Muffels, R. and Dirvan, H.-J. 1999. *The Real Worlds of Welfare Capitalism* (Cambridge: Cambridge University Press).

Gordon, D. 2008. 'Children, Policy and Justice', in G. Craig, T. Burchardt and D. Dordon (eds), *Social Justice and Public Policy: Seeking Fairness in Diverse Societies* (Bristol: Policy Press).

Gordon, D., Nandy, S., Pantazis, C., Pemberton, S. and Townsend, P. 2003. *Child Poverty in the Developing World*, report to UNICEF (Bristol: Policy Press).

Gordon, D., Nandy, S., Pantazis, C. and Pemberton, S. 2009. *Global Estimates of Adult and Child Poverty* (Bristol: Policy Press).

Gore, C. 2000. 'The Rise and Fall of the Washington Consensus as a Paradigm for Developing Countries', *World Development*, 28(5): 789–804.

Gough, I. 2004. 'East Asia: the Limits of Productivist Regimes', in I. Gough and G. Wood (eds), *Insecurity and Welfare Regimes in Asia, Africa, and Latin America* (Cambridge: Cambridge University Press), pp. 169–201.

Gough, I. and G. Wood (eds) 2004. *Insecurity and Welfare Regimes in Asia, Africa and Latin America* (Cambridge: Cambridge University Press).

Government of Kenya. 2007. Government website: http://www.vice-president.go.ke/ (accessed 13 April 2007).

Government of the People's Republic of Bangladesh. 2005. *Unlocking the Potential National Strategy for Accelerated Poverty Reduction*, General Economics Division Planning Commission, Dhaka, Bangladesh.

Government of Zambia, African Union and HelpAge International. 2006. 'Social Cash Transfers for Africa: a Transformative Agenda for the 21st Century', intergovernmental regional conference report, Livingstone, Zambia, 20–23 March (London: HelpAge International).

Graham, C. 2002. *Public Attitudes Matter: a Conceptual Framework for Accounting for Political Economy in Safety Nets and Social Assistance Policies*, Social Protection Discussion Paper 0233 (Washington, DC: World Bank).

Gramlich, E. M. 1997. 'How Does Social Security Affect the Economy?' in E. R. Kingston and J. H. Schulz (eds), *Social Security in the 21st Century* (New York: Oxford University Press), pp. 147–55.

Gray-Molina, G. 1999. *La economía política de reformas institucionales en Bolivia*, Working Paper R-350 (Washington, DC: Inter-American Development Bank).

Grow up Free from Poverty Coalition. 2006. *Achieving Our Dreams for 2015* (London).

Gruskin, S., Mills, E. J. and Tarantola, D. 2007. 'History, Principles and Practice of Health and Human Rights', *The Lancet*, 370: 9585.

Haacker, M. 2004. *The Macroeconomics of HIV/AIDS* (Washington, DC: International Monetary Fund).

Haarmann, C. and Haarmann, D. 2007. 'From Survival to Decent Employment: Basic Income Security in Namibia', *Basic Income Studies*, 2(1), Art. 11.

Haber, W. and Cohen W. J. 1960. *Social Security: Programmes, Problems and Policies: Selected Readings* (Illinois: Irwin).

Hall, A. and Midgeley, J. 2004. *Social Policy for Development* (London: Sage).

Hall, K. 2005. 'Accommodating the Poor? A Review of the Housing Subsidy Scheme and its Implications for Children', in A. Leatt and S. Rosa (eds), *Targeting Poverty Alleviation to Make Children's Rights Real* (Cape Town: Children's Institute, University of Cape Town, CD-ROM).

Haq Mul, K. I. and Grunberg, I. (eds) 1996. *The Tobin Tax* (Oxford: Oxford University Press).

Harrigan, J. 2005. 'Food Security Policies and Starter Packs: a Challenge for Donors?' in S. Levy (ed.), *Starter Packs: a Strategy to Fight Hunger in Developing Countries* (Wallingford: CABI Publishing), pp. 229–48.

Harvey, P. and Savage, K. 2006. *No Small Change: Oxfam GB Malawi and Zambia Emergency Cash Transfer Projects: a Synthesis of Key Learning* (London: Humanitarian Policy Group, Overseas Development Institute).

Hatland, A., Kuhnle, S. and Romøren, T. I. 2001. *Den norske velferdsstaten*, 3rd edn (Oslo: Ad Notam Gyldendal/Gyldendal Akademisk).

Heckman, J. J. 1979. 'Sample Selection Bias as a Specification Error', *Econometrica*, 47(1): 153–61.

Held, D. 1995. *Democracy and the Global Order: From the Modern State to Cosmopolitan Governance* (London: Polity Press).

Held, D. 2004. *Global Covenant: the Social Democratic Alternative to the Washington Consensus* (Cambridge: Polity Press).

HelpAge India. 2003. *Non-contributory Pensions in India: a Case Study of Uttar Pradesh* (London).

HelpAge International. 2004. *Age and Security: How Social Pensions Can Deliver Effective Aid to Poor Older People and their Families* (London).

Hemson, D. and Owusu-Ampomah, K. 2005. 'A Better Life for All? Service Delivery and Poverty Alleviation', in J. Daniel, R. Southall and J. Lutchman (eds), *State of the Nation: South Africa 2004–2005* (Cape Town: HSRC Press).

Hertz, N. 2001. *The Silent Takeover: Global Capitalism and the Death of Bureaucracy* (London: William Heinemann).

Hicks, A. M. and Swank, D. H. 1992. 'Politics, Institutions and Welfare Spending in Industrialized Democracies, 1960–82', *American Political Science Review*, 86(3): 658–74.

Hines, C. 2001. *Localization: a Global Manifesto* (London: Earthscan).

Hirsch, D. (ed.) 1997. *Social Protection and Inclusion: European Challenge for the UK* (York: Joseph Rowntree Foundation).

Hodges, A., Dufay, A. C., Dashdorj, K., Jong, K. Y., Mungun, T. and Budragchaa, U. 2007. 'Child Benefits and Poverty Reduction: Evidence from Mongolia's Child Money Programme', policy research paper presented at the UNICEF Conference, Maastricht, April, Working Paper Maastricht Graduate School of Governance, February.

Hohaus, R. A 1960. 'Income Security for a Free Society,' in W. Haber and W. J. Cohen (eds), *Social Security: Programmes, Problems and Policies* (Illinois: Richard Irwin).

Holzmann, R. and Jorgensen, S. 2000. *Social Risk Management: a New Conceptual Framework for Social Protection and Beyond*, Social Protection Discussion Paper No. 0006 (Washington, DC: World Bank).

Huber, E. 1996. 'Options for Social Policy in Latin America: Neoliberal versus Social Democratic Models', in G. Esping-Andersen (ed.), *Welfare States in Transition: National Adaptations in Global Economies* (London: Sage).

Huber, E. and Stephens, J. D. 2001. *Development and Crisis of the Welfare State: Parties and Policies in Global Markets* (Chicago: Chicago University Press).

Hudson, E. (ed.) 1996. *Merchants of Misery: How Corporate America Profits from Poverty* (Maine: Courage).

Humblet, M. and Silva, R. 2002. *Standards for the XXIst Century: Social Security* (Geneva: ILO).

Hunter, R. 1905. *Poverty* (New York: Macmillan).

Hussain, A. 2002. 'Urban Poverty in China: Incidence and Policy Response', in P. Townsend and D. Gordon (eds), *World Poverty: New Policies to Defeat an Old Enemy* (Bristol: Policy Press).

Hussain, A. 2004. *Overview of Social Security in China*, mimeo (Geneva: ILO).

IFAD. 2001. *Rural Poverty Report* (Rome: International Fund for Agricultural Development).

ILO. 1919. Constitution of the International Labour Organization. Adopted 1919 and subsequently amended, Geneva.

ILO. 1984. *Into the 21st Century: the Development of Social Security*, Geneva.

ILO. 2001a. *Social Security: a New Consensus*, Geneva.

ILO. 2001b. *Social Security: Issues, Challenges and Prospects*, Report VI, International Labour Conference, 89th Session, Geneva.

ILO. 2001c. *The ILO Tripartite Declaration of Principles Concerning Multinational Enterprises and Social Policy*, 3rd edition, Geneva.

ILO. 2002a. *Global Social Trust: Investing in the World's Social Future*, Geneva.

ILO. 2002b. *Women and Men in the Informal Economy: a Statistical Picture*. Geneva: International Labour Office, Employment Sector.

ILO. 2004. *Report of the Director-General on the World Commission on the Social Dimensions of Globalization*, Report to the International Labour Conference, 92nd Session, Geneva.

ILO. 2005. *Social Protection as a Productive Factor*, GB.294/ESP/4, November, Geneva.

ILO. 2006a. *Social Security for All: Investing in Global Social and Economic Development: a Consultation*, Issues in Social Protection, Discussion Paper 16, Geneva.

ILO. 2006b. *The End of Child Labour: Within Reach*, Geneva.

ILO. 2006c. *Social Protection and Inclusion: Experiences and Policy Issues*, STEP Programme of the International Labour Office, Geneva.

ILO. 2007a. Conclusions of the 11th African Regional Conference, Addis Ababa, 24–27 April.

ILO. 2007b. *Social Health Protection: an ILO Strategy towards Universal Access to Health Care – a Consultation*, Issues in Social Protection Discussion Paper 19, Geneva.

ILO. 2008a. *Can Low-income Countries Afford Basic Social Security?* Social Security Policy Briefings 3, Geneva.

ILO. 2008b. *Setting Social Security Standards in a Global Society: an Analysis of Present State, Practice and Future Options for Global Social Security Standard Setting in the International Labour Organization*, Social Security Policy Briefings, Paper 2, Geneva.

ILO. Forthcoming. *Social Security for All: Investing in Social Justice and Economic Development*, Social Security Policy Briefing No. 4, Geneva.

ILO. Various years. *World Employment Report*, Geneva.

IMF. 2003. *World Economic Outlook*, April (Washington, DC: International Monetary Fund).

Innocenti, UNICEF. 2005. *Innocenti Report Card No. 4*, Florence.

International Poverty Centre. 2006. *Social Protection: the Role of Cash Transfers*. Poverty in Focus (Brasilia: International Poverty Centre).

International Poverty Centre. 2008. *Cash Transfers: Lessons from Africa and Latin America*, Poverty in Focus, No. 15 (Brasilia: International Poverty Centre).

Iverson, T. and Soskice, D. 2000. 'An Asset Theory of Social Policy Preferences', paper presented to the annual meeting of the American Political Science Association, Wardman Park.

Iversen, T. and Soskice, D. 2008. 'Electoral Institutions, Parties and the Politics of Class: Explaining the Formation of Redistributive Coalitions', in C. Anderson and P. Beramendi (eds), *Democracy, Inequality and Representation* (New York: Russell Sage), pp. 93–126.

Jazairy, I., Algamir, M. and Panuccio, T. 1995. *The State of World Rural Poverty* (London: IFDA).

Jesuit, D., Rainwater, L. and Smeeding, T. 2002. 'Regional Poverty within Rich Countries', in J. A. Bishop and Y. Amiel (eds), *Inequality, Welfare and Poverty: Theory and Measurement*, Vol. 9 (New York: Elsevier Science).

Johansen, L. N. 1986. 'Denmark', in P. Flora (ed.), *Growth to Limits: the Western European Welfare States since World War II*. Vol. 1: *Sweden, Norway, Finland and Denmark* (Berlin: Walter de Gruyter).

Jones, C. I. 2002. *Introduction to Economic Growth*. 2nd edn (New York and London: W. W. Norton & Company).

Justino, P. 2003. *Social Security in Developing Countries: Myth or Necessity? Evidence from India*, Poverty Research Unit at Sussex Working Paper No. 20 (University of Sussex, Brighton).

Kakwani, N. and Son, H. H. 2006. *New Global Poverty Counts*, Working Paper No. 20 (Brasilia: UNDP International Poverty Centre).

Kakwani, N., Khandker, S. and Son, H. H. 2004. *Pro-Poor Growth: Concepts and Measurement with Country Case Studies*, Working Paper No. 1 (Brasilia: UNDP International Poverty Centre).

Kakwani, N., Soares, F. and Son, H. H. 2005. *Conditional Cash Transfers in African Countries* (Brasilia: UNDP International Poverty Centre).

Kallmann, K. 2005. 'Food for Thought: a Review of the National School Nutrition Progamme', in A. Leatt and S. Rosa (eds), *Targeting Poverty Alleviation to Make*

Children's Rights Real (Cape Town: Children's Institute, University of Cape Town, CD-ROM).

Kanbur, R. 1999. *Income Distribution and Growth*, World Bank Working Papers No. 98–13 (Washington, DC: World Bank).

Kanbur, R. 2000. *Economic Policy, Distribution and Poverty: the Nature of Disagreements*, for the Swedish Parliamentary Commission on Global Development, 22 September.

Kangas, O. 1991. *The Politics of Social Rights: Studies on the Dimensions of Sickness Insurance in OECD Countries* (Stockholm: Swedish Institute for Social Research).

Kaniki, S. and Samson, M. 2007. *Successful Lessons of Southern African Experience in Implementing Social Transfer Programmes to Reduce Poverty*, report commissioned by the Southern Africa Trust (Cape Town: Economic Policy Research Institute).

Kato, J. 2003. *Regressive Taxation and the Welfare State: Path Dependence and Policy Diffusion* (Cambridge: Cambridge University Press).

Kautto, M. 1999. 'Is there a Nordic Model of Financing Social Protection?' in Ministry of Social Affairs and Health, *Financing Social Protection in Europe* (Helsinki: Ministry of Social Affairs and Health).

Kay, S. J. 2000. 'The Politics of Postponement: Political Incentives and the Sequencing of Social Security Expenditures in Argentina and Uruguay', paper presented at the Year 2000 International Research Conference on Social Security, Helsinki, September.

Kay, S. J. and Sinha, T. (eds) 2008. *Lessons from Pension Reform in the Americas* (Oxford: Oxford University Press).

Kebede, E. 2006. 'Moving from Emergency Food Aid to Predictable Cash Transfers: Recent Experience in Ethiopia', *Development Policy Review*, 24(5): 579–99.

Keefer, P. and Khemani, S. 2003. 'The Political Economy of Public Expenditures', unpublished paper (Washington, DC: World Bank).

Kenworthy, L. 2003. *An Equality–Growth Trade-Off?* Luxembourg Income Study Working Paper No. 362.

Kenworthy, L. and Pontusson, J. 2005. 'Rising Inequality and the Politics of Redistribution in Affluent Countries', *Perspectives on Politics*, 3: 449–71.

Keswell, M. 2005. 'Social Networks, Extended Families, and Consumption Smoothing: Field Evidence from South Africa', paper delivered at the 2005 conference of the Economics Society of South Africa.

Kingson, E. R. and Schulz, J. H. (eds) 1997. *Social Security in the 21st Century* (New York: Oxford University Press).

Klasen, S. and Woolard, I. 2005. *Surviving Employment without State Support: Unemployment and Household Formation in South Africa*, Working Paper No. 05/129 (Cape Town: Centre for Social Science Research, University of Cape Town).

Kneller, R., Bleaney, M. and Gemmell, N. 1999. 'Fiscal Policy and Growth: Evidence from OECD Countries', *Journal of Public Economics*, 74: 171–90.

Kornai, J. and Eggleston, K. 2001. *Welfare, Choice, and Solidarity in Transition: Reforming the Health Sector in Eastern Europe* (Cambridge and New York: Cambridge University Press).

Korten, D. C. 1996. *When Corporations Rule the World* (London Earthscan).

Koskela, E. and Viren, M. 1983. 'Social Security and Household Savings in an International Cross Section', *American Economic Review*, 73(1): 212–17.

Kotlikoff, L. J. and Hagist, C. 2005. *Who's Going Broke? Comparing Growth in Healthcare Costs in Ten OECD Countries*, NBER Working Paper No. 11833 (Cambridge, MA: NBER).

Kozul-Wright, R. and Rowthorn, R. 1998. *Transnational Corporations and the Global Economy* (Helsinki, Finland: UNU World Institute for Development Economic Research).

Kramer, M. 1997. 'Social Protection Policies and Safety Nets in East-Central Europe: Dilemmas of the Postcommunist Transformation', in E. B. Kapstein and M. Mandelbaum (eds), *Sustaining the Transition: the Social Safety Net in Postcommunist Europe* (New York: Council on Foreign Relations), pp. 46–123.

Krüger, P. 2006. *Das unberechenbare Europa* (Stuttgart: Kohlhammer).

Kuhnle, S. and Hort, S. E. O. 2004. *The Developmental Welfare State in Scandinavia: Lessons for the Developing World*, Social Policy and Development Programme Paper No. 17 (Geneva: UNRISD).

Kulke, U. and López Morales, G. 2007. 'Social Security – International Standards and the Right to Social Security: Social Security as a Human Right', in E. Riedel (ed.), *Social Security as a Human Right* (Heidelberg: Springer), pp. 91–102.

Kulke, U., Cichon, M. and Pal, K. 2006. 'Changing Tides: a Revival of a Rights-Based Approach to Social Security', unpublished paper, Social Security Department (Geneva: ILO).

Kumaranayake, L., Kurowski, C. and Conteh, L. 2001. *Costs of Scaling up Priority Health Interventions in Low-income and Selected Middle-income Countries: Methodology and Estimates*, Background Paper of Working Group 5 of the Commission on Macroeconomics and Health: Improving Health Outcomes of the Poor (Geneva: World Health Organization).

Kunnermann, R. and Leonhard, R. 2008. *A Human Rights View of Social Cash Transfers for Achieving the Millennium Development Goals* (Stuttgart, Germany: Brot für die Welt).

Kuusi, P. 1964. *Social Policy for the Sixties* (Helsinki: Finnish Social Policy Association).

Kwon, H.-J. 2004. 'The Economic Crisis and the Politics of Welfare Reform in Korea', in T. Mkandawire (ed.), *Social Policy in a Development Context* (Geneva: UNRISD, and Basingstoke: Palgrave Macmillan), pp. 262–83.

Kwon, H.-J. (ed.) 2005. *Transforming the Developmental Welfare State in East Asia* (Basingstoke: Palgrave Macmillan).

Lamiraud, K., Boysen, F. and Scheil-Adlung, X. 2005. *The Impact of Social Health Protection on Access to Health Care, Health Expenditure and Impoverishment: a Case Study of South Africa*, Extension of Social Security (ESS) Paper Series 23 (Geneva: ILO).

Lang, T. and Hines, C. 1993. *The New Protectionism* (London: Earthscan).

Lau, E. and Wallkic, G. 2005. *International Comparison of Productivity: a Technical Note on Revisions and Interpretation* (London: United Kingdom National Statistics).

Leatt, A. and Rosa, S. (eds) 2005. *Targeting Poverty Alleviation to Make Children's Rights Real* (Cape Town: Children's Institute, University of Cape Town, CD-ROM).

Leibfried, S. 1992. 'Towards a European Welfare State? On Integrating Poverty Regimes in the European Community', in Z. Ferge and J. E. Kolberg (eds), *Social Policy in a Changing Europe* (Vienna: Campus).

Leibfried, S. and Pierson, P. (eds) 1995. *European Social Policy: Between Fragmentation and Integration* (Washington, DC: Brookings Institution).

Levy, S. (ed.) 2005. *Starter Packs: a Strategy to Fight Hunger in Developing Countries* (Wallingford: CABI Publishing).

Levy, S. with Barahona, C. and Chisinga, B. 2004. *Food Security, Social Protection, Growth and Poverty Reduction Synergies: the Starter Pack Programme in Malawi*, Natural Resource Perspectives No. 95 (London: Overseas Development Institute).

Limwattananon, S., Tangcharoensathien, V. and Prakongsai, P. 2005. *Equity in Financing Healthcare: Impact of Universal Access to Healthcare in Thailand*, EQUITAP Working Paper 16.

Limwattananon, S., Tangcharoensathien, V. and Prakongsai, P. 2007. 'Catastrophic and Poverty Impacts of Health Payments: Results from the National Household Surveys in Thailand', *Bulletin of the World Health Organization*, 85: 600–6.

Lin, K. and Kangas, O. E. 2006. 'Social Policymaking and its Institutional Basis: Transition of the Chinese Social Security System', *International Social Security Review*, 59(2): 61–76.

Lindert, K. A., Skoufias, E. and Shapiro, J. 2006. *Redistributing Income to the Poor and the Rich: Public Transfers in Latin America and the Caribbean*, SP Discussion Paper 0605 (Washington, DC: World Bank).

Lindert, P. H. 1994. 'The Rise of Social Spending, 1880–1930', *Explorations in Economic History*, 31(1): 1–36.

Lindert, P. H. 2003. 'Voice and Growth: Was Churchill Right?' *Journal of Economic History*, 63(2): 315–50.

Lindert, P. H. 2004. *Growing Public: Social Spending and Economic Growth since the Eighteenth Century*, 2 vols (Cambridge: Cambridge University Press).

Lloyd-Sherlock, P. 2008. 'Doing a Bit More for the Poor? Social Assistance in Latin America', *Journal of Social Policy*, 37: 621–39.

Lødemel, I. and Schulte, B. 1992. 'Social Assistance: a Part of Social Security or the Poor Law in New Disguise?' paper presented at the conference Social Security Fifty Years after Beveridge, University of York, September.

Loprest, P. 1999. 'How Families that Left Welfare are Doing: a National Picture', in *Assessing the New Federalism Project* (Washington, DC: The Urban Institute).

Lund, F. 2002a. 'Crowding in Care, Security and Micro-Enterprise Formation: Revisiting the Role of the State in Poverty Reduction, and in Development', *Journal of International Development*, 14(6): 1–14.

Lund, F. 2002b. 'Social Security and the Changing Labour Market: Access for Nonstandard and Informal Workers in South Africa', *Social Dynamics*, 28(2): 177–206.

Lustig, N. C. and McLeod, D. 1997. 'Minimum Wages and Poverty in Developing Countries: Some Empirical Evidence', in S. Edwards and N. C. Lustig (eds), *Labor Markets in Latin America: Combining Social Protection with Market Flexibility* (Washington, DC: Brookings Institution Press).

Lynes, T. 2006. *The Rape of the National Insurance Fund*, National Pensioners Convention fact sheet (London).

MacDonald, R. 2007. 'An Inspirational Defence of the Right to Health', *The Lancet*, 370: 379–80.

MacDonald, T. H. 2007. *The Global Human Right to Health: Dream or Possibility?* (Oxford: Radcliffe Publishing).

Maddison, A. 1995. *Monitoring the World Economy 1820–1992* (Paris: OECD).

Madeley, J. 1999. *Big Business, Poor Peoples: the Impact of Transnational Corporations on the World's Poor* (London and New York: Zed Books).

Madrid, R. L. 2003. *Retiring the State: the Politics of Pension Privatization in Latin America and Beyond* (Stanford: Stanford University Press).

Mahler, V. A. and Jesuit, D. K. 2006. 'Fiscal Redistribution in the Developed Countries: New Insights from the Luxembourg Income Study', *Socio-Economic Review*, 4(3): 483–511.

Maluccio, J. A. 2005. *Coping with the 'Coffee Crisis' in Central America: the Role of the Nicaraguan Red de Protección Social, Food Consumption and Nutrition Division*, Discussion Paper 188 (Washington: IFPRI).

Manow, P. and van Kersbergen, K. 2008. 'The Welfare State', in D. Caramani (ed.), *Comparative Politics* (Oxford: Oxford University Press), pp. 520–45.

Marlier, E., Atkinson, A. B., Cantillon, B. and Nolan, B. 2007. *The EU and Social Inclusion: Facing the Challenges* (Bristol: Policy Press).

Marshall, T. H. 1950. *Citizenship and Social Class and Other Essays* (Cambridge: Cambridge University Press).

Martinez, S. 2004. *Pensions, Poverty and Household Investments in Bolivia*, mimeo (Berkeley: University of California).

Matin, I. and Hulme, D. 2003. 'Programmes for the Poorest: Learning from the IGVGD Programme in Bangladesh', *World Development*, 31(3): 647–65.

May, J. (ed.). 2000. *Poverty and Inequality in South Africa: Meeting the Challenge* (Cape Town: David Philip, and London and New York: Zed Books).

McCord, A. 2005. *Public Works in the Context of HIV/AIDS: Innovations in Public Works for Reaching the Most Vulnerable Children and Households in East and Southern Africa*, Public Works Research Project (Nairobi: UNICEF).

Medeiros, M., Diniz, D. and Squinca, F. 2006. *Cash Benefits to Disabled Persons in Brazil: an Analysis of the BPC – Continuous Cash Benefit Programme*, International Poverty Centre Working Paper 16.

Medici, A. 2004. *The Political Economy of Reform in Brazil's Civil Servant Pension Scheme*, Technical Report on Pensions No. 002, Inter-American Development Bank.

Mehrotra, J. 2006. 'Job Law with Right to Information Can Cut Poverty in India', in International Poverty Centre, *Social Protection: the Role of Cash Transfers*, Poverty in Focus (Brasilia: International Poverty Centre).

Melgaard, B. 2004. 'Editorial: From Research to Action – a Bridge to be Crossed', *Bulletin of the World Health Organization*, 82: 723.

Mesa-Lago, C. 1978. *Social Security in Latin America: Pressure Groups, Stratification, and Inequality* (Pittsburgh: University of Pittsburgh Press).

Mesa-Lago, C. 1994. *Changing Social Security in Latin America: Toward Alleviating the Social Costs of Economic Reform* (Boulder: Lynne Rienner).

Mesa-Lago, C. 2005. 'Assessing the World Bank Report *Keeping the Promise*', *International Social Security Review*, 58(2–3): 97–117.

Meyer, B. D. 1995. 'Lessons from the US Unemployment Insurance Experiments', *Journal of Economic Literature*, 33(1): 91–131.

Midgeley, J. 1984. *Social Security, Inequality and the Third World* (New York: Wiley).

Miller, S. M. and Markle, J. E. 2002. 'Social Policy in the US: Workfare and the American Low-wage Labour Market', in P. Townsend and D. Gordon (eds), *World Poverty: New Policies to Defeat an Old Enemy* (Bristol: Policy Press).

Mills, A., Bennett, S., Siriwanarangsun, P. and Tangcharoensathien, V. 2000. 'The Response of Providers to Capitation Payment: a Case Study from Thailand', *Health Policy*, 51: 163–80.

Milward, A. S. and Saul, S. B. 1977. *The Development of the Economies of Continental Europe, 1850–1914* (London: Allen & Unwin).

Ministry of Health and Social Services. 2005. *Pension Payout Summary February 2005* (Windhoek: Government of Namibia).

Ministry of Social Affairs and Health, Finland. 1999. *Financing Social Protection in Europe* (Helsinki: Ministry of Social Affairs and Health).

MIRE-DREES (Ministère de l'Emploi et de la Solidarité). 1999. *Comparing Social Welfare Systems in Nordic Europe and France*, Vol. 4 of the Copenhagen Conference, Nantes, Maison des Sciences de l'Homme, Ange Guepin.

Miron, J. A. and Weil, D. N. 1998. 'The Genesis and Evolution of Social Security', in M. D. Bordo, C. Goldin and E. N. White (eds), *The Defining Moment: the Great Depression in the American Economy in the Twentieth Century* (Chicago: University of Chicago Press for the NBER), pp. 297–322.

Misra, R., Chatterjee, R. and Rao, S. 2003. *India Health Report* (New Delhi: Oxford University Press for the World Bank).

Mitchell, O. S. 1996. *Social Security Reform in Uruguay: an Economic Assessment*, Pension Research Council Working Paper 1996–20 (University of Pennsylvania).

Mizunoya, S., Behrendt, C., Pal, K. and Léger, F. 2006. *Can Low-income Countries Afford Basic Social Protection? First Results of a Modelling Exercise for Five Asian Countries*, Issues in Social Protection Discussion Paper 17 (Geneva: International Labour Office).

Mkandawire, T. (ed.) 2004. *Social Policy in a Development Context* (Geneva: UNRISD, and Basingstoke: Palgrave Macmillan).

Mkandawire, T. 2005. *Targeting and Universalism in Poverty Reduction* (Geneva: United Nations Research Institute for Social Development).

Moll, P. 1991. 'What Redistributes and What Doesn't?' in P. Moll, N. Nattrass and L. Loots (eds), *Redistribution: How Can it Work in South Africa?* (Cape Town: David Phillip).

Møller, V. and Devey, R. 2003. 'Trends in Living Conditions and Satisfaction among Poorer Older South Africans: Objective and Subjective Indicators of Quality of Life in the October Household Survey', *Development Southern Africa*, 20(4): 457–76.

Møller, V. and Sotshongaye, A. 1996. 'My Family Eat This Money Too: Pension Sharing and Self-respect among Zulu Grandmothers', *Southern African Journal of Gerontology*, 5(2): 9–19.

Moore, C. 2009. *Impact is Not Enough: Image and CCT Sustainability in Nicaragua*, International Policy Centre One-pager No. 79 (Brasilia: International Poverty Centre).

More, Sir T. 1922 [1516]. *Utopia* (Cambridge: Cambridge University Press).

Morgan, R. 1991. 'State Pensions as an Income Safety Net in Namibia', *Food Policy* 16(5): 351–9.

Morley, S. 1992. 'Poverty and Income Distribution in Latin America: the Story of the 1980s', paper prepared for the conference Poverty and Inequality in Latin America, Brookings Institution, Washington, DC, July.

Morley, S. and Coady, D. 2003. *From Social Assistance to Social Development: Targeted Education Subsidies in Developing Countries* (Washington, DC: Center for Global Development and International Food Policy Research Institute).

Mulligan, C., Gil, R. and Sala-i-Martin, X. 2002. *Social Security and Democracy*, NBER Working Paper 8958 (Cambridge, MA: NBER).

National Statistical Office Thailand. Various years. *Health and Welfare Surveys* (Bangkok: Office of the Prime Minister).

National Statistical Office Thailand. Various years. *Socio-economic Surveys* (Bangkok: Office of the Prime Minister).

National Treasury, South Africa. 2006. *Budget Review 2006* (Pretoria: Government Printers).

Newman, B. and Thomson, R. J. 1989. 'Economic Growth and Social Development: a Longitudinal Analysis of Causal Priority', *World Development*, 17(4): 461–71.

Nicholls, Sir G. 1898. *A History of the English Poor Law*, new edition, 2 vols (London: P. S. King).

Nickell, S. J. 1997. 'Unemployment and Labor Market Rigidities: Europe versus North America', *Journal of Economic Perspectives*, 11(3): 55–74.

Noble, M., Wright, G. and Cluver, L. 2008. *Conceptualizing, Defining and Measuring Child Poverty in South Africa: an Argument for a Multi-Dimensional Approach*, Department of Social Development, Republic of South Africa.

Nordhaus, W. 2002. *The Health of Nations: the Contribution of Improved Health to Living Standards*, NBER Working Paper 8818 (Cambridge, MA: NBER).

Notten, G. and de Neubourg, C. 2007. *Relative or Absolute Poverty in the US and EU? The Battle of the Rates*. Working Paper 2007/01 (Maastricht: Maastricht Graduate School of Governance, www.governance.unimaas.nl).

O'Donnell, O., van Doorslaer, E., Rannan-Eliya, R. et al. 2007. 'The Incidence of Public Spending on Healthcare: Comparative Evidence from Asia', *World Bank Economic Review*, 21: 93–123.

Obinger, H., Leibfried, S. and Castles, F. G. 2005. 'Bypasses to a Social Europe? Lessons from Federal Experience', *Journal of European Public Policy*, 12(3): 545–71.

OECD. 1985. *Social Expenditure 1960–1990*, Paris.

OECD. 1992. *Historical Statistics 1960–1990*, Paris.

OECD. 1994. *The OECD Jobs Study: Evidence and Explanations*, 2 vols, Paris.

OECD. 1999. *Social Expenditure Database, 1980–1996*, Paris.

OECD. 2000. *Economic Outlook*, Paris.

OECD. 2001a. *The OECD Guidelines for Multinational Enterprises 2001: Focus: Global Instruments for Corporate Responsibility*, Paris (first adopted 1976 and amended 1991).

OECD. 2001b. *Historical Statistics: 1970–2000* (www.sourceoecd.org).

OECD. 2003. *Social Expenditures Data Set* (accessed November 2008).

OECD. 2004. Social Expenditure Database, SOCX (www.oecd.org/els/social/expenditure).

OECD. 2005a. *National Accounts of OECD Countries*, Paris.

OECD. 2005b. 'DAC Members' Net ODA 1990–2004 and DAC Secretariat Simulations of Net ODA in 2006 and 2010', OECD website 12 September.

OECD. 2005c. Social Expenditure Database, SOCX (www.oecd.org/els/social/expenditure).

OECD. 2006a. *National Accounts of OECD Countries*, Paris.

OECD. 2006b. *Promoting Pro-poor Growth: Key Policy Messages*, Development Assistance Committee, Paris.

OECD. 2007. *OECD Economic Outlook: Sources and Methods* (http://www.oecd.org/eco/sources-and-methods).

Offenheiser, R. C. and Holcombe, S. H. 2003. 'Challenges and Opportunities in Implementing a Rights-Based Approach to Development: an Oxfam America Prospect', *Nonprofit and Voluntary Sector Quarterly*, 32(2): 268–306.

Ogden, J., Esim, S. and Grown, C. 2004. *Expanding the Care Continuum for HIV/AIDS: Bringing Carers into Focus. Horizons Report* (Washington, DC: Population Council and International Centre for Research on Women).

Olson, S. 1986. 'Sweden', in P. Flora (ed.), *Growth to Limits: the Western European Welfare States Since World War II*. Vol. 1: *Sweden, Norway, Finland and Denmark* (Berlin: Walter de Gruyter).

Oorschot, W. van 2002. 'Targeting Welfare: On the Functions and Dysfunctions of Means Testing in Social Policy', in P. Townsend and D. Gordon (eds), *World Poverty: New Policies to Defeat an Old Enemy* (Bristol: Policy Press).

Oorschot, W. van 2006. 'The Dutch Welfare State', paper presented at the conference: CCWS Working Paper, Aalborg.

Or, Z. 2000. 'Determinants of Health Outcomes in Industrialized Countries: a Pooled, Cross-Country, Time-Series Analysis', *OECD Economic Studies*, 30(1): 53–77.

Orero, M. B., Heime, C., Jarvis Cutler, S. and Mohaupt, S. 2006. *The Impact of Conflict on the Intergenerational Transmission of Chronic Poverty: an Overview and Annotated Bibliography*, Working Paper 71/Annotated Bibliography 4 (Manchester, IDPM/Chronic Poverty Research Centre).

Organization of African Unity. 1990. 'African Charter on the Rights and Welfare of the Child', OAU Doc. Cab/Leg/24.9/49 (1990), entered into force 29 November 1999.

Osberg, L. (ed.) 1991. *Economic Inequality and Poverty: International Perspectives* (New York: M. E. Sharpe).

Osborne, D. and Gaebler, T. 1992. *Reinventing Government: How the Entrepreneurial Spirit is Transforming the Public Sector* (New York, Tokyo, Paris and Amsterdam: Addison-Wesley).

Oyen, E., Miller, S. M. and Samad, S. A. (eds) 1996. *Poverty: a Global Review. Handbook on International Poverty Research* (Oslo: Scandinavian University Press).

Paakjaer Martinussen, H. 2006. 'A Need for a New Balance: Views of the Stakeholders', paper presented at the conference: The EU's Evolving Social Policy and National Models: Seeking a New Balance, Helsinki: Finnish Presidency of the European Union.

Paes de Barros, R. and Foguel, M. N. 2002. 'Focalização dos gastos públicos sociais e erradicação da probreza', in R. Henriques (ed.), *Desigualdade e Pobreza no Brasil* (Rio de Janeiro: IPEA), pp. 719–39.

Pal, K., Behrendt, C., Léger, F., Cichon, M. and Hagemejer, K. 2005. *Can Low-income Countries Afford Basic Social Protection? First Results of a Modelling Exercise*, Issues in Social Protection Discussion Paper 13 (Geneva: International Labour Office).

Palacios, R. and Pallarès-Miralles, M. 2000. *International Patterns of Pension Provision* (Washington, DC: World Bank: http://www.worldbank.org/pensions).

Palier, B. 2005. *Gouverner la sécurité sociale* (Paris: Presses Universitaires de France).

Palme, J. 1999. *The Nordic Model and the Modernization of Social Protection in Europe* (Copenhagen: Nordic Council of Ministers).

Pannarunothai, S. 2002. 'Medical Welfare Scheme: Financing and Targeting the Poor', in P. Pramualratana and S. Wibulpolprasert (eds), *Health Insurance Systems in Thailand* (Nonthaburi: Health Systems Research Institute).

Papatheodorou, C. and Petmesidou, M. 2004. 'Inequality, Poverty and Redistribution through Social Transfers in Greece in Comparative Perspective', in M. Petmesidou and C. Papatheodorou (eds), *Poverty and Social Exclusion* (Athens: Exandas (in Greek)).

Park, Y. S. 2008. 'Revisiting the Welfare State System in the Republic of Korea', *International Social Security Review*, 61(2): 3–19.

Parry, R. 1986. 'United Kingdom', in Peter Flora (ed.), *Growth to Limits: the Western European Welfare States Since World War II*. Vol. 2: *Germany, United Kingdom, Ireland and Italy* (Berlin: Walter de Gruyter).

Pemberton, S., Gordon, D., Nandy, S., Pantazis, C. and Townsend, P. 2005. 'The Relationship between Child Poverty and Child Rights: the Role of Indicators', in A. Minujin, E. Delamonica and M. Komarecki (eds), *Human Rights and Social Policies for Children and Women: the MICS in Practice* (New York: UNICEF/New School University).

Pemberton, S., Gordon, D., Nandy, S., Pantazis, C. and Townsend, P. 2007. 'Child Rights and Child Poverty: Can the International Framework of Children's Rights be Used to Improve Child Survival Rates?' *Plos Medicine*, 4(10): e307 (www.plosmedecine.org).

Perle, L. 1998. *Krise des Wohlfahrtsstaates. Abbau oder Systemwechsel?* (Göttingen Universität Göttingen).

Peters, D. H., Yazbeck, A. S., Sharma, R. R., Ramana, G. N. V., Pritchett, L. H. and Wagstaff, A. 2002. *Better Health Systems for India's Poor: Findings, Analysis, and Options* (Washington, DC: World Bank).

Petmesidou, M. and Papatheodorou, C. (eds) 2004. *Poverty and Social Deprivation in the Mediterranean Area: Trends, Policies and Welfare Prospects in the New Millennium* (London: Zed Books/CROP Series).

PhilHealth. 2007. *Synthesis Report: Conference on Extending Social Health Insurance to Informal Economy Workers, 18–20 October 2006* (Manila: PhilHealth, GTZ, ILO, WHO, and World Bank).

Pierson, C. 2004. 'Late Industrializers and the Development of the Welfare State: Social Policy in a Development Context', in T. Mkandawire (ed.), *Social Policy in a Development Context* (Geneva: UNRISD, and Basingstoke: Palgrave Macmillan), pp. 215–45.

Pitayarangsarit, S. 2005. 'Agenda Setting Process', in V. Tangcharoensathien and P. Jongudomsuk (eds), *From Policy to Implementation: Historical Events during 2001–2004 of Universal Coverage in Thailand* (Bangkok: SRC Envelope).

Piven, F. F. and Cloward, R. A. 1971. *Regulating the Poor: the Functions of Public Welfare* (New York: Pantheon).

Pogge, T. and Reddy, S. 2003. *Unknown: the Extent, Distribution and Trend of Global Income Poverty* (www.socialanalysis.org).

Posel, D., Fairburn, J. and Lund, F. 2006. 'Labour Migration and Households: a Reconsideration of the Effects of the Social Pension on Labour Supply in South Africa', *Economic Modelling*, 23(5): 836–53.

Prakongsai, P., Limwattananon, S., Tisayatikom, K. et al. Forthcoming. 'Equity in Financing Healthcare: How Well has the Thai Health System Performed?'

Prakongsai, P., Tangcharoensathien, V. and Tisayatikom, K. 2007. 'Who Benefits from Government Health Spending Before and After Universal Coverage in Thailand?' *Journal of Health Science*, 16: S20–S36.

Pressman, S. 2003. *Income Guarantees and the Equity–Efficiency Trade-off*, Luxembourg Income Study, Working Paper No. 348, Luxembourg.

Pritchett, L. 2005. *The Political Economy of Targeted Safety Nets*, Social Protection Discussion Paper 0501 (Washington, DC: World Bank).

Rajan, S. I. 2001. 'Social Assistance for Poor Elderly: How Effective?' *Economic and Political Weekly*, 36(8): 613–17.

Rajan, S. I. 2003. 'Old Age Allowance Program in Nepal', Staying Poor: Chronic Poverty and Development Policy, Manchester (United Kingdom), 7–9 April (http://www.chronicpoverty.org/pdfs/conferencepapers/rajan.pdf).

Ravallion, M. 1997. 'Can High Inequality Developing Countries Escape Absolute Poverty?' *Economics Letters*, 56: 51–7.

Ravallion, M. 1998. *Poverty Lines in Theory and Practice*, LSMS Working Paper No. 133 (Washington, DC: World Bank).

Ravallion M. 2008. *Global Poverty Reassessed: a Reply to Reddy* (One Pager, Brasilia: International Poverty Centre).

Ravallion, M. and Datt, G. 1999. *When is Growth Pro-Poor? Evidence from the Diverse Experience of India's States*, Policy Research Working Paper WPS 2263 (Washington, DC: World Bank).

Rawlings, L. B. 2005. 'A New Approach to Social Assistance: Latin America's Experience with Conditional Cash Transfer Programmes', *International Social Security Review*, 58(2–3): 133–62.

Rawlings, L. B. and Rubio, L. 2005. 'Evaluating the Impact of Conditional Cash Transfer Programs', *World Bank Research Observer*, 20(1): 29–55.

Reardon, T., Berdegue, J. and Escobar, G. 2001. 'Rural Non-farm Employment and Incomes in Latin America: Overview and Policy Implications', *World Development*, 29(3): 395–409.

Reddy, S. G. 2008. *The New Global Poverty Estimates: Digging Deeper into a Hole* (One Pager, Brasilia: International Poverty Centre).

Reddy, S. G. and Pogge, T. W. 2001. *How Not to Count the Poor*, Departments of Economics and Philosophy, University of Columbia.

Reddy, S. G. and Pogge, T. W. 2009. 'How Not to Count the Poor', in J. Stiglitz, S. Anand and P. Segal (eds), *Debates on the Measurement of Global Poverty* (Oxford: Oxford University Press).

Reynaud, E. 2001. *The Extension of Social Security Coverage: the Approach of the ILO*, Extension of Social Security Working Paper No. 3 (Geneva: ILO).

Rice, X. 2007. 'Net Giveaway Halves Kenya's Child Deaths from Malaria', *The Guardian*, 17 August.

Riis, J. A. 1902. *The Battle with the Slum* (New York: Macmillan).

Robinson, M. 2003. Address at launch of a report on *Child Poverty in the Developing World*, London School of Economics.

Rodgers, G. (ed.) 1995. *The Poverty Agenda and the ILO: Issues for Research and Action* (Geneva: International Institute for Labour Studies).

Rokkan, S., Cox, K. R. and Reynolds, D. R. 1974. *Locational Approaches to Power and Conflict* (New York: Sage Publications, Halsted Press).

Rokkan, S., Salen, S. and Warmburnn, J. 1973. *Nation Building: a Review of Recent Comparative Research and a Select Bibliography of Analytical Studies* (The Hague: Mouton).

Room, G. (ed.) 1995. *Beyond the Threshold* (Bristol: Policy Press).

Rose-Ackerman, S. 1999. *Corruption and Government: Causes, Consequences and Reform* (Cambridge: Cambridge University Press).

Ruiz-Huerta, J. et al. 1999. *Earnings Inequality, Unemployment and Income Distribution in the OECD, Luxembourg Income Study*, Working Paper No. 214, Luxembourg.

Russett, B. M., Alker, H. R., Deutsch, K.W. and Lasswell, H. D. 1964. *World Handbook of Political and Social Indicators* (New Haven: Yale University Press).

Sala-i-Martin, X. 1996. 'A Positive Theory of Social Security', *Journal of Economic Growth*, 1(2): 277–304.

Samson, M. 2002. 'The Social, Economic and Fiscal Impact of Comprehensive Social Security Reform for South Africa', *Social Dynamics*, 28(2): 69–97.

Samson, M. 2005. *Fieldwork Notes from the EPRI Western Cape Household Survey* (Cape Town: Economic Policy Research Institute).

Samson, M. and Williams, M. 2007. *Social Grants and Labour Market Behaviour: Evidence from South Africa's Household Surveys*, Economic Policy Research Institute Research Paper 43.

Samson, M., Babson, O., Haarman, C., Haarman, D., Khathi, G., Mac Quene, K. and van Niekerk, I. 2001. *The Economic Impact of a Basic Income Grant for South Africa*, report commissioned by the Committee of Enquiry into Comprehensive Social Security (Cape Town: Economic Policy Research Institute).

Samson, M., Babson, O., Haarman, C., Haarman, D., Khathi, G., Mac Quene, K. and van Niekerk, I. 2002. *Research Review on Social Security Reform and the Basic Income Grant for South Africa*, EPRI Research Paper No. 31 (Cape Town: Economic Policy Research Institute).

Samson, M., Lee, U., Mac Quene, K., van Niekerk, I. and Gandhi, V. 2003. *The Social and Economic Impact of Social Assistance Grants*, report commissioned by the Department of Social Development (Cape Town: Economic Policy Research Institute).

Samson, M., Lee, U., Ndlebe, Mac Quene, K., van Niekerk, I., Ghandi, V., Harigaya, T. and Abrahams, C. 2004. *The Social and Economic Impact of South Africa's Social*

Security System, commissioned by the Department of Social Development (Cape Town: Economic Policy Research Institute).

Samson, M., Mac Quene, K. and van Niekerk, I. 2005. *An Assessment of the Government's Microeconomic Reform Strategy and Overview of Developments and Outlook of South Africa's Real Economy*, report commissioned by the Ministry of Trade and Industry's Office of the Director-General for the 2005 South African Cabinet Lekgotla (Cape Town: Economic Policy Research Institute).

Samson, M., Mac Quene, K., and van Niekerk, I. 2007. *Southern African Models of Social Protection* (Cape Town: Economic Policy Research Institute).

Save the Children UK, HelpAge International and Institute for Development Studies. 2005. *Making Cash Count: Lessons from Cash Transfer Schemes in East and Southern Africa for Supporting the Most Vulnerable Children and Households* (London: Save the Children UK, HelpAge International, Institute for Development Studies).

Schefczyk, M. 2005. *Umverteilung als Legitimationsproblem* (Freiburg [Breisgau]: Alber).

Scheil-Adlung, X., Booysen, F., Lamiraud, K., Reynaud, E., Jütting, J., Asfaw, A., Xu, K., Carrin, G., Chatterji, S., Evans, D., James, C. and Muchiri, S. 2006. *What is the Impact of Social Health Protection on Access to Health Care, Health Expenditure and Impoverishment? A Comparative Analysis of Three African Countries* (Geneva and Paris: ILO, OECD and WHO).

Schmidt, M. G. 1997. 'Determinants of Social Expenditure in Liberal Democracies: the Post World War II Experience', *Acta Política*.

Schmitt, J. and Zipperer, B. 2007. *Dropping the Ax: Illegal Firings during Union Election Campaigns* (Washington, DC: Center for Economic and Policy Research).

Schubert, B. 2004. *Social Cash Transfers – Reaching the Poorest: a Contribution to the International Debate based on Experience in Zambia* (Eschborn: GTZ).

Schubert, B. 2005. *The Pilot Social Cash Transfer Scheme, Kalomo District, Zambia*, Working Paper 52 (Manchester: Chronic Poverty Research Centre).

Scott, J., Stokman, F. N. and Ziegler, R. 1985. *Networks of Corporate Power* (London: Polity Press).

Scruggs, L. and Allan, J. P. 2005. *The Material Consequences of Welfare States: Benefit Generosity and Absolute Poverty in 16 OECD Countries*, LIS Working Paper No. 409.

Sen, A. K. 2001. *Development as Freedom* (Oxford and New York: Oxford University Press).

Sharp, K., Brown, T. and Teshome, A. 2006. *Targeting Ethiopia's Productive Safety Net Programme*, report prepared for DFID Ethiopia.

Shin, D.-M. 2000. 'Financial Crisis and Social Security: the Paradox of the Republic of Korea', *International Social Security Review*, 53(3): 83–107.

Singh, A. 1996. 'Pension Reform, the Stock Market, Capital Formation, and Economic Growth: a Critical Commentary on the World Bank's Proposals', *International Social Security Review*, 49(1): 21–44.

Singh, J. A., Govender, M. and Mills, E. J. 2007. 'Do Human Rights Matter to Health?' *The Lancet*, 370: 9586.

SIPRI (Stockholm International Peace Research Institute). 2004. *Yearbook, 2004*. 'Armaments, Disarmaments and International Security', Stockholm (http://www.sipri.org).

Sklair, L. 2001. *The Transnational Capitalist Class* (Oxford: Basil Blackwell).

Slater, R., Ashley, S., Tefera, M., Buta, M. and Escubalew, D. 2006. *Ethiopia Productive Safety Net Programme (PSNP): Policy, Programme and Institutional Linkages*, Final Report for DFID Ethiopia.

Slemrod, J. 1995. 'What Do Cross-Country Studies Teach about Government Involvement, Prosperity, and Economic Growth?' *Brookings Papers in Economic Activity*, 2: 373–431.

Smeeding, T. M. 2002. 'Globalization, Inequality and the Rich Countries of the G-20: Evidence from the Luxembourg Income Study (LIS)', Sydney, May.

Smeeding, T. M. and Phillips, K. R. 2001. 'Social Protection for the Poor in the Developed World', in N. Lustig (ed.), *Shielding the Poor: Social Protection in the Developing World* (Washington, DC: Brookings Institution).

Smeeding, T. M., O'Higgins, M. and Rainwater, L. 1990. *Poverty, Inequality and Income Distribution in Comparative Perspective: the Luxembourg Income Study* (London and New York: Harvester Wheatsheaf).

Smeeding, T. M., Rainwater, L. and Burtless, G. 2001. 'US Poverty in a Cross-National Context', in S. H. Danziger and R. H. Haveman (eds), *Understanding Poverty* (Cambridge, MA: Russell Sage Foundation and Harvard University Press).

Smith, W. J. and Subbarao, K. 2003. *What Role for Safety Net Transfers in Very Low-Income Countries?* Social Protection Discussion Paper 0301 (Washington, DC: World Bank).

Snyder, J. M. and Yackovlev, I. 2000. *Political and Economic Determinants of Changes in Government Spending in Social Protection Programmes*, mimeo (Cambridge, MA: MIT).

Social Security Committee. 1999. *The Contributory Principle*, House of Commons Session 1998–9, Minutes of Evidence, 14 July (London: TSO).

Son, H. H. and Kakwani, N. 2004. *Economic Growth and Poverty Reduction: Initial Conditions Matter*, Working Paper 2 (Brasilia: UNDP International Poverty Centre).

Son, H. H. and Kakwani, N. 2006. *Global Estimates of Pro-Poor Growth*, Working Paper 31 (Brasilia: UNDP International Poverty Centre).

Srithamrongsawat, S, 2002. 'The Health Card Scheme: a Subsidized Voluntary Health Insurance Scheme', in P. Pramualratana and S. Wibulpolprasert (eds), *Health Insurance Systems in Thailand* (Nonthaburi: Health Systems Research Institute).

Start, D. 2001. 'The Rise and Fall of the Rural Non-farm Economy: Poverty Impacts and Policy Options', *Development Policy Review*, 19(4): 491–505.

Statistisk Sentralbyrå (Norwegian Statistics Office).

Subbarao, K., Bonnerjee, A., Braithwaite, J., Carvalho, S., Ezemenari, K., Graham, C. and Thompson, A. 1997. *Safety Net Programs and Poverty Reduction: Lessons from Cross-Country Experience* (Washington, DC: World Bank).

Suplicy, E. M. 2003. 'President Lula's Zero Hunger Programme and the Trend toward a Citizen's Basic Income in Brazil' (London: LSE).

Swank, D. H. and Hicks, A. 1985. 'The Determinants and Redistributive Impacts of State Welfare Spending in the Advanced Capitalist Democracies, 1960–80', in N. J. Vig, and S. E. Schier (eds), *Political Economy in Western Democracies* (New York: Allen & Unwin).

Tabatabai, H. 2006. *Eliminating Child Labour: the Promise of Conditional Cash Transfers* (Geneva: ILO).

Tabor, S. R. 2002. *Assisting the Poor with Cash: Design and Implementation of Social Transfer Programs*, Social Protection Discussion Paper 0223 (Washington, DC: World Bank).

Tangcharoensathien, V. 1990. 'Community Financing: the Urban Health Card in Chiangmai, Thailand', PhD dissertation, London School of Hygiene and Tropical Medicine.

Tangcharoensathien, V., Laixuthai, A., Vasavit, J. et al. 1999a. 'National Health Account Development: Lessons from Thailand', *Health Policy and Planning*, 14(4): 342–53.

Tangcharoensathien, V., Supachutikul, A. and Lertiendumrong, J. 1999b. 'The Social Security Scheme in Thailand: What Lessons Can Be Drawn?', *Social Science & Medicine*, 48: 913–23.

Tangcharoensathien, V., Pitayarangsarit, S. and Srithamrongswat, S. 2003. 'Mapping Health Insurance in Thailand: Directions for Reform', *Global Forum for Health Research*: 109–35.

Tangcharoensathien, V., Wibulpolprasert, S. and Nitayarampong, S. 2004. 'Knowledge-based Changes to Health Systems: the Thai Experience in Policy Development', *Bulletin of the World Health Organization*, 82(10): 750–6.

Tangcharoensathien, V., Teokul, W. and Chanwongpaisarn, L. 2005. 'Challenges of Implementing Universal Health Care in Thailand', in H.-J. Kwon (ed.), *Transforming the Developmental Welfare State in East Asia* (Basingstoke: Palgrave Macmillan and UNRISD).

Tangcharoensathien, V., Limwattananon, S., Pannarunothai, S. et al. 2006. 'Reviews of Existing Databases for Monitoring and Evaluation of Equity in Health in Thailand', ASEM Trust Fund: Work Package 3.

Tanzi, V. 2000. *Globalization and the Future of Social Protection*, IMF Working Paper WP/00/12 (Washington, DC: IMF).

Therborn, G. 1986. 'The Working Class and the Welfare State', in P. Kettune (ed.), *Det nordiska i den nordiska arbetarrorelsen* (Helsinki: Finnish Society for Labour History).

Timmons, J. F. 2005. *Left, Right, and Center: Partisanship, Taxes, and the Welfare State* (Mexico, DF: ITAM).

Townsend, P. 1979. *Poverty in the United Kingdom* (Harmondsworth: Allen Lane).

Townsend, P. 2004a. 'From Universalism to Safety Nets: the Rise and Fall of Keynesian Influence on Social Development Policies', in T. Mkandawire (ed.), *Social Policy in a Development Context* (Geneva: UNRISD, and Basingstoke: Palgrave Macmillan).

Townsend, P. 2004b. 'Direct Policies to Fight Child Poverty', *In Focus* (Rio de Janeiro: International Poverty Centre, UNDP).

Townsend, P. 2007. *The Right to Social Security and National Development: Lessons from OECD Experience for Low-income Countries*, Issues in Social Protection Discussion Paper 18 (Geneva: ILO).

Townsend, P. 2009. 'The 2009 Minority Report on the World Bank', in Fabian Society, *Fighting Poverty and Inequality in an Age of Affluence* (London: Fabian Society).

Townsend, P. and Gordon, D. (eds) 2002. *World Poverty: New Policies to Defeat an Old Enemy* (Bristol: Policy Press).

Towse, A., Mills, A. and Tangcharoensathien, V. 2004. 'Learning from Thailand's Health Reforms', *British Medical Journal*, 328: 103–5.

UN. 1948. The Universal Declaration of Human Rights, New York.

UN. 1988. *Transnational Corporations in World Development* (New York: UN).

UN. 1995. *The Copenhagen Declaration and Programme of Action: the World Summit for Social Development 6–12 March 1995* (New York: UN Department of Publications).

UN. 1996. 'Special Issue on the Social Summit', in *Social Policy and Social Progress*, 1(1) (New York: UN).

UN. 1997. *Sustaining Social Security*, Department for Economic and Social Information and Analysis (New York: UN).

UN. 2001. *Report of the High-Level Panel on Financing for Development*, 28 June (New York: UN).

UN. 2003. *Economic, Social and Cultural Rights: Norms on the Responsibilities of Transnational Corporations and Other Business Enterprises with Regard to Human Rights*, Economic and Social Council, Commission on Human Rights (New York: UN).

UN. 2009. *Youth Development Indicators*, Department of Economic and Social Affairs, Expert Group (New York: UNDESA).

UNAIDS, UNICEF and USAID. 2004. *Children on the Brink 2004: a Joint Report of New Orphan Estimates and a Framework for Action* (New York: UNICEF).

UNCRC. 2003. *General Measures of Implementation for the Convention on the Rights of the Child 03/10/2003*, General Comment No. 5, CRC/GC/2003/5 (Geneva).

UNCTAD. 1996. *Globalization and Liberalization* (New York and Geneva).

UNDP. 1998a. *Overcoming Human Poverty: UNDP Poverty Report 1998* (New York).

UNDP. 1998b. *Poverty in Transition?* (New York: Regional Bureau for Europe and the CIS).

UNDP. 2000. *Overcoming Human Poverty: UNDP Poverty Report 2000* (New York).

UNDP. 2004a. *Children and Poverty, In Focus*, Newsletter of the International Poverty Centre (Rio de Janeiro: UNDP).

UNDP. 2004b. *The State of the World's Children 2005* (New York: UNICEF).

UNICEF. 2004. *The State of the World's Children 2005* (New York: UNICEF).

UNICEF. 2005. *The State of the World's Children 2006* (New York: UNICEF).

UNICEF. 2007. *State of the World's Children 2008* (New York: UNICEF).

UNICEF. Innocenti Research Centre, 2006a. 'Child Poverty in Rich Countries, Part I', *International Journal of Health Services*, 36(2): 235–69.

UNICEF. Innocenti Research Centre, 2006b. 'Child Poverty in Rich Countries, Part II', *International Journal of Health Services*, 36(3): 455–79.

Vagts, D. F. 2003. 'The UN Norms for Transnational Corporations', *Leiden Journal of International Law*, 16: 795–802.

van Ark, B. 2005. 'Does the European Union Need to Revive Productivity Growth?' Research Memorandum, GD-75, Groningen.

van de Ven, W. P. M. M. and Van Praag, B. M. S. 1981. *The Demand for Deductibles in Private Health Insurance: a Probit Model with Sample Selection* (Leiden, The Netherlands: Leiden University).

van den Bosch, K. 2002. 'Convergence in Poverty Outcomes and Social Income Transfers in Member States of the EU', paper for the Fifteenth World Congress of Sociology, Brisbane, July.

van der Berg, S. 1997. 'Social Security under Apartheid and Beyond', *Development Southern Africa*, 14(4): 481–503.

van der Berg, S. and Bredenkamp, C. 2002. 'Devising Social Security Interventions for Maximum Poverty Impact', *Social Dynamics*, 28(2): 39–68.

van Doorslaer, E., O'Donnell, O., Rannan-Eliya, R. et al. 2006. 'Effect of Payments for Health Care on Poverty Estimates in 11 countries in Asia: an Analysis of Household Survey Data', *The Lancet*, 368: 1357–64.

van Doorslaer, E., O'Donnell, O., Rannan-Eliya, R. et al. 2007. 'Catastrophic Payments for Health Care in Asia', *Health Econ* DOI 10.1002/hec. 1209.

van Ginneken, W. 1999. *Social Security for the Excluded Majority: Case Studies of Developing Countries* (Geneva: ILO).

van Ginneken, W. 2003. *Extending Social Security: Policies for Developing Countries*, ESS Paper No. 13 (Geneva: ILO).

van Parijs, P. 2006. 'Bottom-up Social Europe', paper presented at the conference: The EU's Evolving Social Policy and National Models: Seeking a New Balance, Helsinki: Finnish Presidency of the European Union.

Vandemoortele, J. 2002. 'Are we Really Reducing Global Poverty?' in P. Townsend and D. Gordon (eds), *World Poverty: New Policies to Defeat an Old Enemy* (Bristol: Policy Press).

Vandemoortele, J. 2004. *The MDGs and Pro-Poor Policies: Related But Not Synonymous*, Working Paper No. 3 (Brasilia: UNDP International Poverty Centre).

Wade, R. H. 2004. 'Is Globalization Reducing Poverty and Inequality?' *International Journal of Health Services*, 34(3): 381–414.

Watkins, K. 2002. *Rigged Rules and Double Standards: Trade, Globalization and the Fight against Poverty*, Oxfam International, New York (www.maketradefair.com and advocacy@oxfaminternational.org).

Webb, S. and Webb, B. 1929. *English Poor Law History: Part II. The Last Hundred Years* (London, Longmans, Green and Co.).

Weber, M. 1976 [1920 in German]. *The Protestant Ethic and the Spirit of Capitalism*, 2nd edn (London: Allen & Unwin).

WFP. 2005. Reports of the Executive Director on Operational Matters, Agenda Item 8 Ethiopia PRRO 10362.0, Executive Board First Regular Session, Rome, 31 January–2 February (Rome: World Food Programme).

Whiteside, N., Dreyfuss, M., Nijhoff, E. and Pasture, P. 2005. 'Syndicalisme et Etat social', paper presented at the conference: Organized Labour and the Welfare State: New Perspectives on an Old Couple, ESPAnet Young Researcher Workshop, 30 June–2 July (Paris: CEVIPOFO).

WHO. 2000. *The World Health Report: Investing in Health* (Geneva: World Health Organization).

WHO. 2005a. *Achieving Universal Health Coverage: Developing the Health Financing System*, Technical Briefs for Policy Makers No. 1 (Geneva: World Health Organization) (available at: http://www.who.int/health_financing/documents/pb_e_05_1-universal_coverage.pdf).

WHO. 2005b. World Health Assembly Resolution 58.33 (Geneva: World Health Organization) (available at: http://www.who.int/gb/ebwha/pdf_files/WHA58/WHA58_33-en.pdf).

WHO. 2007. *World Health Statistics 2007* (Geneva).

Wibulpolprasert, S. (ed.) 2005. *Thailand Health Profile 2001–2004* (Nonthaburi: Ministry of Public Health, Thai Health Promotion Foundation).

Wilensky, H. 2002. *Rich Democracies: Political Economy, Public Policy, and Performance* (Berkeley: University of California Press).

World Bank. 1990. *World Development Report 1990: Poverty* (Washington, DC: World Bank).

World Bank. 1993a. *Implementing the World Bank's Strategy to Reduce Poverty: Progress and Challenges* (Washington, DC: World Bank).

World Bank. 1993b. *World Development Report 1993: Investing in Health* (Washington, DC and Oxford: Oxford University Press for the World Bank).

World Bank. 1994. *Averting the Old Age Crisis* (New York: Oxford University Press).

World Bank. 1996. *Poverty Reduction and the World Bank: Progress and Challenges in the 1990s* (Washington, DC: World Bank).

World Bank. 1997. *Poverty Reduction and the World Bank: Progress in Fiscal 1996 and 1997* (Washington, DC: World Bank).

World Bank. 2000a. *Balancing Protection and Opportunity: a Strategy for Social Protection in the Transition Economies* (Washington, DC: World Bank).

World Bank. 2000b. *Emerging Directions for a Social Protection Sector Strategy: From Safety Net to Spring Board*, Social Protection Sector (Washington, DC: World Bank).

World Bank. 2001. *World Development Report 2000/2001: Attacking Poverty* (Washington, DC: World Bank).

World Bank. 2003. *India: Sustaining Reform, Reducing Poverty* (New Delhi: Oxford University Press).

World Bank. 2004a. Ethiopia Productive Safety Net Programme Project Information Document (PID) No. 30875 (Washington, DC: World Bank).

World Bank. 2004b. *Inequality and Economic Development in Brazil* (Washington, DC: World Bank).

World Bank. 2006. *World Development Report 2006* (Washington, DC: World Bank).

World Bank. 2008a. *World Development Report 2008* (Washington, DC: World Bank).

World Bank. 2008b. *Annual Report* (Washington, DC: World Bank).

World Bank. Annually. *World Development Reports* (Washington, DC: World Bank).

World Health Organization. 2007. *World Health Statistics* (Geneva: WHO).

World Health Organization. 2008. *Closing the Gap in a Generation: Health Equity through Action on the Social Determinants of Health,* Marmot Commission on the Social Determinants of Health (Geneva: WHO).

Wu, K. 2005. *How Social Security Keeps Older Persons out of Poverty across Developed Countries,* LIS Working Paper No. 410 (Luxembourg: LIS).

Xu, K., Evans, D., Carrin, G., Aguilar-Rivera, A. M., Musgrove, P. and Evans, T. 2007. 'Protecting Households from Catastrophic Health Spending', *Health Affairs,* 26(4): 972–83.

Zacher, H. F. 2005. 'Das "Soziale" als Begriff des deutschen und des europäischen Rechts', in Forschungs-Netzwerk Alterssicherung (ed.), *FNA-Jahrestagung 2005 'Das Soziale in der Alterssicherung'* (Berlin: Deutsche Rentenversicherung Bund), Vol. 66, pp. 11–22.

Zambia Ministry of Community Development and Social Services and German Technical Cooperation. 2006. *Evaluation Report – Kalomo Social Cash Transfer Scheme* (Lusaka, Zambia, Ministry of Community Development and Social Services (MCDSS) and German Technical Cooperation (GTZ)).

Index

NB: Page numbers in **bold** refer to boxes, figures and tables